D1135093

Scout Record

ADDRESS:

_____

_____

_____

I was awarded my:

SECOND CLASS RANK

ON_____

BY_____

FIRST CLASS RANK

ON_____

BY_____

CURVED BAR RANK

ON_____

BY_____

Girl Scout Handbook

The Girl Scout Promise

ON MY HONOR, I WILL TRY:

To do my duty to God and my country,

To help other people at all times,

To obey the Girl Scout Laws.

The Girl Scout Laws

1. A Girl Scout's honor is to be trusted.
2. A Girl Scout is loyal.
3. A Girl Scout's duty is to be useful and to help others.
4. A Girl Scout is a friend to all and a sister to every other Girl Scout.
5. A Girl Scout is courteous.
6. A Girl Scout is a friend to animals.
7. A Girl Scout obeys orders.
8. A Girl Scout is cheerful.
9. A Girl Scout is thrifty.
10. A Girl Scout is clean in thought, word, and deed.

Girl Scout Handbook

INTERMEDIATE
PROGRAM

GIRL SCOUTS OF THE U.S.A.
830 THIRD AVENUE
NEW YORK 22, N.Y.

ATALOG NO. 20-100, $1

Copyright 1953, 1955 by
Girl Scouts of the United States of America

NEW EDITION

First Impression, September, 1953
Second Impression, November, 1953
Third Impression, January, 1954
Fourth Impression, March, 1954
Fifth Impression, August, 1954
Sixth Impression, January, 1955
Seventh Impression, April, 1955
Eighth Impression, November, 1955
Ninth Impression, May, 1956
Tenth Impression, August, 1956
Eleventh Impression, November, 1956
Twelfth Impression, January, 1957
Thirteenth Impression, April, 1957
Fourteenth Impression, July, 1957
Fifteenth Impression, September, 1957
Sixteenth Impression, December, 1957
Seventeenth Impression, March, 1958

Printed in the United States of America

Introduction

DO YOU know about Anna Shaw? She was an American pioneer girl. As a young girl she traveled with her family by ox-cart to Michigan. She educated herself and became a preacher and a physician. Do you know the story of the English woman, Florence Nightingale, who made nursing a profession? She knew the meaning of service and worked hard to relieve the suffering of soldiers during the Crimean War. Today every registered nurse in the world takes the Nightingale Pledge. Have you heard about the work of Marie Curie? She and her husband were the discoverers of radium. These French scientists met with many setbacks in their work but they had courage and finally succeeded. And what do you know about Phyllis Wheatley, the first Negro woman poet in America? Her poetry was praised by George Washington.

Some of the girls of earlier days became explorers, settlers, builders, others were scientists, authors, nurses, and homemakers. They knew the meaning of "Be Prepared." They gave their service to help others.

Sacajawea One of the most remarkable of these girls was Sacajawea, the "Bird Woman." She served as interpreter between the members of the Lewis and Clark expedition and the Indian tribes they met on their way to the Northwest. She was their only guide from the Jefferson River to the Yellow River. She read the sun, the stars, and the trees. The life of the whole party depended on her skill. When the men became ill, she nursed them; when they became discouraged, she cheered them.

The women of Oregon have raised a statue to this young scout. It stands in Portland facing the coast and pointing to where the Columbia River empties into the sea.

Louisa Alcott Louisa Alcott, the author of *Little Women*, was born in Germantown, Pennsylvania, in 1832. She was as skilled in the home as Sacajawea was skilled on the trail.

Her father, although brilliant, was impractical. Much of Louisa's writing was done to help provide for her mother and sisters. She often had to drop the pen for the needle, the dish-cloth, and the broom. She turned carpets, trimmed hats, papered the rooms, made party dresses for her sisters, nursed anyone who was sick, and took part in all the daily home-making tasks. Her home did not have the comforts and conveniences of other homes and there were often emergencies. But Louisa was calm and cheerful.

Amelia Earhart "The first lady of the air" was born in Atchison, Kansas, in 1898. As a young girl and later as an adult she had many interests. She was a splendid lecturer and stimulating teacher. She wrote well. She enjoyed gardening and tried her hand at dress designing. She often made her own clothes. But her chief interest was always aviation.

"A. E." as she was nicknamed, started her flying lessons in California. In 1923, she received her pilot's license. In 1928, she became the first woman to cross the Atlantic in a plane. In 1929, she obtained the prized transport license then held by only three other women. In 1931, she became the first woman to fly an autogyro and on her second ascent established an altitude record. In 1932, "A. E." piloted herself across the Atlantic. In 1935, she piloted the first plane across the Pacific Ocean from Pearl Harbor in Hawaii to Oakland, California. In 1937, she set out to circle the globe. On July 2, 1937, she sent her message from near Howland Island in the Pacific. It read: "Circling . . . cannot see island . . . gas running low." With these words "the first lady of the air" vanished from our world.

A Girl Scout has kinship with these famous people. They met challenges and proved that they could overcome them. They enjoyed adventure and learning new things. They put others ahead of themselves. They knew the satisfaction of giving service. Doing these things belongs to the girls of today just as much as it did to Sacajawea, Louisa Alcott, and Amelia Earhart, and the many others.

There may be no new lands in which to pioneer, but as a Girl Scout you can explore new fields of knowledge. You can learn new skills and share these with others. You can make your contribution today as a citizen of your troop, school, and community. You can prepare to make your contribution in the future as a homemaker, a business woman, or a professional woman.

CONTENTS

		PAGE
Introduction		v

PART I

Your Path in Girl Scouting

1.	The Girl Scouts	1
2.	Tenderfoot Rank	4
3.	Your Girl Scout Troop	32
4.	Second Class Rank	47
5.	Proficiency Badges	81
6.	First Class Rank	87
7.	Older Intermediate Girl Scouts and the Curved Bar Rank	99

PART II

Adventuring in the Arts

8.	Arts and Crafts	115
9.	Literature and Dramatics	145
10.	Music and Dancing	173

PART III

Citizens Here and Abroad

PAGE

11. Community Life   189

12. International Friendship   207

PART IV

Fun and Exploration in the Out-of-Doors

13. Nature   233

14. Out-of-Doors   263

15. Sports and Games   290

PART V

You and Your Home

16. Agriculture   309

17. Health and Safety   320

18. Homemaking   349

PART VI

Proficiency Badge Activities

PAGE

19. Adventuring in the Arts 379
    Arts and Crafts, Literature and Dramatics, Music and Dancing
20. Citizens Here and Abroad 412
    Community Life, International Friendship
21. Fun and Exploration in the Out-of-Doors 433
    Nature, Out-of-Doors, Sports and Games
22. You and Your Home 463
    Agriculture, Health and Safety, Homemaking
Index 495

This edition of the *Girl Scout Handbook* was written by CATHARINE C. REILEY from material compiled by MARGARITE HALL and other members of the Program Department.

The book was illustrated by ELEANOR DART and ALISON CUMMINGS. It was designed by ANDOR BRAUN. The cover was designed by ALVIN LUSTIG.

PART I

Your Path in Girl Scouting

CHAPTER 1   The Girl Scouts

CHAPTER 2   Tenderfoot Rank

CHAPTER 3   Your Girl Scout Troop

CHAPTER 4   Second Class Rank

CHAPTER 5   Proficiency Badges

CHAPTER 6   First Class Rank

CHAPTER 7   Older Intermediate Girl Scouts and the
            Curved Bar Rank

The Star-Spangled Banner

Oh, say, can you see, by the dawn's early light,
  What so proudly we hailed at the twilight's last gleaming,
Whose broad stripes and bright stars, through the perilous fight,
  O'er the ramparts we watched were so gallantly streaming!
And the rocket's red glare, the bombs bursting in air,
  Gave proof through the night that our flag was still there;
Oh! say, does that star-spangled banner yet wave,
  O'er the land of the free, and the home of the brave?

On that shore dimly seen through the mists of the deep,
  Where the foe's haughty host in dread silence reposes.
What is that which the breeze, o'er the towering steep,
  As it fitfully blows, now conceals, now discloses?
Now it catches the gleam of the morning's first beam,
  In full glory reflected now shines on the stream;
'Tis the star-spangled banner; Oh, long may it wave,
  O'er the land of the free and the home of the brave!

Oh, thus be it ever, when freemen shall stand
  Between their loved homes and the war's desolation;
Blessed with victory and peace, may the heav'n-rescued land
  Praise the power that hath made and preserved us a nation.
Then conquer we must, when our cause it is just,
  And this be our motto—"In God is our trust";
And the star-spangled banner in triumph shall wave
  O'er the land of the free and the home of the brave.

FRANCIS SCOTT KEY, 1814.

CHAPTER 1

The Girl Scouts

THE scouts who lived long ago blazed the trails for the Girl Scouts of today. They ventured ahead and led and helped others. They were trusted by the people. They prepared themselves for any emergency. They tracked and stalked. They built overnight shelters and cooked over open fires. They made friends with all the things of nature. They cared for themselves and others. Their tasks required skill, courage, and knowledge. Their lives were often marked by hardship. Yet they were happy and full of the joy that comes from helping others.

Girl Scouts Today

The Girl Scouts of today have great pride in their name. They, too, like to do things. They have fun and adventure. They hike, cook outdoors, and camp. They explore and learn about the wonders of nature. They dance and sing, play games and tell stories. They make friends with girls in their community. They write to girls who live in other parts of the United States or who live in other countries. They put on plays. They have fun making things—a dress, an airplane model, a birdhouse, a bracelet or pin, a puppet. They enjoy doing many things to help others.

You can do these things, too. There is a place for every girl in the Girl Scouts. When you become a member you will find hundreds of other exciting things to do too. You will receive a warm welcome. You will make new friends and have lots of fun.

A Girl Scout troop is different from other clubs. Every member makes the Girl Scout Promise. She puts into practice the Girl Scout Laws. She chooses her good times from among the Girl Scout activities. She belongs to a national and international organization. She wears the Girl Scout pin.

Girl Scouting in the United States is for girls from seven through seventeen years of age. Brownies are the youngest members, from seven through nine years, and wear brown uniforms. Intermediate Girl Scouts are from about ten through thirteen or in the fifth, sixth, seventh, or eighth grades. They wear green uniforms. The Senior Girl Scouts are the oldest. They are girls of about fourteen through seventeen years of age and in the ninth grade or high school. Some wear green uniforms and others blue.

How You Can Join the Girl Scouts

If you are a Brownie Scout, you are already a member of the Girl Scouts. During the last months in your Brownie troop, you may complete your Tenderfoot rank requirements. You will then be ready to join an Intermediate troop. You will find that some of the things you do as an Intermediate will be the same as those things you did as a Brownie Scout. However, since you are older, you will be able to do them better. You can share what you already know with the girls who are new to Girl Scouting. You can help them to complete their Tenderfoot rank requirements. You will find many other ways to help, too.

If you have never been a Girl Scout, you may find a troop in your school, church or synagogue, or neighborhood. Ask the leader if you may go to a troop meeting. Or, if there is a Girl Scout office listed in your telephone book, call up and ask how you can join a troop. You must have your parents' permission to become a Girl Scout. Your leader will give you a form which your parents fill out.

If there is no troop in your neighborhood, you and your friends may ask a favorite teacher or other adult friend to help you get started. She can find out how to go about it from the Girl Scout office, or from the National Organization if there is no office in your community. You will find the address on the title page of your handbook.

CHAPTER 2

Tenderfoot Rank

Tenderfoot Rank Requirements

1. Learn the Girl Scout Promise, Laws, slogan, motto.

2. Learn the history of Girl Scouting.

3. Be able to give the Girl Scout salute, sign, handshake.

4. Learn how to display and use the flag of the United States of America.

5. Know about the World Association of Girl Guides and Girl Scouts. Be able to explain the meaning of its pin.

6. Choose one activity from each of the following groups and show by the way you do them that you understand the Girl Scout Laws:

a. Homemaking

Know how to set a table and do it at home.

Know how to make a bed and make your own bed.

Make something useful for your home.

Take care of a household pet.

b. Out-of-doors

Use a compass and make a rough sketch map of the way you go from home to school and from school to troop meeting.

Lay a trail for others to follow.

Use a jackknife to make shavings for a fire.

7. Pay your Girl Scout annual membership dues and know something about why you pay these dues.

8. Attend your troop meetings for four or more weeks.

9. Make the Girl Scout Promise and be invested as a Girl Scout.

You may think that Tenderfoot is a strange name. It was used in pioneer days. The word means someone who has just started out in a new country. The early settlers had to hike for many hours before they found a camp site. They carried all their belongings. Their feet soon ached. The old-timers called them "tenderfeet."

When you join the Girl Scouts, you are also starting out on a new adventure. You will find that there are certain things which have a special meaning to the members of your troop and to all Girl Scouts. While you are learning these things you are completing your Tenderfoot rank requirements.

1. **Learn the Girl Scout Promise, Laws, slogan, motto.**

The Promise

On my honor, I will try:
To do my duty to God and my country,
To help other people at all times,
To obey the Girl Scout Laws.

All over the world Girl Scouts and Guides make this Promise. It is made in many different languages. The words will be different in French, Japanese, Spanish, and Swedish but the meaning will be the same.

There have always been special promises, pledges, or oaths. The knights of the Middle Ages had their code of chivalry. Your doctor took the Oath of Hippocrates when he started in his profession. Nurses take the Florence Nightingale Pledge. Ministers, priests, and rabbis have their special pledges. New American citizens take the naturalization oath.

5

It is easy to make a promise. To keep a promise may be difficult unless you understand it. When you are invested as a Girl Scout and make this Promise, you are saying:

On my honor—I can be trusted to do and to mean what I say.

I will try—I know it is not easy to live up to the Promise at all times, but I will try hard.

To do my duty to God—I will honor God in the finest way I know and will be faithful to my own religion.

. . . and my country—I will try to make my country a place where everyone can live and work in safety and freedom. I will respect my country's laws.

To help other people at all times—I will think of ways I can help others. I will think of others first and not myself.

To obey the Girl Scout Laws—I know that I have taken a code of honor. I will try to live by the code.

The Girl Scout Laws The Laws serve as daily reminders of the way you would like to act at home, at school, in your community—and even when you are alone. The pictures on the following pages are some imaginary happenings that may help you understand their meaning.

1. *A Girl Scout's honor is to be trusted.*

"A party after school? Oh, I'd love to come. Oh no, I'm sorry I can't . . . I forgot . . . I have my troop meeting that day."

2. *A Girl Scout is loyal.*

"I know Sally is your friend but does she *have* to come? She's a slow poke."

"Sure she is . . . but that's because she finds interesting things to look at. We're always in such a hurry that we never stop to look at a thing. Sally knows a lot about nature."

3. *A Girl Scout's duty is to be useful and to help others.*

"Here, let me give you a hand with your bedroll. I'll teach you how to make a bowline and then we can tie it."

6

4. *A Girl Scout is a friend to all and a sister to every other Girl Scout.*

"No, I didn't go to the movies with Jane. I thought it would be good fun to have a picnic here."

5. *A Girl Scout is courteous.*

"Oh, excuse me. I got so excited I forgot it wasn't my turn to speak."

6. *A Girl Scout is a friend to animals.*

"Wait a second. I must feed Duchess first."

7. *A Girl Scout obeys orders.*

"I used to 'jaywalk' but I don't any more."

8. *A Girl Scout is cheerful.*

"Let's sing 'Donkey Riding' and these dishes will be finished in a flash."

9. *A Girl Scout is thrifty.*

"A few more stitches and this will be as good as new."

10. *A Girl Scout is clean in thought, word, and deed.*

"Yes, I did hear that story, but let's skip it."

Do a good turn daily

Scouts and Guides are known for the help they give other *The slogan* people. Good turns are extra acts of kindness. They are small, thoughtful things which give others pleasure. They may also be big things. The important point is that good turns are done without expecting praise. Try to do at least one good turn a day. Let good turns become a habit.

Be prepared

A Girl Scout is ready to help when she is needed. The *The motto* desire to help is not enough. You must also be trained. You must know how to do the job well, even in an emergency. For example, if a person is drowning you cannot rescue him un-

9

less you know lifesaving. Have you read about the ways your heroes and heroines trained themselves?

As you look through this book you will find hundreds of interesting activities. All of them will help you be prepared.

2. Learn the history of Girl Scouting.

Lord Baden-Powell

ROBERT BADEN-POWELL was a British officer. During the Boer War he was sent to South Africa to defend Mafeking. He found that the soldiers under his command were not prepared for life in the open. To help them learn how to get along out-of-doors he made up a series of games. He called these "Stunts for Scouting." He divided the soldiers into teams, called patrols. Each patrol elected its own leader. The men enjoyed these games and learned a great deal from them. Soon boys in England began playing them. In 1908, Baden-Powell rewrote his games into a program for boys and founded the Boy Scouts.

The girls saw what fun their brothers were having and wanted a club of their own. In 1909, a Boy Scout rally was held in the Crystal Palace in London. The King proclaimed Sir Robert Baden-Powell "The Hero of Mafeking." Imagine the surprise to everyone to see a group of girls marching with the boys. They were dressed in khaki shirts and skirts and wide-brimmed hats. They were determined to be Scouts.

Almost before Sir Robert knew what was happening, some six thousand English girls had taken up Scouting. Something had to be done. At the end of 1909, the Girl Guide organization was founded. Sir Robert's sister, Agnes Baden-Powell, became the first president.

Soon Girl Guiding spread to other parts of the Commonwealth—Scotland, Wales, Australia, South Africa, and Canada. In less than a year, organizations were started in other countries—Suomi-Finland, Sweden, Denmark, Poland.

In some countries the name Girl Guides was kept; in others, the name Girl Scouts was used.

JULIETTE GORDON Low, the Founder of the Girl Scouts in the United States, was born in Savannah, Georgia, in 1860. Her friends called her Daisy. She had a great talent as a sculptor and painter, and enjoyed these activities throughout her life. She loved animals, especially dogs and cats, and had many pets.

Juliette Low

At the age of twenty-five, Daisy Gordon married William Low and made her home in England and Scotland. There she met Sir Robert (later Lord) and Agnes Baden-Powell. They interested her in the newly organized Girl Guides. She first became the leader of a Guide company in a small village in Scotland. There were only seven Guides, some of whom had to walk six miles to meetings. She taught them to raise poultry, spin and weave, and found a market for their home-spun. Later she led two Guide companies in London.

Before sailing to the United States in 1912, she sent a cable to her family which read: "I am bringing home the biggest thing yet." They were puzzled. When she arrived in Savannah, she telephoned a friend and said: "Come right over, Nina, I've got something for the girls of Savannah and all America, and all the world, and we are going to start it to-night." That was the way Juliette Low, our Founder, brought Girl Guiding to the United States.

The phone call was followed by a meeting with a group of girls from Miss Nina Pape's school. On March 12, 1912, the first Girl Guide company was organized. The first camp was held the next summer. In 1913, the name was changed to Girl Scouts. The uniform of that first troop was blue. The first Girl Scout handbook was called *How Girls Can Help Their Country.*

The story of the Girl Scouts during the early years is the story of the tireless energy and enthusiasm of one woman—Juliette Low. She was handicapped by ill health and almost total deafness. But nothing could stop her. Wherever she went she started Girl Scout troops. She traveled all over the United States sharing her idea with others. For four years she financed Girl Scouting herself. She was not wealthy, but she found the money that was needed, even when it meant selling a treasured heirloom—her pearls.

By the end of 1915, there were five thousand Girl Scouts. The organization had a national council, a constitution and bylaws, and a charter. Mrs. Low became the first president. Girl Scouts became known for their services during the First World War. By the end of 1918 there were 34,081 members. By the end of 1952—forty years after its founding—there were 1,931,253 Girl Scouts in the United States.

3. Be able to give the Girl Scout salute, sign, handshake.

The salute   The Girl Scout salute is made by raising the right hand to the forehead, three fingers extended, the thumb holding down the little finger.

The salute is always given when the Promise is made or repeated. It does not matter whether you are in uniform or not. The salute is also given when the flag is raised or lowered or passes you on parade if you are in uniform. If you are in a public place but not in uniform, face the flag and stand at attention with your right hand over your heart.

The sign    To make the Girl Scout sign, bring your right hand up shoulder high with palm forward. The three extended fingers stand for the three parts of your Promise. The sign is used as a greeting when Girl Scouts meet, whether friends or strangers.

The Girl Scout handshake is given by shaking hands with your left hand while the sign (or salute) is given with your right hand. It is the form of greeting used all over the world by Girl Scouts and Girl Guides when they meet whether they are in uniform or not.

The handshake

It was Baden-Powell who introduced the custom of the left handshake. While serving in West Africa he learned the legend of two neighboring tribes who were always fighting each other. One day they realized that it would be much better to live as good neighbors. They flung down their shields and their spears. As they met one another they held out their left hands to show that they were without weapons and came to greet someone they could trust and wished to treat as a friend.

4. Learn how to display and use the flag of the United States of America.

The word flag covers all kinds of banners and standards. It is thought to come from the Anglo-Saxon word *fleogan*, "to fly or float in the wind." Originally a banner was used by a country and a standard by a particular person.

The flag

The flag of the United States of America is the symbol of the oneness of the nation. The thirteen stripes stand for the thirteen original states. The stars stand for the states in the Union today. The colors of the flag are red for valor; white for purity; blue for justice. The five-pointed stars originally meant "a new constellation" arisen in the skies of the world —a new nation.

THE DISPLAY AND USE OF THE FLAG. Public Law 829 tells civilians how to display and use the flag of the United States. The flag should be displayed on flagpoles only from sunrise to sunset. It should be raised quickly and low-

13

ered slowly. It should be flown on all days when the weather permits. It should not be displayed in bad weather.

When flown at half-mast, the flag should be hoisted to the top and then lowered to the middle of the pole. It should be raised to the top before it is lowered for the day.

When flags of two or more nations are displayed, they must be flown from separate poles of the same height. The flags should be the same size.

When the flag is carried with another flag, the flag of the United States must be on the right. When it is carried with two other flags, it should be in the center.

When the flag is hung against a wall, the blue field should be uppermost and to the flag's own right. When it is hung against the wall with another flag, the flag of the United States should be at the spectator's left. If there are three or more flags, the flag of the United States should be in the center.

The flag should never be used as a drapery or cover. No object should ever be placed on the flag. It should not be allowed to touch the floor or ground. An old flag should be destroyed by burning.

Pledge of Allegiance "I pledge allegiance to the flag of the United States of America and to the Republic for which it stands; one Nation under God, indivisible, with liberty and justice for all."

At Girl Scout gatherings you give the Girl Scout salute

while repeating the Pledge of Allegiance. At other gatherings where the Pledge is used, such as school assemblies, Girl Scouts are expected to follow the custom practiced in that place.

5. Know about the World Association of Girl Guides and Girl Scouts. Be able to explain the meaning of its pin.

Because Scouts and Guides have so much in common, the World Association of Girl Guides and Girl Scouts was formed in 1928. One of its purposes is to encourage friendship between girls of all nations. As a member of the Girl Scout movement in the United States you are a part of the World Association.

The Girl Guide or Girl Scout organization of a country applies for admission to the World Association. First it is a Tenderfoot member. After it has met all the qualifications it becomes a full member. The Girl Scouts of the U.S.A. is a full member.

Delegates from all member organizations meet together every other year. This is called the World Conference. In between conferences, the business of the World Association is carried on by the World Committee.

The headquarters of the World Association of Girl Guides and Girl Scouts is called the World Bureau. It is located in London. The headquarters for the Western Hemisphere Committee of the World Association is in New York City.

The World pin is a symbol of the world-wide bond of Scouting. It can be worn by all Girl Guides or Girl Scouts whose organizations are members of the World Association. When "World pin" and "World flag" are mentioned in other parts of this book, they mean the pin and flag of the World Association of Girl Guides and Girl Scouts.

The World pin has a bright blue background with a gold

trefoil on it. The blue stands for the sky which is over us all. The gold stands for the sun which shines on all. The stars in the leaves of the trefoil remind us of our Promise and Laws. The vein is the compass needle which guides us. The base of the trefoil is shaped like a flame—the flame of the love of mankind.

6. Choose one activity from each of the following groups and show by the way you do them that you understand the Girl Scout Laws.

   a. Homemaking
   Know how to set a table and do it at home.
   Know how to make a bed and make your own bed.
   Make something useful for your home.
   Take care of a household pet.
   b. Out-of-doors
   Use your compass and make a rough sketch map of the way you go from home to school and from school to troop meeting.
   Lay a trail for others to follow.
   Use your jackknife to make shavings for a fire.

   Do you wonder how you can "show that you understand the Girl Scout Laws" while you work on activities? The activities themselves give you an opportunity. Making something for someone else is an expression of friendliness. Setting the table at home is useful. So is making your bed. Caring for a pet is being a friend to animals. Are you cheerful while you wait for your turn to use the crayon and scissors to make your map? Are you courteous to all the girls in your troop? Do you obey the "no trespassing" signs and rules of the road when laying trails? Are you loyal to your troop and a friend to all troop members?

Care in setting a table helps to make any meal a success. It is good to know various pieces of silver and their uses. You will find pictures of them in magazines and catalogs. You can see them in jewelry or department stores. Most homes have the pieces illustrated in this picture, with the addition of soup spoon, server, tablespoon, and gravy spoon. *Set a table*

In setting the table, all china and silver are placed about one inch from the edge of the table. The table should be large enough to allow ample room for each place.

Special events—holidays, birthdays, and so forth—call for special arrangements of flowers and tableware. Many cookbooks and magazines have pictures to show how a tea table, a buffet table, or a breakfast-in-bed tray should be set.

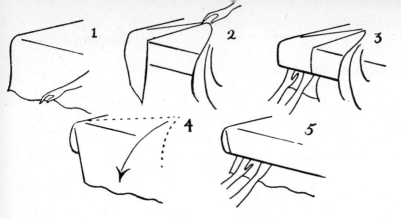

A well-made bed will hold firm and smooth when used.

Make a bed

1. Cover the mattress with a pad.

2. Put the bottom sheet on the bed right side up. Tuck in the sheet at the head first, then at the foot. Miter the corners as shown in the illustration. Tuck in the sides.

3. Place the top sheet on the bed right side down. Leave enough sheet at the top so that it can be folded over the blankets. Tuck the sheet in at the foot and miter the bottom corners.

4. Put on the blankets. Turn the top sheet down over the blankets. Tuck the blankets in at the foot, miter the corners, and tuck the sheet and blankets in along the sides.

5. Put the bedspread on smoothly.

6. Shake and smooth the pillow. Put the pillow case on the pillow as it lies on the bed. Place the pillow flat at the head of the bed, and cover with the bedspread.

Make a useful article

You are the best judge of what will be useful in your own home. It may be that you will make a recipe file box for your mother, a toy chest for a younger brother or sister, a tool rack for your father, napkin rings for your family, or a garment bag for your own closet.

Model a pottery bowl, embroider a guest towel, or make some gay potholders. Do you have an emergency telephone list near your phone? Design an attractive card and list the family doctor, the police and fire departments, the ambulance service and the local hospital.

Your father might help you get started on a little carpentry. Would another shelf, bench, stool, or simple bookcase be useful? Do your pets have homes? Could you help construct a chicken coop, rabbit hutch, or doghouse?

A pet is good company and great fun to watch. There are *Care of a pet* many different kinds of household pets such as dogs, cats, birds, hamsters, white mice, and turtles. It is unfair to have a pet and not take good care of it. Their needs are simple but constant. They are much the same as your own, that is, daily exercise, nourishing food, pure water, body cleanliness, proper elimination, and a clean place to live. All pets need regular attention and kind treatment. If a pet belongs to you, it is your job to keep it well and happy. It should not be left to other members of the family.

A compass is an instrument used to determine direction. *The compass* Every compass has a magnetized needle that always points north. Every compass has a face on which you will find the four cardinal points: north, east, south, and west. You will also see the degree readings. Hold your compass in one hand waist high. Look to see where the magnetic needle comes to rest. Now point out north with your other hand. Can you also point out south, east, and west?

Different kinds of compasses are used by sailors, explorers, and aviators. The picture on the next page shows a compass used by Girl Guides and Girl Scouts in many countries.

Around the compass housing there are letters and numbers. These are the four cardinal points and the 360 degree readings. North is 0 degrees, east is 90 degrees, south is 180 degrees, and west is 270 degrees. These degree readings show the 360 different ways you can travel.

To find a specific degree reading with your compass follow these steps:

1. Turn the housing until the degree reading you wish to follow is in line with the direction of travel arrow. For exam-

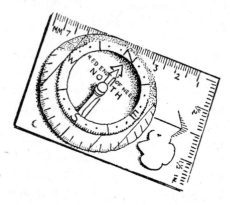

ple, if 120 degrees is the direction you wish to go, turn the housing until the figure 120 is in line with the direction of the travel arrow.

2. Hold your compass level and about waist high. The direction of travel arrow should point away from you and straight ahead. Next turn *yourself* around slowly until the magnetic needle is directly over the orienting arrow and points to the letter N on top of the housing. Now you are facing the direction you wish to go which is 120 degrees.

You can also use your compass to find the degree reading for an object.

1. Hold your compass level and waist high. The direction of travel arrow should point away from you and in the direction of the object. This is called "sighting."

2. Turn the *compass housing,* by itself, until the magnetic needle is directly over the orienting arrow and points to the letter N. Now the degree reading for the object is in line with the direction of travel arrow on the plastic base.

A compass is not dependable when used near cars, railroad

tracks, or much steel because metal attracts the magnetic needle. Test the truth of this statement for yourself.

This type of map shows a route from one spot to another. *A rough* The main points are outstanding landmarks, types of roads *sketch map* and their names, and arrows showing where turns are made. Here is an illustration.

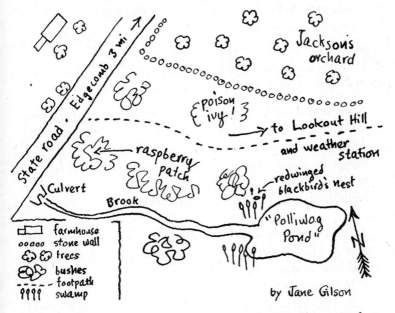

by Jane Gilson

Have you ever noticed that road and city maps have north, east, south, and west marked in one corner? After you finish your sketch, use your compass to find North. Put in an arrow pointing north on your map.

In laying trails you can use rocks, twigs, grass, white peb- *Trail signs* bles, bits of colored yarn, or anything that is easily seen. The Indians and early American settlers used simple trail signs. When you lay a trail, be sure the signs are not too far apart, and point the way clearly.

21

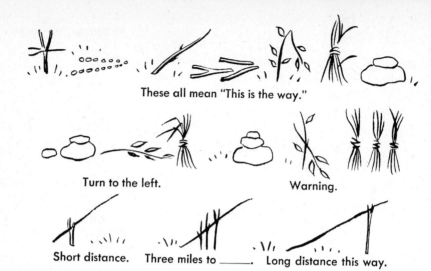

These all mean "This is the way."

Turn to the left.   Warning.

Short distance.   Three miles to _____.   Long distance this way.

Be careful not to move or destroy a temporary trail sign unless you are the last person to need it or have been asked to destroy it. If several people are following a trail, one girl stands by a trail sign while the others scout ahead for the next sign. When it is found, they call or signal to the girl left behind. She destroys the sign and moves up to the new one.

Your jackknife   A jackknife must be clean, sharp, and easily opened and closed. This illustration shows different types of jackknives and how to use and care for them.

In using a knife:

1. Whittle or cut away from the body, until you are skillful.

2. Keep the fingers behind the blade.

3. Do not carry an open knife.

4. Keep the knife clean. Keep the knife out of fire. Do not run the blade of the knife into the ground to clean it.

5. Do not pry things open with the blade or use it as a screwdriver.

6. Do not hammer with the handle of a knife.

22   7. Know how to oil the hinges and sharpen the blades.

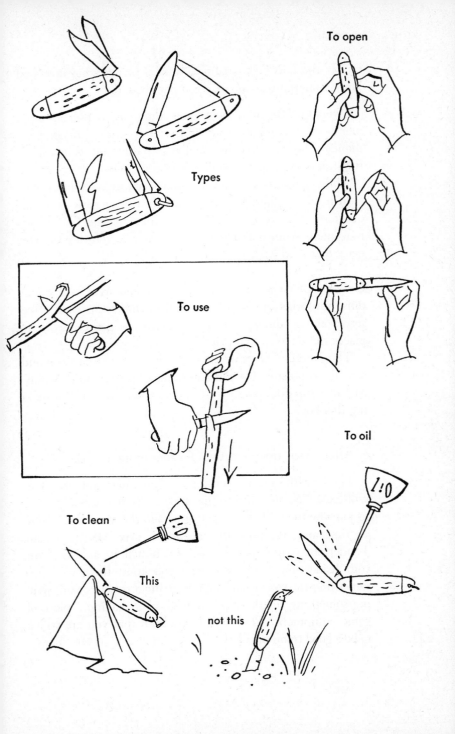

Types

To open

To use

To oil

To clean

This

not this

7. Pay the Girl Scout national annual membership dues and know something about why you pay these dues.

Every Girl Scout, both girl and adult, pays national annual membership dues of one dollar. Your leader collects this money. She sees that the membership dues and your troop's registration are sent to national headquarters.

Many girls earn money for their own dues. Some troops earn it all together. When the dues arrive at national headquarters, you are enrolled as a member of the Girl Scout movement. Your membership card is sent to your leader. You get a new card each year when you register.

The card shows that you are a member in good standing. Only people who hold cards can buy and wear Girl Scout pins, uniforms, and badges. Your membership card often serves as an admission card to Girl Scout gatherings or to places that give special privileges to Girl Scouts.

The National Organization uses the money to carry on and to make it possible for you and other girls to be Girl Scouts. Membership dues paid by Girl Scouts helped to pay for making this book.

8. Attend your troop meetings for four or more weeks.

The first four meetings you attend are important ones. You will have a chance during that time to see if you really want to join the troop. Take an active part in the meetings. Arrive on time and stay until the meeting is over. Work on your Tenderfoot requirements so that you will be able to show your leader and your troop that you know them well. Do something for your troop such as laying a treasure trail, writing something for the troop notebook, or making a piece of game equipment. They will know then that you are trying to be a good troop member.

Above all you will need this time to think about your Girl Scout Promise and Laws. You will want to know them not *by* heart but *with* your heart. Try to understand every word. Make up examples of how the Laws apply to your life. Then when the time comes you will really know whether you want to try to live up to the Girl Scout Promise and Laws. You will be prepared to make your Promise and be invested.

9. Make the Girl Scout Promise and be invested as a Girl Scout.

Your investiture as a Girl Scout is important. It marks a milestone along your trail. It is the goal for which you have been working. It shows that you are ready to become a member of a great world-wide movement. Your gold trefoil pin is a symbol of membership. The trefoil identifies Girl Scouting and Girl Guiding all over the world. The three parts of the trefoil stand for the three parts of the Girl Scout Promise.

This ceremony is used by all troops when taking in a new member. Investitures are not always alike but certain things are always included. All members of the troop should be present to welcome the new member officially. This may be done through the salute, handshake, a song, or in some other way. The new member makes her Promise in front of the troop and receives her pin. *Your investiture ceremony*

The ceremony is carried out in different ways. The troop forms either a horseshoe or a circle. Most troops like to start with a flag ceremony. After the flag ceremony, your patrol leader or an older Girl Scout brings you forward to the troop leader. Or the friend who introduced you to the troop brings you forward. If there are several new girls, you may come forward together.

25

The leader greets you and asks you whether you are ready to make your Promise. You then officially make your Promise. Repeat it slowly and think about what you are saying. As you make your Promise, your leader salutes and all the other Girl Scouts do the same. In giving the salute, they know that they are renewing their own Promise.

Your leader then places the trefoil pin on the knot of your Girl Scout tie, or on the left side of your dress if you are not in uniform. As she does this she may say a few words to you. Generally the World pin is presented at the same time. It is fastened just above the breast pocket of the uniform or just above the Girl Scout pin if you are not in uniform. Your leader may give you the Girl Scout handshake, after which you return to your place.

You have become an official member of the Girl Scout movement in the United States.

Your Girl Scout Uniform and Insignia

As soon as you have completed the first eight Tenderfoot rank requirements and are ready to be invested you may wear the Girl Scout uniform. Usually you wear it for the first time to your investiture ceremony. It is one way of saying to everyone who sees you, "I am a Girl Scout." It is a bond between you and the Scouts and Guides all over the world. On page 216 are pictures of the uniforms girls wear in some other countries. The colors and styles are different but wearing a uniform is part of Guiding and Scouting.

The uniform for Intermediate Girl Scouts is a dress of green cotton covert, with a dark green web belt, a tie of a color chosen by the troop, and a dark green beret with the trefoil emblem. Green anklets with trefoil-trimmed cuffs match the dress.

Girl Scouts in the seventh and eighth grades may wear the alternate Senior Girl Scout blouse-and-skirt uniform if their council approves. With this the green beret, troop tie, and badge sash are worn.

All Girl Scouts like to own and wear a uniform, but it is not necessary to have one in order to be a Girl Scout. If you have no uniform, wear a white blouse, dark skirt, and Girl Scout pin.

Be sure that your uniform fits properly. Wear the full uniform as described above. Shoes with flat heels and rounded toes are worn with either uniform. *How to wear your uniform*

Keep your uniform and tie in good condition. Be neat yourself, with hair brushed, nails and hands clean.

Remember that the things you say and do while in uniform reflect credit (or discredit) on all Girl Scouts.

27

When to wear your uniform You may begin to wear your uniform the day you are invested as a Girl Scout (see page 25). Wear it to all troop meetings and Girl Scout gatherings or to public meetings where you represent the Girl Scouts.

How to get a uniform You need either your membership card or a note signed by your leader in order to buy a uniform, uniform materials, or any other official equipment. These items are sold only to registered Girl Scouts.

Uniforms may be bought through a local store that carries Girl Scout equipment or through the Girl Scout National Equipment Service. Or you may make your uniform. You can get the materials and a pattern from the National Equipment Service.

When you outgrow your uniform, remove your badges and pass it on to another Girl Scout. Remove all insignia, including buttons, if the uniform is to be used by a girl who is not a Scout.

Your insignia The picture on the opposite page shows you where to place your insignia.

The Girl Scout pin is worn on the knot of the Girl Scout tie.

The World pin is worn just above the breast pocket.

The Second Class badge is worn on the left sleeve of the uniform, one inch below the troop numeral.

The First Class badge replaces the Second Class badge on the left sleeve.

The First Class pin is only worn when *not* in uniform.

The Curved Bar pin is worn on the breast pocket, just below the flap. This pin may be worn at any time.

Proficiency badges are worn on the right sleeve. Sew the

28

first one just above the cuff, and as badges are added, make rows of three each up the sleeve.

A troop crest is an embroidered oval symbol chosen by a troop as its special insignia. It is worn on the right sleeve just below the shoulder seam. Many different designs are available, or a troop may make up and embroider its own.

An identification emblem is a curved strip of cloth embroidered with the name of the troop's town or city. It is worn on the left shoulder, with the bottom edge touching the sleeve seam.

A troop numeral with the troop's own number on it may be worn on the left sleeve, one inch below the identification emblem.

A membership star may be worn by a Girl Scout who has been a member for one year. Stars are placed in a row on the flap of the breast pocket. Membership stars received as a Brownie are also worn on the Intermediate Girl Scout uniform.

Brownie Scout wings are worn by Girl Scouts who have been Brownie Scouts. They are worn on the right sleeve one inch below the troop crest.

The badge sash is a four-inch band of Girl Scout cloth and is worn over the right shoulder and fastened on the left hip. If you wear a uniform with short sleeves or the alternate uniform, or if you have no uniform, you may wear your proficiency and rank badges on a badge sash.

Your Girl Scout Magazine

The American Girl is your official Girl Scout magazine. It is published monthly by the Girl Scouts of the U.S.A. It has many special features. You can read about the activities of Girl Scouts all over the world. You will find ideas for your own patrol and troop programs. There is a special section for readers' contributions. You can send in your poems, short stories, cooking recipes, drawings and jokes. It is a thrill to see what you have written in print. Its pages are full of enjoyable short stories and serials. There are special articles on sports, hobbies, good grooming, and careers. The magazine always gives tips on teen-age fashions and accessories.

Subscriptions to *The American Girl* are available to registered Girl Scouts at a special low rate. You can find out more about the magazine from your leader. She will also have a subscription blank. Or you can write to the National Organization. The address is on the title page of this book.

CHAPTER 3

Your

Girl Scout Troop

A TROOP is the name Girl Scouts use for a club. It is made up of girls and their leader. Troops are of different sizes. In some rural areas troops may have as few as eight girls. Most troops have twenty-four to thirty members.

Generally troops meet once a week for two hours. They hold their meetings in schools, churches and synagogues, homes, community buildings, or in their own club rooms. Whenever possible, Girl Scouts meet out-of-doors.

One of the nicest things about a Girl Scout troop is that it belongs to the members. You plan what you want to do at troop meetings. Your leader helps. The success of your troop depends on *you*. Your troop meetings will be fun if you take part in the work, play, and government of the troop.

Your troop can be a small democracy. This means that you welcome all girls as members. Everyone feels free to speak. Every member respects the ideas of other members even when they are different from her own. Everyone votes. The majority vote wins. The minority has its share in the program too. Every member is ready to carry out her share in troop projects.

Girl Scouts use the patrol system or the club meeting types of government. Your troop decides which one to use.

The Patrol System

Girl Scouts, Girl Guides, and Boy Scouts use the patrol system. It is the kind of government used by troops all over the world. It is used at international gatherings. It is one of the many things Scouts and Guides have in common. It helps unite us in one great movement.

The patrols and Court of Honor together are called the patrol system. The patrols take care of patrol matters. The Court of Honor takes care of troop matters. If your troop has patrol meetings and no Court of Honor meetings, or vice versa, it is not using the patrol system. The strength of the patrol system is in having regular and good patrol and Court of Honor meetings.

A patrol is made up of six to eight girls. A patrol may choose *The patrol* a special name, such as Caballeros, Gypsies, Redwing, or Oak. The meaning of a patrol name is only known to the patrol members. For example, Caballeros might stand for happiness, Gypsies for adventure, Redwing for cheerfulness, and Oak for sturdiness.

Every patrol has its special meeting place. These are called "corners" or "homes." If the troop meets indoors, "corners" may be particular places in the room. Out-of-doors they are often favorite spots.

Patrol treasures and belongings are kept in patrol corners. You might build a bookcase or a chest in which to store them. If you cannot keep your things at your meeting place, members of your patrol may be responsible for different pieces of equipment. It is fun to make and keep your own patrol corner distinctive and attractive.

Patrols hold meetings during a part of every troop meeting. This is the time when you make plans for future meetings

33

and carry out the plans you have already made. You talk over the report from your patrol leader of the Court of Honor meeting. You learn, practice, and use Girl Scout skills that will help you with your ranks, badges, and service. You take attendance and collect dues. Patrols may also have meetings at other times than the regular troop meeting time.

For a part of every meeting, the troop as a whole does things together. Each patrol may present a skit, or the troop may go on a hike, or work on arts and crafts, or do a service project. What you do as a troop depends on the suggestions that each patrol presents to the Court of Honor.

At times girls from different patrols get together to serve on a committee. This is fun because you get to know more troop members. Committees are often needed for troop events such as an investiture, parties, service projects, and a Court of Awards.

The patrol leader is elected by her patrol to serve for one *Patrol leader* year. It is a great honor and responsibility to be a patrol leader. It means that patrol members think you are fair, have ideas, and know how to get things done without being bossy. They feel you will listen to their ideas and speak for the patrol, and not for yourself, at Court of Honor meetings. They expect you to work well with other elected officers. They know that you will take time to help all patrol members, especially the new ones.

As a patrol leader you want the patrol to have a good time working together. You will be in charge of all patrol meetings. Your troop leader will teach you how to make an agenda and lead a patrol discussion. She will also show you skills that you can share with your patrol.

A patrol leader wants her patrol to get along with members of other patrols. She is interested in the good of the whole troop. Lord Baden-Powell said that a patrol leader puts her patrol ahead of herself and her troop ahead of her patrol. Can you do this?

Each patrol has an assistant who takes the place of the patrol *Assistant* leader when she is absent. She helps the patrol leader with *patrol leader* all her duties and may have special jobs, such as collecting dues or taking charge of games or songs or patrol equipment.

The assistant is also elected by the patrol and serves for a year. She attends the Court of Honor meeting if the patrol leader is absent. At other times she attends when invited. An assistant may be elected as the patrol leader the following year.

Patrol
Your patrol is like a team. Each member must do her share. *members*
Everyone has a job. First, you are responsible for electing a 35

good leader and assistant. That means that you do not vote for a girl just because she is your friend or nice looking or good at games. You vote for the girl who can help your patrol. You vote for the girl you think can do the job.

As a patrol member, try to be a good follower. You have ideas. Talk them over, and be willing to change or combine them with other people's ideas. Carry through on patrol jobs. Do your level best to live up to the Promise and Laws.

You also help your patrol leader do a good job. It makes no difference whether you voted for the patrol leader or not. You know the majority wanted her so you stick by her and help her.

All the girls in your patrol help each other and are friendly to everyone in the troop. You do not blame others when things go wrong. You are quick to admit your own faults and slow to point out the faults of others. You do your best in everything and accept praise for a job well done. At the same time you let others have their share of honor and glory.

The Court of Honor The Court of Honor is made up of patrol leaders, assistant patrol leaders (by invitation), the troop scribe, the troop treasurer, and the troop leader. It meets from ten to thirty minutes before or after each troop meeting. In addition, the Court of Honor holds longer meetings every month. These take place on a different day from the troop meeting. They are held at the troop meeting place, the home of one of the girls, the leader, or a troop committee member.

The chairman of the Court of Honor in a new troop is generally the leader. Later the patrol leaders may take turns conducting the meetings. When a patrol leader acts as chairman, the assistant patrol leader attends the Court of Honor meeting and speaks for the patrol.

The Court of Honor deals with matters that affect the whole troop. It discusses the ideas from the patrols and leaders and works them into a program for the troop. It has ideas of its own which it submits to patrols for approval. Each of its members is expected to speak freely and say what she thinks. Decisions made in the Court of Honor are taken back to the patrols by patrol leaders. In addition, at these meetings patrol leaders learn new things which they can teach to their patrols.

In representative government each citizen has the right to elect a person to represent him and his interests. This is the form of government we use in the United States today. Our president, senators, representatives, and governors are elected by the citizens to represent them.

Representative government

When you vote for a patrol leader, you are doing the same thing. You are electing her to represent your interests at the Court of Honor meeting. That is why the patrol system is called the representative type of troop government.

The Club Form

The club form of government is sometimes used by small troops. As the troop grows larger, it generally changes to the patrol system.

In the club meeting all the girls in the troop plan together. In the very beginning your leader may act as chairman. After a time the troop elects a president or chairman. She then presides at meetings. There will be other elected officers, too. The elected officers and the troop leader make up the "executive committee." The executive committee may appoint committees to make plans for special events. These are called "special committees."

The club meeting is like the form of government used in many organizations such as the parent-teacher association. Every member has a chance to stand up and speak before the whole group. Every member votes directly for or against any matter of importance. Every member is responsible for seeing that anything the group has decided on is carried out. Because every member speaks and votes directly, the club meeting is called the direct type of democratic government.

The Scribe

Every troop needs a scribe or secretary. She takes the minutes of the Court of Honor or business meetings. She writes and answers invitations and letters. She writes thank-you notes for the use of property, for gifts, and so on. She is responsible for the troop log of pictures, sketches, and written accounts of troop activities.

The scribe may keep the record of each girl's progress in ranks and badges. Some scribes help fill out the troop registration form that is sent to national headquarters. There may be an assistant scribe to help with this work.

When your troop elects a scribe, choose someone who likes

to write and keep records. Her handwriting should be neat and easy to read. A scribe serves for a year.

The Treasurer

The troop treasurer is elected to serve for a year. She should like to work with numbers and keep accounts. She keeps a book and enters all incoming and outgoing money. She gives a regular monthly report. In addition, she should be ready to report on the troop's finances whenever asked.

The treasurer receives the dues from the patrols and records who paid them. The money itself is usually given to the troop leader or a troop committee member for safekeeping. It may be put in a bank to the troop's account.

The Troop Treasury

Any group that wants to do things needs money for some activities. The place where clubs keep their money is called a treasury. You have a troop treasury.

A budget is a plan by which you decide how much money you will need, how you will get it, and how you will spend it. You have your own budget. You know your allowance or the money you earn determines the things you can buy. Your family has a budget, too, to cover rent, food, clothing. *The troop budget*

A troop usually gets its money in two ways: (1) dues paid each week by members; (2) money earned by the troop. The amount of dues is decided on by the whole troop. They are your main source of income. Try to plan your troop program so that you will not need additional money. If there is something special you want to do, you may have to raise money. Earn this by doing something worth while by which you can use the skills you have learned in your troop. Your money-raising project must be approved by your Girl Scout council.

39

Here is a troop budget form. It has two parts: income (the money you receive) and expenditure (the money you pay out). There are also two columns, one for the amount you expect to receive or pay out, and the second for the amount you actually receive or pay out.

Troop Budget Form

Income	Amount Estimated	Amount Received
Troop Dues		
(Multiply total weekly dues by number of weeks the troop meets.)	_____	_____
Other Sources		
(List money-raising project, contributions, and so forth.)	_____	_____
A. _____	_____	_____
B. _____	_____	_____
Total	_____	_____

Expenditures	Amount Estimated	Amount Spent
(Based on the number of members, and needed troop supplies.)		
National Annual Membership Dues		
___ girls at $1.00 each Total	_____	_____
Troop Supplies		
(List books, flags, outdoor games, and crafts equipment, record forms, and so forth.)		
A. _____	_____	_____
B. _____	_____	_____
C. _____	_____	_____

Troop Activities

(List outdoor and
indoor activities,
service projects,
and so forth.)

———————	———————	———————
———————	———————	———————
———————	———————	———————

Total ——————— ———————
Grand Total ——————— ———————

The Troop Leader

Your Girl Scout troop has an adult leader who is interested in you and your troop. Your leader wants you to have a good time and do interesting things. She will help you learn how to run your troop and plan your programs.

Because she likes you, she gives her time to your troop. Her only "pay" is the fun she gets from working with you. She takes special training to become a good leader. She will share her skills and hobbies with your troop. When you choose activities in which she is not skilled, she will have fun learning with you. Sometimes she will invite people with special skills to help the troop. These people are called program consultants. Large troops may have one or more adult assistant leaders, who are there to help the girls and the leader.

Other People Who Help Your Troop

The troop committee is a group of mothers, fathers, or other adult friends who are interested in you. These grown-ups are there to help your troop when you need them.

The Girl Scout council is a group of men and women who are responsible for Girl Scouting in your town. They have different committees. They organize troops and find meeting places. They train leaders and operate camps. They work

41

with other community groups. They raise money and do many other things. They keep the wheels of Girl Scouting turning in your community. Ask your leader about your council.

Your Troop Meetings

Every troop meeting is special and every one is different. Some of the time is spent in patrol corners, committees, or other groups. Some of the time the troop does things all together.

The meeting may start with a flag ceremony or game. You will collect dues and take attendance. Your patrol may work on a service project or do some crafts. The entire troop may join together for folk dancing. Perhaps patrols will lay trails and come together for a troop cook-out. The troop meeting may close with some favorite songs or a special ceremony. What you do at each meeting depends on you. There are hundreds of things that you can do. You must plan for the ones that you want to do.

Any meeting or activity is more fun if it is well planned. You will need to spend part of each meeting planning for future meetings. It takes time and skill to make good plans. At first you may make mistakes but with practice you will gain skill. The more experienced you become, the further ahead you can plan.

Big events like parties, plays, and troop camps take a lot of planning. They take preparation too. There are some things you need to learn and others you just need to review or practice. No event is a success unless you are prepared.

Troop meetings include the work you do on ranks and badges. It is fun to learn new skills with others. Perhaps you can show the others how to do something you know. Most of the badges include service activities. This gives you a chance to help others. Service is as much a part of Scouting

42

as good times are. Allow time at troop meetings for planning and doing little and big acts of service.

Between troop meetings you can go ahead on your own. You may finish articles you have started, start a new activity, or practice a song or dance, work on a collection, or do some reading. When you work on your ranks and badges in between meetings you will find that troop meetings are even more fun. You will have more to share with troop members.

Most troops meet out-of-doors in good weather. They play tracking and stalking games, go on hikes, cook-outs, and camping trips. Girl Scouting is an outdoor program. Such activities as crafts, dramatics, dancing, songs, and many more can easily be done outdoors. You will find them more fun that way.

Special Troop Occasions

In every troop there are certain events that are important. Ceremonies are one way of celebrating these special occasions. Ceremonies that you make up yourself have more meaning than those you get from books. You can read about ceremonies in Chapter 9.

The registration date of your troop is the troop birthday. At this time most troops have a celebration with candles and cake. By this time all members should have paid their national annual membership dues. Membership cards are usually given out at this birthday party. *Troop birthday*

The presentation of ranks and badges is called a Court of Awards. It can be held at any time of the year and whenever there are badges to be awarded. You may do this at a regular troop meeting, join with another troop, or plan a special pro- *Court of Awards*

43

gram to which you invite your parents. It may be part of a troop party.

Your Court of Awards may include skits which show the things you learned and enjoyed doing for the badges. Perhaps the girls who are to receive the badges plan the troop meeting. If they have earned badges in "Fun in the Out-of-Doors," they may lay a nature trail, hold a playday, or have a cookout. If their badges are in "Adventuring in the Arts," they may lead songs or dances, hold a storytelling period, or arrange an exhibit.

Awarding the badges is the highlight. Plan a ceremony which gives recognition to every troop member's progress. Keep it short, simple, and direct. Include in it some favorite songs and, if you wish, a flag ceremony. This is a fine time to repeat your Promise and Laws as a troop.

Brownie Scout fly-up This ceremony takes place when a Brownie troop becomes an Intermediate troop or when one Brownie graduates to an Intermediate troop. It is called a fly-up because this is the time that Brownie Scouts receive their Brownie wings. When part of a troop flies up into an Intermediate troop, both the Brownie troop and the Intermediate troop come together for the ceremony.

Graduation to a Senior troop Sometimes a whole Intermediate troop is ready to become a Senior troop, and sometimes a few members graduate to a Senior troop. This, also, is occasion for a ceremony.

When part of an Intermediate troop graduates into a Senior troop, both the Intermediate and Senior troop come together, with their leaders, for the occasion.

This is a Girl Scout meeting held in the troop, at camp, or by *Scouts' Own* two or more troops together in which Girl Scouts reaffirm their ideals. It is planned by the girls and their leaders. The Scouts' Own program may grow out of experiences the group have shared together, or books, songs, and poems they have enjoyed. It is held at a time and place agreeable to everyone taking part.

Girl Scout National Occasions

There are certain national events which your troop will want to know about and take part in. You plan for these in your own troop.

Girl Scout Week is celebrated each year during the week of *Girl Scout* March 12, the birthday of Girl Scouts in this country. The *Week* days are called the Seven Service Days. On these days Girl Scout troops make a special effort to show their community what they are doing.

The week includes Girl Scout Sunday, Homemaking Day (Monday), Citizenship Day (Tuesday), Health and Safety Day (Wednesday), International Friendship Day (Thursday), Arts and Crafts Day (Friday), and Out-of-Doors Day (Saturday).

The Girl Scout Birthday, March 12, is the day the first *Girl Scout* troop was started by Juliette Low in Savannah, Georgia. *Birthday* Girl Scout troops often give their contribution to the Juliette Low World Friendship Fund (see page 214) on this day or during Girl Scout Week.

Juliette Low's birthday, October 31, is recognized by Girl *Juliette Low's* Scouts as a special day. The girls often give their contribution *Birthday* to the Juliette Low World Friendship Fund (see page 214) on this day or during Girl Scout Week in March.

45

Girl Scout International Occasions

Girl Scouts and Guides have some special occasions which they celebrate in common. Their plans for these events are part of their troop programs.

International Month February is International Month wherever there are Girl Scouts or Girl Guides. During this month we try to give special thought to the things which are of importance to all people, such as good will, peace, and health.

Many troops plan to do things with people of different national and racial backgrounds during the month. International parties with folk dancing games, and songs are fun. You might exchange recipes with another group or try outdoor dishes from other countries. The activities in the international friendship field will give ideas. In doing these things, try to learn more about other countries and your own country. Share the things that you have learned with others.

Thinking Day Thinking Day falls during International Month on February 22. This day is the birthday of Lord Baden-Powell, Founder of all Scouting. It is the same as the birthday of George Washington, the first president of our country, which is a national holiday. It is celebrated also by Scouts and Guides in memory of Lord Baden-Powell. Lady Olave Baden-Powell, the World Chief Guide, was also born on this day. Thinking Day reminds us of the friendship that exists among the countries that have Scouts and Guides. On this day members of the movement send their greetings to other members all over the world.

CHAPTER 4

Second Class Rank

Second Class Rank Requirements

Choose one activity from each of the following eleven fields to earn the Second Class rank.

Arts and Crafts

1. Make an original design and use it in one of the following: basketry, pottery, wood carving, weaving, textile work, needlecraft, leather, or metal.

2. Make and bind a notebook or scrapbook.

Literature and Dramatics

1. Select a book or story about each of the eleven program fields. Use the book about each field as you work on the Second Class rank requirements.

2. With others, dramatize a story and present it at a troop meeting or before some audience.

Music and Dancing

1. Learn to sing with your troop at least five Girl Scout songs. Teach a simple dance to someone else.

2. Listen to symphonic music. Recognize, by sound, two instruments of a symphony orchestra. Recognize, by sight, ten other instruments.

Community Life

1. Take part as a member of the color guard in a flag ceremony at a troop meeting or other gathering. Help to plan and direct one in your troop meeting.

2. Do something to improve your troop meeting place or help with a project for local improvement that will add to the comfort and happiness of other people.

International Friendship

1. Get acquainted with someone in your own community who was brought up in another country and have him tell you about that country.

2. Learn about the Girl Scouts or Girl Guides of one country other than the U.S.A. Learn about the purpose of our Juliette Low World Friendship Fund and what its projects are.

Nature

1. Choose two of the following and identify, out-of-doors, six kinds of each: trees, birds, wild plants, garden flowers, or constellations.

2. Recognize three kinds of cloud formations; make the five weather flags and know their meaning in combinations.

Out-of-Doors

1. Go on a hike with your troop and be responsible for one of the following: where to go and what to wear; games or songs along the way; the program at the site; collecting and packing first aid equipment and any supplies; keeping a record of the trip; laying a trail using compass directions.

2. Help build a fire for a campfire or cook-out. Do one of the following and demonstrate safety precautions: select a suitable spot and clear it; gather fuel and arrange the

48

woodpile; lay and light a fire; put out the fire and fix the fireplace.

Sports and Games

1. Teach your troop how to play an indoor or outdoor game.

2. Learn how to make and use the following knots: bowline, clove hitch, square, sheetbend, sheepshank.

Agriculture

1. Take full charge of an animal, a garden, or three different kinds of house plants for a week; or help with the care of one of these for at least four weeks.

2. Plant a seed or bulb, or root a cutting. Take care of it for at least four weeks.

Health and Safety

1. Show how to give first aid for fainting, simple cuts, burns, and splinters, and how to use a triangular bandage.

2. Show that you know how to take care of your hair, hands, and teeth. Know the number of hours you should sleep and the amount of water you should drink, and keep a record about yourself for two weeks. Know the kinds of food you *should* eat and keep a record of what you *do* eat for two weeks.

Homemaking

1. Invite some other Girl Scouts or friends to visit your troop meeting. Plan ways to make them feel at home and activities you think they would enjoy. Help prepare and serve simple refreshments.

2. Show that you know how to do one of these: darn, mend a triangular tear, put on a patch, turn a hem, or sew on snaps and buttons.

A girl who wears the Second Class rank badge has explored many interests and has skill in a few. This rank is a sampling. It is an introduction to the hundreds of interesting activities you will find in the proficiency badges.

There are eleven different fields of interest in the Girl Scout program and they are grouped this way:

Adventuring in the Arts	Fun in the Out-of-Doors
Arts and crafts	Nature
Literature and dramatics	Out-of-doors
Music and dancing	Sports and games

Citizens Here and Abroad	You and Your Home
Community life	Agriculture
International friendship	Health and safety
	Homemaking

The best place to work on Second Class is at your troop meetings. Read over the requirements and choose activities that will give you a chance to try something new. The ones that you can do with your patrol or friends are the most fun. Your leader can help you decide how to begin. She will also have tips on the best way to do the activities you choose.

To become a Second Class Scout you must do one activity under each program field—a total of eleven activities. If you wish, you may do both activities in some or all of the fields.

Arts and Crafts

1. **Make an original design and use it in one of the following: basketry, pottery, wood carving, weaving, textile work, needle-craft, leather, or metal.**

Make a design

Line and color are important in design. All designs are made with straight or curved lines or both. Color combinations can be found in anything in nature. What colors do you see in a rainbow, flowers, a butterfly wing, an autumn leaf, a sea shell, or a bird?

Every day you are making designs. What design do your footprints make as you run, skip, and jump? What design do

you and your friends make as you play dodge ball? Have you watched someone lead a song? Her hands make a design.

All around you are many things which will give you ideas for design combinations. Try to make designs from punctuation marks, music notes, snowflakes, leaves, animal footprints, shells, and the petals of flowers.

Practice making all kinds of designs. Choose the design you like best and use it in the craft you select.

2. Make and bind a notebook or scrapbook.

Why not keep a record of the fun you have in your troop? *Make a book* You can make and bind your own scrapbook or notebook. Decide on the size and thickness of your book. Choose paper and binding that will last. Decorate the cover of your book. Try finger painting or printing with linoleum, wood block,

51

potato, or shells. Or make a needlework sampler cover. Turn to your palette and brush to paint a picture which represents the name and symbol of your patrol and troop.

Chapter 8 on arts and crafts will help you on this part of your Second Class rank.

Literature and Dramatics

1. Select a book or story about each of the eleven program fields. As you work on each Second Class rank requirement, use the book about each field.

Books Have you read anything about animals lately or children in other lands? *Smoky: The Story of a Cow Pony* and *Hans Brinker* have long been favorites. The first is related to the nature field and the second to the international friendship field. What other books and fields can you think of? You'll find it fun to browse in the library and find books on different subjects. And it will be even more fun telling your patrol about your discoveries and hearing about theirs.

The more you read and handle books, the greater will be your respect for books. You will understand why some people make a life work of printing and binding books. You may want to learn about the discovery of paper, the invention of printing, early picture writing, and the first alphabet.

Nobody likes to read a book that is dog-eared, torn, and soiled: be careful of the way you treat a book, whether it is your own or borrowed. Dust jackets help keep your books in good condition. You can make them of any heavy paper.

Learn how to make simple repairs on a book. The best way to do this is to visit the mending department of your library or a bookbindery. You will see ways to mend, bind, and re-bind books and can learn about the materials which are used.

We all have the pleasure, now and then, of handling a new book. There is a way to open a new book so that the

binding will not be injured. Open a few pages at a time, first at the front, then at the back, and press the middle of the book gently. Repeat this until you have reached the center of the book.

2. With others, dramatize a story and present it at a troop meeting or before some audience.

Good times are in store for patrols who try their skill at dramatizations. No long rehearsals and preparation are needed. A stage can be made at one corner of the room. Effective costumes can be made from the things found in your meeting room. In no time at all a bit of red sash and a pair of brass curtain rings can turn you into a pirate. A string of beads and a bandanna are all that are needed to become a gypsy.

Dramatizations

Each member of the patrol will, no doubt, have a favorite story. It will be necessary to decide which one can be dramatized most effectively. Try to work out the details for several. Then select the one that will be the most fun to prepare and will bring the most pleasure to your audience.

You will find songs and ballads to dramatize in your Girl Scout songbook. Here are the steps to follow: choose the characters; plan the properties, costumes, and scenery; decide on the action; rehearse the dramatization. You will find helpful information in Chapter 9.

Music and Dancing

1. Learn to sing with your troop at least five Girl Scout songs. Teach a simple dance to someone else.

Singing together Girl Scouts love to sing. They have hundreds of favorites. There are some songs, however, that are popular in every section of the United States. It is good to know these songs for then you can sing with Girl Scouts wherever you may be.

Here are some songs for an investiture, a flag ceremony, for outdoor activities, a world friendship program, a campfire, or a Scout's Own.

When E'er You Make a Promise
FOUR-PART ROUND
W. W. Shield, 1828

When e'er you make a prom-ise Con-sid- er well its im-

port-ance And when made, en-grave it up-on your heart.

54

O Beautiful Banner

This is a Concord Song
Homer H. Harbour and Birdsall Otis Edey   German Folk Song

O beautiful banner all splendid with stars,
That in the breeze is flying,
Proud emblem of the free! My heart and hand salute you,
Dear flag of liberty!

From ocean to ocean you brighten our land,
O'er prairie, forest, mountain,
Superb against the sky. Oh flag for which men labor!
Oh flag for which men die!

From *A Book of Songs* (Concord Series No. 14). Copyright, 1924, by E. C.
Schirmer Music Company, Boston, Mass. Used by permission.

The Wayfarer's Grace

M. Elizabeth Worsfold   *G. C. E. Ryley*

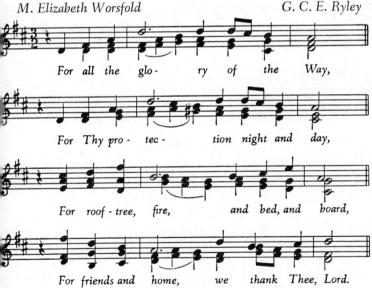

For all the glo - ry of the Way,

For Thy pro - tec - tion night and day,

For roof - tree, fire, and bed, and board,

For friends and home, we thank Thee, Lord.

Copyright 1938 by The Kent Girl Guides Association; from the Kent County Hymn
Book and the Kent County Song Book. Used by permission.

Peace of the River

(Written on the Kentucky River)

Glendora Gosling   Viola Wood

Slowly with expression

Peace I ask of thee, O Riv-er, Peace, peace, peace.

When I learn to live se-rene-ly Cares will cease.

cresc.

From the hills I gath-er cour-age, Vi-sion of the day to be,

Strength to lead, and faith to fol-low, All are giv-en un-to me.

Peace I ask of thee, O Riv-er, Peace, peace, peace.

Our Chalet Song

English version by Betty Askwith   *Joseph Bovet*

High up, high on the mountain,
We've founded our Chalet;
High up, high on the mountain,
We've founded our Chalet;
Its sloping roof and wide
Shall shelter us without a care,
And each Girl Scout and Guide
Shall find a welcome there.

High up, high on the mountain,
We've founded our Chalet;
High up, high on the mountain,
We've founded our Chalet;
And this its dedication
Shall never fail nor be undone:
Each race, each creed, each nation,
Beneath its roof are one.

Words reprinted by permission from *The Kent County Song Book,* Novello and Company, Ltd., London, England.

Gypsy Song

English version by V. M. S.   *German-Swiss*

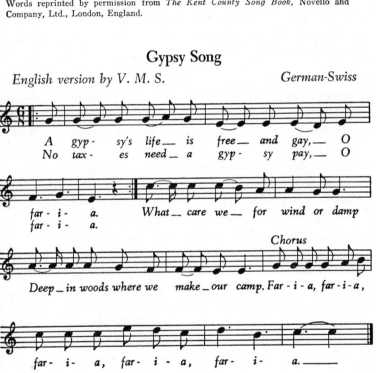

From *"Pfadfinderinnenlieder"* by permission of the Swiss Girl Guides Federation.

All join hands How many circle dances or singing games do you know? Can you teach a folk dance and call a square dance?

Dancing helps to make troop meetings gay and fun. Singing games, folk, square, and modern dances are always popular. Teach the dances you already know to your troop. Learn some of the dances other troop members know. Together, try some new dances. Don't forget to find out about the people who first enjoyed these dances and the countries in which they lived.

2. Listen to symphonic music. Recognize, by sound, two instruments of a symphony orchestra. Recognize, by sight, ten other instruments.

Listening to music What kind of music do you like? Do you ever listen to music alone or with a friend or two? The more you listen to music, the more you will feel at home with it and learn to appreciate its fine points. Soon you will begin to "feel" changes in tempo, time, and volume.

Can you recognize stringed, wind, and percussion instruments in a symphony orchestra? Among the stringed instruments are violins, cellos, harp, and piano. Flutes, oboes, French horns, clarinets, and trumpets make up the wind section. Percussion instruments are the easiest to pick out, such as the deep notes of the bass drum, the roll of trap drums, the clash of cymbals, and the jingle of xylophones.

You can listen to symphonic music on the radio, television, phonograph, or at a concert. Play your records over and over again until you can pick out their main characteristics. Many public libraries have record collections that you can borrow.

Try to discover what the composer is saying to you in his music. Is he describing the gentle winds in spring, a summer thunder shower, the gaiety of a fiesta, or a happy reunion?

Invite some of your friends or patrol to a "listening" party at your home. Discuss your feelings about the music. There will be times when you can hold a concert party with your family or friends.

Community Life

1. Take part as a member of the color guard in a flag ceremony at a troop meeting or other gathering. Help to plan and direct one in your troop meeting.

The flag ceremony is used for investitures, Court of Awards, Thinking Day, patriotic events, and occasional openings and closings of meetings.

The flag ceremony

Every flag ceremony must be carefully planned. Your program may include a song or two, an inspirational reading, a short choral reading, or a brief story. You may wish to say the Laws and repeat the Promise. The Pledge of Allegiance to

the Flag is also included. A short, simple ceremony is most effective. The spirit and the way in which any ceremony is carried out are the things which make you remember them.

A color guard must be selected. If only the flag of the United States is used, a guard of three is chosen—a color bearer who carries the flag and two guards who walk on either side of her. If there is also a troop flag or the flag of the World Association of Girl Guides and Girl Scouts (called the World flag), additional color bearers will be needed.

Here are two ways to bring the flag of the United States before the troop:

1. If the girls in the color guard are standing with the troop, they step back out of the circle or horseshoe and go to the place where the flag is standing. They line up three abreast. At a word from the color bearer they take a few steps toward the flag, stop, and salute. The color bearer steps forward, picks up the flag, and steps back. The color guard then wheels to the right, in unison, and marches to a place in front of the troop.

2. The color guard may remain outside the horseshoe or circle at a spot near the flag. At a signal they come forward and stand in front of the troop.

The same method may be used when there are additional flags. If the flag of the United States is used with another flag, the flag of the United States must be on the right and is the first to be picked up. If three flags are used, the flag of the United States must be in the center.

During the ceremony the color guard stands at attention and takes no part in the singing or speaking.

When the ceremony is over, the color guard wheels to the right and replaces the flag in its original position. The members of the color guard salute the flag and return to their places with the troop.

2. Do something to improve your troop meeting place or help with a project for local improvement that will add to the comfort and happiness of other people.

What can you do to improve your troop meeting place? *Your troop* Get ideas from other troop members and your leader. Present *and town* these to your patrol and then make plans. Are new curtains needed? Do the present ones need laundering? Would some pictures make the room brighter? Does any of the paint need touching up or the floor a good waxing? Have you enough storage space or could your patrol make a chest for troop equipment? And don't forget to look outside, too. Can you do anything to improve the grounds? Would a few flowers or shrubs add a gay note? Does the grass need cutting or the garden need weeding? If your meeting place is a school playground, are there enough trash cans? Is the game equipment in good condition or could it be improved by sanding and revarnishing? Be alert and you will find lots of ways to improve your troop meeting place.

Take a look at your own block. What can you do to beautify it? Can you join forces with a group that has already organized to improve the streets, vacant lots, and properties? Or does your troop want to start its own project? You might clean up a vacant lot, repair a neighborhood tennis court, or direct a "Clean-Up-the-Block" campaign. If you look around you will see many things that you can do to add to the comfort and happiness of your neighbors.

International Friendship

1. Get acquainted with someone in your own community who was brought up in another country and have him tell you about that country.

People from other countries

In every community there are people who have come to the United States from another country.

When they came they brought along customs from their homeland—family traditions, language, law, crafts, music, religion. These they have given to the United States. They have been woven into the folkways that we call American.

The very best way to learn about another country is to talk with someone who was brought up in that country. Natives of another land can tell you how they celebrated holidays and holydays. They can tell stories they heard at home as children. They can sing and hum for you the favorite lullabies and songs. They may give you a recipe for a national dish. They can teach you a folk dance or two. They can tell you of their school days and vacations, of their household chores and family celebrations. They may have pictures, china, linen, or furniture from their native land. Through them you will learn to know their former country, not as a visitor or sight-seer, but as a friend of the family.

If every member of your patrol makes friends with someone who comes from a different country, you can have a fine time exchanging notes. You might combine your knowledge and plan an international party. It would be fun to invite the people who have helped you learn about their native lands to share in the program.

There are other ways of learning about another country. You can talk with people who have traveled. You can listen to radio programs, read newspapers, magazines, and books. You can see travelogues at the movies, attend exhibitions of paintings, crafts, and household arts. You can start a collection of articles from your chosen country such as postage stamps, pieces of embroidery, and pictures of national costumes.

2. Learn about the Girl Scouts or Girl Guides of at least one association on each of the continents. Know their uniform, pin, be familiar with their Laws and Promise; find out how they camp and what other things they do.

It is thrilling to think that you have sister Scouts and Guides living, playing, and working in every continent of the world. You will always recognize a member of the movement by the World pin and the trefoil pin. The latter may differ slightly in size and shape and decoration. But everywhere it

Guiding the world over

stands for the three-fold Promise. In many countries, the Girl Scouts and Guides wear their pin all the time.

The words of the Laws and Promise may differ in various languages but the meaning is the same and all are taken from Lord Baden-Powell's original Laws and Promise. The motto in the Netherlands is *Wees Bereid;* in Denmark *Vær beredt;* in Haiti *Prête;* in Italy, *Estote Parati* and *Sii Preparata;* in Great Britain and the United States, *Be prepared.* The beginning letters of the motto for English-speaking countries are the same as Lord Baden-Powell's initials—B. P.

The uniforms of Girl Scouts and Guides vary with the customs and the climate of their country. The Girl Scouts of the Philippines wear jade green uniforms, the Norges K.F.U.K. Speidere in Norway wear khaki dresses, the Eclaireuse of France brown skirts and white blouses with a tie of a color selected by the company. The Bandeirantes of Brazil have adopted white, the Girl Guides of South Africa appear in navy blue, and the Guides of India wear saris. On pages 216 and 217 you will see pictures of the uniforms and pins of a few of the member countries of the World Association.

Camping is popular all over the world. In Malta the girls sleep in old stone forts. In the Philippines, the Scouts often use shelters made of straw. The girls in France may borrow land near an old chateau on which to pitch their camp. The Padvindsters of the Netherlands use barns. Swedish Guides like tents with four bamboo poles which form an arch. The British Guides use "bell" tents. The Danish Guides like "wall" tents.

Around the world Girl Guides and Scouts are good homemakers, craftsmen, lovers of folk dancing, and makers of music. They enjoy games. They love to be out-of-doors and to become friends with the things of nature. They are ready to give service in their home, community, and country.

Nature

1. Choose two of the following and identify, out-of-doors, six kinds of each: trees, birds, wild plants, garden flowers, or constellations.

To be friends with all the wonderful things in the out-of-doors means much more than just knowing a great many names. Think of all that you know about your friends at school—where they live, what they eat, what they like to do, the color of their hair and eyes, and many other things. *Our out-of-door friends*

If you were asked these same questions about your outdoor friends, could you answer them? Start with some of the things you see every day in the city or the country, such as the fruits and vegetables you eat, the things in flower shops, pet shops, and fish markets, the trees and birds, and don't forget the weeds in a vacant lot or your own garden. Yes, a sparrow enjoying his dinner of dandelion seeds in a back yard is nature. What do you know about the sparrow and the dandelion?

Resolve now that the next time you watch a bird, look at a maple, or examine a jack-in-the-pulpit or a rose, you will really open *your* eyes. You'll be surprised at how many new things there are to discover. Learn to use your five senses—sight, hearing, taste, touch, and smell—in making friends out-of-doors. Chapter 13 is filled with interesting material.

2. Recognize three kinds of cloud formations; make the five weather flags and know their meaning in combination.

Weather is always a topic of conversation. There have been many jingles written about it, too. How many do you know? Are they all true? Test the weather sayings you know against your own observations. *Weather wisdom*

Here is a rhyme about clouds. Is it really true?

> *When the clouds appear like rocks and towers,*
> *The earth's refreshed by frequent showers.*

65

We use Latin words to describe the shape of clouds. The major types are: *cirrus,* feather-like clouds, often called *mare's tails; stratus,* clouds in a layer formation; *cumulus,* clouds in big heaps like masses of white fluff. Before a storm these different types of clouds are apt to cross the sky in quick succession. Be on the lookout for them.

On a hot summer's day you may see the cumulus clouds getting larger and larger. When this happens they are called cumulo-nimbus clouds. Instead of looking like masses of white fluff, they change their shape and resemble rocks and towers. When you see this happening, better take shelter because showers are apt to follow. So you see the little rhyme above is founded in fact.

Out-of-Doors

1. On a hike with your troop, be responsible for one of the following: where to go and what to wear; games or songs along the way; the program at the site; collecting and packing first aid equipment and any supplies; keeping a record of the trip; laying a trail using compass directions.

Hiking Hike short distances first—possibly a mile. Increase the length of your hikes gradually. Three miles an hour is a good average speed. Go slower if you find interesting things along the way.

It's more fun to hike with nothing in your hands, so carry only what you can put in your pockets, strap to your waist, or carry in a knapsack or packbasket. Why not make your own hike first aid kit?

RULES OF THE ROAD. Take Your Girl Scout Laws with you. If you remember "a Girl Scout's honor is to be trusted," you will respect the property of others—you will not pick fruits or flowers without permission, trample cultivated fields, or leave gates open if you found them shut, or shut them if you found them open.

Never accept lifts from strangers, even if you should be tired and late. *Never* thumb a ride.

If you remember "a Girl Scout is courteous," you will not disturb people you meet along the way. You will hike quietly in two's or three's; and you will save the shouts, songs, and lively activities until you are by yourselves.

If you are going to use or cross private property, you must get permission. If you wish to visit or use any building not generally open to the public, arrangements must be made in advance.

Along an automobile highway or traveled road, walk singly on the left side of the road, facing oncoming traffic. When walking on a public highway after dark, wear something white that can be seen easily. Avoid all areas that may be swampy or otherwise dangerous. Never walk along railroad tracks or trestles.

Most experienced hikers drink little water on the trail. A sensible hiker *never* drinks from an untested supply. Unless you are sure you can get tested water, take it with you or purify it. Here are some methods: (a) boil for ten minutes, (b) dissolve one Halazone tablet in a pint of water, (c) add ten drops of chlorine solution to a gallon of water.

REST. Rest for five or ten minutes about once an hour. You may need to rest more often if hiking in hilly country or mountains. In the middle of the day, especially after you have eaten, you will need a longer rest. The best way to relax is to lie flat on your back, with your legs raised and propped against a tree or rock. Always put your sweater or "sit-upon" under you. A sit-upon is a piece of waterproof material (oilcloth is good) about eighteen inches square that you can roll and carry on your belt.

2. Help build a fire for a campfire or cook-out. Do one of the following and demonstrate safety precautions: select a suitable spot and clear it; gather fuel and arrange the woodpile; lay and light a fire, put out the fire and fix the fireplace.

Firebuilding Fire is our friend and servant. It has many uses. We may build our fires to cook food, to give warmth, to set up smoke signals, to burn rubbish, or to gather around in the evening.

Every Girl Scout should be able to make a foundation fire and build it into different kinds of fires. The kind of fire you make depends on the type of fuel, the weather, where you build it, and the purpose for which you build it. It may be necessary to use charcoal. A charcoal fire is started with paper rolled into tight wads.

SELECTING A SITE. You may find a fireplace already built in a state or city park, on a public reservation, or in a neighbor's back yard. In many places you can make a fire only in the fireplaces. In others you will have the responsibility of selecting a good and safe site. No matter where you build a fire, know your local fire regulations.

Your site should be in a clear, open space. Never build a fire against or under a tree. Remove all dried leaves, grass, sticks, and leaf mold. Clear the site down to hard dirt, sand, or rocks for an area of six square feet.

FIXING A FIREPLACE. Build a fireplace of rocks, bricks, clay, or green logs. In windy or dry weather, dig a ditch or hole. A good safety precaution is to wet a circle of ground around the fireplace. Always have a bucket of water or sand or a broom handy. If you are alone or with a small group, gather all the wood you will need before lighting the fire. A fire should never be left unwatched.

GATHERING MATERIAL. Three types of material are needed: tinder, kindling, and fuel.

Tinder is any material which catches fire easily. It should be about as thick as a match and as long as a new pencil. It must have enough body to really burn.

Kindling should vary in size from twigs which are a little bigger than tinder to those that are about as thick as your thumb. Kindling must be dry and should snap when broken.

Fuel is the material which keeps fires burning. It should be firm wood graduated in size from pieces slightly bigger than kindling to good-sized logs.

THE WOODPILE. As the wood is gathered and cut or broken, divide it into piles of tinder, kindling, and fuel. Place the woodpile four feet from the fire and on the side where sparks will not fall on it.

The Basic A fire is easy to build.

1. Lay two good sized sticks of kindling in a V formation with the open end of the V facing the wind.
2. Lay a smaller stick across these to form an A.
3. Place a handful or two of tinder on this crossbar.
4. Kneel and strike your match with your back to the wind. Tip it down so the flame catches the wood. If windy, cup your hands. When the match is burning well, light the tinder from *underneath*.

The foundation fire

69

5. As your fire catches, add more tinder gradually. When it is burning briskly, place pieces of kindling in a tepee or wigwam formation, allowing for a draft.

THE TEPEE OR WIGWAM FIRE. This fire is quick, hot, and compact. It is the best for boiling as the heat is concentrated. After the Basic A fire is burning well, add wood in a tepee shape.

THE CRISS-CROSS FIRE. This is used for campfire or broiling. It burns steadily, produces good coals, and does not need much feeding. Start with the Basic A fire and add wood in a criss-cross formation. Put thick sticks at bottom and smaller ones across the top. In this way the wood will burn and fall, making a bed of coals.

Firebuilding wisdom Keep your fire small. Build it only large enough to serve its purpose. If rubbish or garbage is to be burned, crush papers into hard balls to prevent lighted papers from flying out of the fireplace.

To put out the fire Put the fire out as soon as you have finished using it. Let it die and then scatter the coals. Sprinkle water until there are no live coals. Check again to be sure there are no coals or smoldering logs left. Make a final test by placing your hands on the remains for one minute. "Practically out" will not do; the fire must be *out*.

70   You will find more helps in Chapter 14.

Sports and Games

1. Teach your troop how to play an outdoor or indoor game.

There are many kinds of games—active ones for out-of-doors or a big room, get-acquainted games called "ice-breakers," quiet games that may be played around the campfire or in the living room at home. There are team games as well as individual games. *Games*

You might teach your patrol or troop a game you already know and have played. Suggestions for teaching games are on page 292. Or you might teach a new game. Here are some that are fun to play.

WORLD ASSOCIATION GALLERY.

Equipment: Pictures of Girl Guides and Scouts cut from the *Guides and Girl Scouts Painting Book.* Have paper and pencil for each girl.

Method: Number the pictures and post them around the meeting room. Each player numbers her paper and at a signal starts around the room. She writes the country opposite the correct number on her paper. To score, girls switch papers.

Scoring: Score a point for each picture correctly identified. The patrol that has the highest total score is the winner.

LEAF HUNT.

Equipment: Have 8 to 10 leaves on hand.

Method: Explain the various points in identifying a tree and the difference between simple and compound leaves, and alternates and opposites. Show all the leaves to the group and let them study them. At a signal have the patrols go out and get a similar set.

Scoring: The first patrol to return with a complete set wins.

WHIFFLEPOOF.

Equipment: Each patrol leader makes a whifflepoof from a log approximately 3 inches in diameter and 12 inches long with nails driven into it and a rope attached.

Method: During a hike patrol leaders go ahead of the troop leaving a trail behind them, made by the whifflepoof being pulled over dirt or grass. Each patrol leader takes a different route to the same destination. At a signal each patrol then follows one of the trails.

Scoring: The first patrol to reach the destination wins.

BUZZ.

Equipment: None.

Method: Troop sits in a circle. Each girl counts off a number in turn. When the number seven is reached the girl must say "Buzz" instead of the number. Every time the number is a multiple of seven or has a seven in it such as 14, 17, 21, 27, the player must say "Buzz." If she fails, she drops out of the game. The last people left in are the winners.

2. Learn how to make and use the following knots: bowline; clove hitch; square; sheetbend; sheepshank.

Knotcraft A Girl Scout should be able to tie her own parcels, rope her own blanket roll, tie up her boat, put together a broken string, hitch an animal. A good knot should be tied quickly and untied easily.

The square knot is used to put together two ropes or pieces of string of equal thickness. Use it to tie bundles; to fasten a sling, bandage, or splint; to mend broken strings, ropes, or cords; or to lengthen guard, mooring, or lifelines.

The *sheetbend* is used to put together two ropes of un-equal thickness; or for fastening an end to a permanent loop.

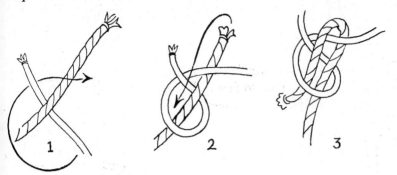

The *sheepshank* is used to take up the slack in a rope.

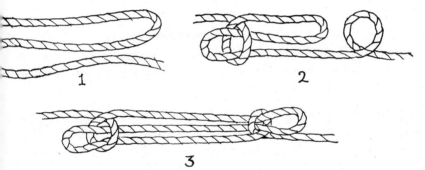

The *bowline* is used for a halter or a lifeline. The loop can be made any size and will not jam or give.

73

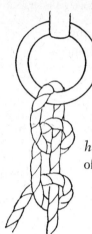

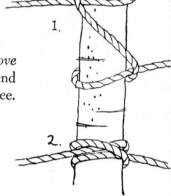

Two half hitches or a *clove hitch* are used to fasten the end of a rope to a ring, post, or tree.

Agriculture

1. Take full charge of an animal, a garden, or three different kinds of house plants for a week; or help with the care of one of these for at least four weeks.

The care of living things An animal, a garden, and house plants all require regular attention if they are to thrive. Ask the person who generally cares for them what things are needed. Read about these things in Chapters 14 and 17. Work out a schedule for yourself and stick to it. Record the interesting things that happen and discuss them with the person who has helped you. Share your findings with your patrol or troop.

2. Plant a seed or bulb, or root a cutting. Take care of it for at least four weeks.

Starting plants Try planting such things as birdseed, orange seeds, beans and peas, onions and potatoes, a slice from the top of a carrot with about an inch of the green left on. Plant them in a pot with any kind of soil and watch the results.

Take a little section of the yard and cultivate the soil. Then plant the seeds of your favorite flower or vegetables or put out some bulbs of daffodils, tulips, and so forth. Have you ever tried growing narcissus bulbs indoors in the winter?

Make cuttings from many different types of plants. The ivy, coleus, begonia, and geranium are especially easy to grow from cuttings. This picture shows you how to make a cutting.

Health and Safety

1. Show how to give first aid for fainting, simple cuts, burns, and splinters and how to use a triangular bandage.

FAINTING. A person faints when there is an insufficient *Simple first* supply of blood to the brain. Keep the patient lying flat. *aid* Loosen any tight clothing. After she recovers she may be given a drink of water. If the person does not regain consciousness in a short period of time, a doctor should be called.

CUTS. Cuts are technically called wounds. A wound is any injury in which the skin is cut or penetrated. In every wound, no matter how small, there is danger of infection.

Wash the surface of minor wounds with mild soap and water. Stop the bleeding by placing gauze over the wound and holding it firmly in place. Apply an antiseptic and a dry, *sterile* dressing. Adhesive tape or any application which keeps out all the air should never be used directly over a wound.

75

BURNS. In mild burns the skin is reddened but not destroyed. Apply sterile petrolatum ointment to the affected part and cover with a sterile gauze dressing.

SPLINTERS. Sterilize a needle by passing it through a flame, an antiseptic, or alcohol. Use the needle to lift the skin over the splinter. Remove the splinter and apply an antiseptic. Cover the wound with sterile gauze and bandage.

TRIANGULAR BANDAGE. Two triangular bandages can be made from a 40-inch square of unbleached muslin cut diagonally. The bandage has many uses in first aid treatment. In its triangular form it is used for an arm sling and in bandaging a head, hand, or a foot.

A cravat bandage is made by making several folds in a triangular bandage. It is frequently used as an emergency support for a sprained ankle.

2. Show that you know how to take care of your hair, hands, and teeth. Know the number of hours you should sleep and the amount of water you should drink, and keep a record of yourself for two weeks. Know the kinds of food you *should* eat and keep a record of what you *do* eat for two weeks.

Your health
76

To have the best possible health, we should all strive for a balanced diet. A balanced diet means having the right kind and amount of food for our own needs. Chapters 16 and 18 contain much information on foods.

Spend at least one hour a day in exercise out-of-doors. Select the kind of exercise you like and take as much of it as possible, considering your physical condition, age, things you have to do, and the climate and time of year.

You should sleep in a well-ventilated room at least nine hours out of every twenty-four.

Try to take a bath every day. Use warm water, plenty of soap, rinse and dry thoroughly.

Your bowel movements should be regular. They will be helped by proper diet, plenty of the right kind of exercise, and sufficient sleep and rest.

Your state of health and bodily cleanliness is seen in the condition of your hair, skin, and nails. Keep your combs and brushes clean, shampoo your hair frequently and brush it daily.

A good complexion comes from good health and a clean skin.

Keep fingernails short and filed to suit the shape of your fingers and hand. Push cuticle back. Cut toenails straight across the top and keep them short. Keep your nails clean by frequent use of soap, water, and a nailbrush.

Protect your own health and that of others by not borrowing or lending such things as your comb, brush, clothes, towel, face cloth, drinking cup, powder puff, or lipstick.

The ten commonest carriers of disease are your ten fingers. Be sure to keep them clean; wash your hands thoroughly, especially before eating and after using the toilet.

Homemaking

1. Invite some other Girl Scouts or friends to visit your troop meeting. Plan ways to make them feel at home and activities

you think they would enjoy. Help prepare and serve simple refreshments.

Entertaining others What do you like to do when you visit another group? How do you like to be greeted? What things make you feel at home? Answer these questions and then make your plans. Your answers will serve as guides. You will find ideas to help you in the Hospitality and Games badges. If everyone has had a good time, guests and hostesses, then you will know the affair was a success.

2. Show that you know how to do one of these: darn, mend a triangular tear, put on a patch, turn a hem, or sew on snaps and buttons.

A stitch in time The old slogan "a stitch in time saves nine" is as true as ever. Many people can help you learn to sew—your mother, a home economics teacher, your leaders, or a friend who likes to sew. Start by learning to do one of the things in Activity 2, but don't stop there. You will find all of them are important. They are skills you will use all your life.

The Girl Scout Promise and Laws

How often have you thought about your Girl Scout Promise and Laws since you were invested? Have you consciously tried to put them into practice? Are they part of everything you do every day?

Why not make a chart for yourself? On the left side of the page write the Promise and Laws. Then on the right side opposite the Promise and each Law, write down the things you have done which show that you are practicing your Girl Scout code. This is your own personal record. It is not something you share with anyone else. If you do this over a period of time, you will find that your Promise and Laws are always with you—at home, at school, in your troop, and in the community. At the same time you will gain a better understanding of their meaning.

Let's take a look at the Laws again.

1. *A Girl Scout's honor is to be trusted.*

She tells the truth, plays fair, and does her work honestly. She can be trusted with other people's money, possessions, or confidences. She keeps her promises.

2. *A Girl Scout is loyal.*

She is true to the things she thinks are right and good. She is faithful to her family, her friends, school, and religion.

3. *A Girl Scout's duty is to be useful and to help others.*

She does her share of duties wherever she may be. She looks for opportunities to help other people in many ways, and prepares herself to do this through her Girl Scout activities.

4. *A Girl Scout is a friend to all and a sister to every other Girl Scout.*

She has a feeling of good will toward people, regardless of nationality, creed, or color. She tries to be friendly to all the members of her troop and to Girl Scouts everywhere.

5. *A Girl Scout is courteous.*

She is thoughtful of other people's feelings. Courtesy is more than saying "Thank you" and "Excuse me." It is consideration for others, although their ideas, ways of living, and beliefs may be different from yours.

6. *A Girl Scout is a friend to animals.*

She sees that her own pets receive good care, and she protects all animals from neglect, cruelty, and unfair treatment. She does not kill any creature unnecessarily.

7. *A Girl Scout obeys orders.*

She respects the rules of her troop, school, home, and community, and does the things she is asked to do by those who are responsible for her.

8. *A Girl Scout is cheerful.*

She does her daily jobs pleasantly. She is not discouraged when things seem hard. She never grumbles or whines when things go against her.

9. *A Girl Scout is thrifty.*

She uses materials, money, time, and energy wisely so that she may have them when she needs them and have some to spare for others.

10. *A Girl Scout is clean in thought, word, and deed.*

She directs her thoughts toward worth-while things so that she will not stoop to words or deeds that would bring shame upon her or upon others.

CHAPTER 5

Proficiency Badges

E ARNING proficiency badges gives you a chance to increase your skill and ability in a particular subject. The word proficiency means "progress, as in acquiring a skill." Proficiency badges help you move forward and progress.

There are many proficiency badges in the Girl Scout program. They are different from the ranks. The ranks deal with a variety of subjects. When you received your Second Class rank, you did one activity from eleven different fields. Do you remember? When you work on a badge, you do several activities in one subject only, such as Photography in arts and crafts, My Troop in community life, Conservation in nature, or Good Grooming in homemaking.

In order to work on these badges, you must finish your Tenderfoot rank first. Most girls also complete their Second Class rank. However, while you are working on your Second Class rank, you and your friends may find one activity very interesting. If you do, and if you want to learn more about it, turn to the program field from which it was taken and you will find a badge that will help you. You may start to work on this badge and earn it before you finish your Second Class rank. But you must finish the Second Class rank requirements before you can become a First Class Scout.

Proficiency badges show that you are prepared to use what you have learned to serve others as well as yourself. Your goal in proficiency badge work is quality rather than quantity. To learn how to do something well and have fun while doing it is much more worth while than having a large number of badges.

Choosing badges It is more fun to choose a badge with activities that you have never done before, even in school. If you do choose a badge that has activities you have already done, do them again but in a different way. Try especially to use your knowledge to serve others.

There are six or more badges in each of the program fields. These are arranged so the ones that are easier to do come first. You will find that the first badges in each field are good starting points, such as Rambler, Games, Adventurer, Active Citizen, Minstrel, and so forth. As you gain skill and knowledge, you can select any badge you wish. If a badge is marked "junior high," it is best to wait until you are in the seventh or eighth grade in school.

As you look over the proficiency badges, make a list of the ones you would like to try. Ask yourself these questions:

Am I really interested in this badge?

Will it be fun to work on with my troop, patrol, and by myself?

Can I work on it at the troop meeting place, at home, or some other place in the community?

Will it help me to be a better person now and prepare me for something I want to do in the future?

Compare your list with other girls in your patrol. Talk over the badges that you have selected. Choose one or two that you could work on together. Through your Court of Honor plan the ways you will work on the activities during troop meetings and in between meetings. Decide what outside help you will need and where you can get it. Talk over the trips you will take in connection with the badge. Make plans to use in your program what you have learned.

Working with others

Every badge has some activities that are done best in a group and others that you can do alone. Most of the badge activities are planned for you to do at troop meetings with your patrol or a group of friends, or at home with your family. Many times you will become particularly interested in an activity and will want to do more work on it by yourself. In general, the ones you work on with others are more fun and better preparation for being useful.

Sometimes you will work on badges with your family. Your mother and your leader together decide what part of the badge you have earned at home. Do the work by yourself and on your own initiative. After you have completed the activities, plan some way of sharing your knowledge or skill with your patrol or troop.

Occasionally, you may work on an entire badge by yourself with the help of an adult. Examples of these badges are Reader, Writer, Musician. You will find, however, that there

83

◀ If you have the Storyteller badge, you can give service.

are many activities in any badge that you can do with your patrol. In any event you show your proficiency by doing something with or for your troop.

Working on a badge Read carefully the note at the beginning of each badge before you start. It tells you how many activities to do. Did you notice that some of the activities have stars? The starred activities are required of every girl who earns the badge. You may choose among the others until you have done as many as you need to earn that badge. It generally takes about three months to complete a badge.

The work you do in school is a good base on which to plan many badge activities. Use what you have learned at school in your troop. Use your Girl Scout knowledge in class.

Finding help Your *Girl Scout Handbook* is your greatest help in working on badges. Turn to the Index and you will find listed the various program fields and the page numbers for illustrations, directions, and other material on your chosen subject. Each program chapter is written to help you earn the badges in that field. For instance, if you want to work on the World Trefoil badge, you will find the required activities under the badge and some information to help you in the international friendship chapter under World Trefoil. All the other information in the chapter will help you too.

Do you know other Girl Scout publications? There is *Hands Around the World* which will help you with international friendship, *Sing Together—A Girl Scout Songbook,* the *Weather Handbook, Arts and Crafts with Inexpensive Materials,* and many others. Your leader has a *Publications Catalog,* ask her about these resources.

Look for material in current magazines. Let your public and school librarians know what you want. You will find

84

If you have the Cook badge, you can give ▶
service.

they are willing to lend you material for your program. For some of the program fields such as agriculture, homemaking, and health and safety, your federal government has many inexpensive bulletins. Write to the Superintendent of Documents, Government Printing Office, Washington 25, D.C., and ask for a list of bulletins on subjects you are interested in. Be sure to state your request clearly.

Finally what about the people you know? Many of them have hobbies and are willing to share them. Ask some of these people to help you and your patrol or troop with your proficiency badges.

Giving service is an important part of your Promise. When *Giving* you say "to help other people at all times," you mean that *service* you are willing and ready to give service. Every badge has suggestions for service projects.

Keep your eyes and ears open and be on the look-out for worth-while things to do. Some service attracts lots of attention. Most service does not. It is more the "see-a-job-and-do-it" sort of thing. This is easy to understand if you just make a list of all the things your mother and father do in a day to make your home pleasant. Look over the list and ask yourself what would happen if they only did those things which brought attention.

Have you ever thought that service is proof that you are important? It is citizenship in action. Service shows that you

have grown up enough to think of someone besides yourself. Service is your way of making a contribution to your community. Service is being able to help someone else because of the skills you have learned.

Wearing your badge Your leader and program consultant will help you decide when you are really skilled enough and are entitled to wear the badge. When you wear the embroidered symbol on your sleeve, you are saying, "I am prepared to be of service in this subject." After you receive your badge, use your new skills and knowledge as much as possible. In that way you will not forget them.

In presenting badges at a Court of Awards, Juliette Low once said: "Every badge you earn is tied up to your motto. This badge is not a reward for something you have done once or for an examination you have passed. Badges are not medals to wear on your sleeve to show what a smart girl you are. A badge is a symbol that you have done the thing it stands for often enough, thoroughly enough, and well enough to be prepared to give service in it. You wear the badge to let people know that you are prepared and willing to be called on because you are a Girl Scout. And Girl Scouting is not just knowing but doing—not just doing but being. A First Class Girl Scout is a first class person."

If you have the My Community badge, you can give service.

CHAPTER 6

First Class Rank

First Class Rank Requirements

1. Complete the Second Class rank.

2. Earn ten proficiency badges, of which no fewer than four, no more than five, are chosen from one field and the remainder from other fields.

3. Complete the Citizens Here and Abroad Requirement.

4. Complete the Fun in the Out-of-Doors Requirement.

5. Complete the Adventuring in the Arts Requirement.

6. Complete the You and Your Home Requirement.

To become a First Class Girl Scout is a high honor. It means that you are an "all-round" girl. You have some skill in many fields and have become proficient in one. You are not only willing but prepared to use your knowledge to help others. You are a first class person.

The First Class rank will take you longer to attain than Tenderfoot or Second Class. It requires hard work, and the ability to stick at a job once started. Generally it takes two

87

years to complete the First Class rank. When you wear your emblem you will be proud of your achievement.

Before you start to work on the requirements, take stock of yourself as a troop member. The following questions will help you:

Do you welcome newcomers to your troop and make them feel at home?

Do you accept responsibility when asked? Do you volunteer to do jobs?

Do you think before you speak and give others a chance to express their opinions, too?

Do you help to make troop meetings run smoothly?

Do you help to make and keep your meeting room attractive?

Do you arrive at meetings on time?

1. Complete the Second Class rank.

This shows that you have some knowledge of each of the eleven program fields. You are able to base your First Class work on the interests you have found as you completed the Second Class rank. You have enjoyed working with other members of your patrol and troop.

2. Earn ten proficiency badges, of which no fewer than four, no more than five, are chosen from one field and the remainder from other fields.

The four or five badges from one field represent your chief interest. Earning that many badges in one field helps you become especially skilled along one line and enables you to take more responsibility and give service or pleasure to others. For this reason before you decide on one field, ask yourself these questions:

Is this a field to which I want to devote a great deal of time?

Are my hobbies along this line?

Is this the subject in which I have my greatest ability?

Will I enjoy sharing these skills with other people?

Does my community offer plenty of opportunities for these activities?

Your parents and leader will help you make a wise choice. Discuss your interests with them and then make your plans.

There are some badges that belong to more than one field. On the first page of some of the badge sections in Part VI there is a list of these badges. For example, the First Aid badge is included in the health and safety field. It also applies equally well to the out-of-doors, and sports and games fields. If you have selected any one of these three fields, First Aid may be counted toward the four to five badges. However, if you decide to work on only four badges in one field, at least three of them should be badges included in your chosen field.

The rest of your ten badges may come from any of the other fields in any combination that you and your leader consider good. It is generally best to choose these badges from several fields for then you will be a girl with a variety of interests and skills.

Some of them may be used to add to your knowledge of your chief interest. For example, if you choose four to five badges in music and dancing, you may earn the Reader or Writer badge in connection with your musical interests. Others might be chosen to help you prepare for something you or your troop wants to do. For example, you might be working in community life, but in preparation for a troop camp you may earn, along with the rest of the troop, the Outdoor Cook or Campcraft badge.

After you have completed your proficiency badges you will be ready to use the skills and knowledge you have learned as you work on the rest of your First Class rank requirements.

3. Complete the Citizens Here and Abroad Requirement.

Check yourself as a citizen here and abroad. Use the "A Friend to All" questionnaire on page 221 and study the skills of an active citizen on page 190. Then do one of the following:

a. Double check the questions you can answer because of what you have learned through your badges. Choose one question that is important to you, and help others in your troop get a better understanding of its importance.

b. Plan a new adventure in friendship that you and your troop can carry out. Do it in a way that shows your thoughtful understanding of people in your community and the world.

4. Complete the Fun in the Out-of-Doors Requirement.

Take part in a troop camp or spend a total of four days in the out-of-doors doing one or more of the following:

a. Teach the Tenderfoot and Second Class rank activities in the out-of-doors field.

b. Be responsible for an afternoon program which includes tracking, stalking, or wide games and teach the Second Class activities in the sports and games field in knotcraft.

c. Take major responsibility for a patrol or troop conservation project.

5. Complete the Adventuring in the Arts Requirement.

With others who are interested, give a play or puppet show for a community group. If you do a puppet show, help make the puppets. Take major responsibility for one of the following:

a. Read a variety of plays from which you select one and direct it.

b. Make and paint the props and scenery.

c. Collect or make the costumes and make up the actresses.

or

With others in your troop, help set up a plan for a story-telling or entertainment hour for a nursery school, playground, or some younger children's group. Tell stories, teach songs, games, simple folk dances, or direct informal dramatics with the children. Continue this at intervals over a period of time.

6. Complete the You and Your Home Requirement.

Make and equip a first aid kit to use in your home for treatment of burns, abrasions, cuts, and other minor injuries which might occur. Teach new girls in your troop or another

91

troop the first aid they will need on an outing and help them
make their first aid kit.

or

Take entire responsibility for planning menus and cooking
at least one meal a day for your family for a week or more.

or

Arrange with your family to assume full responsibility for
some part of managing your home such as caring for a
younger child, taking charge of the shopping, or doing the
house cleaning over a period of two weeks or more.

The Girl Scout Promise and Laws

As you grow, your understanding of the Promise and Laws
should grow too. However, understanding is not something
which comes automatically with another birthday. It is something you have to work for and think about.

*The
Promise*

On my honor, I will try . . . Having honor means having
a sense of what is right, just, and true, and showing it in your
daily actions. It means that you can be trusted. You really
have the intention of being trustworthy or else you would
not have taken the Promise. But good intentions are not
enough. Your aim is to become one of those people who can
always be counted on to carry through an assignment. The
best way to do this is to "Be Prepared."

To do my duty to God . . . You honor God in the finest
way you know, by the things you say, do, and think. You are
a faithful member of your religious group and take part in
the activities of your church or synagogue. Lord Baden-
Powell said: "Thank God for everything you enjoy as you
go about your work each day; a good friend, a good swim, a
good game, a good view, and pray silently for His blessing on
other people as you wish them goodbye."

. . . *and my country*. You are proud of your country. Do you know its history? Remember the courage it took the first settlers to establish their homes in America. You can be proud of the beauty of your country, its greatness, and its resources. How much do you know about the government? Respect the laws and traditions of your country. You will grow in your understanding of democracy by practicing it every day—in your home, troop, school, and community. Do all in your power to make the United States a place where all people may live happily. Take part in projects to improve your community such as bicycle safety program, conservation activities, back-yard playgrounds, and other activities.

To help other people at all times . . . You think of others first. You remember your slogan, "Do a good turn daily." You know it is more fun to discover for yourself something that needs doing than to wait to be asked. Develop your powers of imagination, observation, and sympathy. Try to put yourself in other people's shoes. You know how easy it is to think only of your own interests and wishes and forget how they may affect others.

To obey the Girl Scout Laws . . . You know, understand, and practice the Laws which you have accepted of your own free will. They become for you a code of honor by which to live.

Have you ever stopped to think about the girls you admire *The Laws* most? What makes you admire them? Your answer will be a combination of many things. On the top of the list, however, will be such things as "She is thoughtful of others," "You can count on her," "She's gay," "She'll lend a hand." These are the very qualities that the Girl Scout Laws help you attain.

93

1. *A Girl Scout's honor is to be trusted.*

Your friends know that when you say you will do something it is as good as a promise. Your word can be counted on. You do not accept a job unless you are willing to give time and effort to doing a *good* job. You are known as a person who can always be trusted.

2. *A Girl Scout is loyal.*

You are true to your family, friends, troop, school, religion, and country. You try to understand the reasons why they are as they are and you may see ways they can be better. You admit mistakes and human failings. At the same time you have the courage and loyalty to stand up for what you believe even when you are in the minority.

You are careful not to repeat stories and gossip which may hurt another person or group. "My absent friends have learned that they are safe in my hands," said Florence Nightingale when someone was gossiping about a fellow worker. Do your friends feel that way about you?

3. *A Girl Scout's duty is to be useful and to help others.*

To live up to this Law you must "Be Prepared." Did you ever try to help someone and not know what to do? It is not enough to just *want* to be helpful. You must also know *how* to be helpful and stand ready to lend a hand whenever needed. Try to develop the habit of doing something over and above what is expected of you each day. The more you do, the more you will see to do, and the more prepared you will become to do things well.

4. *A Girl Scout is a friend to all and a sister to every other Girl Scout.*

Look for the best in everyone. Give of yourself freely. It

may be a smile, some extra help at home, or the sharing of a special treat with others.

You know that every person is different in appearance, beliefs, and ideas. You respect those differences. You know that the world would be a dreary place if everything in nature were green. You realize the same applies to people. It is more exciting to have friends with different backgrounds and interests just as it is more interesting to have a meal with meat, vegetables, and a dessert, rather than one which is just a series of ice cream sodas.

You believe in yourself and other people. You try to develop sound values. You try to spread happiness wherever you go. You value your old friends and new friends. King Solomon the Wise said: "He that would have friends must show himself friendly."

5. *A Girl Scout is courteous.*

However kind you want to be, it is by your manners that you will be judged, liked, or disliked. They show wherever you go and often when you are least aware of the fact.

A Girl Scout knows that true courtesy is a sign of consideration of others. A gentle manner and pleasant voice are great assets in life. And the best part is that any girl can acquire them. Look over these questions and see where you can improve:

Are you a good "conversationalist"—one who listens to others and does not monopolize the conversation?

Do you do everything you can as a hostess or a guest?

Can your friends count on you to be a good sport, to be prompt in keeping appointments and in answering letters; to see that there are two sides to every question?

Can your family count on you to practice simple rules of courtesy wherever you may be?

6. *A Girl Scout is a friend to animals.*

You are interested in *all* animals. You try to learn more about their homes and their habits. You work with others in your community to see that all animals are protected from neglect, cruelty, and unfair treatment. Learn about the work of such organizations as the Audubon Society, the Defenders of Furbearers, the Society for Prevention of Cruelty to Animals. They are national organizations interested in the welfare of animals.

7. *A Girl Scout obeys orders.*

You obey those who are responsible for your welfare. Even if you are asked to do something you do not like, you do it when it is right and is your duty. The self-discipline that comes from obeying orders is just as important as courage. Unless you learn how and when to obey an order, it is doubtful that you can ever become a good leader.

You learn about and obey the laws of your community. You know the traffic regulations that affect you as a pedestrian and a cyclist. You know where you can build fires, what permits are necessary, and where to get them. You take time to discover the reasons behind the laws.

8. *A Girl Scout is cheerful.*

Joy and happiness are catching. If you can laugh easily and show others the funny side of things, you will be surrounded by friends.

Happiness does not depend on money, clothes, or other external things. It depends on *you*. A happy person is cheerful even when things do not go her way. A happy person knows the value of a good laugh and sometimes her gayest laughs are on herself.

9. *A Girl Scout is thrifty.*

Learn how to make the best use of your possessions. Thrift does not mean saving things without thought or purpose. Thrift means using what you have wisely—your time, your health, your money, and other possessions.

The most valuable thing you have in life is time. Have you ever thought of how many hours are wasted each week by daydreaming, doing nothing, or just listening to the radio or television when you are not really interested? These are the minutes and the hours that could be spent learning new things, reading, practicing an instrument, painting, sketching, or helping others.

You are apt to take health for granted. Yet if you stay up late, eat the wrong foods, never exercise in the fresh air, and slump and slouch, you will tear down your health. You will be wasting a valuable resource.

Some girls make a budget and stick to it. This is wise and requires discipline. It's not the easiest thing to give up a soda just because you did not put it in your budget. You cannot hope to save for camping equipment or photography gadgets or a new dress if you spend your money on pop, candy, and knicknacks.

If you want to look smart, take time to repair, wash, and press your clothes. Put them away neatly. Take care of your accessories, such as shoes, hats, scarves, and gloves. Keep your books, games, musical instruments, and sporting equipment in good condition.

10. *A Girl Scout is clean in thought, word, and deed.*

You respect your body and your mind; your actions are such that others respect them, too. You have learned what is meant by clean living from your church or synagogue and your family. You use this knowledge in your daily life.

97

You spend your time and thoughts on things that make you a finer person. You enjoy books and activities that you would be willing to share with others. You have the courage to refuse to follow the crowd when you know what they are doing is wrong. You speak, listen, or act in ways that will not hurt other people. You know you are made by God in His image and likeness, and to fulfill His purpose, and therefore, all your thoughts, words, and deeds must be worthy of your Creator.

CHAPTER 7

Older Intermediate Girl Scouts and the Curved Bar Rank

IF YOU are twelve or thirteen years old and in the seventh and eighth grades in school, this chapter is especially for you. It does not matter what rank you have attained for it is filled with ideas to help you have fun as an older Intermediate Scout. Read the whole chapter carefully. After you have earned your First Class rank you can start work on your Curved Bar rank. This is the highest rank in the Intermediate program. Pages 106 to 108 will give you help.

As you grow older and become more experienced, your program in Girl Scouting must also grow and keep pace with your changing interests. Now that you are twelve or thirteen you have new ideas; you like to do things in a different way; you are more selective of your hobbies and interests. You are concerned about *you*.

Do you ever take time out to think about yourself? You have a number of needs and desires which are the same for every girl. In fact they are the same for every human being whether they are old or young or whether they live in Iraq, India, or Italy.

Of course everyone needs to feel that she is an individual. Everyone wants to be recognized for what she does and says.

She wants an opportunity to find out new things and learn to do some things well. Each girl wants a chance to express herself in words and action. She wants people to like her, especially the boys and girls of her own age. Being "one of the gang" is important.

Young people change their ideas about adults as they grow older. A teen-ager wants adults to accept her as a more responsible person—to work in partnership with her. She wants a larger share in planning her own life. She wants more independence.

You are probably no different. Like everyone else, you have your moods. It is natural to feel bright, happy, and gay one day and blue as indigo the next. The important thing is to get better acquainted with yourself so you can control your moods.

All these things are a natural part of growing up. In your troop you can take greater initiative in planning and carrying out the program. You need your leader to be on hand to help you over the rough spots, but you want the program to be your own. This chapter will help you put your ideas into action.

How do I look to others? This question has led many older Intermediate troops into a variety of activities. Your answers are a looking-glass. They will help you pick out your best points and decide what you should do to improve. Ask yourself:

Do I make friends easily?

Do I get along with both boys and girls?

Am I able to work with people whether I like them or not?

Am I a loyal friend? Am I dependable? Do I keep my word?

Do I try to get more than my share of attention at school, troop meetings, home?

Am I overly shy? Do I become confused when I meet new people?

Am I able to express my appreciation?

Can I write a good thank-you letter? Can I make guests feel at ease in my home?

Can I understand my parents' point of view when they think differently than I?

Do I get along with all the members of my family?

Do I have hobbies? Can I do several things well?

Do I get pleasure from helping others?

After looking at yourself, decide on a plan of action. There are some things that you may work on by yourself and others that are fun to do with your patrol or troop.

Ask outside consultants to come to your troop and discuss health, etiquette, good grooming, and attitudes. Ask your leader or librarian to suggest current magazine articles, pamphlets, and books that will help you.

Creative dramatics, a posture or good grooming clinic, activities and parties with other groups of boys and girls, a dad-daughter box supper, or a fashion show will help you put into practice the things you discuss. At the same time, you may finish Play Producer, Good Grooming, Dancer, Nutrition, Clothing, Speaker, or other related badges.

Badges for Older Intermediate Scouts

Have you noticed that some of the proficiency badges are starred and labeled "junior high"? Many of these were suggested and developed by Girl Scouts of junior high age. It makes no difference if you are in a junior high troop, a member of a patrol of older Intermediates, or one individual in a troop of younger girls, these badges are yours. In addition, you find in the following lists other badges that are of interest to older Intermediates.

Adventuring in the Arts

Bibliophile
Journalist
Dramatic Appreciation
Play Producer
Dancer
Any of the badges in the arts and crafts field

Fun and Exploration in the Out-of-Doors

Explorer
Pioneer
Athlete
Sports
Life Saving
Any of the badges in the nature field

Citizens Here and Abroad

My Government
Speaker
Radio
Aviation
My World
Pen Pal

You and Your Home

Public Health
Home Nurse
First Aid
Dressmaker
Good Grooming
Clothing
Nutrition

The badges in each of the eleven fields are arranged according to difficulty. The simpler ones always come first. The last badges in each field are for older Intermediate girls who have completed some of the less difficult ones. This does not mean that you cannot earn other badges. However, most

Girl Scouts prefer to work on the less difficult ones first. Then the others are more fun.

The Good Grooming badge means more to you if you have already earned the Hospitality and Personal Health badges. The Seamstress, Dressmaker, or Textile Design badges prepare you to work on the Clothing badge. The activities in Active Citizen, My Troop, and My Country badges give you a good foundation for the My World badge.

After exploring the Dabbler badge you may develop an interest in weaving, wood, metal, pottery, or glass. The girls who earned Conservation, Explorer, Pioneer, Athlete, and Life Saver badges could never have perfected their skills easily had they not finished their work on the Rambler, Foot Traveler, Campcraft, Games, and Swimmer badges. With a good foundation all kinds of activities are possible now that you are older and more experienced.

Perhaps you have long been a lover of the out-of-doors. If so, you are now ready to do more advanced things. Your skills in nature and outdoor living are improved with use. Only through repetition and practice does anyone develop real skill in any subject. Teach and share them with less experienced members of your troop. *The out-of-doors*

Prepare and plan with other troop members for a troop camp. Make it different from others you have had. Select a new site, go for a longer time, or try a primitive camp. Hold cook-outs and hikes to increase your skills. Learn how to pitch and strike a camp and when you are proficient try a trip camp.

Look into the Conservation, Weather, Pioneer, Explorer, Sports, Canoeing, and Cyclist badges. They will help you become an all-round outdoor person.

Coed activities Softball games, bowling, roller and ice skating, skiing, pot luck suppers, square dances, and service projects can be lots of fun with a neighborhood boys' club, a Boy Scout troop, or a group of boys in your school. Bring the boys in on the planning and give them jobs, too.

Find out some of their hobbies. It is fun to work on such things as photography, first aid, skiing, ice skating, and sports together. You might form a Junior Audubon Club and do some nature badges.

Many boys love to sing. Why not form a mixed chorus and join forces for a simple operetta? A radio workshop is benefited if the boys are on hand to help. You might enjoy exploring together the vocational possibilities in radio or television. Any kind of dancing is more fun with boys and girls. Some of the boys may be just as anxious to improve their skill as you are. Why not ask them?

Service and citizenship Every human being wishes to be useful. Service to others is part of your Girl Scout motto, Promise, and Laws. As you have advanced in Girl Scouting, your ability to serve has grown. Investigate the needs for service in your community. Select and carry out a service project that you can and would like to do.

Older Intermediate Scouts have served as baby sitters while mothers have gone to the polls on election day. They have launched and carried out home and community safety campaigns. They have landscaped the grounds around their schools or troop meeting places. Some troops have carried out conservation projects on their camp sites. All these projects have been related to the badge interests of the troops.

If you are interested in storytelling, why not give service at a children's hospital or in a Brownie troop? A neighborhood playground would welcome your help in teaching

games and songs. Reading aloud to elderly persons or those who are confined is a splendid service project.

You have had many experiences in working with girls, boys, and other adults. Through practice you have learned how to plan with others and how to arrive at group decisions. You have acquired skill in managing your own troop program.

Working with others

105

This business of getting along with people and of working so that everyone can make her best contribution is one of the most important things you can learn. As you plan and work with your troop, you will learn how to plan and work better with representatives from other troops.

Intertroop and community-wide activities are popular with older Intermediate Scouts. Often there is a girls' planning group or a temporary girls' committee in a community which takes charge of these events. You may be elected to represent your troop. You will be expected to plan with representatives from other troops for intertroop programs, to exchange program ideas, and to take action on those things which are of concern to all troops. Every chance you have to plan and work with others is a preparation for becoming a more thoughtful and active citizen.

Curved Bar Rank Requirements

1. Complete the First Class rank.

2. Earn at least four badges from one of the following groups, none of which you earned before. The starred badges in each group are required. If you already have the starred badges, select another badge from the same program field.

Curved Bar in the Arts
    * Reader
    * Minstrel
    * Prints

Plus one additional badge from the arts and crafts, literature and dramatics, or music and dancing fields.

Curved Bar in Citizenship
 * My Government
 * World Trefoil
 * Pioneer

Plus one additional badge from the community life or international friendship fields.

Curved Bar in Homemaking
 * Child Care
 * Personal Health
 * Conservation

Plus one additional badge from the agriculture, homemaking, or health and safety fields.

Curved Bar in the Out-of-Doors
 * Conservation
 * Sports
 * Pioneer

Plus one additional badge from the nature, out-of-doors, or sports and games fields.

The Curved Bar is the highest rank in the Intermediate program. When you wear a Curved Bar, it shows that you are a First Class Scout plus. Your leader and program consultant will expect you to show a high standard of work and to give continuous service in connection with this rank. It will take you about a year to earn your Curved Bar rank. You are awarded only one Curved Bar.

The Curved Bar groups are arranged to correspond with the Senior program. If you complete your Curved Bar in the area in which you are most interested, you will find that you are better prepared to enjoy activities related to your interests as a Senior Girl Scout. Your Curved Bar badges link together the things you have done as an Intermediate Scout and the things you wish to do as a Senior Scout. They help you get ready for the kind of fun older girls enjoy. They prepare you for advanced service.

Bridge to Senior Scouting

As you look ahead to the adventures of Senior Girl Scouting, take a look at yourself: Where are you today? How far have you come? What will you take with you?

What did you do as a Brownie? How did you use those things as an Intermediate Girl Scout? What are the most important things you have learned in your Intermediate troop?

Can you get along with people better? Have you become a better patrol leader, committee chairman, troop member? What new skills and hobbies have you acquired? Do you enjoy sharing the things you have learned with others?

Do you take more responsibility in your troop than you did at ten or eleven? Are you a person who can be counted on to see a job through?

Do your Girl Scout Promise and Laws have deeper meaning to you as you take part in religious, school, and civic activities?

You, yourself, are the best judge of whether you are living up to your Girl Scout ideals. If you feel you are falling short at any point, now is the time to try to pull yourself up again. Remember, the first part of your Promise states: "On my honor, I will try." The saying, "If at first you don't succeed, try, try, again" applies as well to your Girl Scout Promise and Laws as to any skill activity.

Senior Scouting Ahead

And what of the future? Senior Girl Scouting offers you four more years of fun and friendship with girls and boys your own age. The Senior program provides you with opportunities to serve others in grown-up ways, to explore vocations, to work with adults in partnership, and to participate in community, state, regional, national, and international events. As a Senior Scout you have a chance to enjoy the skills you have achieved and acquire new ones.

While there are no ranks and badges in the Senior program, Senior Scouts follow their keenest interests in adventuresome and challenging ways. Each troop has the privilege of naming and being identified by its special interests. Thus we have Mariners, Wing Scouts, Rangers, Trail Blazers, Mountaineers, and many others. You will find that once you have discovered an interest, you can explore it in Senior Scouting and build your program round it.

Those who love the lakes, rivers, and the sea choose Mariner Scouting as their special pursuit. Those who find fascination in the "wild blue yonder" will learn more about aviation in Wing Scouting. Those who love growing and living things, sleeping under the stars, and the glow of campfires follow the steps of the Campcrafter and Woodsman in the Trail Blazer program. The Ranger Aide lives close to nature and serves as its guardian through conservation activities. Mountaineers may climb over rugged terrain in summer and slip down white fields of snow on skis in winter.

Woven through all Senior Scout activities is service to others. While serving others, Senior Scouts have an opportunity to explore vocations. The Hospital Aide serves and works in a hospital performing many of the duties of a nurse. The Child Care Aide learns how to care for children under expert instruction and guidance. Program Aides are trained to help Brownie and Intermediate Scouts in learning new skills in the out-of-doors, music, dancing, arts, and crafts. Museum Aides receive special training to serve in art and natural history museums. Office Aides learn about secretarial and clerical work while giving valuable help in the Girl Scout office or other community agencies.

No matter what Aide program you choose as a Senior Scout, you will receive training, you will serve, you will learn skills for the present and future. No matter what your special interest is, or what phase of the Senior program you are following, you will be joined with all other Girl Scouts the world over through your belief in the Promise and Laws. They will continue to enrich your life, to grow with you, and to offer you a code to live by.

Invite Senior Scouts to visit your troop. Talk to them about their activities. Read the Senior handbook. Discuss Senior Scouting with your leader. Select activities which will increase your skill and knowledge in the part of the Senior program you like best.

PART II

Adventuring in the Arts

CHAPTER 8   Arts and Crafts

CHAPTER 9   Literature and Dramatics

CHAPTER 10   Music and Dancing

CHAPTER 8

Arts and Crafts

HAVE you ever shaped a lump of clay into a bowl, turned a block of wood into an animal, or made a gay lantern from a piece of tin? It is a thrill to say, "I made it myself." Your article may not be as beautiful as one made by an expert but you can be proud of it because it is your own.

In everything you do in arts and crafts you want to be true and honest. If you make something from wood, finish it to look like wood and not like metal. If you use paper, let it look like paper and not leather. When we try to make one material look like another, we lose the beauty of both.

Your design should be your own. You would not sign your name to a poem Shakespeare wrote, or a painting of Rembrandt's, or a song of Stephen Foster's. Learn to design your own work and make it yourself. Then you will know the joy and satisfaction that comes from creative work.

Every human being has the desire to make things. Primitive man started by making tools and useful articles. Later, he decorated these things. Later still, he created articles for beauty and pleasure rather than from need alone. He began to paint scenes on the walls of his cave home. He wove designs into his fabrics. He fashioned jewelry from the materials near at hand. Man's joy in creative work has continued through the centuries.

115

Dabbler

Earning this badge will give you a chance to dabble with a purpose. You can explore and experiment in the use of many kinds of materials. It will help you find out what you like best in arts and crafts. This is your opportunity to draw and paint, to try your hand at puppetry and design, and to make articles from clay, wood, and metal. Find in this badge what you like, and then work on the more specialized badges.

Chalk and crayon Did you know that you can get different widths and shadings with crayons and chalks? It depends on how you use them. Peel the paper off your crayon and break it in two. Draw with the point and then the side and notice the difference in the lines. Split the point of your crayon or chalk and you will get an interesting double line. Try pressing down hard with your crayon and then lightly. Is there a difference in the shade? Use your chalk on wet construction paper. The colors will be brighter and the chalk will go on more easily.

Try pottery Pinch pots are made from a mass of clay. Take a round ball of clay and with your thumb work from the center out, pinching and molding a pot or bowl. Try for even thickness around the sides and the bottom. When the bowl is thoroughly dry, rub it with the side of your pencil or a smooth stone. This will bring out the lovely color of the clay and will give the bowl a highly polished effect.

Make use of wire Interesting three-dimensional forms can be made from thin pliable wire. Bend the wire into the form of some imaginative animal. Hammer parts of it. Cut other materials to attach to it such as copper screening or colored glass.

116

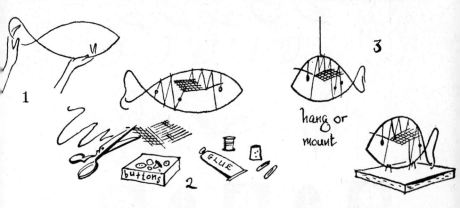

Shoeboxes make wonderful peepshows. Cut away a part of *Build a* the cover and paste colored cellophane over the opening. Cut *peepshow* a one-inch square opening at one end of the shoebox. This will be the peephole.

Now you are ready to build your scene. What type do you want? Will it be a scene from a favorite story, song, or poem? Will you select an historical event? Do you want to make a camp scene?

Bits of sponge, coffee grounds, pebbles, twigs, feathers, cotton, spools, corks, toothpicks, sand, and many other things can be used in building your scenery. As your properties are built, set them in place, and paste them down securely. Decorate the outside of your box with your own designs.

The peepshow is held near the light when viewing. Young children enjoy these toys.

Try new things. *Hints for the*
Sketch several ideas. *dabbler*
Choose one idea and take time to work it carefully.
Use your tools with respect and care.
Be interested in other people's work.
Teach someone else what you have learned. 117

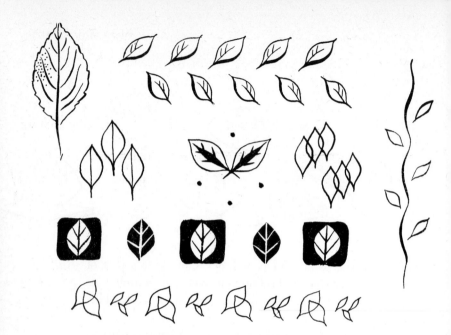

Drawing and Painting

Through drawing and painting you can talk to people all over the world and be understood. You paint a picture to say something about the way you feel. It is like writing a letter or telling a story, but you do it with color, form, and line.

There is a design in everything you do, everything you wear, everything you see. Books on a shelf, the pattern in your dress, the shadows on a wall—all suggest designs. To have fun at troop meetings you need to organize your program, to write a letter you need to organize your thoughts, to make a design you need to organize your lines and your colors.

Try drawing some lines. Do they express your feelings? What different effects can you achieve? Lines that go up and down (vertical) give a feeling of height, strength, power—like tall trees. Lines that go across (horizontal) whether straight or wavy, give a feeling of calmness—like a river. The jagged, broken line gives a feeling of fast movement—like lightning.

Sketches can be made with soft pencils, chalk, or charcoal. *Sketching*
You will find some charcoal in the fireplace after you use a fire. Keep wax paper between your sketches so that they will not blur. Those that you wish to keep for some time must be "fixed." You can buy a prepared fixative, with a pipe for blowing it onto the paper at art stores. Fixative is a mixture of shellac and wood alcohol.

It is fun to experiment with colors. Your uniform is green and so are grasses and leaves. But each is a different green. Some are light, others are dark. Light and dark in colors is called "value." You can get different values of one color by adding black, white, or another color, or a combination of colors. Poster paint (tempera) is fine to use for these experiments.

Finger painting is an exciting way to experiment with colors. *Finger*
You can make your own finger-painting base. Here is a rec- *painting*
ipe:

2 cups laundry starch
1 quart boiling water
1 cup soap flakes

Mix the starch with cold water to make a creamy paste. Add the boiling water and stir while cooking over a low flame until clear. Let cool slightly and stir in soap flakes. Keep covered.

Use slick paper for finger painting. Regular shelf paper, eighteen inches wide, is good. Put your starch medium onto the paper and add your poster paint color. Use your knuckles, fingers, and palms, and jar lids, shells, and combs to get different patterns in your painting. Study the different effects.

Textures "Texture" is the way the surface of things feels and looks. Arrange some of the following textured materials on a piece of paper: feathers, coffee grounds, black-eyed peas, wood, straw, copper, screening, sandpaper, felt, satin, colored yarn, burlap, leather. Combine them in an interesting design. Then paste them on the paper. As you work with these tex-, tured materials, notice the difference between them, for example, between the smoothness of paper, wood, satin. Decide which textures seem to go well together and which do not.

Bookbinding

Did you ever bind a book yourself? You can make your own scrapbooks and photograph albums. Some of these may have leather covers. Others can be made from wood or cloth.

A sewed book is usually divided into sections called "signatures." A signature is a folded sheet of paper or a series of folded sheets ready for sewing. There are usually sixteen pages, but there may be four, eight, sixteen, thirty-two, or sixty-four pages. How many signatures do some of your books have?

A portfolio is useful for all sorts of collections. See if you can follow these steps.

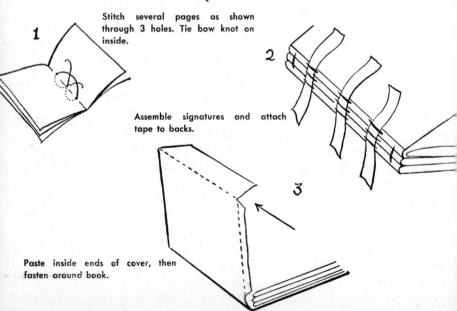

1 Stitch several pages as shown through 3 holes. Tie bow knot on inside.

2 Assemble signatures and attach tape to backs.

3 Paste inside ends of cover, then fasten around book.

Wood

You can make many things of wood. The wood from cigar boxes can be turned into pins, buckles, and buttons. Dogs, penguins, and other animals can be whittled from small pieces of scrap lumber. Larger pieces can be combined with the smooth ends of orange crates to make homes for your animal friends. Birdhouses, bookcases, and magazine racks are good wood-working projects. Wooden spools, button molds, and dowel sticks can be easily made into a child's toy. Dowels are smooth, round sticks that come in different lengths and thicknesses.

When you are out-of-doors, look for interesting pieces of wood. Driftwood, old roots, and burls can be carved into centerpieces or lamp bases. Small limbs that have fallen on the ground but have not rotted make excellent hike sticks.

There are hardwoods and softwoods. Most hardwoods are from the kinds of trees that grow slowly such as the white ash. The softwoods are from quick growing trees such as the red maple. Softwoods are much easier to carve than hardwoods. A fallen softwood tree is a real find. It will furnish a great deal of material.

Before you start whittling, turn to page 22 and check on the care and use of your jackknife. Next, turn to page 75, and see what to do in case of a cut.

Select a piece of softwood about the size of the object you wish to make. Study its shape and grain. Draw your design on the wood so that it runs parallel with the grain. Hold your knife firmly and guide the blade through the wood away from you. Cut the general outline first. Gradually put in the details and round out the shape.

Here is the way to finish a pin or other small objects made of wood:

1. Sandpaper it until it is smooth. Use a medium sandpaper first and finish it with a fine sandpaper.

2. Rub linseed oil into the wood; then wipe off the extra oil.

3. Rub with a mixture of pumice and oil.

4. Rub with wax until it is shiny.

There are other methods of finishing wood, especially in refinishing furniture. Ask the man at the paint store or the librarian where you can get this information. In some of these methods you use stain, varnish, and/or shellac. You put these on the wood after you wipe off the extra oil. Then finish it the same way.

If you have made a pin, you will need a clasp. Cut a slot in the center of the back. Fill the slot with plastic wood. Press the back of a safety pin into the plastic wood. Let it dry for at least two hours before you wear the pin.

Woodcarvers use different kinds of tools. The picture on page 366 shows you a worktable and various tools used in woodworking and carpentry. Ask someone to show you how to saw wood and clamp it safely into a vise, how to hold a nail when driving it with a hammer. If a hammer head seems to loosen a little, hold is upright and strike the end of the handle on a bench or block.

Decorating wood The early Egyptians invented a method of decorating wood. It is called gesso craft and is very popular today. If you follow these steps, you can decorate a box, book ends, napkin rings, or other wooden articles.

Take sixteen tablespoons of whiting and mix with water into thick cream. Whiting is a powder used in making putty and is sold in paint stores.

Stir in twelve tablespoons of liquid glue. Mix thoroughly. Add two tablespoons of varnish and eight of linseed oil. Boil in a double boiler for ten minutes. This makes a little more than one pint of mixture. Sketch your design lightly on the wood. Then fill in the design with brush loads of gesso. Drip little spots or beads for extra designs. You can add tempera color to gesso to tint it. Metallic powders may also be used.

Glass

Many things in your home are made from glass—mirrors, windows, and glasses themselves. The glass in each of these articles is different. Each has been made for a special purpose.

Here are some terms that every glass lover knows:

"Cut glass" is glassware decorated by cutting figures or patterns into the surface. This is done by pressing the glass against a revolving wheel.

In "pressed glass" the glass is not blown but forced mechanically into a mold. This was started in America around 1825. There is hand-pressed glassware as well.

"Milk glass" is opaque white glass. The most familiar is opaque-white pressed glass which was popular at the end of the last century.

Crystal and fine glass are synonymous. It has quite a bit of lead in it which makes it brighter, stronger, and sound like a bell if you tap the glass with your fingernail.

Sandwich is one of the best-known names in American glass. A man named Deming Jarves first founded a factory in Sandwich, Massachusetts, in 1825. It was known as the Sandwich Manufacturing Company. This factory produced such good pressed glass that now the names pressed glass and Sandwich glass mean the same thing.

Monogramming by etching, or engraving on glassware is an ancient art. Glassware treated this way has long been popular but expensive. It required special equipment and chemicals. It could only be done by trained experts. Today a new method has been discovered so that you can decorate your own glassware. These are the steps:

1. Purchase etching cream and a thin aluminum stencil at a crafts supply house.

2. Draw your design on the stencil and cut out the design itself.

3. Attach the stencil to the glass. Apply etching cream to the cutout area.

4. In about two minutes, hold the glass, with stencil and cream on it, under running warm water. Or hold it in a pan of warm water.

5. Remove the stencil and cream. Your initial, monogram, or design remains etched for the life of the glass.

Pottery

The term pottery applies broadly to all articles made from clay and hardened by heat or fired. These articles range from ordinary bricks to the finest porcelain.

Here are some common terms used in pottery:

Slip. Clay mixed with water to a thick cream consistency. It is used to paint designs on pottery or to weld two pieces of clay together.

Sgraffito. Decoration made by scratching through a layer of slip. Used by early Pennsylvania German potters.

Biscuit or bisque. Clay which has been fired once but is unglazed.

Under-glaze. Paints or metallic oxides are added to clay slip and then painted or sprayed on bisque ware. A clear glaze is then painted, dipped, sprayed, or poured over the entire piece and fired.

Glaze. A coating used to cover clay articles. When fired it melts and forms a glassy coating which makes clay waterproof.

All clay must be wedged to get rid of air bubbles and to press the particles of clay closer together. If this isn't done, the article will break when it is heated. The picture above shows how to make and use a wedging board.

Clay will stick to a table top. So you should make plaster bats to work on or cover the table with oilcloth or linoleum.

Orange sticks, bobby pins, meat skewers, or tongue depressors are good modeling tools. You can also whittle your own from pieces of wood.

Two of the methods used in pottery-making are the "mass" and the "coil." In the mass method, the object to be molded

125

is worked directly from a mass of wedged clay. It may be a figure, dish, bowl, tile, or plaque. In this method some of the work is done by hand and some with the help of the potter's wheel.

The second method is called the coil method. It is often used for making bowls. The object is built from coils of wedged clay. In this method all the modeling is done by hand. Make a pinch pot with walls one-half inch thick, add coils of soft clay and shape. If you wish, you may build from a base of clay by using coils. Be sure the inside of the bowl is smooth. The outside may be smoothed, or you may leave the coils showing, or you may put interesting texture on it with a saw blade or other tool.

You can model all kinds of things. Mold the clay into the rough form of what you wish to make. Gradually add more clay in some places or take it away in others. This will bring out the important parts like head, legs, arms, wings, and so forth. Pushing clay through copper screening makes texture for hair, flower centers, and so on.

Leather

A book cover, a purse or wallet, a camera case, a belt, or a sheath for your hatchet are a few of the things you can make from leather.

Get the feel of working with leather by practicing on leather scraps. Try using different types of leather. Make small articles which look well without decoration such as matchbox covers, bookmarks, or coasters. Make a paper pattern first and then cut the leather. Articles such as these make useful and attractive gifts.

Tooling leathers are used for articles which are to be decorated. Calfskin and cowhide are popular. A bookmark is something simple to start with. Here are the steps to follow:

1. Make a paper pattern and decide which parts of the article are to be decorated.

2. Draw a simple design for these parts on another piece of paper.

3. Dampen your leather with a cloth or sponge. This should be done on the flesh side until damp on the finished side. Always dampen the whole piece of leather in order to avoid water spots. If it is too wet, the water will ooze when you start to work.

4. Lay the paper design on the front of the leather and trace the design with a pencil.

5. Place the leather on a piece of glass. With the flat end of a modeling tool, press down gently around the edges of the design. Use firm, even strokes. Gradually the whole background will be pressed down and only the design will be raised, or embossed.

6. With the broad end of your modeling tool press the design up from the underside of the leather.

7. When the leather is dry, paint the back with a coat of shellac. This holds the tooling firm.

8. Finish the article by rubbing with a good floor wax, either liquid or paste. When it is dry, polish it with a soft cloth.

There is a big thrill in designing and making your own moccasins, jerkins, handbags, and belts. A "handmade original" is a prized possession.

Needlecraft

On this page are some of the common embroidery stitches. You can learn them easily. You will find dozens of others as well as many things to make in needlework books. Borrow one of these books from your library.

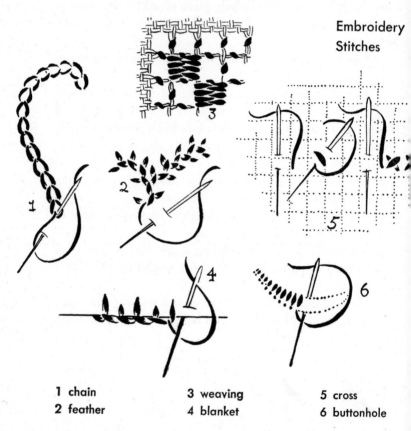

Embroidery Stitches

1 chain	3 weaving	5 cross
2 feather	4 blanket	6 buttonhole

Florentine embroidery comes to us from Florence, Italy. It is done on coarse linen or canvas with floss silk or fine wool. Many variations are possible from a simple weave pattern to a floral stitch.

Assisi embroidery also comes to us from Italy. It is a variation of cross-stitch embroidery. The background is embroidered with crosses and the pattern is left plain.

Hedebo embroidery comes from Denmark. It is cut and drawn work done in white on white linen. The name comes from *heden* meaning heath and *bo* to live, because the people who lived on the heath did this kind of embroidery.

Jacobean embroidery is characterized by designs rather than any particular stitches. It uses delicate floral forms. It was first done in England but shows the influence of the Orient.

It is a good idea to have a box or basket in which to keep your sewing things: thread, needles, thimble, scissors, tape measure, and so on. Make your own sewing basket (see page 136). Or, make a sewing box out of any kind of pasteboard or wooden box painted or covered with wallpaper or cloth. Perhaps you would like to use plain paper or cloth that you have blockprinted (see page 130).

Textile Design

The frontier wife in America had to be a chemist and botanist. She spent long hours over steaming kettles, dipping and wringing fabrics. She had to solve the mysteries of the vegetable and chemical dyes of her day.

Today we no longer decorate materials ourselves because we have to. We do it because we want to. It is fun to see our own designs on luncheon cloths, place mats, draperies, camp ties, and many other things. There are many methods from which we can choose. You can try different methods and become skilled in several.

129

Stenciling Stenciling is one of the oldest and easiest ways of putting a design on paper, fabric, or wood. First you draw a design on cardboard or stencil paper; now cut out the design. This is your stencil. Pin it tightly over the material and paint the part that shows through the hole. Use a stiff brush, and paint from the edges to the middle.

Silk screening The silk screen process was developed in this country. It is based on the same principle as the paper stencil and is used on paper as well as textiles. A coat of lacquer is placed on the silk, leaving only the design uncovered. A tool called a squeegee is used to push the color through the silk screen on to the cloth. It is easier to get different shades in your designs by using the silk screen method than by using a paper stencil.

Batik Batik work comes to us from Java. The design is put on the cloth with carbon paper. The cloth is then attached to a frame and the design is painted on both sides of the cloth with a wax mixture. After the wax has dried, the cloth is crumpled and immersed in a dye bath. Finally the cloth is ironed to remove the wax.

Tied-and-dyed Interesting effects in color and design can be obtained through the tied-and-dyed method. The cloth is knotted in several spots and put in a pot of dye. When the cloth is dry, undo the knots and tie in different spots. Put the cloth in a pot of dye of another color. Keep doing this until you like the way your material looks.

Block printing Woodblock printing was used in the early days of the cotton printing industry in this country. Wood blocks were made from basswood or other softwoods.

130

Today linoleum blocks are more popular in textile work. They are easier to make and do not require woodcutting tools. You can use battleship linoleum or purchase mounted blocks at an art supply store. Warm the linoleum before you start to work. It will become softer and easier to cut. Cut your design

deeply so that it will print clearly. Use a simple design on a coarse fabric. If you select a smooth textured fabric, you can use a more detailed design.

As you print, place layers of newspaper under the cloth on which you are printing. Ink the block with a brayer. This is a rubber-covered roller. When in place the block must be tapped with a wooden mallet. If you do not have a mallet, place your cloth and block on the floor and step on it. This will give you a clear print. Remember to use textile paints when printing on fabrics.

Weaving

The North American Indian contributed much to the art of weaving. He developed the warp-weighted loom, the two-barred upright loom, and the small horizontal loom on which decorative belts were woven. Today there are many standard harness looms on the market that weave fabric eight to thirty-

131

six inches wide. These looms have rollers for the finished fabric. The weaver can make a pattern in the material by the way he threads the heddles and moves the harnesses.

However, like the Indian and our colonial forefathers, you can easily make your own loom to weave such things as table runners, mats, bags, scarves.

Simple loom Get a fruit or seedling box about five inches deep. Cut out long sides as indicated by dotted lines, and sand off rough edges.

With heavy wire (coat hangers) make four holders for the warp beams. Make a space at the end no more than one-quarter inch between the wires. Attach them to the top of the four corners of the box.

Bend holders around the end of the box so that the loop lies close to the side.

The two warp beams can be cut from flat strips of wood— old yardsticks make good ones. They must be two inches longer than the outside width of the box.

Now you are ready to make the heddle frame and heddles, which will lift and lower the warp.

The length of the frame must be one inch shorter than the *inside* width of the box.

Cut fifty pieces of twine, each fourteen inches long. Double a piece and attach it to the top of the frame (A). Take the double twine and knot it two inches below the frame (B). Pull tight and tie another knot one-half inch below the first one (C). Attach the twine firmly to the bottom of the frame (D). Each piece of twine is put on this way.

Warp threads should be cut at least seven inches longer than the final length of weaving. Colored twine is good to use as a starter.

132 Fasten about eight warp threads at a time to warp beam B

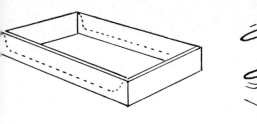

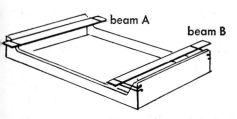

beam A

beam B

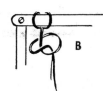

heddle frame — thin strips
of wood screwed together

A

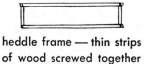

B

C

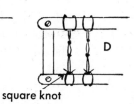

D

square knot

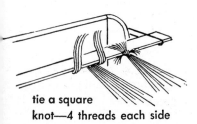

tie a square
knot—4 threads each side

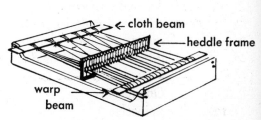

← cloth beam

← heddle frame

warp
beam

(nearest you). Continue tying on eight at a time until all are attached to beam B.

Allow eight to ten threads of twine to the inch in the finished weaving.

Slip the beam out of its holders and roll the warp tightly until only enough remains to stretch easily across the loom. Put beam back in holders.

Now begin threading the warp threads through the heddle frame.

Thread number one goes through the first heddle (the eye between the knots). Thread number two goes *between* the first two heddles. Thread number three goes through the eye of heddle number two, and so on.

When all the warp is threaded past the heddle frame, attach it, eight threads at a time, to the warp beam A. Be sure to pull it tight before tying the knots.

Now your loom is ready to operate. When the frame is pulled up, the odd-numbered threads are raised above the even ones, making a "shed" between beam A and the heddle, where the shuttle can be slipped through. When the heddle is pushed down, the even-numbered threads are left above the odd ones and the shuttle is returned to its starting position.

As the weaving progresses the rolled-up warp is unwound from beam B and the finished cloth wound up on beam A.

Natural dyeing To make weaving even more interesting, try dyeing your yarns and materials with dyes made from native plants. Be sure to use only common plants. Here are a few common things that can be used and the colors they make.

Onion skins	light brown, yellow, orange
Spinach	green

Beets	rose
Goldenrod flowers	gold
Coffee	brown
Red sumac (leaves)	black
Red sumac (berries)	red
Carrots	yellow

To make natural dyes you will need this equipment: enamel pan, rubber gloves, stirring rods (dowels, or stick), paper towels, cheesecloth.

Follow these directions:

1. Chop leaves, grind roots or crush berries; soak overnight in enough water to cover.

2. Boil slowly for an hour.

3. Strain dye, removing plant material.

4. Add mordant (alum).

5. Dampen material, wring.

6. Put in dye bath to cover.

7. Simmer slowly until material is right color (a little darker when wet than dry).

It is nearly impossible to give exact proportions, as so much depends on what shade you want and what plant material you are using. However, the following proportions should give you some idea of amounts. If you use 1 quart berries, roots, or leaves, 2 quarts of water, and 1 ounce of alum, you can dye ¼ pound of fabric.

Basketry

Among the many kinds of baskets are sewing baskets, flower baskets, market baskets, wastebaskets, and packbaskets. Baskets are made of bark, grasses, raffia, reeds, rushes, pine needles, palmetto, vines, or splints.

Different parts of the country produce different types of baskets. Certain tribes of American Indians were and still are noted as fine basket makers. Some of their baskets are so tight and firm that they are used for water jugs. The Indian frequently uses baskets as a part of his tribal rituals. Symbols of rain clouds and sun, the eagle's flight, and other tribal designs appear on his baskets.

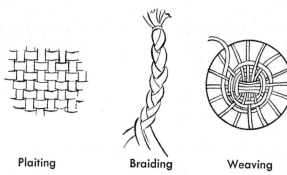

Plaiting   Braiding   Weaving

These are the general methods of basket making: weaving, coiling, braiding, and plaiting. In the weaving method, round materials are usually used such as vines, roots, reeds, and branches. The spokes form the basket framework and should be stronger than the weavers so they will hold the shape of the basket. The base is usually shaped like an inverted saucer. The coil method is used for grasses, pine needles, husks, and other short length materials. In the braiding method the materials are first braided and then they are coiled and sewn together. The plaiting method is illustrated by the grocer's delivery basket. Usually flat materials are used, such as rushes, splints, and corn husks.

All things used in basket making must be prepared in some way. The picture on the opposite page gives directions for preparing some basketry materials.

In your camp or in your town, you may be able to find some of the things growing that can be used for making baskets. Splint baskets are usually made from oak or ash.

136

How to Prepare Basketry Materials

Red cedar bark

1. Strip from dead trees only.

2. Boil for 10 or 15 minutes in water and wood ashes.

3. Rinse off and lay on board to dry.

Grasses

1. Cut.

2. Dry.

Corn

1. Husk.

2. Tear husks into ½-inch strips.

3. Soak.

Metal

Every metal has its own characteristics. Some are easier to bend and shape than others. If a metal can be molded easily, it is called "malleable." Lead is the most malleable metal and nickel silver is the least malleable. In between these two are: pewter, tin, aluminum, copper, silver, iron, and brass. Learn what it is like to work with as many of these metals as possible.

Start with a bowl or tray made from lead, pewter, or aluminum. Irregular shapes make interesting pieces. It is exciting to see a flat sheet of metal change to a hollow form under the blows of your hammer.

You will need the following tools: flat wood block or stump or old flatiron, ball peen hammer, jeweler's saw and blades, bench pin or notched board, half round file—No. 2 cut, and emery paper or fine steel wool.

Soldering is the method used to hold two pieces of metal together. There are hard and soft solders. The kind of solder you use depends on the malleability of the metal. A simple blow torch is used with hard solder.

Metal can be decorated by etching. Draw a simple design on paper. Transfer the design on to the metal. Use a covering, such as asphaltum, that will resist the acid. Paint all the parts of your design that you do not want to be eaten away by the acid. The type of acid you use depends on the metal. This is mixed in a glass dish and the article to be etched placed in the acid bath. All acids are dangerous. Great care must be taken in using them.

Prints

A print is an impression made from a metal plate, wooden block, or stone on which a design has been cut, etched, or engraved.

138

There are three kinds of prints:

1. Prints in which the design to be printed is *raised* and the background is cut away. These are called relief prints. Blockprints belong to this group.

2. Prints in which the design is *sunk in*. These are called intaglio prints. Etchings, dry points, mezzotints, and aquatints belong to this group.

3. Prints made from a *flat* surface which is neither raised nor sunk in. These are called planograph prints. Lithographs, monotypes, and stencils belong to this group.

Blockprint designs are generally cut out of wood or linoleum. However, you can start by using potatoes, turnips, carrots, cork, sticks, shells, and the ends of spools.

When using vegetables it is necessary to use a blotter to dry up the moisture or "juice" before starting to print. If you want to keep your vegetable printer overnight, place the printing end in water. When you print, remove the excess moisture with your blotter.

Blockprint designs should be kept simple. Remember that the lines that you want to print must be raised. Cut away all the background. Lettering is not very effective unless you are very skilled. All lettering must be cut backward on the block.

For printing with any of the blocks mentioned above, use water paints on paper and textile paint on textile.

In addition to the kinds of prints mentioned so far, you may like to try others, such as smoke, ozalid, ink, stamp pad, spatter, and blue prints. You can use some to record your nature observations. With others you can make greeting cards, bookplates, end papers, and napkins.

Interior Decoration

Let's start with a "decorator's survey" of a room you would like to change. See it as an empty box, with no furniture, no color, no radiators, no glass in the windows, no paintings—nothing! Sketch a new plan, add color, make a scale model, and then get to work on the room itself.

A well-decorated room, like a well-dressed person, will present a complete, pleasing, well-thought-out picture. It should be furnished and decorated to fit a purpose such as a meeting room, sleeping room, or living room. A good interior decorator tries to express personality through the furnishings she plans and the colors she selects.

A room is disturbing when there are too many mixed patterns—on furniture, in the carpet, in the wallpaper, in the draperies. A restful and harmonious room is created by avoiding clashing colors and patterns. Floors are meant to stay underfoot. When the wood is too light, or the rug too patterned, the floor immediately rises up and hits you. A room becomes bright and cheerful through the use of pretty things. The choice and placement of pillows, lights, mirrors, paintings, and plants provide comfort, warmth, and brightness. A room is more interesting when it is orderly, well balanced, and there is ample space.

One of the most exciting things about interior decoration is the taking of an old piece of furniture and refinishing it

yourself. You can find inexpensive items at auctions, antique shops or second hand shops. Try to find something rather simple without too much carving or detail—a plain chair, chest, table or even a wooden bowl. Usually the old finish must be removed first. Sometimes it is necessary to use paint or varnish remover.

Photography

Everywhere you go you are likely to find people with cameras busy photographing their friends, the scenery, their pets, or anything they enjoy. Almost everyone knows how to take pictures, but it requires knowledge to take good pictures.

The most inexpensive camera can take good pictures if the person using it knows a few everyday facts about composition, light, exposure, distance, and what that camera can do.

The amount of light, time of exposure, and distance at which the camera takes a good picture varies with types of cameras. But good composition is the same for all.

"Composition" means the arrangement of the subject in the picture. Every good picture has a focal point. That is the point to which your eye is immediately attracted.

Here is a method you can use to get practice in composition. Outline on a piece of cardboard the dimensions of the picture your camera takes. Cut away this area. You now have a frame which is called a "finder."

Hold your finder in front of you at arm's length. Look around for a subject that will make a good picture. Decide what the focal point is to be. Keep moving the finder and yourself until you get a well-balanced arrangement. Practice in your house, back yard, on a trip, at camp, along a street— anywhere. The position of such things as trees, lakes, and mountains cannot be changed, but we *can* move ourselves and our cameras.

If you have a room in your house that you can make com-   141 pletely dark, you can develop and print your own pictures. Someone in your community knows where to get an inexpensive developing and printing apparatus and will help you and your troop. You can make parts of this apparatus yourself. Developing and printing is half the fun of photography.

Architecture

Architecture is the science and art of designing and constructing buildings. Every building should be strong, beautiful, and suitable for a purpose. Whether it is a house, factory, school, or hospital, it should show these three marks of a good building.

Styles of architecture change with the times like the clothes we wear and the utensils we use. Building materials also change as new materials are developed. Floor plans and exteriors follow the changes made by the invention of new conveniences. For example, the invention of the elevator made the tall office building or apartment house possible.

The architecture of the interior of our homes and the decoration of them is called interior architecture. It has been affected by the use of gas, electricity, and central heating which replaced the oil lamps, wood-burning stoves, and fireplaces of our ancestors.

The way we want to live also brings about changes in architecture. The desire to live informally has simplified both the exterior and interior of our homes. Can you find some of the differences between the oldest house in your community and some of the new ones?

Some buildings have outstanding characteristics. Often they are said to be built in a certain style. Would you recognize an Elizabethan cottage, a log-cabin home, a Colonial house? Could you give examples of Moorish, Greek, and Roman architecture? Do you know the differences between Gothic and Renaissance buildings? In what parts of the

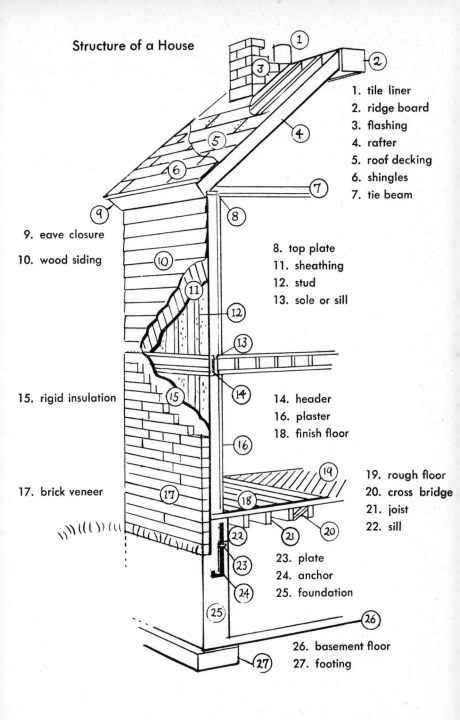

Structure of a House

1. tile liner
2. ridge board
3. flashing
4. rafter
5. roof decking
6. shingles
7. tie beam

9. eave closure
10. wood siding

8. top plate
11. sheathing
12. stud
13. sole or sill

15. rigid insulation

14. header
16. plaster
18. finish floor

19. rough floor
20. cross bridge
21. joist
22. sill

17. brick veneer

23. plate
24. anchor
25. foundation

26. basement floor
27. footing

United States would you find the influence of the French, the Spanish, or the English on architecture? Do any buildings in your community have outstanding characteristics?

It is useful to be able to read a blueprint and know the names for the different parts of the structure of a house. You will also find floor plans and helpful information on architecture in many popular magazines.

CHAPTER 9

Literature and Dramatics

BOOKS and plays spell adventure, romance, discovery. They are magic carpets taking you to exciting places to meet interesting people, see unusual sights, and enjoy wonderful experiences.

As you read a book or watch a play you forget the everyday world. The people in the story come alive. They become friends and you live with them. You grow to love some more than others. You can imagine yourself as some of your favorites. You feel their joys and sorrows. You share their adventures.

Literature and dramatics have much in common. Both are great arts requiring skill and talent to be effective. In both, the writers share with you their ideas and feelings. The writer of books uses the written word. The playwright or dramatist uses the written word. All writers seek to capture your imagination with their tales.

LITERATURE

Literature opens whole new worlds to you in the land of books. Emilie Poulsson sums this up when she says:

> Books are keys to wisdom's treasure,
> Books are gates to lands of pleasure,
> Books are paths that upwards lead,
> Books are friends. Come, let us read.*

---

* Inscription in the Children's Reading Room, Hopkinson Public Library, Hopkinson, Mass.

Yes, hours of pleasure are in store for booklovers. You can find anything you want in books. Taste in reading is just like taste in foods. It varies with each individual, and there are books to suit every taste.

Books add interest and value to any hobby. In them, you can find all sorts of information. Books bring to your armchair pictures of faraway places. You may never visit these lands but you can become friends with the people who live across the seas. Through your reading you can be a member of a Japanese family, or visit in an Eskimo igloo, or skate with the Dutch boys and girls on the canals of the Netherlands. You can share in the fun and adventures of people all over the world. You can learn more about the daily life and customs of your neighbors. Many will hold your interest through the beauty of their language. There is music in words. Look for it as you read and write.

Magic Carpet

Right at your own doorstep you can find the pleasure of reading and the fun of acting. Many of your favorite tales can be dramatized by your friends, patrol members, or troop.

You do not have to look far to find interesting books. You can find them at home, at school, among your friends, and at the public library. There are all kinds, too—travel, adventure, romance, mystery, exploration, history, poetry, fiction, and so forth. You may already have a favorite kind of book. Most people do. But explore them all. There may be some kinds of books which you may not like at first. However, you often find that your interest and enjoyment grow. The more well-rounded your reading habits are the greater will be your pleasure as you explore the land of books.

Start to make a collection of your special favorites. Bring a few of these to your troop meeting and exchange some of your books with other members of your patrol. It is fun to design your own bookplate and make an original book jacket with picture, title, and author's name. You might build a bookcase for your meeting room and start a small library. You will need a system for marking the books and for checking when someone borrows or returns them.

When many books are gathered together in one place, they are put on shelves in a special way. The majority of libraries use the Dewey decimal system. This was introduced in 1876 by Melvil Dewey, who was also the founder of the American Library Association. The librarian at your school or public library will show you how to use the card catalog to find a book. She can also give you suggestions on books you might like to read. Ask her for help when you set up a troop library.

If you find a piece of poetry or a descriptive paragraph or a saying that you especially like, what do you do? Many people make anthologies. The word "anthology" comes from the Greek *anthos* flower and *lego* gather. You gather together in one place your own favorites. You can start your anthology in a notebook. Make a special cover for it and illustrate some of your favorites.

You often read the word "folklore." Do you know what it means? It is used to describe the traditions, customs, and beliefs of people. Folklore is handed down from one generation to another. When folklore is woven into a story, it is called a folk tale.

Folk tales are interesting to read. They can also be dramatized and are excellent for storytelling. You will find help on dramatics on page 159 and storytelling on page 151.

If you are interested in American folklore, you will enjoy "Johnny Appleseed" by Vachel Lindsay. This poem tells the story of a half-historical, half-legendary character who made his way across the wilderness leaving behind him the seeds of our apple orchards. Also look up *Paul Bunyan* by Esther Shepard and *Yankee Doodle Cousins* by Ann Malcolmson.

Reader

Have you visited with the *Little Women* or gone with Alice on her *Adventures in Wonderland?* Are you a friend of *Heidi, Hans Brinker, Terisita of the Valley,* or *Ho Ming, Girl of New China?* Have you shared life with *The Moffats, The Meleny Family,* or the *Strawberry Girl?* Have you read *Black Beauty, Bambi,* or *The Yearling?* Do you know about the *Merry Adventures of Robin Hood* and *Gulliver's Travels?*

When the first settlers came to America, there was little for the children to read. Their books were wooden paddles. They were called horn books because there was a piece of transparent horn, made from the horn of an animal, nailed over the paper pasted to a board to keep it clean. And there were no exciting stories to read on the horn books.

Did you know that the first fairy tale was written in 1697? It was published in France. Yes, you guessed it. It was Charles Perrault's *Tales of Mother Goose* or as the French would say *Contes de ma Mere l'Oye.* The brothers Grimm gave us the first folk tales in 1812. They were called *Kinder and Hausmarchen* or *Children's and Household Stories.* From Denmark came *The Wonder Story* in 1835 written by Hans Christian Andersen.

The History of Goody Two Shoes was written by Oliver Goldsmith and published in England in 1765. It is not like the history books of today but you will find it interesting. And from England came the first poetry for children when William Blake wrote *Songs of Innocence* in 1789 and William Wordsworth completed his *Lyrical Ballads* in 1798. Can you name "firsts" from other countries—Norway, Italy, Mexico, the United States?

Many stories have been written about Girl Scouts and Girl Guides. Here are a few favorites: *Here Come the Girl Guides* by Kitty Barne, *Juliette Low* by Mildred Mastin Pace, *Shanty Brook Lodge* and *Toplofty* by Fjeril Hess, *On My Honor* edited by Marjorie Vetter, *A Wish for Tomorrow* and *For a Brave Tomorrow* by Jean Dupont Miller, *Abbie Higgins, Young Group Work Executive* by Constance Rittenhouse and Iris Vinton. *Girl Scout stories*

There are many good anthologies of poetry. They contain poems that tell stories, poems about animals, poems about our country, and poems which tell our feelings about things. There are humorous poems and sad ones. There are those about love and romance. There is poetry for everyone. Some good collections are: *This Singing World* compiled by Louis Untermeyer, *Love's Enchantment* compiled by Helen Ferris, *Silver Pennies* compiled by Blanche J. Thompson, *Bells and Grass* compiled by Walter de la Mare. *Poetry*

There are good books on every interest. For example, if you want to read about Girl Scouts and Girl Guides all over the world you will enjoy *Hands Around the World*. Ask your librarian to help you select books. She can suggest camping and sports stories, mystery novels, science and crafts books, animal stories, and adventure tales. *Special subjects*

149

As you read try to classify the books under the headings that are used in your library; for example, history, biography, fiction, poetry, and so forth. This will help you judge whether your reading is well rounded. Ask your librarian to show you some booklists. They will help you to make your own selections.

Adventures in Reading by May Lamberton Becker is an excellent guide for any girl interested in the Reader badge.

Standards for reading   How can you find out whether a book is "good," interesting, and well written? One of the best ways is to get into the habit of reading the book reviews in such magazines as *The American Girl, The Horn Book, The Saturday Review* and the book sections of your own local paper.

Buying books   There are times when you want to buy a book. Whatever it is, make sure that it will be a real addition to your library. Ask yourself these questions: Is it a book I can and want to read? Will I want to read it more than once? What is it about and who wrote it? Is it well illustrated and do the pictures really tell me something? Is the book well printed and attractively bound? Is there a better book on the same subject? Will this book make my library more interesting and varied? Do I really want to own this book?

Collections   There are many reasons why girls like yourself collect books. You may have a special interest in American history or art. You may collect folk tales or poetry. You may want books on airplanes, dolls, or birds. You may try to find first editions or rare bindings. Perhaps you would like a collection of books written by your favorite author or illustrated by a famous illustrator.

Storyteller

From earliest times storytellers have had a place of honor. The art of telling a tale that holds the interest of listeners is rare and to be treasured. A good storyteller is always welcome whether a group is gathered in the living room, back yard, or around a campfire.

Every girl can learn to tell stories well if she really wishes to. As you become a storyteller, you will gain poise and confidence and learn how to say clearly and vividly just what you vant to say.

Selecting stories

There are many different kinds of stories—true, fairy, legend, biographical, and so forth. There are the legends and tales of your own section of the country. There are the stories you have heard others tell. Begin by telling a story that you like and know well.

Your librarian or other storytellers can help you select stories. Look through several books. Select a story you like and one that will appeal to the people who will be your listeners.

Once you have found the right story for the group, read it over several times. Put the book down and think through the story. Then try telling it to yourself out loud. Reread it again. You must know the story forward and backward.

Telling the tale

Here are a few tips:

Be natural. Tell the story in your own words and your own way.

Be sure your listeners are comfortably seated and can see your face.

Use your voice well, speak clearly, and pronounce the words correctly.

151

Avoid gestures unless they come naturally.

Speak slowly or rapidly to suit the action of the story.

Beware of letting the story drag. Know where it is to end and end it.

Enjoy yourself and the story as you tell it.

Stop spinning yarns while your audience is still eager to hear more.

Read and practice There are many good books on storytelling. Ask your librarian to recommend one. Ask her to tell you about the story leagues in various cities, what they do, and if there is one in your own town. Find out whether you can visit the children's library during story hour. Observe the storyteller. Watch how she keeps the interest of the children. Talk to her afterwards and she will give you some tips.

Practice telling stories every time you have the opportunity. You might start a regular story-hour period for your neighborhood. Above all, when you are chatting with your friends, practice making every account you tell as interesting and concise as possible.

Writer

Everyone needs to be able to write easily and correctly. Can you compose a good letter, take minutes of a meeting easily, and write an interesting report?

You gain great satisfaction when you can express your own thoughts and feelings clearly or tell a story well. The first thing that a writer must do is to decide what he wants to write about and to know something about his subject. That is not difficult, for every minute of every day we are having new experiences. Think of all the things you do in your classes, on your way back and forth to school, at troop meetings, and with your family.

152

After you have decided exactly what you wish to write about, you must decide how you wish to say it. In what form will it be most effective—as a poem, a story, a report, a composition, an article, or a play?

No matter what form your writing takes there are certain points to remember. The words and phrases you use should have color and flavor. Try describing the same thing in different ways. Then decide which has greater meaning and feeling, such as "the dancing snowflakes," "the white snowflakes," "the slowly falling snowflakes." Simple words, correctly put together, give writing clearness, strength, and beauty.

Sentences and paragraphs in writing should have rhythm. Read the works of different authors aloud and you will soon discover what is meant by rhythm in writing.

Avoid writing about things in general. Try to write about things that have really happened to you or particularly interest you. It is far more interesting to others if you describe a special family picnic that was fun and tell why, rather than write a composition on family picnics.

A good writer feels deeply, uses all five senses, and is able to make the reader see and feel what he writes about. Can you describe the last person you met today? Can you write a paragraph about your feelings when you were invested? Can you express for others the joy of watching the sunrise or the adventures of a cross-country hike?

All you need for writing are a pencil, some paper, something to write about, and the ability to use words correctly and effectively. Take advantage of every opportunity to write and use different forms. You will find that the more you write, the more you will want to write and the better your writing will become. Submit some of your finished work to a magazine, such as *The American Girl* or *The Horn Book*, or to your school, troop, or camp paper, or local newspaper.

Bibliophile

The word "bibliophile" comes from the Greek and means lover of books. When you once start looking up words in the dictionary, you will find it fascinating. Did you know, for example, that the word "alphabet" comes from the first two letters of the Greek alphabet—*alpha* and *beta*?

Early writing

The alphabet came into existence about 2,000 B.C. The Latin alphabet was spread throughout Western Europe during the days of the Roman Empire. Before that time many other forms of writing were used. The earliest was called pictograph and was actually picture writing. It took a long time to write in this way and later ideograms were substituted. Today we still use ideograms when we write $ for dollars and ¢ for cent. Then followed the period when hieroglyphics and syllable writing were used. Did you know that the word "hieroglyphics" comes from the Greek *hieros* meaning sacred and *glyphinin* meaning carve. Hieroglyphics were first used to carve religious texts on stone. Later other things were carved. There are examples on the obelisks and pyramids of Egypt.

The first books

The Chinese made books many, many years ago. Some have been found which date back to 868 A.D. They were made from wood blocks and printed on very thin tissue paper. Books of this type were popular in European countries in the fourteenth century. The first books made from printed impressions of engravings on copper were discovered in Italy. They were made about the year 1400.

The earliest examples of printing using movable type come from the Rhine Valley. Johannes Gutenberg of Mainz, Ger-

Early printing many, is usually given the credit for inventing it and printing the first book. It was published on August 24, 1456, and is known as the forty-two line or Gutenberg Bible. By 1500, most books were printed from movable type.

You will find it interesting to read about some of the other great printers such as Nicholas Jensen, William Caxton, Aldus Manutius, Christophe Plantin, and William Caslon. Some great American printers and type designers of more recent years are D. B. Updike, Bruce Rogers, Rudolph Ruzicka (who designed the type face used in this book), and Frederic Goudy. Look in some of your favorite books and see whether the designer is mentioned.

Famous illustrators Have you ever seen the spirited drawings of horses, dogs, pigs, and cows that made Randolph Caldecott famous in the eighteenth century? Look for a copy of *Alice in Wonderland* that was illustrated by Sir John Tenniel. The illustrations by A. B. Frost for *Uncle Remus* and those of Dorothy Lathrop for Rachel Field's *Hitty* are also famous. Wesley Dennis is well known for his illustrations of horses. They appear in such books as *King of the Wind, Misty*, and *Sea Orphans*.

Some authors do their own illustrations. They are called artist-authors. Among those who are well known are Lois Lenski, Kate Seredy, Robert Lawson, and Marguerite de Angeli.

Exhibits and collections Oftentimes you will find interesting exhibits at your own library. It may be that they will feature the development of writing through the ages, early editions of books, or the work of some famous illustrators. Be on the lookout for these exhibits.

Throughout the United States there are libraries and museums which have famous collections. Some examples are the Huntington Library in Pasadena, California; the Folger

Shakespeare Library in Washington, D.C.; and university libraries, such as Yale which owns many of the original letters and manuscripts of James Boswell, and the University of Michigan where you will find the Clements Library of History.

Many people collect noteworthy illustrations, old volumes, first editions, original letters and manuscripts. Do you know of any privately owned collections in your town?

The most prized awards in the field of young people's literature are given by the American Library Association and presented in the spring of each year. They are: *Literary awards*

1. The Newbery Award for the most distinguished contribution to literature for children. This award is named in honor of John Newbery, who first published storybooks for children in England in the middle of the eighteenth century.

2. The Caldecott Award for the most distinguished Ameri-

157

can picture book for children. This is named for Randolph Caldecott, the famous illustrator.

The Nobel prize is the highest award in value and honor for adult literature. It is given annually on December 10 by the Swedish Academy in Stockholm. In addition to the prize in literature there are four others: physics, chemistry, medicine, and peace.

The most important American award is the Pulitzer Prize in Letters. Joseph Pulitzer, the newspaper editor, set up a fund for this purpose.

Journalist

The journalist is the person who manages, edits, or writes for a newspaper. He records the what, who, when, where, why, and how of events. It requires a special style of writing For that reason, there are schools of journalism throughout the country.

Visit a newspaper A visit to your newspaper will be most worth while. Prepare for your visit beforehand by doing some of the other activities suggested in this badge. You will get much more out of your visit if you are well informed.

Do you know, for example, when the first newspaper was published? Have you heard of *The Tatler* and *The Spectator* and Johnson's *Rambler*? Do you know when the printing machine was invented? Have you ever thought of what goes into the preparation of the paper on which the news is printed?

Visit the various departments of your newspaper. Try to be there when the press is in operation. If possible, arrange to interview some of the people who work on the newspaper, such as the editor, a reporter, a feature writer, and a typesetter. List the questions that you would like to ask in advance. Afterward, write up your interviews and visit as if you were writing for a newspaper.

158

Study the common proofreader's marks in this illustration. Then take the report of your visit and edit it, using the correct symbols.

⊙   Period

⊥   Push down space

‿   Close up entirely

Λ   Insert at this point

℧   Turn over

[or]   Move over

stet.   Let it stand

℞   Take out

¶   Make paragraph

≡ or *caps.*   Capitals

lc.   Lower-case letter

___ or *ital.*   Italic

DRAMATICS

Dramatics is an art in which all other arts play a part. It makes use of music, literature, dance, and art itself. Its history is that of the human race. From earliest days man has sought to express his feelings and emotions through drama.

Do you know why a mask is associated with drama? In ancient Greece, the performers hid their true identity behind masks. Actors and actresses no longer do this. Instead, they strive to lose their identity in the part they are playing. This is not easy to do. It is natural for us to act and to do things in our own way rather than to act like another person.

Actors and actresses must be sensitive to other people. They learn to understand other people by observing them closely. They must, through the use of their voice and body, be able to show us different types of people, different emotions, and different feelings.

We start acting early in life. Do you remember when you gave tea parties? Have you imagined you were a policeman

159

at a street corner? Did you ever dress up and play the part of a queen or knight? Have you and your friends imitated your parents' conversations? If so, you were acting. You were putting yourself in the place of another. That is what everyone must do who wants to be in a play.

Troop Dramatics

One of the best preparations for any actress is to watch other people. Watch all kinds of people. Do you know how an old man walks with a cane, a five-year-old runs into a room, or how a person picks up a heavy bundle? Can you express these actions in pantomime so that troop members can guess who you are? Try it. It's lots of fun and much harder than you think.

"Nosebag" dramatics Each patrol gathers together five to eight different articles and puts them into a paper bag. The bags are exchanged with another patrol. Allow about five minutes for each patrol to open its bag, think up a story to go with the articles, and cast the parts. Each patrol then presents its skit. The girls must use all the articles in the paper bag but cannot add any others.

Troop entertainments The Girl Scout songbook has many songs that can be dramatized and used for troop entertainment. You will find many other resources in your library. You will discover it is most fun, though, when you make up your own entertainment. For instance, you might dramatize for your guests some of the things that you do at Girl Scout meetings. You will be able to make up your own stage and acting directions, experiment with casting the roles (have girls play the part of other girls in the troop), plan the properties and costumes, and decide what action, movement, and script are necessary.

Every person interested in acting needs to know the lan- *Acting terms*
guage of the stage. Here are a few common terms:

Downstage: Toward the audience

Upstage: Away from the audience

Stage right: The actress's right as she faces the audience

Stage left: The actress's left as she faces the audience

As you rehearse your dramatizations of fairy tales, legends,
scenes from favorite books, or historical events, learn and use
these terms and others such as apron, exit, entrance, cue, and
script.

A square yard of material can make many costumes.

Ceremonies are important in any troop. They mark special *Ceremonies* occasions such as the welcoming of new members, the presentation of ranks and badges, the troop's birthday, the graduation of members into Senior Girl Scouting and other events.

Ceremonies in the troop are an excellent opportunity for dramatics. Try writing your own. They will then have a very special meaning. Remember the following points:

1. Ceremonies should be simple and sincere.

2. They should be short and dignified.

3. Every ceremony has a pattern, such as a horseshoe, circle, hollow square.

Player

The player must be skilled in the use of her body alone in conveying feeling and also in the use of her body and voice.

Pantomime is the oldest of the dramatic arts. It is the method *Pantomime* the very first hunters used to recount their adventures to tribesmen. In pantomime, the actors interpret feelings and ideas without using any words. There was a time during the days of silent movies when actors were so clever at pantomime that drama was in danger of being overshadowed.

Pantomime is the basis of characterization. You express yourself in action before you express yourself in speech. Every movement is important. Pantomime is bodily speech. The movies and the modern dance are good examples of its importance today.

You can have great fun at troop meetings pantomiming such actions as knitting, spilling a glass of milk, arranging a vase of flowers. Do you think you could fill the vase with roses in pantomime so that an audience would know just what you were doing? How would you show that the flowers were roses?

After you have done a few simple pantomimes, make them more difficult. For instance, you might be a child learning to knit or an older person who already knits well. You might be a boy arranging flowers, or a grandfather or grandmother. When you knock over a glass of milk, do you do it in the same way as a baby in a high chair?

Pantomime is often used in playing charades—guessing games in which each syllable of a word is represented by a description, picture, tableau, or dramatic action. It is also used in a pageant where one person reads the lines.

When you can read lines well and act with your whole body, including facial expressions, then you are really learning to act.

Impromptu *dramatics* Short skits or scenes that have no long rehearsals are called impromptu or informal dramatics. A stage can be made in one corner and you can create your own costumes from coats, newspapers, and other things found in the room.

In this type of dramatics you need only one thing to let people know what you represent. A rabbit may be suggested by long paper ears, a donkey by a long rope tail, an elephant by a stuffed stocking trunk, an old man by white cotton whiskers, an angel by wings. A crown of tin or paper with gumdrops for jewels can suggest a king.

Impromptu dramatics can be done using songs, book titles, proverbs, advertising slogans, or names of people. It's good fun to act out your favorite stories. Before you dramatize a story, read it through several times and talk it over with your patrol. Ask yourselves these questions:

Is there plenty of action?

Is it a story we can tell others through action? Will they enjoy it?

What must we tell the audience in advance?

How shall we divide the story into scenes?

Where shall we put our stage? Where shall we make our entrances and exits?

What type of costumes shall we make?

How shall we compose our script?

Do we have enough players to play the parts or too many?

As you answer these questions, you can decide whether the story can be dramatized and which members of the patrol will take care of costume, script, scenery, and so forth. Here are two books that have many stories that can be dramatized: *The King of the Golden River,* by John Ruskin, and *Children of the Handcrafts,* by Caroline Sherwin Bailey. Look for them in your library.

Choral reading is a form of dramatics. A chorus speaks verse or rhythmic prose in unison, much as songs are sung in unison by a group. The chorus is divided into two parts; one has the higher-pitched voices (called light voices), and the other has the deeper voices (dark voices). Parts may be worked out for solo speech, duet, or small groups to lend variety and force to the choral speech. Beginning groups should have between eighteen and twenty-four members. *Choral reading*

Try choral reading with one of your favorite poems or ballads. Or look in *Sing Together—A Girl Scout Songbook.* Experiment with different combinations and effects. You'll get lots of pleasure from this form of dramatic art, and you don't have to be able to carry a tune!

Puppeteer

There are many types of puppets. For an afternoon of fun try making puppets from paper bags. Select a bag that fits over your hand. Draw a face with crayons on the top third of the bag. Make hair from crepe paper or old wool, and paste

165

it on the top of the bag. Make holes in the bag for your thumb and little finger. They will be the puppet's arms. Put the bag over your hand and tie a string around it two-thirds up from the bottom. For a costume, you can drape pieces of material around the string. Your stage can be the edge of any table. Make up your own story or adapt a favorite tale. Then . . . on with the show!

More permanent puppets can be made by carving heads from a block of soft pine or by using potatoes which already have "noses," "ears," or "chins." Paint the faces with water colors.

If you wish, you can make puppets from hollow dolls' heads or by drawing a pattern, cutting it out of muslin and then stuffing it. The face can be embroidered or painted to suit the character represented.

A hole must be made in the bottom of the head to admit your forefinger. Fasten on a wig headdress. Make the hands from small potato lumps, soft pine, or cloth wound with wire. The costume sleeves should be hollow and attached to the hands of the puppets. In this way, you will be able to put your own thumb and third finger in the sleeves to become the puppet's arms.

The costume may be attached to the head and draped over the hand of the puppeteer. It should be long enough to hide the hand or the arm.

A stage for puppets may be made from a large packing box. Remove the top and one side. Use bits of cloth for the backdrops and attach your scenery to them. Christmas tree lights will serve for footlights. Get a sturdy table that you can stand on if you are using puppets worked from above. Place the table in a doorway and use curtains that will hide you from your audience.

Shadowgraphs are little figures cut out of cardboard mounted *Shadow-* on flat sticks or strips of heavy cardboard. They are worked *graphs* behind, and flat against, a screen covered with a sheet or a piece of unbleached muslin. To move heads, arms, and legs, these parts must be cut out separately. Attach them with brass paper fasteners to the trunk of the figure so that each piece overlaps. Next attach a thread to the overlapping parts so that when you pull it the arm, head, or leg will lift and fall again of its own weight.

Start with plain silhouettes. Then experiment with color. Cut out the area to be colored and paste tissue paper or cellophane over the hole. For example, you may put a red kerchief on a pirate's head. Cut out the shape of the kerchief and leave a small margin of cardboard all around the head. Then paste red cellophane over the cutout place.

SHADOWGRAPH SCREEN. A shadowgraph screen may be as simple as an old sheet stretched across the doorway, with newspaper covering the space above and below the screen. Or, a permanent screen can be made from a discarded window screen. Remove the wire screening and tack cardboard over the lower half and a piece of unbleached muslin or sheeting over the top half. Nail a couple of blocks of wood to the bottom of the screen so that it will stand upright.

All scenery or properties are cut from cardboard and tacked to the sides of the frame against the screen and away from the audience.

SHADOWGRAPH PLAYS. In producing a shadowgraph play it is important to remember several things.

1. The figures must be kept close to the screen at all times.
2. The actions of the figures must be timed with the story.
3. Those working the figures must stay below the screen.
4. The light is placed behind the screen and should be spread out and not in one spot.
5. The room should be darkened as much as possible.
6. The words of the story or song must be spoken clearly. Dialogue (the words of a play) for puppets or shadowgraphs may be presented in several ways. Each performer may work a figure and do the speaking for that character. One person or several may tell the whole story, or a group may sing the song while others work the figures. Or, the audience may be given an outline of the story, omitting the dialogue completely.

Marionettes   Marionettes are similar to dolls and have strings or wires attached from their hands, elbows, feet, knees, back, and head to a wooden crosspiece. The operator stands above the marionette and by pulling the different strings can make it dance, walk, bow, and do many other things.

You can make a marionette from an old stuffed doll or by drawing a pattern, cutting it out of muslin, and stuffing it. There should be no stuffing or very little stuffing at the waist, neck, elbows, knees, hips, and shoulders so that the marionette can be moved with ease. If you use an old doll, you will have to remove some of the stuffing and sew the doll up again. This illustration will help you to do this and also shows you how to attach the strings to your crosspiece.

The marionettes, their scenery, and their properties must all be in proportion. A good scale to use is two inches to a foot. A marionette representing a man who is six feet tall would be twelve inches high. Think of your marionette in terms of his bed and his door, and you will see what his best scale will be. In one play all the marionettes must be made in scale with one another. It is wise for a troop to decide on a scale and have every member use it to make her marionettes. Then you can use them together for any show.

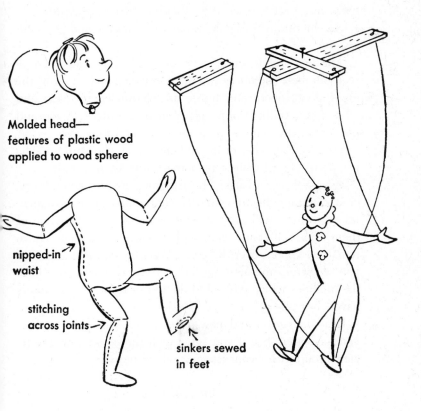

Molded head—
features of plastic wood
applied to wood sphere

nipped-in
waist

stitching
across joints →

sinkers sewed
in feet

Dramatic Appreciation

Did you realize that much of the world's greatest thought and action is presented through the drama. As you read about its development you will see how it traces the history of mankind. The great plays you read and see on stage, screen, and television today enact the emotion, action, interest, and achievement of the people, their social setting, and period of history.

The first storytellers, players, and minstrels had to go directly to their audiences and many traveled on foot. Now the finest plays, opera and music are channeled by radio and television to millions of people in many countries. Actors and musicians must choose their media of performance.

You, as a member of an audience, may choose the media you prefer—legitimate stage, movies, television, or radio.

Why not join a Little Theatre group in your community, or start a troop theatre yourself? Your appreciation of dramatics and music will grow as you assist in the production of them. Find out about actors and actresses whose names have remained famous over the years. What made them great? As you see actors and actresses today, try to decide if they have the qualities which will stand the test of time as these others have.

Read magazine and newspaper reviews of performances you have seen. See if you agree with the reporter. Write reviews yourself for your troop or school newspaper.

Producer

There are many angles to play production and all are fascinating. However, do not let your own enthusiasm tempt you to try something which is way beyond the ability of your troop. Start with simple dramatics and then try a one-act play. After that you will be ready for a longer one.

Study the play carefully—its plot, its meaning, its characters. Girls who can draw should be asked to make sketches for settings, costumes, and properties. Those who are handy with a hammer or who are musical-minded can make properties, arrange for stage lighting, and handle sound effects, such as snowstorms, and the noise of galloping horses.

For many of these activities you may need help and advice from someone with experience in directing plays, but do try to work out his suggestions in the troop by yourselves. A trip to a theatre with someone to explain what goes on backstage will be a great advantage at the start, especially if you want to make a model stage-set for the play you have chosen. You cannot organize a backstage crew until you know what jobs must be done.

Don't worry too much about stage-sets. If the acting is good enough and the play interesting, few stage effects are needed. In Elizabethan times, stage directors were masters at setting a play without scenery. It is, of course, satisfying to be able to set a stage with real scenery and properties. If you cannot do this well, merely suggest them and let your good acting make up for the lack of a stage-set.

One fascinating part of play production is make-up. To be successful at it, you must be exceedingly observant. Just where are the deepest lines in the face of a very old person? How do you make a naturally gay person look very sad? Study pictures of different kinds of people and make a collection of faces that represent all types and nationalities. The materials for make-up—grease paints, powder, crepe hair, and so forth—have no value unless you know how to use them.

The same need for study and observation is also true in regard to costumes. It is important to know what kinds of clothes were worn at different periods of history or by people who have different occupations. It is not usual to dress the characters in a play of colonial days in modern dress, or a doctor in a pair of blue jeans. Collections of pictures of costumes are helpful if you are interested in this part of play production.

The person who wants to direct a play should get, first of all, as much experience as possible in different backstage jobs. The director has to be able to see the production as a whole and to know where each person's job fits in.

CHAPTER 10

Music and Dancing

E VERYONE loves to sing and dance. It matters not how old or young you are or whether you live in Africa, Asia, or America. Music and dancing are the universal language of all people. They are as old as mankind. Through them we express our feelings without words. Through them we speak from heart to heart.

There are two ways of enjoying music and dancing. One is by doing something yourself—singing in a chorus, dancing with friends, playing in an orchestra. The other way is by listening and observing—watching a ballet, listening to a concert, a recital, the radio or television, or recordings.

MUSIC

Some of the oldest fables tell us of the power of music. Do you know the story of the Greek hero Orpheus? He is said to have charmed even trees and stones with his music.

The word "music" comes from a Greek word meaning the "art of the Muses." To the Greeks the Muses were goddesses who helped men create beauty in the arts.

There is music to fit every mood. There are lullabies, hymns of grief, love songs, marching songs, and others. Music is written in many forms such as symphonies, fugues, sonatas, tone poems, and operas. The skillful song leader or musician can make an audience feel emotion through the music she selects and the way she directs or plays it.

173

Minstrel

The wandering singers and musicians of the Middle Ages were a colorful and gay group. They were found in almost every country of Europe. In England and Ireland they were called minstrels. In the Scandinavian countries they were known as skalds. In Germany they were named meistersingers, and in France troubadours. They wandered from country to country and their songs traveled with them. These were picked up by other singers. Each group added and changed tunes and words as they wished and their collection of songs, stories, and dances grew ever larger. They were also the news reporters of the period, singing of the happenings they heard about or saw in their wanderings. These singers and musicians were responsible for handing down many of the folk tunes we love today.

Among the minstrels of our day are Susan Reed and Burl Ives. They sing both long-forgotten and familiar folk tunes of many countries. Joseph Marais is chiefly known for his songs of the South African veldt. John Jacob Niles has given us collections of beautiful folk music of early England. He found these in remote sections of the Southern Highlands of the United States. They had never been written down. Arrange to listen to the recordings of these artists.

A Girl Scout minstrel can sing almost anywhere. She can bring gaiety and happiness to all kinds of gatherings. Singing is a favorite part of every campfire, a natural for hiking, and a friendly tie at social events. Dishes are washed and dried in no time as you sing a rollicking tune. When Girl Scouts from different troops, communities, states, or countries get together, the bond of friendship is quickly woven as they lift their voices in songs everyone of them knows.

A minstrel will need a good collection of songs. Here are four types that should be included. In these four types you

will find ballads, spirituals, lullabies, religious, working, hiking, cowboy, Indian, and love songs.

1. *Rounds:* These are part songs such as "When E'er You Make a Promise," "Rise Up O Flame," and "Sweet the Evening Air of May." They are fun to use in a large group because they are easy to learn and have pleasing harmony.

2. *Folk Songs:* These are the songs which were not written down for many years. Their source cannot be traced and the composers are unknown. They were passed on from one generation to the next. Folk songs are found in every country. They tell of the life of the people such as "The Erie Canal" from New York State, "The Riddle Song" from the Kentucky mountains, "The Weggis Song" from Switzerland, "Tancuj" from Czechoslovakia, and "Mi Chacra" from South America. Even today there are still many songs which have not been written down.

3. *Art Songs:* These are more modern than folk songs but old enough to have stood the test of time. Their composers are known. Examples are Sibelius's "Finlandia," Brahms's "Lullaby," and the works of Gilbert and Sullivan.

4. *Patriotic Songs:* These are the ones that we sing at flag ceremonies and other special events. Examples are "The Star Spangled Banner," "America the Beautiful," and "O Beautiful Banner."

There will be times when you and your friends may wish to write an original song. It may be a patrol song or one to celebrate a special troop event. You may feel like composing a tune while hiking or watching a beautiful sunset. You may write the words to music someone else has composed, or you may compose the tune and words for your song. If you decide to write the words only, choose music that has no words of its own. When you use someone else's music or words, secure his permission. See page 180 for the copyright law.

Group Musician

Music most enjoyed is that which you share. Take every opportunity to lead songs for various occasions. Unless you have already had experience in choosing songs and arranging them into a varied program, ask someone who has had experience to help you, such as a music teacher, your leader, or a troop member.

These are some points to help you:

Selecting songs

1. Begin with some songs the group already knows.
2. If the group has not sung together before, choose short rounds and folk songs with tra-la-la choruses.
3. If the group sings together frequently and enjoys singing, choose longer folk and art songs, longer rounds, simple part songs, and songs with descants.
4. Choose songs which fit the occasion.
5. If you are singing a number of songs, select different types of songs.

If you know a song and a friend knows a song, and you teach them to each other, both of you will know two songs. Sharing songs you know with your troop helps everyone learn more.

Check on these points before you teach a song. If you follow them, you will be sure that everyone will have fun.

Teaching songs

1. Know the song well—words and music. Try not to use a book.
2. Tell the group who wrote the song, if the composer is known, and when it was written. Explain the meaning of unusual words. Tell something about the country from which the song came.
3. Sing the song through yourself (or the first stanza if it is long).

177

4. Sing the song one phrase at a time. After singing the first phrase have the group sing it. Then sing the first and second phrases together, and let the group sing. Continue adding one phrase at a time until you have taught the complete song.

5. If the group is singing a round, try it all together several times before dividing. Be sure each group knows when it comes in and how often it is to sing the song.

In a part song or when using a descant, be sure each group knows its part before putting all parts together.

Leading songs After teaching your song, you can lead it along with other songs your troop knows. As a song leader, see that:

1. The group keeps to the tempo—not too fast or too slow.

2. Everyone enunciates the *d's, t's* and *ing's.*

3. The song is modulated, loud to soft and vice versa, as indicated by the music.

4. The pitch is a comfortable one for the group—not too high or too low.

5. Everyone starts and ends together (except in rounds).

6. Your signals are plain and that everyone watches you.

The tempo and the shading of music depend upon the leader. You get your lead from the way the music is written. Before you begin directing, look at your music and find the time signature. The top number tells how many beats there are to each measure. The bottom number tells what kind of note gets one beat. The first note or beat in each measure gets the strong accent. In leading a chorus or orchestra, the hand or baton comes down on the first strong beat.

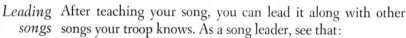

Select a song you know for each time and tempo and practice them until you can beat time easily. Practice in front of a mirror and make your strokes clear. Try keeping time with your right hand and use your left hand to indicate where to hold, release, and soften notes.

Many troops enjoy this game. Have different girls tap out the rhythm of a familiar tune. The others try to guess the song from the tapping.

Learn to recognize by sight and ear some of the instruments that are used to make music. It's fun to know about the history of different instruments too. There are records and books that will help you. Or you can visit a music store, someone who has a collection, or a museum. There are many people in your community who can explain the instruments to you.

Musician

The Girl Scout who wears her Musician badge has spent time and effort in the study of music. If you have this badge, you want others to enjoy your music. Music, along with dancing, is best when it is shared.

Why not start sharing your skill with your troop? Serving as accompanist for troop singing, furnishing some of the music for dancing, contributing your talent to special programs are a few ways you can demonstrate your proficiency.

You will find that it is fun to play with others. Why not start a troop orchestra or chorus? You may be surprised at the number of boys and girls who can play some instrument or who enjoy singing.

A "mixed" chorus which sings well will find many demands for its services. A string trio or quartet will have command performances at school, in their churches, and for community gatherings. The people in your town will enjoy dancing to a good dance band. Through your love of music and your skill you can bring happiness to shut-ins, to children, to adults, to those in hospitals—to just everyone.

179

Copyright Every musician must know about copyright law. Copyright
law means the exclusive legal right of a person to publish and
dispose of his work for a limited time. The sole right to copy
material is usually given by law to a business firm that pub-
lishes an author's or composer's work, although the individual
may hold the copyright if she prefers. No one may copy such
published material without first getting permission from the
copyright owner.

This means that songs, poetry, or any other copyrighted
material cannot be copied in any way without the permis-
180   sion of the copyright owner. It makes no difference whether

the copies are sold or given away. If you break this law, you may be punished whether you understand it or not.

The term of copyright protection is fifty-six years (twenty-eight years plus twenty-eight years renewal term). After that the material is said to be "in the public domain," that is, public property.

Look in your Girl Scout songbook and find out which songs are copyrighted and which are in the public domain.

Music Appreciation

Music, you know, is like food. You can't tell what you like until you taste it. And some foods you have to try more than once before you enjoy them. Music is the same. Start with the things that you know you like and then add others.

Appreciation of music is increased through listening and through making music yourself. Many libraries have records you can borrow, or your school may have some. The nice part about records is that you can play over and over again the pieces or parts of pieces you like best. If there are parts you do not quite understand, you can play those parts over too until you do understand them. Plan to listen to them with your friends. Have varied programs and include symphonies, concertos, oratorios, chorales, and instrumental, vocal, religious, and popular music.

The time you spend listening to music will deepen your enjoyment of its beauty and bring you hours of happiness. An appreciation of music also develops your appreciation for the beauties of sound and rhythm in nature such as the songs of the birds, the babbling of a brook, the chirp of crickets, the dance of leaves, the thundering of ocean breakers.

Repeated listening will increase your awareness of the effort that goes into a good musical performance, and the contribution that composer, director, and the musician must make. If you become interested in the works of a particular composer you will want to learn about his country and people. You might enjoy finding a pen pal in that country. Through correspondence you will learn much more about the music and other arts characteristic of the country.

DANCING

From the earliest time people have expressed their feelings through some form of the dance. They have expressed reverence and worship in religious ceremonies, joy and thanksgiving in folk dances, friendliness and gaiety at social gatherings. For this reason you will hear people call dancing the Mother of the Arts.

Folk Dancer

Just as people in different countries compose their own tunes, called folk music, they also make up their own dance steps, called folk dancing. It becomes traditional in a country and is danced by the people who live there.

The best-known folk dances in the United States are called square or country dances. The Highland fling and schottische came from Scotland, the jig from Ireland, the morris dance and hornpipe from England, the gavotte from Brittany, the bolero from Spain, the tarantella from Italy, the waltz from Austria, the polka from Czechoslovakia, the mazurka from Poland.

Folk dances are handed down from parents to children. Each generation may change them slightly. Some have never been recorded. Some have been written down and you can find good directions in books.

Just as folk songs are more vivid if you know something of their background, a folk dance also means more when you know about the people who danced it first.

In this country, folk dancing is increasing in popularity. Many good square and folk dances have been put on records. These have the calls and directions. You can find records and

books in your local music store or library. Arrange to borrow them for a troop meeting.

Singing games

Singing games are the simplest form of folk dancing. They are fun and easy to learn. You can make your own music by singing while you do the dance steps and motions.

Circle singing games require a single or double circle. Examples are, "Skip to My Lou," "Sandy Land," "Shoo Fly," "Captain Jinks," and "Duck of the Meadow."

A longway formation for a singing game means that you must have two long lines or sets of two lines with four, six, or eight sets of partners. Examples are, "The Noble Duke of York," "Jennie Crack Corn," and "The Paw Paw Patch."

Folk dance definitions

Every folk dancer needs to know these definitions:

Swing your partner—turn partner swiftly around once or several times.

Reel—couple hooks right or left elbow and turns swiftly.

183

Cast off—partners separate and each goes down outside of own line.

Slip step—a sideways gallop.

Promenade—couple joins hands in double handclasp and walks, shuffles, or skips around together.

Grand right and left—partners face each other, clasp right hands, and pass each other on the right. The left hand is given to the next person and they pass on the left. The right hand goes to the next in the same manner and so on. You continue alternating right and left around the circle until you meet your original partner.

You will find that folk dancing is more fun if you invite a group of boys to dance with you. Find out if there is a boys' club or a group of boys in your school who would like to join your troop in a barn dance or international dancing party.

Dancer

In rhythmic dancing the entire body is used to interpret the rhythm, time, and melody of music. The modern dance is characterized by very free interpretation; the ballet dance is more stylized.

Listen, with some of your friends, to a favorite piece of music. Get the feel of its rhythm and melody. Try walking, swaying, hopping, and leaping to the music. Then move your hands and arms in rhythm with your feet. Soon you will find you are creating dance patterns for your favorite music. Listen to other types of music, and let your body express what the music is saying.

Combine your dance steps with those your friends have composed. Make up a story to go with the dance. Perhaps you can find a dance teacher or someone who likes to dance who will help you. Group dancing, such as ballet and modern, will do much to help you develop good posture, poise, grace, and confidence.

This type of dancing is a favorite when boys and girls get *Social* together. Devote some time at troop meetings to mastering *dancing* the popular dance steps. Combine forces with a group of boys who want to improve their dancing. Start with dances that are familiar, such as the fox trot and waltz. Then try the tango, samba, rhumba, and other dance steps. All you need are a portable phonograph, some good dance records, and an interested adult or a Senior Girl Scout to teach you the basic steps.

A trip to a department store, followed by a clothes clinic and fashion show, will help you decide on the right outfit for the barn dance, the junior high informal, or the very special "dress up dance."

It takes more imagination than money to give a successful dance. Be thrifty and clever in planning invitations, decorations, and refreshments. Invite people who will get along well together—more boys than girls if possible—and you are off to a good start.

As hostess at a dance, plan to include Paul Joneses, Grand Marches, and double circle congas. Have some games up your sleeve like "Musical Chairs," "Fruit Basket Upset," and "Laughing Hat." Get books that tell you how to plan parties and games you can play.

The vocations in music and dancing are many and varied. You may become a teacher, director, performer, choreographer, or composer. Build on the interest you have discovered in this field. Practice the things that you enjoy now. By doing this you will be laying the foundation for a future career in music or the dance.

PART III

Citizens Here and Abroad

CHAPTER 11 *Community Life*

CHAPTER 12 *International Friendship*

Community Life

YOUR home is your first and most important community. It is the place where you first learn how to plan for and get along with other people. There are two important things that make a community—place and people. There is no community without them.

Let's begin by looking at the "place" part. What places can you think of besides your home? What about your school and Girl Scout troop? These are two places where you get experience in community life all the time. And how about your synagogue or church? Naturally you will think of your own neighborhood and town as the wider circles of your community.

Now, let's look at the "people" part of the definition. Who are they? They are the people who live in your city or town. They are the people you pass in your neighborhood. They are the people you meet at religious services. They are the boys and girls at school, the other Scouts at troop meetings, your brothers and sisters and parents at home. Each of these people is different. Some are tall, others short; some have red hair, others black, brown, or blonde; some are old, others young; some have brown skin, others have white, or yellow. Some worship in temples, others worship in synagogues and churches. Some build homes, others run homes; some make our clothes, others help us keep our clothes in condition. Some are teachers, others are students.

189

Each of these people has a contribution to make. Yes, the ideas and actions that make you proud of your country come from the millions of people living in communities all over the United States. The strength of our country rests on the work, belief, and actions of every individual. *E Pluribus Unum,* "from the many, one." This is the meaning of that Latin phrase found on our American coins.

Finally, where do *you* fit into the definition? When we say the "people" make the community, it means you. You are the people. Everything you do affects the life of the community whether it be home, school, troop, or the community in general. If you do thoughtful, little things that make your home a happier place, you are contributing to the welfare of your town or city, state, country, and the world. The greatness of any country and the peace of the world depend to a large extent on the strength of each family and the happiness of every home.

If you are friendly and helpful to people who are different from yourself, you are learning how to know and like people in other parts of the world where language, clothes, beliefs, customs, food, and looks are different from your own. You are preparing yourself to be a "friend to all."

Active Citizen

Citizenship takes practice. All of us, not just grown-ups, are citizens. Sharing in the fun and work of your troop is just as real citizenship as sharing in the election of the president, or of the members of the school board, when you are older. The skills are the same. And just as with any other skill such as playing the piano, swimming, or cooking, the skills have to be practiced.

These are some of the skills needed by active citizens:

1. *Learn your facts.* You must know the facts. Learn to listen. Ask questions when things do not seem right or fair.

"Why" is a very powerful word. Avoid gossip and idle chatter. At times you may want to read about a subject. At other times you may want to look, and listen, while others discuss a question.

Be sure you have all the facts and then form your own opinion. This opinion should be one you understand, believe in, and can explain.

2. *Develop sound attitudes.* Your attitudes are your personal feelings about something or someone. Like your opinions, they must be your own. They cannot be borrowed from others. Like your opinions, they also must be based on facts.

3. *Learn to act.* Action is the result of the first two steps. Without action, knowledge and thought are of little use. Our American way of life depends upon each one doing his share. Throughout the years we must work to make this possible. It can be compared to a ball game. It is fun and successful only when every member knows the rules of the game and plays well. And that takes practice. See how you would answer these questions:

Can you get along with people?

Can you put your finger on the question or the problem?

Can you get the facts that are needed to answer the question?

Can you use those facts to make a plan?

Can you present your plan so others will like it?

Can you take your part in carrying out the plan?

Can you take your share in judging the good and bad points of the plan?

You use these citizenship skills in many ways because under your country's Constitution you and your family enjoy many privileges and freedoms. Read the Bill of Rights on page 192. Can you see how these freedoms affect you, your family, and all the people in your country? With these freedoms go responsibilities so that an active citizen's job is never done.

THE BILL OF RIGHTS
AMENDMENTS I TO X OF THE CONSTITUTION OF THE UNITED STATES

DRAFTED BY JAMES MADISON AND PROPOSED AND AP-
PROVED AT THE FIRST SESSION OF CONGRESS IN
1789. ADOPTED BY THE REQUIRED NUMBER OF
STATE LEGISLATURES UNDER ARTICLE V OF
THE CONSTITUTION AND DECLARED
IN FORCE DECEMBER 15, 1791

Congress shall make no law respecting an establishment of religion, or prohibiting the free exercise thereof; or abridging the freedom of speech, or of the press; or the right of the people peacefully to assemble, and to petition the government for a redress of grievances.

II
A well-regulated militia, being necessary to the security of a free State, the right of the people to keep and bear arms, shall not be infringed.

III
No soldier shall, in time of peace, be quartered in any house without the consent of the owner, nor in time of war, but in a manner to be prescribed by law.

IV
The right of the people to be secure in their persons, houses, papers, and effects, against unreasonable searches and seizures, shall not be violated, and no warrants shall issue but upon probable cause, supported by oath or affirmation, and particularly describing the place to be searched, and the persons or things to be seized.

V
No person shall be held to answer for a capital, or otherwise infamous crime, unless on a presentment or indictment of a grand jury except in cases arising in the land or naval forces, or in the militia, when in actual service in time of war or public danger; nor shall any person be subject for the same offence to be twice put in jeopardy of life or limb; nor shall be compelled in any criminal case to be a witness against himself, nor be deprived of life, liberty, or property, without due process of law; nor shall private property be taken for public use without just compensation.

VI
In all criminal prosecutions the accused shall enjoy the right to a speedy and public trial, by an impartial jury of the State and district wherein the crime shall have been committed, which district shall have been previously ascertained by law, and to be informed of the nature and cause of the accusation; to be confronted with the witnesses against him; to have compulsory process for obtaining witnesses in his favor, and to have the assistance of counsel for his defence.

VII
In suits at common law, where the value in controversy shall exceed twenty dollars, the right of trial by jury shall be preserved, and no fact tried by a jury shall be otherwise re-examined in any court of the United States, than according to the rules of the common law.

VIII
Excessive bail shall not be required, nor excessive fines imposed, nor cruel and unusual punishments inflicted.

IX
The enumeration in the Constitution, of certain rights, shall not be construed to deny or disparage others retained by the people.

X
The powers not delegated to the United States by the Constitution, nor prohibited by it to the States, are reserved to the States respectively, or to the people.

My Troop

You have thoughts about what you would like to do when your patrol meets to plan future activities. Other patrol members have thoughts too. So each patrol member must speak up and express her ideas. This is called group discussion. The result of group discussion is group thinking. From the many ideas expressed a plan is made and agreed upon by the patrol. When the plan is carried out, it is called group action. Group discussion is used by your Court of Honor, the Girl Scout planning board, senior conferences, and committee meetings of adults.

This

not this

Certain things are necessary for a good discussion. Everyone should be comfortable and should be able to see each other. All should take part in the discussion and should speak *on the subject*. It is important to listen carefully to what others have to say. Before speaking, you should be recognized by the chairman. No one should monopolize the discussion. Everyone should leave a discussion feeling that something has been accomplished.

As a patrol leader, or as the chairman of a special committee, you may be called on to lead a discussion. Here are some tips:

1. Think about the question to be discussed in advance.
2. Explain the question to the group. If possible, write

it on a blackboard, a large sheet of paper, or slips of paper for each person.

3. Do not let one person monopolize the discussion. Interrupt politely by saying: "Can we hear from another member now?" "Does anyone have another point of view?" or something like that.

4. Keep the discussion on the question. It is easier to do this if you summarize the discussion and mention the important points once or twice during the discussion period.

5. Do not present your own views and do not do all the talking yourself.

6. Encourage different points of view.

7. Close the discussion as soon as the group has reached a decision.

My Community

Who were the first settlers in your community? Were they fishermen, farmers, hunters, traders, homesteaders? Where was the first house built? Do you know what your street looked like 25, 50, 100 years ago? How did it get its name? How were the streets lighted before the invention of electricity? Did the coming of the car and plane alter your community? What effect did the city water system, gas, and the telephone have on the lives of the people? Where did the children of fifty years ago go to school?

There is an exciting story in your community. If you find the answers to the above questions, you will discover it for yourself. There is drama in its settling, in its growth, and in its changes. There is drama in the people—where they came from, what skills they brought, their struggles in building your community.

Your community is the result of the work of many people over many years. It is not enough to know that there are hospitals, schools, libraries, municipal buildings. You also need to know something about the people who made them possible. What is the history behind your library? Where does the money come from? What services does the library give you? What can you give the library in return?

What about your own Girl Scout troop? How did your leader become interested in Girl Scouting? Why did she volunteer? Who helped her learn about the program? Are other adults interested in Girl Scouting? When was the first troop formed in your community? Who started Girl Scouting in your town? How did she go about it?

Old maps, newspapers, picture collections are good ways to start exploring the early days of your community. Talk with people, read articles, visit historical spots, and ask lots of questions. Interview some of the older citizens. They may tell you about the music, dance, clothes, food, and recreation of the olden days. Through them you will discover interesting stories and legends.

But don't stop with the past. Bring yourself up to date. Get your friends to ask you questions about your community, such as how many parks there are, who represents you in the town or city or federal government, the bed capacity of the hospital, how much it costs to support the fire department, and so on. Take the questions you cannot answer to your troop and see what the other girls do with them.

It is always a good idea to see whether we are helping to make our community a pleasanter place in which to live. Can you tune in the radio or television without breaking the eardrums of others in the room? Can you use the telephone without annoying the family or giving the operator gray hair? Can you ride in a bus or trolley without stepping all over people, shouting and giggling? Do you help new students and new troop members? Are you willing to accept jobs in your troop and class? Do you put your orange peels and candy papers in a trash can? Do you respect other people's property? Are you a gossip?

There are dozens of other questions you can ask yourself. Some may have to do with laws, others with rules, and others with good manners. Does it matter much? Rules, laws, and good manners all imply an understanding of the rights of others. Are we as conscious of our rudeness in stepping on someone else's ideas or beliefs as we are of stepping on their feet?

My Country

In the expression "my country," the word "my" is a possessive pronoun. You use it in combination with many other words such as "my dress," "my dog," "my book." When you say "my country," you are telling people that the United States belongs to you, you feel responsible for its well-being, you are proud of it.

What is America? Here is one description that you know well:

O beautiful for spacious skies, For amber waves of grain,
For purple mountain majesties Above the fruited plain!
America, America! God shed His grace on thee,
And crown thy good with brotherhood, From sea to
shining sea!

How much do you know about the symbols which, wherever they are found, stand for "the United States of America"? Do you know why the eagle, the Liberty Bell, and the Statue of Liberty are symbols of freedom? Look at your money. The insignia on the coins reminds us of American traditions and historical events. Our stamps bear pictures of important people and happenings.

And what of the people? Where do they live and who are they? They live on peaceful farms, large ranches, in quiet villages, growing towns, and bustling cities. Their ancestors came from many parts of the world. They brought with them customs which we now call American. In the Southwest, California, and Florida, you will discover names, foods, architecture, and traditions which remind you that the Spaniards once claimed this land. The old French Quarter of New Orleans is still called *Vieux Carre* and the city still reflects the influence of the original settlers from France. Along the eastern coast you find many traces of the early English settlers. Look at a map and find New London, Exeter, Bedford, Northampton. What other names do you see that were brought across the waters? The Germans left their influence around Pennsylvania in furniture and pottery. Their designs are called "Pennsylvania Dutch." And as the years rolled by and the colonies grew, still others came. Do you know the contributions of the Negroes, Italians, Irish, and other cultural and national groups?

And even today as we welcome more people to our country they continue to give of themselves. They bring customs and traditions. They bring skill and knowledge. Their new gifts are forever being woven in among older gifts to make our American folkways.

Do you know the stories behind some of our legendary American heroes? Read about Paul Bunyan, Pecos Bill, Johnny Appleseed, Old Stormalong, and Joe Magarac. What do you know about "Uncle Sam"?

Do you know the stories behind songs such as the "National Anthem," "America the Beautiful," "Yankee Doodle," the "Battle Hymn of the Republic," "Oh Susanna," and "Dixie"? As you learn about them, you will also learn more about the history of your country.

Can you locate on a map the Natural Bridge, Old Faithful, Niagara Falls, the Grand Canyon, and the Sequoia National Forest?

Do you know when Patrick Henry said: "Give me liberty or give me death," and Franklin Delano Roosevelt said: "The only thing we have to fear is fear itself"? Do you know some

197

famous words of Nathan Hale, Benjamin Franklin, George Washington, Abraham Lincoln, or Horace Greeley?

To be a good citizen of your country you need to know more about its history, its form of government, its needs, and its people. In school, by reading, and from people you will learn its history. From the same sources and by being an active member of your troop and community you will learn more about its form of government. Through your friendship with people in your community, and through correspondence, travel, and reading, you will begin to understand the people of this country.

Corresponding with a Girl Scout who lives in another region of the United States is one way of learning more about your country. If you do not already know someone, ask your leader, a neighbor, someone in your church or synagogue, or a member of your Girl Scout council to help you find a pen friend. Your leader may know of a Girl Scout troop in another part of our country, or you may write to the Girl Scout office in any large city for information.

The map on page 376 shows the twelve Girl Scout regions in the United States. It is called a pictorial map.

Traveler

A Girl Scout can no longer think of herself only as a citizen of a certain town or city. Modern methods of transportation and communication—the train, airplane, bus, automobile, radio, telegraph, and telephone—have brought all parts of our country and the world closer together.

Right now you are a traveler in your own community—back and forth to school, or to the store, or to a friend's house. Later, you may travel to other parts of your state or other sections of your country.

Learn about the modern methods of communication and transportation and how to use them. Dramatize incidents

that might happen in a car, bus, train, plane, or boat. How do you call a porter on a train, a hostess on a plane, a steward on a boat? Where do you eat? How do you sleep?

Whenever and however you travel, take along your Girl Scout Promise and Laws. They will help you to be a courteous traveler.

There is a knack to packing a neat suitcase. On this page is a picture that may help you. Practice packing a suitcase until you can do it easily and quickly. Then you will be a well-groomed and efficient traveler.

When we think of communication, we usually think of writing, the telephone, and the radio. If you live near the water or near a railroad or if you travel on either of these, you will discover that trains and boats have a language all

199

their own. On page 266 you will see the methods used by other people to communicate with lights, buzzers, flags, and so forth.

Speaker

Have you ever really listened to other people talk? Have you noticed their enunciation, the tone of their voice, their facial expressions, and mannerisms? Each of these contributes something to the impression you receive about them as a person. Try saying: "I'd love to" or "Thank you" as a shy person, a bored person, or someone who is enthusiastic. What is the difference?

Your speech has a great effect on those about you. The same words can be understood when clearly spoken and go unnoticed or unheard when mumbled. The same words can be spoken harshly or pleasantly; they can make people feel badly or they can make them feel happy. Have you watched a person talk without opening his mouth, or while giggling, or with his hand in front of his face?

Sooner or later everyone has to take part in discussions. You will find help on how to be a good member or the leader of a group discussion on page 192. At times you may be called on to act as chairman or a toastmistress of a special event. You may be called on to give an introduction and present a special guest to your troop. Often you will want to be able to think quickly and speak well before a group.

When you are planning to give a talk or a speech, keep these points in mind:

1. *Believe in your subject.* If you do not really believe in what you are saying, you cannot get your thoughts across to an audience. Choose a subject that you know about, find exciting or interesting, and are eager to share with others.

2. *Warm up to your subject.* When you meet someone on the street, you say "hello" or "how-do-you-do" before starting in on a story. The same principle holds when you make a

speech. Your opening remarks are like "how-do-you-do's." They will give you time to get used to the audience and at the same time the audience will get used to you.

3. *Plan your speech.* Making a speech or talk is like taking a trip. You must know where you are going, which means that you must have a purpose and a plan. On any trip there must be markers along the way and so in making a speech you need a few points which are clearly made. It is always more fun to travel at a comfortable speed, neither too fast nor too slow. The same applies to your speech. Deliver it clearly, distinctly, and neither too quickly nor too slowly. Often the driver of a car does not realize how rapidly he is going. When you give a speech, you will find the same thing is true. The audience may become restless and miss what you have to say if you talk too fast. And finally, a pleasant trip comes to a close before the travelers are tired. Be sure to close your speech while the audience is still attentive.

4. *Know your closing.* A planned closing makes it easier to stop. It will leave the audience with the feeling of a strong ending. Some speakers close with a quotation which can be read. Try various endings and find the one most suited to you and your subject.

Clerk

Every office has special equipment. It takes knowledge and skill to use it correctly. You may find typewriters, duplicating machines, postal scales, stapling machines, and many different types of records such as ledgers, journals, cashbooks, and so forth.

It is important to know how to use these tools well. More important, however, is to be able to work well with other people. You must be aware of the interests and needs of those who work with you. You must be courteous and thoughtful. You must be efficient and calm. You must be accurate. You must be willing to do more than your share. And never forget that in an office, as in your home, troop or school, a smile and a pleasant word will bring happiness to your co-workers.

My Government

"We hold these truths to be self-evident, that all men are created equal; that they are endowed by their Creator with certain inalienable rights, that among these are life, liberty and the pursuit of happiness. That to secure these rights governments are instituted among men deriving their powers from the consent of the governed. . . ."

These words from the Declaration of Independence are the cornerstone of the My Government badge. Your government is *you* and all the other citizens. Yours is a representative government in which every individual has rights and privileges. Every individual has responsibilities.

Like the patrol system in your troop, everyone has to help make government work—for the good of all. In both your troop and your country, government can be only as good as the people who make it.

Right now, as an active citizen, you have certain responsibilities which in turn ensure you of "life, liberty and the pursuit of happiness." In your school and troop elections:

1. *Use your right to vote.* Give thought to the abilities of the candidates. Vote for the one whom you feel can best represent you.

2. *Support your elected representative.* You may not have voted for the person who was elected but you have a responsibility to support her. That means that you will do everything you can to help her become a good representative. You will tell her about your ideas and opinions so that she will know how to speak and act for you.

Find out all you can about your city, county, state, and federal governments. Who are your city officials and what do they do? What taxes do *you* pay? What taxes do your parents

It starts with people who elect candidates from their ranks

representatives who serve

national, state and local

PEOPLE
ARE THEIR
GOVERNMENT

who have party or
independent support

VOTE FOR

Editorial
Our Choice

Every eligible citizen votes to elect

ELECTION

Ballot

National party conventions nominate presidential candidates

CONVENTION

Primary

Candidates in some states are elected in the primary or by state party conventions or committees

pay? What services do you receive in return?

No one is too young or too old to be an active citizen. Your Girl Scout Promise and Laws embody the spirit and principles of good citizenship. Your program activities give you opportunities for being an active citizen.

How can you be of service to your town government? In some places Girl Scouts serve as aides to voters. They find out what services they may give during elections and throughout the year and then make a plan to carry them out.

You might care for small children in your home or neighborhood while the adults get out the vote. You could offer your services to a child care center where younger children stay while their parents assist in some volunteer capacity during election.

Why not find out if there is a nonpartisan organization in your town interested in good government. Ask one of these organizations to help you and your troop as you do the activities in this badge. They may advise you, too, as you set up a plan to serve as Aides to Voters.

Aviation

Men have always wanted to fly. Throughout the ages you will find stories of man's attempts to fashion a set of wings. The best-known legend is that of Daedalus and his son Icarus. They escaped from the island of Crete by wearing a set of wings. These were made with light frames and covered with wax and feathers. The legend goes on to tell that at a later date Icarus was showing off and flew so high that the sun melted the wax and the feathers fell off his wings. Icarus dropped into the sea and was never seen again.

Throughout the seventeenth, eighteenth, and nineteenth centuries, you will find records of attempts of the French, Germans, and English to build a flying machine. The story of the first plane really commenced in 1878, in Dayton, Ohio. It was during that year that the Wright brothers received a toy "helicoptere."

At first Wilbur and Orville flew their toy in the house. Later they tried it outdoors. It was destroyed in the branch of a tree. They decided to build themselves a larger model. They did and this led to more and more experimentation. Twenty-five years later, in 1903, they became the first men to fly a real plane.

Air has substance and weight. The air supports a plane just as water supports a boat. When the plane flies, the wings, curved on top, strike and separate the air. They press the air down and the air pushes the wings up. This force is called "lift" and keeps a plane aloft. The "lift" overcomes gravity which tends to pull the plane earthward. The force which

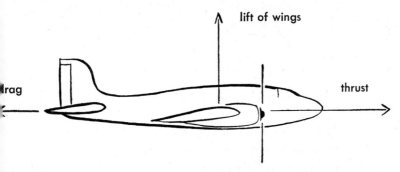

lift of wings

drag

thrust

pulls a plane through the air is the "thrust." "Drag," or the resistance built up by the plane, as it moves through the air, is overcome by the "thrust."

There are two methods which are used to create the "thrust" or force which pushes a plane through the air. These are: (1) the propellor rotated by an engine, and (2) jet propulsion. The last device was invented recently. This force is produced by expelling air or gas through a jet, or nozzle, at extremely high pressure.

Radio and Television

Radio and television bring the world to your hearthstone. Knowledge and entertainment are brought with the turn of a dial. Because radio and television programs are so available and the selection is so wide, it is smart to train your ear and eye for the best. Listen to and watch many broadcast and telecast programs. Talk with your friends, parents, teachers, and Girl Scout leader to find out the kind of programs they

Move closer.   Move away.   Cut.

Watch me.   On schedule.   Stretch it out.   Slow up.

Okay.

Speed up.

like. Decide which ones you enjoy most and why you like them.

If you like to write, if you sing or read well, if you like dramatics, radio and television will have their appeal. Radio and television workshops give aspiring writers, musicians, and dramatists a chance to put into practice many of their skills. Before you start such a workshop, visit one or several broadcasting stations. Observe the techniques of your favorite commentators and announcers. Find out how sound effects are produced and study studio manners and etiquette which ensure a smooth, effective performance.

On this page are pictures of a few of the most commonly used broadcasting signals.

Your radio and television workshops will need boys for the masculine roles. Team up with a boys' club or your neighborhood group to bring boys in to take their parts and help with script writing and production.

This is a badge with a future. There are many vocations open to women in radio and television. Have someone who works in this field visit your troop and tell you about opportunities.

CHAPTER 12

International Friendship

INTERNATIONAL FRIENDSHIP—what do those two words mean? Do you think of travel and faraway places? Do you think of adventure and excitement? Do you think of folk dances and songs, of works of art, of interesting customs, and different languages? Many people do. But international friendship is much greater than the sum total of all those things. It stands for friendship among people of many nations. It is based on understanding and love. It begins within your own heart and in your own home. It spreads from home to home, community to community, and country to country. As it spreads it grows stronger. It brings with it peace among all the people of one nation and all the peoples of the world. It is an exciting adventure in getting to know yourself and your neighbors, whether they live next door or thousands of miles away.

World Gifts

America is often called the "melting pot" of the world. The only native Americans are the American Indians. The rest of us have come to America from all the countries of the world. Our ancestors, at one time or another, were called immigrants. Every day you meet people whose parents or grandparents immigrated to the United States from a different country than the one your ancestors left. Perhaps they, themselves, were "born on the other side."

207

As each group has come and continues to come they bring with them the customs and traditions of the old country. These they adapt to their new country as they become citizens. That is why America is called "the melting pot." You can also think of it as a symphony orchestra. Each group makes a contribution. Each contribution is beautiful in itself but it increases in beauty as it blends in unity and harmony with the total orchestra. For over three hundred years, the United States has been molding together the culture and contributions of other nations.

Have you ever thought of the gifts we have received from all over the world? Often, we take them for granted. The picture on page 209 shows some of them. What others can you think of? What others can you discover? They are all around you—in your own home, neighborhood, and town. You do not have to travel to find these gifts. The people who have them are your neighbors. Make friends with them.

What people are like The only thing that is exactly the same in all people is that they are human beings. In other things they may agree or differ.

There are people all over the world who like the same things. It may be cabbage, collecting postage stamps, hiking, camping, cooking, books, playing with dolls, swimming—anything. No matter what you are interested in, you will find some people in your country and in other countries who are interested in the same things.

All human beings have similar needs. They want to love and be loved; they want to be dependent and independent; they want to create; they want to worship; they want to feel secure. All people are sad sometimes and happy other times. They have "troubles" of a kind. They all get cross once in a while. They want friends and good times. They need food

Gifts of the World

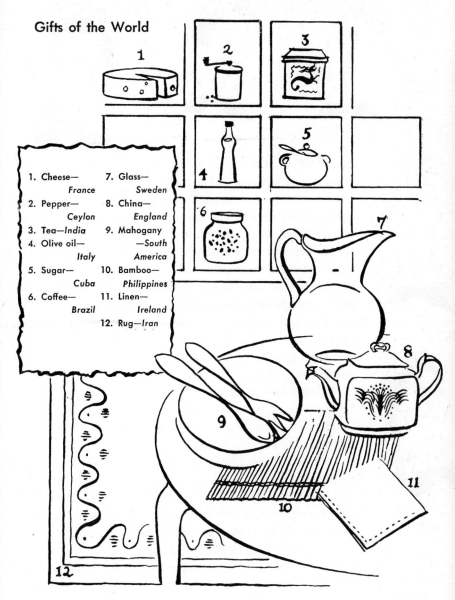

1. Cheese— France
2. Pepper— Ceylon
3. Tea—India
4. Olive oil— Italy
5. Sugar— Cuba
6. Coffee— Brazil
7. Glass— Sweden
8. China— England
9. Mahogany —South America
10. Bamboo— Philippines
11. Linen— Ireland
12. Rug—Iran

and clothing. They want to feel free and safe in their own homes, communities, and country.

Differences, such as night and day, summer and winter, sun and rain, in color and sound, help make the world beautiful. Differences do not mean that something is better or worse, superior or inferior. Differences in people are what make the world interesting.

Members of your family think differently and do not do things exactly alike. Some like blue, and some like red. Some like fish, and some do not. Some like the movies better than books, and some do not. Some like active games, and some like quiet games. All these things are known as differences of opinion and action.

Probably no two members of your family look exactly alike. Some are dark, some are medium, some light. Some are tall, some short, some thin, some stout. These things are known as physical or outward differences.

You would not like it if every member of your family looked exactly the same, acted the same, thought the same, and said the same things. Can you imagine your troop, your school, your community with only people who were exactly the same? Or the United States? Or the world?

You do not like, equally well, every dress you have. You do not find equally companionable all the people in your school or troop. It is natural to like some people, as individuals, better than others.

However, you can learn that every group of people has its own way of life. You can try to understand and respect that way even though it is quite different from your own. You can practice good will toward all races, creeds, and national backgrounds in your home town. It is easy to be friends with people you like. Start now by making *new* friends.

Every one of us has a wonderful chance to be a "world neighbor" by simply getting to know our own neighbors— the people we go to school with and those who live in our town.

World Trefoil

The World pin is the emblem of the World Association of Girl Guides and Girl Scouts. It may be worn by all Girl Guides and Girl Scouts whose countries are members of the World Association. When you are invested as a Girl Scout you may wear it. As a Tenderfoot Girl Scout you learned about the pin and the World Association (see page 15). Now, as you work on the World Trefoil badge, you will want to become more familiar with the World Association, its work, and the activities of its member associations.

The flag of the World Association of Girl Guides and Girl Scouts symbolizes the world-wide bond of Girl Scouting. It is flown at all international meetings and camps. Your own troop may wish to make or buy one of these to use in troop meetings along with the flags of your country and your troop.

The World flag has a bright blue field with a gold trefoil on it. The design is exactly like the one that appears on your World pin. On page 15 you will find the explanation of what it means.

211

Our Chalet On the slope of a mountain near Adelboden, Switzerland, in the heart of the Alps, stands Our Chalet. (See page 213.) It was given to the World Association by an American Girl Scout, Mrs. James J. Storrow. Our Chalet was built as an international home so that Girl Guides and Scouts from all over the world could come together to meet and make friends. They enjoy excursions, mountain climbing, winter sports, and discussions around the campfire. The motto painted on Our Chalet reads *Gott behute dieses Hus, Und All die gehen yn und us* ("God bless this house and all who go in and out of it").

The Juliette Low World Friendship Fund (page 214) sends girls from a different group of countries every summer to a gathering at Our Chalet. There are always representatives of the United States at the gathering. Here they live, work, and play together. They grow to understand each other. Each girl learns more about the lives, customs, traditions, education, art, and economic conditions of the countries of her new friends.

International hostels In addition to Our Chalet, there are now five other international hostels open to Girl Guides and Girl Scouts. They are Our Ark, in London, England; *La Nef* in Paris, France; *Buitenzorg* in Baarn, the Netherlands; the Guide Cottage in Enniskerry, Ireland; and the *Pigespejderhuset* in Copenhagen, Denmark.

Thinking Day International friendship goes on every day of the year. However, February is the month that Girl Guides and Girl Scouts set aside for special emphasis on this part of their program. February 22 is the birthday of both Lord and Lady Baden-Powell and since 1926 it has been set aside as Thinking Day.

Exchange counselors

International Gatherings
at Our Chalet

Girl Scout books and periodicals,
office supplies, uniform material
for re-establishment
of Guide associations

Food, clothing,
blankets, money for relief
in Europe, Africa,
and the Far East

Sanatorium
in France

Juliette Low World Friendship Fund

Scouts and Guides the world over celebrate this day. Your troop may want to plan a special program. These are some of the things that your sister Girl Guides like to do. In Belgium, the troops in each community gather together for a campfire program. In Australia, at a certain time of the day the Guides stop whatever they are doing and pray for their sister Guides in other countries. In Ireland, the Guides write to pen friends. In New Zealand you will find that every year a group of Rangers climbs to the summit of Mt. Eden, near Auckland, to hold a sunrise service. In the Netherlands, all the Guides of a town gather together in the morning to renew their Promise and to receive snowdrops and an ivy leaf. The ivy stands for friendship which is always fresh and strong. The snowdrops stand for our ideals which must always be kept pure and white like these little blossoms.

International Friendship Troops — A troop of girls in junior or senior high school that has met special requirements and is ready to have a direct link with a troop in another part of the world is eligible to become an International Friendship Troop. The Program Department, at Girl Scout national headquarters, can tell you how to go about becoming one.

World Friendship Fund — Juliette Low, our founder, was a great traveler and knew the far parts of the earth almost as well as her beloved Georgia and the England that she had adopted at her marriage. Her hope had always been to unite the children of many countries in common ideals and interests. The concept of "international friendship" had taken shape in her lively mind long before the phrase became familiar to everyone.

At her death, it was felt that no more fitting memorial to her could be established than one that fostered friendship among the young people of many countries. And so the

214

Juliette Low World Friendship Fund was started. Girl Scouts of the U.S.A. of all ages and living in all parts of the world contribute to the fund.

On page 213 is a picture showing some of the things this money has made possible. You can find out more about the fund from *The American Girl* and by borrowing your leader's February copy of *The Girl Scout Leader*. Every Girl Scout gives what she can to this fund at a special ceremony held either for her whole community or in her own troop.

JULIETTE LOW REPRESENTATIVE. Your troop may have a Juliette Low representative. The Juliette Low chairman of your Girl Scout council meets with her and other troop representatives in your community to plan Juliette Low world friendship work at intertroop and city-wide activities.

A Juliette Low representative should learn all she can about our Founder and the fund. She should work with her leader to promote interest in the fund and to tell the troop how it is used. She should report to the troop all information and plans she has learned about at meetings with other representatives.

INTERNATIONAL GATHERINGS. The Juliette Low World Friendship Fund makes it possible for some Senior Girl Scouts to meet with other Girl Guides and Girl Scouts. Every year a gathering is held at Our Chalet. Frequently, gatherings are also held in the United States. At other times, the fund enables Senior Girl Scouts to participate in events sponsored by other members of the World Association. Your leader can tell you about these opportunities. Although they are only for older girls, you and your troop can begin to prepare for them now. Proficiency badges in the international friendship, community life, and out-of-doors fields are very helpful.

215

Great Britain

Mexico

Brazil

Canada

Egypt

Australia

India

Representatives from full member countries of the World Association of Girl Guides and Girl Scouts meet every two years at the World Conference to decide Association matters. Each full member may send two delegates. Each full member country has one vote, regardless of its size. Tenderfoot members may send two representatives to the conference. They have no vote.

The Council Fire *The Council Fire* is the official Girl Guide and Girl Scout magazine published four times a year by the World Association. It contains news of Girl Scouts all over the world, pictures of events and people in Guiding and Scouting, and accounts of special occasions. The articles are written in English and French.

Pen Pal

One of the ways to get acquainted with girls throughout the United States and in other countries is through correspondence. If you are twelve years old or over, you can correspond through the International Post Box. You can find out how to locate a pen pal in this country by reading page 198.

Juliette Low started the first International Post Box. Many members of the World Association have an International Post Box Secretary, who helps find pen friends for Girl Scouts and their leaders all over the world.

Our International Post Box (located at Girl Scout national headquarters) has on file the names, ages, and addresses of a limited number of girls from abroad who want pen pals. If you are twelve or over, you may write to the Post Box direct. Give your age, address, country preferred, if any, and the language you read (in addition to English) or for which you have a translator. Be sure to include a large self-addressed, stamped envelope for Post Box reply. Don't be discouraged if you do not receive an immediate reply. It takes time to make the arrangements.

When you start a correspondence, you become a kind of ambassador for your country. Not you alone but your troop, all Girl Scouts, and your country, will be judged by the things you write, the way you write, and the neatness of your letter. *Tips on letters*

Here are some pointers that you will want to check when you write to your pen pal:

1. Write the letter with care.

2. Tell your pen pal about the things that you do in your troop and with your family, at school and in your town. Write about your pets, your hobbies, your everyday life, and special celebrations.

3. Include snapshots of yourself, your family, your troop and so forth. Postcards of your town and clippings from *The American Girl* and other magazines will be popular, too.

4. Include directions for favorite games and crafts projects. Exchange troop albums, camp notebooks, stamp collections, or pictures or prints of birds, trees, and flowers.

5. Describe special holidays, such as Thanksgiving and the Fourth of July. Tell why and how we celebrate these days and ask your friend to tell you about the holidays in her country.

6. On special occasions, send your pen pal a small gift that you have made. Be sure to make something that will have real meaning to her and will help her to learn more about the United States.

Western Hemisphere

It is fun to get to know your neighbors to the north and south of you. Have you ever stopped to think that the term American includes everyone who lives in North, Central, and

219

South America? Did you realize that the longest unguarded frontiers in the world lie between the United States and Canada and the United States and Mexico? Do you know how this came about? It shows that trust and cooperation between nations can become a reality.

Mexico and other Latin-American countries have played an important part in the history of our country. Even today you can see and feel the impact of their culture as you travel through the Southwest and California.

Because the world is so large, there is a subcommittee of the World Association known as the Western Hemisphere Regional Committee. Its headquarters are located in the same building as our own national headquarters in New York City.

The Canadian Girl Guides are one of the members of the Western Hemisphere Regional Committee. Did you know that they are also linked to all the Guides in all parts of the far-flung British Empire and Commonwealth through the Imperial Girl Guide Headquarters in London?

Travel in Canada and Mexico is a dream that may come true for many of you, especially if you live along the northern border of the United States or in the Southwest. It may be that you will visit these countries with your family on a holiday, or travel or camp with your Senior Girl Scout troop. You will find that a visit to any country is much more fun when you know about the life of that country. Prepare today by working on the Western Hemisphere badge and others in the international friendship, community life, and out-of-doors fields.

World Neighbor

In the preamble to the Charter of the United Nations there is a clause which must make us think. It states that one of the purposes for which the nations of the world have united is "to practice tolerance and live together in peace with one another as good neighbors."

Our Fourth Girl Scout Law states: A Girl Scout is a friend to all and a sister to every other Girl Scout. What is a friend to all? This check list will help you to find the answer. Check it today, then a month from now, two months from now, and so on. Gradually you will discover that you can check the right answers more and more frequently. You will become aware of the things that make a person a friend to all. You will be on your way to becoming a world-minded citizen.

How Do You Rate As a Friend to All?

Work To Get All Check Marks Under "No"

	Yes	No	Sometimes
1. Do I make fun of other people's religious beliefs?	☐	☐	☐
2. Am I jealous of other people's possessions?	☐	☐	☐
3. Do I call names that might hurt people's feelings?	☐	☐	☐
4. Do I make fun of people's accents?	☐	☐	☐
5. Do I shun people who are not "like me"?	☐	☐	☐
6. Do I say that all people of any one group are any one thing, such as stingy, dishonest, stubborn?	☐	☐	☐

Work To Get All Check Marks Under "Yes"
In My Family

	Yes	No	Sometimes
1. Do I keep my temper under control?	☐	☐	☐
2. Do I try not to insist on having my own way all the time?	☐	☐	☐
3. Do I respect the wishes of other members of my family?	☐	☐	☐

221

	Yes	No	Sometimes

4. Do I keep from saying mean things about members of my family? ☐ ☐ ☐

5. Do I share my possessions with others in the family? ☐ ☐ ☐

6. Am I courteous to my family, young and old? ☐ ☐ ☐

In My Troop

1. Do I help new members of my troop to understand Girl Scouting? ☐ ☐ ☐

2. Do I treat all my troop mates in the spirit of the Fifth Law? ☐ ☐ ☐

3. Do I "come through" with all the jobs that are given to me? ☐ ☐ ☐

4. Do I bring new ideas of things to do to my troop? ☐ ☐ ☐

5. Do I pay attention to the wishes and ideas of the other members? ☐ ☐ ☐

6. Do I express my opinions in meetings and not after meetings? ☐ ☐ ☐

In My Community

1. Am I helpful and courteous to new Americans in my community? ☐ ☐ ☐

2. Do I give service to the hospital, fire department, school, orphanage, and so forth? ☐ ☐ ☐

	Yes	No	Sometimes
3. Do I know interesting things about the history of my own town?	☐	☐	☐
4. Am I courteous and considerate to people who give me service?	☐	☐	☐
5. Do I respect other people's property and public property?	☐	☐	☐
6. Do I know how, and by whom, my town is governed?	☐	☐	☐

In My Country

	Yes	No	Sometimes
1. Do I listen to other people's ideas and opinions?	☐	☐	☐
2. Do I help with things when it isn't what I want to do?	☐	☐	☐
3. Do I stand up for the right of other people to have *their* opinions?	☐	☐	☐
4. Do I go out of my way to welcome new citizens to my country?	☐	☐	☐
5. Do I make friends with people different from myself—richer or poorer, or another race or creed?	☐	☐	☐

In the World

	Yes	No	Sometimes
1. Do I believe there is some good in every person?	☐	☐	☐
2. Do I believe the United States can learn helpful things from other nations?	☐	☐	☐

223

	Yes	No	Sometimes
3. Do I contribute, regularly, to the Juliette Low World Friendship Fund?	☐	☐	☐
4. Do I wear my World pin as well as my Girl Scout pin, and understand what they mean?	☐	☐	☐
5. Do I go out of my way to learn about other countries?	☐	☐	☐

Language

Do you call a thing to fry eggs in a "skillet," a "frying pan," or a "spider"? Do you call a burlap bag a "tow sack," a "croker sack," or a "gunny sack"? The words you use for many everyday items vary, depending on the part of the country from which you come. When you meet someone who uses a different term for a familiar object, a small barrier arises between you. When you learn to use his terms as easily as your own, you find that a bond has brought you closer together.

The same is true with languages. Learning to speak the language of another country makes you feel more friendly toward its people, and makes them feel more friendly toward you.

Most people in our country are slow to learn other languages because we are an English-speaking nation throughout, and our borders are wide. In small countries of the world, people have to learn several languages in order to communicate because their neighbors are so close to them.

When people of other parts of the world visit us, they are usually able to talk with us in our own language. One of the things we can do to show our friendliness toward another country is to learn to speak its language.

fogata

la feu de camp

Some Girl Scouts have in their families people who are able to speak another language. If you are one of those fortunate girls, take advantage of the opportunity to practice both languages at home, and share what you learn with others in your troop. The English language, like the rest of our culture, is rich in gifts from other countries.

el trebol

la trèfle

la tienda

la tente

la linterna electrica

la lampe de poche

Conversationalist

To master the ordinary, everyday phrases and to be able to express yourself slowly is the first step in learning any language—even our own native tongue. But to really be able to speak another language requires study, practice, and concentration. One of the frequently quoted tests of a person's ability to converse in a language other than his own is his ability to think in that language.

A conversationalist is a girl who has mastered another tongue. She can speak it with ease—frequently and accurately. She can think in that language. When talking she has no need to translate what is said to her into English and then translate her English answer into the other language. It just comes naturally. In addition to speaking well, a conversationalist can read and write well, too.

A girl who has recently come to the United States, with

225

only a little knowledge of English, might first work on her Language badge and then go on to the Conversationalist badge.

If you want to learn a language, you *can*. Take a course in school. Try to get a set of language records. Sometimes you will find courses given over the radio. Talk with a person who can speak the language. And after you have mastered the language, keep on practicing.

My World

When the first people voyaged over the oceans to reach our country, it took them months and months to travel. Today, fast steamers and planes have brought all nations of the world close together. It now is just a matter of hours to get to Paris or London from New York. It does not take much longer to fly to Sidney or New Delhi. Modern transportation has made it possible to move easily and quickly around the world.

At the same time it has also brought to our shores many things. It is fun to visit a grocery or delicatessen store and

---

ILO International Labor Organization

FAO Food and Agriculture Organization

UNESCO United Nations Educational, Scientific, and Cultural Organization

ICAO International Civil Aviation Organization

IBRD International Bank for Reconstruction and Development

IMF International Monetary Fund

WHO World Health Organization

UPU Universal Postal Union

ITU International Telecommunication Union

WMO World Meteorological Organization

IMCO Inter-Governmental Maritime Consultative Organization

ITO International Trade Organization

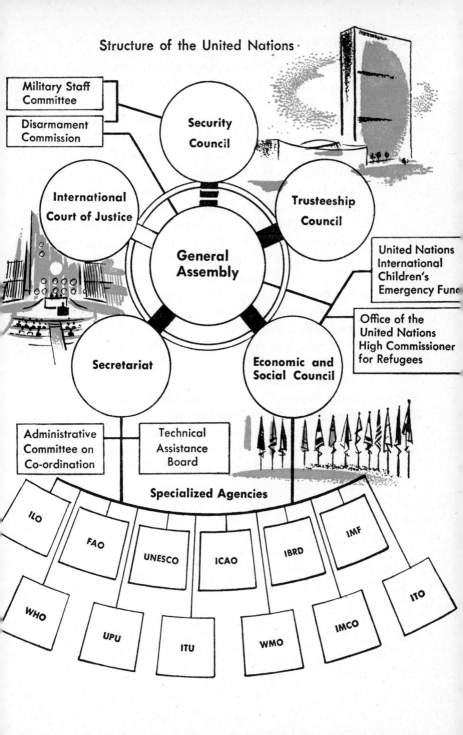

Structure of the United Nations

Military Staff Committee

Disarmament Commission

Security Council

International Court of Justice

Trusteeship Council

General Assembly

United Nations International Children's Emergency Fund

Office of the United Nations High Commissioner for Refugees

Secretariat

Economic and Social Council

Administrative Committee on Co-ordination

Technical Assistance Board

Specialized Agencies

ILO
FAO
UNESCO
ICAO
IBRD
IMF
WHO
UPU
ITU
WMO
IMCO
ITO

locate the many things that have been imported. In other stores, too, you will find more things that come from other countries.

It is no longer unusual to hear broadcasts from other countries. You can turn the dial of your radio and pick up many interesting programs. Our own stations often broadcast special programs in other languages, such as French and Spanish. Today, one can hear by telephone the voices of friends and loved ones in a matter of minutes.

In the United Nations organization, delegates from various countries of the world can meet together. Since the United States of America is a member of the United Nations, you will want to know about the work of the United Nations and its specialized agencies. Girl Scouts are particularly concerned with that part of the United Nations work which deals with the welfare of children and youth.

As you have already learned, the World Association of Girl Guides and Girl Scouts works to encourage friendship among Girl Scouts and Girl Guides. This association is made up of national associations of Girl Guides and Girl Scouts that fulfill certain membership requirements. One of its objectives is to promote understanding of the fundamental principles of Girl Scouting and Guiding throughout the world. The associations in the World Association work together on common interests and concerns.

CHAPTER 13

CHAPTER 14

CHAPTER 15

PART IV

Fun and Exploration
in the Out-of-Doors

Nature

Out-of-Doors

Sports and Games

Nature

D O TREES have flowers? Are some
plants square stemmed? Do cats
have eyelashes? Do earthworms have eyes? What kind of
teeth does a hamster have—or a cow? Do turtles have
tongues? What is the family name for African violets and
snake plants? Have you ever wondered about these things?

Nature is not confined by time or place. It is everywhere.
However, nature does charge a price for admission. It opens
its doors only to you who open your eyes and ears, who feel,
taste, and smell. In return, Nature unfolds before you its
mysteries and wonders. It brings you the excitement of discovery and the joy of finding new interests and friends.

Rambler

A rambler enjoys exploring off the beaten path. If you are
a rambler you stop, look, and listen every time you find anything of interest. You walk slowly and halt frequently so you
will not miss anything.

When you are out-of-doors, are you interested in all the
things you see? Why not learn a little about each? Learn
the way some things depend on others for their growth. A
tree must have sun, water, and a certain kind of soil. A rabbit
must have water and green things to eat and bushes for
shelter. A bird may need a certain kind of berry and will live
only where that berry is found.

233

As a rambler you will get to know where certain kinds of plants, birds, mammals, and insects are found. You know that mosquitoes, frogs, and water turtles can be found in swamps. You look for trillium and violets in woodsy, shady spots and for hummingbirds and yellow warblers along the lake.

You will discover that nature rotates plant growth as a farmer rotates his crops. If a piece of land is burned over or lumbered, different trees, flowers, and ferns will start to grow there, taking the place of the ones that did grow there.

People like to collect and take home mementos of their rambles. It does no harm to collect such things as pebbles, shells, leaves of trees and shrubs. But there are other things that must not be disturbed, such as rare plants or their blossoms, birds' eggs, rare insects. However you can make sketches or collections of pictures. Start now and you will always have your own happy memories.

Names in nature Everything in nature has a scientific name. Some things also have "common" names. They are called "common" only because they are familiar. Many times the scientific names are the same as the common such as geranium, nasturtium, phlox, hippopotamus, vireo, sassafras, catalpa, and lynx.

The three kingdoms There are three kingdoms in the world: plant, animal, and mineral. The mineral kingdom includes things that do not have life and therefore do not grow, such as rocks and minerals. They are called inorganic.

Members of the plant and animal kingdoms do have life and do grow. They are called organic. The great difference between these two kingdoms is that members of the animal kingdom can move of their own will and members of the plant kingdom cannot.

A tree is a plant because it has life and grows but cannot move from place to place. An insect is an animal because it

has life and grows and can move about. When most people speak of animals, they really mean mammals, such as the cat, dog, wolf, and skunk. Mammals are one class in the animal kingdom. Find the three kingdoms in the picture.

Tree

Get into the habit when you look at a tree of noticing the leaves, bark, buds, blossoms, and general shape. All but the leaves and blossoms will be there during every season in all parts of the country.

Trees are either deciduous or evergreen. The deciduous trees, such as the maple, shed all their leaves at once. Evergreen trees, such as the spruce, shed their leaves (needles)

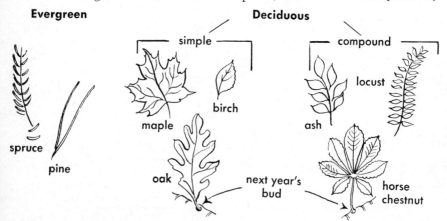

Evergreen

spruce

pine

Deciduous

simple

maple

birch

oak

next year's bud

compound

locust

ash

horse chestnut

from time to time. This difference is very noticeable in cold and temperate climates. In the tropics, it is not so noticeable.

Deciduous trees have two types of leaves—simple and compound. A simple leaf is one leaf. A compound leaf is a leaf that is made up of several leaves.

All trees have both flowers and seeds. Look at the picture of a simple flower and notice the stamens and pistil. The stamens carry the pollen and the pistil receives the pollen.

Some plants have the stamens and pistil in the same flower, like the tulip tree. Others, like the oak, have them on separate flowers on the same plant. Still others have them on separate plants, like the holly. Flowers that have only stamens are

236

called staminate (male) flowers. Those that have only pistils are called pistillate (female) flowers.

Trees can be identified by the buds alone for they are different on every tree. Leaf scars, too, are different on each type of tree. They are little scars left on the twigs where the leaves were attached.

A tree that is crowded in with many other trees rarely shows its characteristic shape. To learn the shape of trees pick those that you find growing in fairly open places.

Most people like to include some of the shrubs in their study of trees. A shrub is also a woody plant. It is smaller than a tree and has many main stems instead of one stem or a trunk like a tree. Japanese barberry, flowering quince, and hydrangeas are common shrubs.

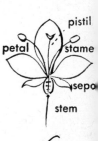

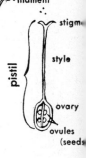

Garden Flower

Did you know that all cultivated plants grown in our houses or gardens can be found growing wild in some part of the world? In some cases, horticulturists have improved the original form by careful breeding and cross-breeding. The carnation is an example. In other cases, cultivated plants have in no way changed. The jade plant is an example of this type.

All flowering plants have seeds, but they are not all grown from seeds. Some are grown from bulbs (Easter lily), some from seeds (pansy), some from corms (some of the begonias), some from roots or cuttings (ivy), and some throw out new plants from the parent plant (strawberry begonia).

Not everyone can have a garden of his own but everyone can learn lots of interesting things about flowers and plants. A potted plant or a bunch of flowers comes to many homes some time during the year. Can you care for them?

237

Find out from what part of the world the cultivated plants in your house come. If you know this, you will know what your plants need and will be able to take better care of them. A plant that grows wild in a swamp in the tropics needs

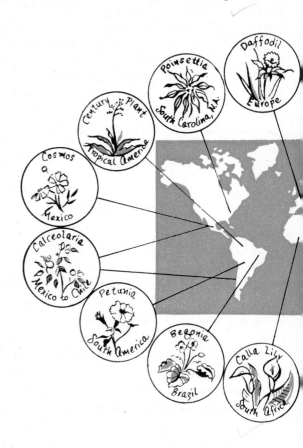

quite different care than one that grows wild in the side of a mountain.

Try growing some plants in your home. The picture on page 240 will help you select the kinds to grow.

238

If you already have house plants, look at them every day to see whether they need water. About once a week stir up the top soil with a fork. Watch them carefully for pests, such as plant lice, red mites, and mealy bugs. A plant responds

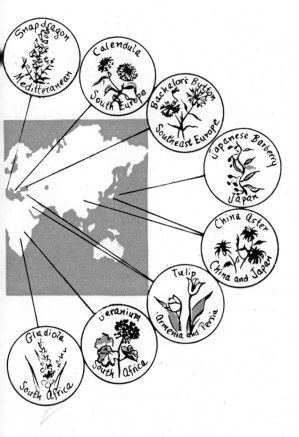

quickly to kind and understanding treatment and returns to us in beauty all we give it in service.

Don't stop with plants and flowers in the house. Try a window box out-of-doors.

EAST	1. inch plant	4. strawberry be-
	2. Kenilworth ivy	gonia
	3. spider plant	5. jade plant
	6. pick-a-back plant	

NORTH	1. asparagus	3. holly fern
	fern	4. philoden-
	2. ivy	dron
		5. sword fern

Wild Plant

Wild plants have been used by man throughout the centuries for food and medicine. Do you know what plants the early settlers and Indians used in your community? How many of them do you think are still used in medicine today?

The plant kingdom is a large one. Get to know the flowering plants, such as dandelions and orchids, and also the ferns, mosses, mushrooms, and seaweeds.

It is useful to know the parts of a flower. On page 237 is a drawing of a simple flower. By simple we mean not complicated in structure, as, for example, some of the mints and orchids. Look closely at several different types of flowers and see how the parts are arranged. If you look quickly at an Easter lily or tulip, you might say it has six petals. But you would be wrong for there are only three. The three petals and three sepals are usually alike or nearly alike in both color

240

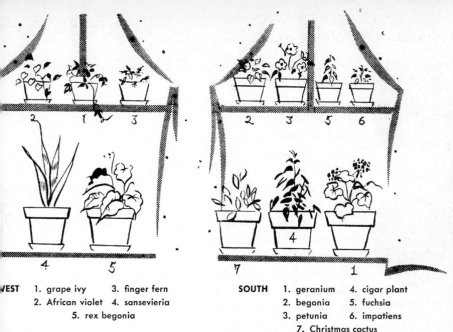

WEST   1. grape ivy   3. finger fern
       2. African violet 4. sansevieria
                5. rex begonia

SOUTH   1. geranium   4. cigar plant
        2. begonia   5. fuchsia
        3. petunia   6. impatiens
            7. Christmas cactus

and shape. Can you find the pistil and stamens in a carnation? What are they like in the snapdragon, the onion flower, or the begonia?

The ovary is the part of the plant that carries the seeds. It is at the base of the pistil. The pollen, which is contained in the stamens, falls upon the pistil, and a pollen grain, provided it is from the same species of plant, sends a tube down the pistil to fertilize a seed.

It is possible to cross-pollinate different kinds of begonias and the pollen will work. However, it is impossible to make the pollen from a rose work on a begonia. A plant needs a pollen grain to fertilize each seed. If it is two-seeded, it needs two pollen grains; if it is three-seeded, three pollen grains; and so on.

Pollen is carried from one flower to another in different ways. It may be by the wind, by insects, by water, or by birds. Some plants are self-pollinated, which means that the

241

poison ivy

poison oak

poison sumac

poison wood

blossom's own pollen falls on the pistil of the same flower and fertilizes the seeds in the ovary.

Try to look at different pollen grains under a microscope. They are very interesting and come in all shapes—round, oval, triangular. Some are smooth and others have spines.

You will find old legends and superstitions about plants as exciting as any story. Do you know why the anemone is sometimes called the "windflower" and the hepatica is referred to as "liverwort"?

Some of your favorite wild flowers have cultivated relatives that you will find growing in many a garden. For example, the snapdragon and "butter and eggs," baby's breath and "chickweed," iris and "blue-eyed grass."

Some plants are called weeds. A weed is simply a plant that grows where you want something else to grow. The weeds in our garden are nature's way of covering up a scar we have made in the face of the earth. They are as interesting to know as the things you have planted. You will discover that some weeds are beneficial to a garden and should be controlled but not eradicated. Did you know that a plant that is a weed in one part of the country may be a rare plant in another part?

There are only four plants that are poisonous to touch. They are poison ivy, poison oak, poison sumac, and poison wood. Poison ivy, oak, and sumac all belong to the same family genus, namely *Rhus*. The poison "oak" is not an oak. The poison sumac is sometimes called "poison dogwood" but it is not a dogwood. Poison wood is found only in Florida.

Learn to recognize these plants and stay away from them. The picture here will help you. The best first aid treatment is prevention, but if you should happen to come in contact with these plants follow the directions outlined on page 342.

Cat and Dog

Cats and dogs are the most common household pets throughout the world. They have been favorite pets for thousands of years. All the different breeds have been developed by man from a few wild ancestors. Cats belong to the same family as lions, jaguars, leopards, and tigers. Dogs belong to the same family as wolves and foxes.

Members of the cat family are lone hunters. They stalk their prey and jump with sureness and speed. Look at a cat's paws. They are sharp and sheathed. This sheathing serves two purposes; one, the claws are kept sharp because they are sheathed; two, the cat walks only on the cushions of the feet. You do not hear a cat walking around the house; he moves silently.

The entire dog family pursues its prey by running it down. Look at a dog's paw. The claws are unsheathed and serve the same purpose as spikes on a track shoe—to keep from skidding and increase speed. When the dog walks around the house, you hear his claws on the floor.

Notice the paw marks of the cat and dog in snow or moist earth. The dog's prints always show at least two of the claws while the cat's prints do not show any claws.

There are a few simple things to remember when you have one of these animals as a pet. Their needs are almost like your own, that is, regular exercise, nourishing food served regularly, proper elimination, bodily cleanliness, and kind treatment.

Dogs and cats need exercise to keep their bodies in good condition. If you live in a community where your dog must be kept on a leash, you can go out together for your daily exercise.

Meat is the natural food for both animals, but must be supplemented by vegetables, fish, and cereals. It is important that they receive their meals or meal regularly—as near the same time each day as possible. This helps them form regular habits of elimination. It is a good idea to exercise the dog before feeding because it will stimulate his appetite. An animal likes to rest and sleep after a good meal.

Keep your dog and cat as clean as possible. This does not mean bathing, but does mean a thorough brushing daily. It is not a good idea to bathe dogs too often because it destroys the oil in the skin and takes away the luster from their coats.

It is unfair to own a cat or dog and not treat it well. One of the most important things is to try to understand your pets and help them to understand you. Screaming at an animal or hitting him is not the way to teach understanding. Dogs and cats have sensitive ears and feelings. Screaming or hitting hurts and confuses them and they will learn nothing but fear. Kindness, patience, and perseverance are the only ways in which you and your pet—or other human beings for that matter—can establish understanding.

If a dog or cat does something you do not want him to do, use the same word, always, in correcting him. It does not matter what the word is—"no," "stop," "don't"—but use the same word and only one word. Be consistent. Don't scold a puppy once for climbing on a bed and then later play with him when he is on the same bed. When you correct a pet once for making a mistake, you must correct him every time he makes the same mistake, or he will never learn.

If your pet does something you want him to do, be sure to praise him. "Good dog," "good puss," or just the word "good" becomes music to his ears and he associates the thing you want him to do with a pat on the head. Do not reward dogs or cats with bits of food.

Cats and dogs have a small vocabulary. If your pet understands and responds to ten words, he is very smart and you are doing well in teaching him.

Puppies and dogs can be easily housebroken. Feed them at regular hours and then take them out-of-doors within about ten minutes, or take them to the special box or place you have provided. Do not whip or rub their noses in their mistakes. But say "bad" or "naughty" or "no" and take them outdoors or to their box. If you are patient, kind, and consistent, they will learn quickly.

Be kind, be firm, compliment good behavior, feed and exercise your pet regularly, and he will grow in his devotion and you will grow in your affection. You will then have learned to understand each other.

Bird

Did you realize that birds are the only members of the animal kingdom that have feathers? There are other animals that lay eggs, such as turtles, flies, and toads; and others that can fly, such as bats; but only birds have feathers.

Different kinds of birds have different habits. Watch the birds around your home and notice the different things they eat, the various types of material they use in building their nests, and the different places they select to nest. Their eggs are not the same color or shape either.

Most birds build nests. Some are fancy and some very simple. Some hang from branches; others are in the hollows of trees; others under the eaves of buildings. Still others will be found nestling in the crotch of a tree or among tall grasses in the field. Each type of bird builds its own kind of nest. You can know the bird by its nest. Most birds build a new nest every year but there are a few who return to last year's nest.

245

The bird's nest is used only for holding the eggs and the young.

Some birds, such as ducks, grouse, and pheasants, are ready to travel around with their parents as soon as they are hatched. Other birds, such as robins, sparrows, warblers, remain in their nest for a time as helpless babies.

The kind of bill a bird has is determined by the kind of food it eats. For instance, seed-eating birds have short, chunky bills. Insect-eating birds have small, slender bills. Hawks and owls have curved bills for tearing their food.

No matter how many eggs a bird lays in the nest, it lays only one a day until the set is complete. The bird does not begin "setting" on the eggs until the full set is laid.

Different kinds of birds hatch their eggs differently, too. Sometimes only the female does the hatching, in other cases it is only the male, and in others they both take turns.

Most birds bring up more than one family in a season. They may have as many as three. Birds' nests are always clean no matter how large or how often they have a family. The parent birds carry from the nest the droppings of the baby birds.

Do you know which birds in your community are permanent residents, summer residents, winter residents, or passing visitors? The permanent residents stay the whole year; summer residents winter south of you; winter residents go north for the summer; and passing visitors will stop for a week or two, on their way north or south. Although we do not know exactly why birds migrate, we do know that it has something to do with the kind of food they need. Some birds migrate a great distance—thousands of miles—and follow definite routes. When migrating, small birds travel at night and large birds during the day.

Birds move quickly and often. As you study them, you will become a keen observer. You have only a few minutes,

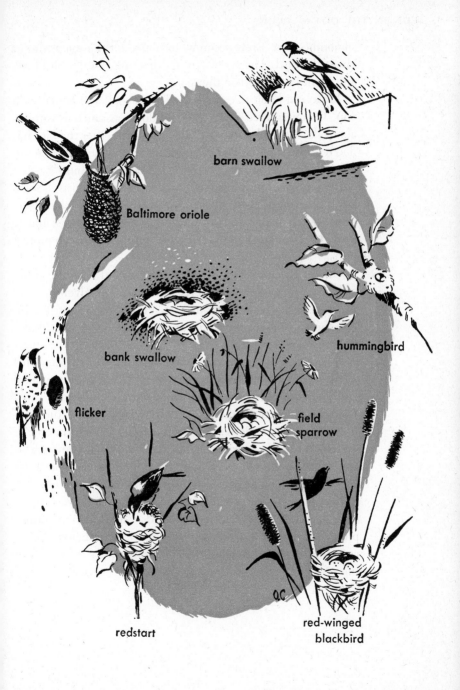

barn swallow

Baltimore oriole

bank swallow

hummingbird

flicker

field sparrow

redstart

red-winged blackbird

sometimes just a few seconds, to notice all the many things about the bird. There is often not time to get out a bird book and identify the bird on the spot.

Make it a habit to carry a small notebook and pencil with you. When you see a new bird, jot down as much as you can about the size, color, type of bill, and so on. After the bird has flown away or when you get home, you can use your notes to identify the bird in a book and read about its habits.

People who study birds are called "ornithologists." Some are interested in every phase of bird study. Others have specialties such as the study of plumage, migration, eggs, and so forth, or are interested in bird photography or laws to protect birds.

One of the most famous names connected with the study of birds is James Audubon. His life was full of adventure and you will enjoy reading about him. His greatest contribution was the painting of the birds of America. Look in the library for reproductions of his work.

Today there is a national organization named after this man—the National Audubon Society. There are many local Audubon societies throughout the country. Find out if there is one in your community. There may be a Junior Audubon Society, too, or perhaps your troop would like to form one.

There are other organizations that will help you such as garden clubs and the state forestry department. What ones can you think of in your community? Any organization that is interested in beautifying a community with flowers, trees, and shrubs helps to attract the birds, since such plantings provide them with nesting places, food, and shelter. What can you do in your neighborhood or community to attract the birds?

Mammal

A mammal is an animal that nurses its young. Many people think that mammals are only those animals that have fur. That is incorrect because whales are mammals, as are mice, lions, elephants, bats, dogs, cats, horses, cows, squirrels, and humans.

Choose for study the cat, dog, horse, and a few zoo mammals. It is better to learn as much as you can about a mammal in your home, the zoo, or circus than it is to study one you cannot see alive.

The kind of teeth that mammals have depends on the food they eat and the way they get their food. The teeth of a horse are shaped differently from those of a cow, mouse, or a cat.

Their feet are different, too. Some mammals have five toes, some four, some three, some two, and some only one. The horse, for example, has only one and the cat has five. How many do the rabbit, the mouse, and the cow have?

Some mammals in cold temperatures hibernate (go to sleep) in the winter, and some of them partially hibernate, which means they sleep during part of the wintertime. When an animal hibernates, very little is happening in the body but the heartbeat, which is faint. It is not a sleep like you have each night. Animals who hibernate add quite a bit of fat to their bodies in the fall to give them energy to last through a long sleep.

Some mammals are abroad during the daytime and others only at night. Those that travel in the daylight are called "diurnal" and those that travel at night are called "nocturnal." For example, the horse and cow are diurnal and the cat and bat are nocturnal. How many can you add?

On page 251 you will see pictures of mammal tracks. Watch for these when you are on a hike or in camp. Try putting a shallow pan filled with moist earth or sand in your yard or near your tent or cabin at camp. Leave it overnight and you may find some interesting tracks. After you learn to recognize them, it is fun to be able to read the tracks and tell how fast the mammal was traveling and how long ago or recently he passed by.

Once upon a time, in this country, all kinds of birds were killed to provide feathers to decorate hats. Now there are strict laws to prevent this. Wild mammals are still killed for their fur. Many of our mammals may be killed off completely some day if something is not done to stop it. Many mammals are trapped for their fur by cruel and painful methods. Many people are interested in improving the laws to prevent this cruelty.

Most mammals are beneficial in one way or another. For instance, the fox eats many field mice, rabbits, woodchucks, and gophers even though he does catch a chicken now and then.

Mammals have different kinds of homes. The gray squirrel lives in a hole in a tree. The deer simply finds shelter under trees or against a rock. The white-footed mouse uses an old bird's nest for its winter home, building a grass roof on top of it. The rabbit lives in some sheltered place, not a hole. The hare does live in a hole and so do the foxes and woodchucks. Most mammals that make their homes in the ground have both a front and a back door.

Mammals are even harder to watch than birds. There are fewer of them and they have such keen eyes, ears, and noses, that they get out of our way before we can see them. So— walk quietly when looking for mammals.

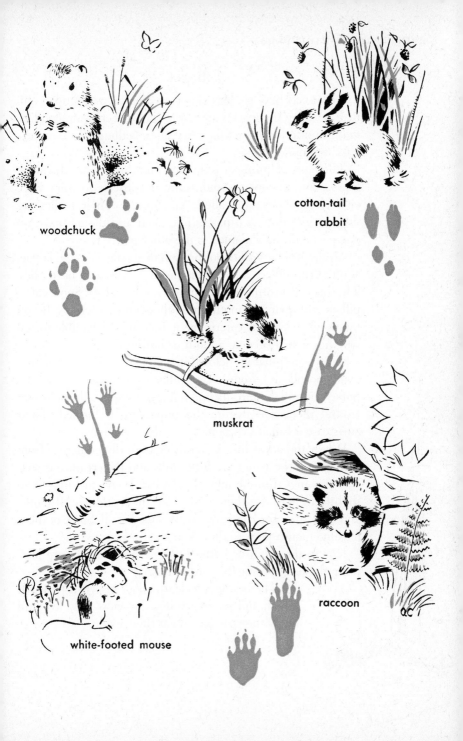

woodchuck

cotton-tail
rabbit

muskrat

white-footed mouse

raccoon

Insect

All insects have six legs. They are the largest group of animals. Among the insects are wasps, bees, beetles, dragonflies, moths, butterflies, houseflies, lice, flies, bedbugs, cockroaches, ants, and mosquitoes.

The body of an insect is divided into three parts: the head, thorax, and abdomen. Spiders are not insects for they have eight legs. They are called "arachnids." Their bodies are divided into only two parts. The head and thorax make up one part and the abdomen is the other part.

Moths and butterflies go through three stages—egg, larvae, adult. Caterpillars are the larvae of moths and butterflies. They are not worms, for worms do not have legs. Some caterpillars will turn into moths and others into butterflies. If you know what kind of caterpillar it is, you will be able to tell whether it will become a moth or butterfly.

Every caterpillar is enclosed in a pupa case when it changes (metamorphosis) from a caterpillar to a moth or butterfly. Some caterpillars spin silk and hairs; some spin silk and leaves around themselves before the pupa case is formed. Their outer case is called a cocoon.

When the adult insect (moth or butterfly) emerges from the cocoon, the wings are little nubs and the creature is wet. These wings unfold and the insect keeps moving them slightly to help dry them and make them strong. All moths and butterflies feed on nectar if they feed at all. Some of them have no mouth parts so they do not eat.

It is in the moth or butterfly stage that the eggs are laid. From these eggs come the caterpillars.

The best way to learn about insects is to watch them and see what they do—how they live and how they catch and eat their food.

Some insects make homes for themselves and their young. Some live in the ground, like certain ants; some have a hive, like the honey bee; some roll up in leaves, like the leaf rollers; some make a home of small pebbles cemented together, like the caddis fly.

Often you will hear people call insects harmful or beneficial. A harmful insect is one that eats things you have planted and want for yourself, such as the Japanese beetle. Beneficial insects are those that eat the insects you call harmful, or that eat only the kinds of plants you do not particularly want for food or decoration, such as the daisy and the milkweed. Some insects pollinate flowers which serve as food for some adult birds and for most baby birds.

Most of the insects found in the fields and woods are harmless to humans. Some bees, wasps, mosquitoes, and flies will sting. Some caterpillars will sting or drop hairs that irritate the skin. Some beetles, especially the very big ones, can nip. Some insects give off a protective odor that is not very pleasant to smell. But the majority of insects are perfectly harmless.

Considering that insects are the largest group of animals and there are many different types, too little is known about their life histories. Here is a chance for you to discover something.

Reptile and Amphibian

The reptiles include alligators, crocodiles, lizards, snakes, and turtles. They have scales and lay their eggs on land except for a few snakes that bear their young alive.

The amphibians include frogs, toads, newts, and salamanders. They do not have scales and lay their eggs in water or damp places.

One of the most interesting things about a snake is the way it sheds its skin. As the snake grows, the skin becomes tight

253

and new skin forms underneath. When the snake is ready to shed, it twines itself around sticks or rocks to help get the skin off. It is shed wrong side out and comes off over the eyes as well as every other part of the body. Rattlesnakes do not get a new rattle every year, but they do get a new one every time they shed their skins, which may be two or three times a year.

Snakes are often called poisonous and nonpoisonous. Nonpoisonous snakes are the most common. Most poisonous snakes have triangular heads, but all snakes with triangular heads are not poisonous. All snakes have teeth.

Poisonous snakes have two fangs in their upper jaws. The fangs are hollow in the center like a hypodermic needle. At the base of the fangs are sacs filled with poison. The snake has these fangs to kill its food and to protect itself. Poisonous snakes do not go out of their way to attack human beings unless they have been frightened or feel themselves in danger.

Snakes do not have ears, but receive vibrations through other parts of their body. The eggs they lay are oval in shape.

Turtles are harmless creatures. They do not have teeth, but their jaws are sharp and strong. Snapping turtles have little undershell and cannot hide themselves within a shell. Therefore they have difficulty protecting themselves. They are the only turtles that really bite.

Some turtles live in the water and others on land. All turtles breathe through lungs and those that live in the water must come up for air. Turtles' eggs are round and the baby turtle has its shell as soon as it is hatched from the egg.

Frogs' eggs are laid in a mass that is surrounded by jelly. Some of the tree frogs lay their eggs separately and cover each one with jelly. Toads lay their eggs in long strings of jelly with the eggs dotted along the strings.

Frogs and toads hatch from the eggs as tadpoles—sometimes called polliwogs. Tadpoles eat only plant life—usually

the green scum (spirogyra) in shallow ditches and in shallow places in ponds and rivers. Toads and frogs eat only animal life—usually insects, small fishes, tadpoles, earthworms, and smaller toads and frogs.

Tadpoles breathe by gills; the adult toad or frog has lungs. They both catch their food by means of the tongue and jaw.

Both toads and frogs shed their skins. You may see snake skins in the woods but you will never see the skin of a frog or toad. The frog's skin is usually shed in the water and floats away in small pieces. The toad swallows its skin as it takes it off.

Frogs and toads take in water through their skins. They must live where it is damp. You can fix a terrarium to house a toad comfortably for a few weeks. Give it a place for shelter during the day, plenty of moisture and food. The common toad will eat earthworms. You may have the experience of seeing the toad shed its skin.

Reptiles and amphibians are not the most beautiful animals in the world but they are valuable and are often needlessly hurt and killed.

Star

Stars are suns that shine by their own light. They are millions of miles away. Constellations are groups of stars that have been given names to honor some god or person or because the grouping looked like something people saw in daily life.

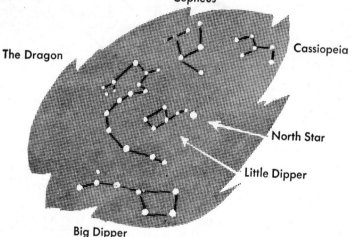

North of the equator there are five constellations visible all year. These are called the Polar Constellations. They are the Great Bear (Big Dipper), the Little Bear (Little Dipper), Cassiopeia (The Queen), Cepheus (The King), and the Dragon.

One of the most brilliant constellations is Orion, the Hunter. The most famous single star is the North Star. It is famous because men found their route on land and sea by its fixed position long before a compass was invented. See the picture on this page.

All the bright spots we see in the sky are not stars. Some are planets. They shine by reflected light. The planet we know the best is the earth. Our nearest planet neighbor is Mars.

There are nine planets in all. Two are not visible to the naked eye—Neptune and Pluto. Mercury is so near the sun that it is barely visible to the naked eye. Perhaps the most beautiful is Venus, which is often called "the evening star."

It is fun to look at the moon through opera or field glasses. When there is a half-moon or one that is three-quarters full, you will be better able to see the dark and light spots which are called mountains, craters, and seas. Most of them have names, and some of them have had these names for hundreds of years.

What can you see in the sky from your yard? From the roof of your house? From your window?

Rock and Mineral

A rock is a combination of two or more minerals. The common rock called granite is made up of feldspar, quartz, and mica; sometimes hornblende or augite is also present. All of these are minerals.

Minerals are identified by their hardness, cleavage, specific gravity, streak, luster, and color.

1. The hardness of a mineral is measured by how difficult it is to scratch.

2. The cleavage means the structure of the mineral, which makes it break more easily in one direction than another.

3. The specific gravity of a mineral is found by comparing its weight with the weight of an equal volume of water.

4. The streak of a mineral means its color when powdered.

5. The luster is the appearance of the surface due to reflected light.

6. The color means just what it says.

All these things are important to notice when you try to name a mineral. Most of them do not show up in a picture.

Many people begin their interest in rocks and minerals by picking up pebbles. These can be found almost anywhere.

257

Wash them and break a piece off each pebble to show a fresh surface. A smooth pebble can often fool you into thinking it is something that it isn't! How would you like to break open an uninteresting-looking pebble and find it filled with beautiful crystals? This kind of pebble is called a "geode."

Interesting rocks and minerals can be found where excavators and contractors are working. Keep your eyes open in places where gravestones and monuments are cut and try to collect samples of the stones used.

A visit to a quarry is the most fun of all. However, it is not always easy to find a quarry and sometimes it is difficult to get permission to visit. But it does no harm to try. In most quarries, there are dump heaps where many good specimens can be found.

It is interesting to know about jewels, too. They are called precious and semiprecious. You can see them in jewelry store windows.

What would you say if you were asked "What is the most precious of all precious jewels?" Have you any idea what soot and a diamond have in common? Do you know your own birthstone?

Weather

Although man has never been able to control the weather, he has learned to forecast it quite well. Weather affects what you wear and what you plan to do. The amount of food produced each year depends to a large extent on the kind of weather we have.

All through man's history, weather forecasting has been vital to the farmer, the traveler, the shipper, and the sailor. It is many times more important now that we have "taken to the air."

Weather forecasting has always been interesting to Girl Scout hikers and campers, as well as to Mariners and Wing Scouts.

Weather forecasting for the whole country is difficult and means that many highly trained scientists have to work closely

258

together. But it is perfectly possible for you, if you watch and practice, to forecast the weather of your local area fairly well. By doing this, you can learn many of the why's and ways of the weather that will increase the fun of living out-of-doors.

The would-be weather prophet must daily collect and record facts about temperature, clouds, winds, and other phases of to-day's weather in order to know about tomorrow's weather.

The equipment you need for weather forecasting is simple: a barometer, a compass or weather vane, a good view of the sky, a pair of sunglasses, and a thermometer. Camp weather bureaus use weather flags to make known their forecasts to the camp.*

Salt Water Life

Sea shells are the house of soft-bodied creatures which live in the sea. They are divided into bivalves and univalves. Oysters, clams, and mussels are bivalves, which means that the two shells are hinged. The whelks, winkles, and conches are univalves, which means one shell. These belong to the order of mollusca. However, not all mollusks are found in the sea. The land snail, shell-less snail or "slug," the squid, and the octopus also belong to this family.

Shells are composed of lime extracted from the sea water by the little inhabitant. These animals can build their shells larger and larger as they grow. Each species always builds its shells in the same pattern.

* From *Weather Handbook*, by Lou Williams, by permission of the author.

Dead shells are burned and crushed to make lime. It is used on poultry farms to supply calcium for egg-laying hens. It is also used in surfacing roads.

Seaweeds are members of the same family as the "green scum" you see on ponds. This is called algae. It is the only form of plant life that lives in the sea. Some seaweeds are large and tough and others are small and delicate.

There are many forms of salt water life in tide pools. These pools are formed by the water left between rocks or in depressions in rocks after a high tide. You will find seaweeds growing, barnacles and mollusks, crabs, and even small fish. You may see a crab eating a little fish or a starfish having its dinner. The starfish puts its stomach around the food rather than putting the food in its stomach!

Look for crabs along the beach. You will find more than one kind. Two of the most interesting are the fiddler crab and the hermit crab. The fiddler has one front claw which is much larger than the other. The hermit lives in the cast-off shell of some mollusk and walks along carrying the shell on top of itself.

Many different types of birds, insects, trees, flowers, and shrubs can only be found along beaches and rocky shores. Notice how many of them blend with the color of the sand or rocks.

Conservation

To conserve means to keep in safe and sound condition. If you want to conserve your strength, you will not use it all at one time. If you want to keep a dress in good condition, you wear it but you take good care of it. To conserve our forests, waterways, soil, flowers, and animals means that you will use them carefully and keep them in sound condition.

Our forests must be replanted and kept free of forest fires if we are to have forests for lumber, for recreation, and to have as homes for plants and animals.

Our rivers and lakes must be kept free from pollution if we are to enjoy them and wildlife is to remain.

Our soil must be kept rich if we are to raise the food we need. We must keep the topsoil on the land, prevent erosion, and replenish the soil with fertilizers.

Some of our wild flowers, mammals, and birds need special protection if others are to enjoy them in the future. Find out which ones they are and become active as an individual or member of an organization to protect them.

Everyone can do something about conservation. Why not take the Conservation Pledge?

The Conservation Pledge

I give my pledge as an American to save and faithfully to defend from waste the natural resources of my country —its soil and minerals, its forests, waters, and wildlife.

"Hurt no living thing." *

---

* Adapted from a drawing by Robert Lawson in *Under the Tent of the Sky* by Brewton. By permission of The Macmillan Company.

You can take care of the soil in your gardens, yards, and camps. You can plant some of the things that birds and mammals need for shelter and food. Refrain from picking wild flowers, unless they are common. Do not needlessly kill anything. You will remember that each living thing has a place in this world and each has a contribution to make. Take care to use natural materials wisely in outdoor activities. Do not start bonfires or campfires in dangerous places, and see that all fires are completely out before you leave. You can learn as much as possible about things out-of-doors, so that you will know how to keep them in safe and sound condition.

You can write to your forestry department and state conservation department for materials on conservation.

If you keep your eyes open, you will find many things to do to practice conservation in your community and camp. Vacant lots, schoolyards, your own yard, paths in camp, river and lake banks are places you can start with first.

LOU HENRY HOOVER MEMORIAL FORESTS AND SANCTUARIES. The National Girl Scout Organization has a project that you and your troop will find interesting. It is a project in conservation as a memorial to Mrs. Herbert Hoover who was president of the Girl Scouts of the U.S.A. for several years. This project is called the Lou Henry Hoover Memorial Forests and Sanctuaries. Any troop, town, or camp may establish such a forest or sanctuary by doing certain things. Ask your leader or camp director to write to the Program Department, Girl Scouts of the U.S.A., to find out about it.

You will find that there are conservation activities in every nature badge.

CHAPTER 14

Out-of-Doors

A RE picnics, hikes, cook-outs, and camping magic words to you? They are for most girls. They spell fun, adventure, winding trails, the smell of woodsmoke, and nights under canvas. Who does not walk taller and see wider when living in the out-of-doors?

The very word "Scout" means a pathfinder, a pioneer, a lover of the open trails. Living in the out-of-doors is an American heritage. The sturdy pioneers who settled the length and breadth of our vast country were one with the earth. You too can learn to live comfortably in the out-of-doors and to make friends with all things you find there.

Adventurer

An adventurer feels at home out-of-doors. She knows how to build a fire and cook a simple meal. She can give simple first aid treatment, use her compass and jackknife, and send and receive simple messages in Morse code. Look in the Index and you will find that there is material throughout this book to help you. Here are some special tips.

Clothing Your clothing should fit well and be suitable for the kind of activity and the weather. Blouses, shirts, or light sweaters worn with skirts, jeans, shorts, or snowsuits are good. Be sure your socks are free from holes. Wear sturdy walking shoes. A ski cap or crew hat will protect your head from the sun, from branches and brambles, and will keep your hair in place.

Take along a sweater even on a hot day. It may turn cold or rain and you will be glad of the extra protection.

Because a bandanna has many uses it is called the adventurer's friend. It can become a kerchief, potholder, bandage, signal flag, trail marker, or a bag in which to carry food or treasures.

Direction As a Tenderfoot you learned to use your compass. Do you remember how to orient it and take degree readings? Read page 19 again. As you know there are times you cannot use a compass. Then you will need to be able to tell directions in other ways.

BY THE SUN. The sun, as we all know, rises in the east and sets in the west. At noon it is overhead, but a little to the south. If you face the sun in the morning, you will be facing nearly east. The north will be on your left hand. If you face the sun at noontime, where will north be? If you watch the sun set, where will north be?

BY THE STARS. At night (north of the equator) there is one constant compass point, the North or Polar Star (see page 256). It is more dependable than a compass needle for it always hangs near the true north. It is in a straight line beyond the two pointer stars at the end of the Big Dipper. It is also the last star in the handle of the Little Dipper.

264

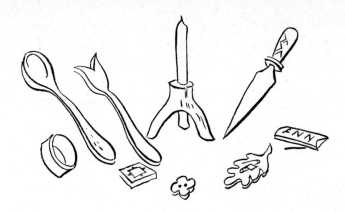

Here are articles you can whittle. Be sure your jackknife *Your*
is sharp before you start. Page 23 shows you how to open, *jackknife*
use, and care for your knife. Finish your whittled article by
sanding and waxing.

A rope that is to be used often must be whipped or the ends *Whipping a*
will fray.   *rope*
   1. Take a piece of string about twelve inches long. Make
a one-inch loop and lay it on one end of the rope so that both
ends of string hang over the rope's end. One end of the string
should be longer than the other.

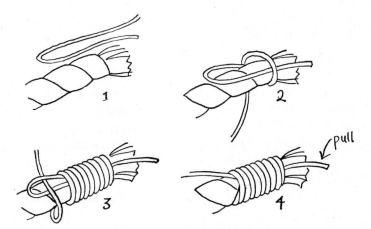

265

2. Take the longer end and start winding back away from the end.

3. Wind the string for about three-quarters of an inch. Tuck the end of the string you have been working with through the loop.

4. Now pull the short end of the string. The loop will disappear under the winding. Clip the ends of the string.

5. Whip the other end of your rope in the same way.

Now you are ready to practice making the knots on pages 72 to 74.

Signaling   It is fun to send messages to your friends in all sorts of ways. Do you know the types of signaling used by other people in their work, such as railroad men, sailors, aviators? In all signaling, accuracy is the important thing.

position

International Morse Code

A ·—	G ——·	N —·	U ··—
B —···	H ····	O ———	V ···—
C —·—·	I ··	P ·——·	W ·——
D —··	J ·———	Q ——·—	X —··—
E ·	K —·—	R ·—·	Y —·——
F ··—·	L ·—··	S ···	Z ——··
	M ——	T —	

dot o

WITH A FLAG. You can make your own flag. Take a piece of cloth twenty-four inches square and sew on an eight-inch square of another color in the center. It may be white with the smaller square red, or vice versa. To make your pole cut a smooth stick about forty-two inches long and one-half inch in diameter.

Position: Hold the flag vertically, and face the person who is to receive the message.

Motions: Right means dot. Swing flag down to right and back to position, making a figure eight.

Left means dash. Same motion on left.

Front means interval. One dip means end of word; two dips, end of sentence; three dips, end of message.

dash ▭

WITH A LANTERN. Swinging the lantern to the right makes a dot; to the left, a dash. The lantern directly in front of sender is "position," lowering once means the end of a word, lowering it twice means end of a sentence, darkening means end of message.

WITH A FLASHLIGHT. A short flash makes a dot; a long flash, a dash. A pause the length of three dots separates letters; a pause the length of five dots separates words. A still longer pause means end of sentence. Darkened for sixty seconds means end of message.

front

WITH A WHISTLE OR BUZZER. A short blast of the whistle or rasp of the buzzer makes a dot; a long blast or buzz, a dash. A pause the length of three dots separates letters; a pause the length of five dots separates words. A still longer pause means end of sentence. A pause for sixty seconds means end of message.

Outdoor cooking is not very different from cooking at home. Before you start, however, you must plan carefully to bring everything you need. You cannot open the door of a kitchen cabinet if you forget a pot, a can opener, or the salt.

Outdoor meals

Start with one-pot meals. They are satisfying and especially good in cold weather. Here are three to try on patrol or troop cook-outs.

Squaw Corn (*serves* 8)

8 slices bacon	3 onions
2 cans of corn	salt
2 green peppers	bread or crackers

Fry the bacon. Add onion and pepper thinly sliced. Fry till light brown. Add corn and salt to taste. Fry till light brown. Serve on toast or crackers.

Blushing Bunny (*serves* 4)

1 tablespoon butter	½ cup diced American cheese
1 tablespoon flour	crackers or bread
1 can tomato soup	

Melt butter and blend it with flour. Add soup. When thoroughly heated, add cheese. Stir until melted. Season and serve over crackers or toast.

Pocket Stew (*per person*)

Each girl brings a handful of cleaned vegetables (carrots, celery, potato, beans), and a piece of meat wrapped in wax paper. Fry bacon and add onions (if any) till light brown. Add a little water, the meat, and finally the vegetables. Simmer slowly. Just before removing from the fire add two bouillon cubes.

What other foods would you include to make your meal well balanced and nutritious? You will find more recipes under Outdoor Cook on pages 279 to 281.

Back-Yard Camper

Do you have a back yard? Is there one in your neighborhood? You can do many things in the smallest of back yards. Have you ever slept under the stars, cooked on tin-can or charcoal stoves, held a cook-out for your family?

A bedroll An outdoor bed is called a bedroll, envelope, or klondike bed. The first thing you will need is a poncho or groundcloth. You can make your groundcloth from a piece of canvas, oilcloth, or by waterproofing muslin. A groundcloth should be a

How To Make a Bedroll

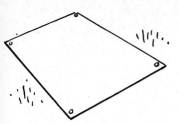

1. Place poncho (ground sheet) flat on ground.

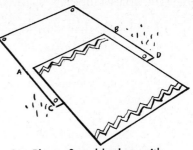

2. Place first blanket with one edge down center of poncho. (A–B)

3. Place second blanket with one edge at middle of first blanket. (C–D)

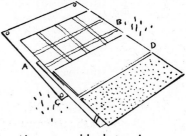

4. Alternate blankets in same way, until all are down. Fold sheet or sleeping blanket in half, and place in middle. (A–B–C–D)

5. Starting with last blanket, fold blankets alternating in reverse order, until all are over middle. (A–B–C–D) Pin at bottom if poncho does not snap together.

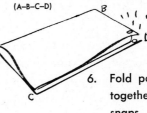

6. Fold poncho over. Snap together if there are snaps on bottom and side.

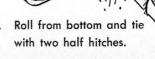

7. Roll from bottom and tie with two half hitches.

foot longer than your longest blanket. It should be the same width as the blanket. Here's how to make a groundcloth.

1. Shave one-half pound of paraffin. Melt the paraffin by placing in a large saucepan set in a larger pan of hot water. Remove from the stove. Add two quarts of turpentine. Mix well.

2. Stretch your material by tacking it to a frame made from four old boards.

3. Use a stiff brush and spread the solution on the cloth evenly but not too heavily. Brush it in well.

4. After it is dry, hem your groundcloth.

The picture on page 269 shows you the steps to follow in making your bedroll.

Prepare for rain Have you ever built a fire in the rain? Try doing it the woodsman's way. Use your jackknife to make shavings and fuzz sticks for tinder. Split some wood with your hatchet and scoop out the dry center for kindling and fuel. Light your fire with waterproofed matches. Keep additional fuel near fire so it will dry.

WATERPROOFED MATCHES. These can be made by painting the tip of each match with nail polish. Another method is to dip the head and about half the matchstick into melted paraffin. This can be done individually or you can tie about ten matches together. A whole box of matches can be waterproofed by placing the match box in a tin container and then pouring the paraffin into the box. Always use the large household matches for waterproofing. Keep your water-proofed matches in a small container.

EMERGENCY FUEL. Trench candles are one of the most popular types of emergency fuel. They are made from news-paper soaked in paraffin.

1. Take about ten sheets of newspaper and roll them into a very tight roll.

2. Tie string around the roll at two- or three-inch intervals. Leave one end of each string about six inches long.

3. Take a small saw and cut the roll into pieces between the ties. Push one end of each piece up in the center so that it looks like a candle without a wick.

4. Melt paraffin in a saucepan set in a larger pan of hot water. Put the trench candles into the paraffin with the strings hanging over the sides of the saucepan. Leave for about ten minutes.

5. Remove the candles and place on newspaper to dry.

6. Store your candles in a cool place until you wish to use them.

Another type of emergency fuel is made from gauze bandage. Use what is left of an opened two-inch roll of bandage that is no longer sterile. Tie a string around the gauze and dip it in kerosene. Let the excess moisture dry. Store it in an old medicine bottle with a close-fitting top. Cut off as much as you need to get your wet-weather fire started.

A tin-can stove provides quick cooking when the fuel is limited or when you want to have a small enclosed fire. To make one you will need a pair of tin snips, some work gloves, and a No. 10 tin can. *A tin-can stove*

A charcoal stove can often be used when no other type of fire is permitted. See page 272. *A charcoal stove*

271

Tin-Can Stove

With a pair of tin shears cut two openings in a No. 10 tin can—one for fuel and one for a chimney. Make small fire and place can over it, or use a Buddy burner.

How To Make and Use a Charcoal Stove

Use a No. 10 tin can for the stove. Remove top with a roll can opener. Put holes around base and top with a punch opener. Leave a small strip of tin between each hole. Fasten a 24-inch wire at top for handle. Force wire screening into base to hold charcoal and ensure a draft. Make a small fire with twigs. When it is burning briskly, add small pieces of charcoal. Swing stove by handle or blow at base to make fire burn. A grate may be made for the top by using crisscross wires or strong screening. Place pan on top and proceed as in any other cooking.

Campcraft

Every camper takes pride in her equipment. She knows how to use a knife, hammer, saw, and hatchet. She can make cooking gadgets, repair a bench or table, build a cache, and split wood. She takes good care of all her equipment so that it will serve her well.

1. The blade of an ax or hatchet should always be kept sharp and be protected by a guard or sheath. Dull tools waste time and strength and are unsafe.

The ax or hatchet

2. An ax or hatchet is carried by grasping the handle close to the head with the blade down. Hold it loosely so that if you trip it can be dropped quickly.

3. In chopping, see that you have a clear space, both around and above where your ax will sweep.

4. Always use a low, solid chopping block or log as a base when splitting wood or kindling.

5. Do not hold a stick of wood in one hand and chop with the other. Do not steady the stick with your foot.

6. Be sure that the head of the ax or hatchet is securely attached to the handle.

7. Always chop wood so you are sure the ax or hatchet will not strike your body if it should slip.

8. When chopping down a tree or cutting off a branch, cut away all the twigs and foliage first so that nothing will interfere with the fall of the ax.

You will often use your knife or hatchet to get wood for cooking gadgets. Do not cut anything without knowing whether it is right for your purpose. Always look to see from what part of the tree or bush the stick can best be spared. Cut close to the branch or tree trunk, and close to the ground if you are cutting from a bush.

273

Lashing In the out-of-doors when nails and hammers are not handy, a knowledge of lashing is useful. Here are three types:

SQUARE LASHING. Square lashing is used to join two sticks together at right angles, as in making coat hangers, washstands, tables, and other articles. Here are steps in making a coat hanger.

1. Take two sticks, one with a fork and the other slightly curved, and cross them. Tie a clove hitch (see page 74) on the forked stick at one end of cord, slipping knot around so that the long length of cord pulls directly out from the knot. Tighten the knot. Check to see that the crossed section of the clove hitch is on top of your stick.

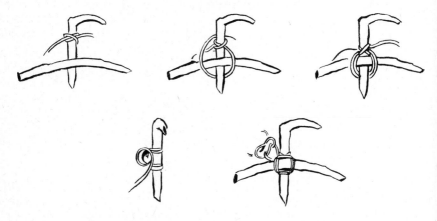

2. Bring the long piece of twine over the curved stick, under and behind the forked stick, up and over the curved stick, and under and behind the forked stick. Follow "the square" you have made three or four times, always pulling twine tightly.

3. When the two sticks are firmly bound, tighten with a frapping. This is done by winding the twine tightly between the two sticks.

4. Finish with a square knot and tuck the ends underneath the lashing.

SHEER OR ROUND LASHING. Sheer or round lashing is used to bind several sticks together, as in making a tripod basin rack. For this you will need sturdy sticks of the same thickness, trimmed to equal lengths with pointed ends.

Hold all three sticks with one hand and spread them apart. Place a basin on the top, and mark the spot for lashing which will make your rack the right height. Next, lash the three sticks together.

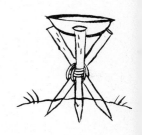

1. Make a clove hitch around one of the sticks.
2. Wrap the twine around all the sticks, three or four times.
3. Pull the twine between each of the three sticks. This is frapping.
4. Finish with a square knot and tuck ends under.
5. Spread the rack to fit your basin and set it in the ground.

CONTINUOUS LASHING. If you know how to do continuous lashing, you can make your own outdoor furniture. Here are directions for a seat.

275

1. Select two trees for the ends of the seat. Measure the distance between the trees and get two strong sticks which are slightly longer for the sides.

2. Lash the side sticks to either side of the trees using square lashing at the height you want your finished seat to be.

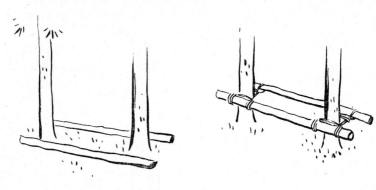

3. Get smaller sticks for the crosspieces. Use your jackknife and notch the side sticks so that your cross sticks will rest in the notches. Trim the crosspieces to equal lengths.

4. Cut off a piece of twine four times longer than your side sticks. Make a clove hitch at the middle of the twine leaving two ends of equal length. The knot should be at the end of your side stick, underneath the crosspiece.

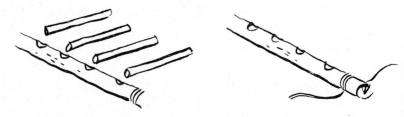

5. Place the cross sticks in the notches. Take the ends of your twine in your right and left hands and pull them up

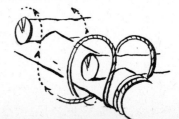

and over the first cross stick. Pull them down and under the side stick crossing them underneath. Continue in this way to end of the cross sticks, pulling the twine tightly. Finish with two half hitches or a square knot. You can build a work table in the same way. If trees are not available, drive four sturdy sticks in the ground for your posts.

Outdoor Cook

Make your outdoor kitchen or dining room attractive. Plan it so that the fireplace and woodpile are convenient and there is space for everyone to be comfortable while cooking and eating. There should be a spot for wraps or equipment where they will be safe and out of the way. It is also a good idea to designate special places for food and cooking utensils. Arrange a place for trash that is to be burned and for garbage that has to be buried or taken home.

Kapers

The work on a cook-out should be divided so that everyone has a share and a chance to learn something new. Make a kaper chart.

Here are some of the jobs: shoppers, packers, wood gatherers, firebuilders, cooks, table setters, clean-ups. It may not be necessary to have all these jobs. It will depend on the kinds of things you are cooking.

When you want to bake, roast, fry, or boil, do you use the same part of your stove? It would be just as silly if we tried to cook all our outdoor meals over one type of fire. As a Second Class Scout you learned the Basic A, the tepee, and crisscross fires (page 70). Now as an outdoor cook you will need to master some more advanced firebuilding methods.

Fires to fit your food

HUNTER'S FIRE gives steady heat and the logs or rocks may be used to support cooking utensils. Place two green logs in a V shape with one end about 7 inches apart and the other end about 4 inches apart. The wider opening should face the wind. Build a foundation fire between the logs. Cooking utensils can be placed near the narrow end.

TRENCH FIRE is the safest type on windy days and is good for hot weather. Dig a trench about 1 foot deep. One end should be about 12 inches wide and the other end 6 inches. The wide end should face the wind. Slope the trench upward toward the wide end.

Build one or more foundation fires. When they are burning well, place fuel across the top in crisscross style. If there is not enough draft, raise sticks by using a long green stick.

Save the soil and sod and replace it after the fire is out.

REFLECTOR FIRE provides high, steady heat for baking, planking, or for barbecues. Use a large, flat-faced rock to reflect heat, or make a fireback by driving two stakes into the ground about a foot apart and slightly sloping. Against these stakes pile green logs, chinking any spaces between them with mud.

Build a foundation fire directly in front of the fireback. Gradually add fuel in crisscross formation. Lean larger fuel at angle against reflector of logs or rock. Place the oven or plank opposite the reflector. It should be placed at the spot where your hand becomes uncomfortably warm at the count of eight.

There are all kinds of things to cook out-of-doors. At the *Meals*
beginning of this chapter you found recipes for one-pot meals. *without*
Here are some suggestions for meals without dishes. These *dishes*
are called nonutensil meals and must be cooked over coals.
The food will then cook slowly, thoroughly, and will not be
smoked or burnt.

Cheese Toast (*serves 4*)

8 slices buttered bread   ¼ pound American cheese
¼ teaspoon paprika   ¼ teaspoon Worcestershire
                                          sauce

Toast the bread. Make paste of the cheese and add seasoning.
Spread the toast generously with the cheese mixture and prop up
in front of the fire to brown.

Kabobs (*serves 4*)

1 pound chuck steak   2 good-sized onions
8 slices bacon   8 buttered rolls

Cut the meat into one-inch squares. Slice the onions. Cut the
slices of bacon in squares. Sharpen and peel a green stick. Place
the beef, onion, and bacon alternately on a stick with a little space
between. Sear quickly to prevent the juices from dripping away.
Broil slowly over coals until done. Kabobs can be made with
lamb, liver, ham, or oysters.

Eggs on a Rock (*serves 1*)

2 slices bread
4 half slices bacon
1 egg

Find a thin (1 or 1½ inches) fairly smooth flat rock, and place it
on two larger rocks. Put a small rock at the back.

Dig a trench under the flat rock, and build a fire in it. It takes
about twenty minutes to heat a rock about 1 foot square and
1½ inches thick. When the rock is hot, place slices of bacon
on it. After they are cooked on one side, turn the bacon. Take
both slices of bread and remove the centers. Place them over

279

**Emergency
Measures**

1 cup

heaping teaspoon

level teaspoon

1 pinch

1 tablespoon

1 tablespoon

the bacon so that two pieces are under the hole. Break an egg and drop it into the hole. Put the remaining bacon on top of the egg, crisp side down. When done on one side, turn. The egg will cling to the bread and the bacon to the egg, forming a sandwich.

Other things can be cooked on a flat rock, such as hamburger, chops, sausages, and (if the rock is smooth and well greased) pancakes.

You can also heat rocks in a regular fire for twenty minutes, pull them out, and cook on them.

Do not use limestone or shale rocks, since they explode when in contact with heat.

Bread Twisters or Doughboys (*serves 1*)

4 tablespoons flour	pinch of salt
½ teaspoon baking powder	2 teaspoons shortening
	4 teaspoons milk or water

Put the dry ingredients in a paper bag and shake. Use your fingers to work in shortening. Pour milk or water into mixture and with a peeled stick mix until flour has absorbed enough moisture to make it stick together well. Use flour on your fingers.

Take a green stick, at least one-inch thick at the larger end. Peel this end for about six inches and heat over the fire. When hot, wrap dough around the heated stick. Bake over coals, turning the stick so the dough bakes evenly. When cooked, the twister will slip off the stick. Fill with butter, brown sugar, or jelly.

For bacon twisters, wrap a piece of bacon around a stick as described above and cook thoroughly. Cover with biscuit dough and bake. A sausage or frankfurter may be used in place of bacon.

For cheese twisters, cut yellow cheese into bits and mix with biscuit dough. Raisins may be used in the same way, if a dash of sugar is added to the dough.

Some-Mores (*serves 1*)

4 squares plain chocolate (thin)	2 graham crackers
	1 marshmallow

Toast a marshmallow slowly over coals until brown. Put chocolate on a graham cracker, then the toasted marshmallow on top, then another graham cracker. Press gently together, and eat. Makes you want "some more"!

This recipe may be varied by using slices of apple (cut cross-wise) or by using pineapple slices or peanut butter in place of chocolate.

Mock Angel Food Cake (*serves 12*)

1 loaf day-old white bread (unsliced)	1 can condensed milk
	1 package shredded coconut

Trim all crust from loaf and divide loaf into twelve pieces. Dip each piece of bread in condensed milk until well covered, then roll it in shredded coconut. Toast on end of stick until golden brown. May also be cooked in a reflector oven.

Foot Traveler

Neither yardstick nor tape measure is available in the woods and yet there are times when you need to know the distance between two points. If you know the length of your own pace, you can judge distance.

Mark off a level stretch of ground exactly 100 feet. Pace it ten times, using your normal walking step. Start each time with your toe on the line. Count the number of steps you used each time and average them. One hundred feet equals 1200 inches. Divide 1200 inches by your average number of steps and you have the length of one pace. You know then that every time you take a normal step you cover that many inches. For example, if your average number of steps is 50, divide 1200 inches by 50 and you have 24 inches, which is your pace. *Your pace*

Scout's pace means walking a certain number of paces, then jog trotting the same number of paces. For example, walk twenty paces, then jog trot twenty paces, and so on. This helps you to cover considerable ground without getting tired and also to measure distance and time another way.

281

Sketch maps   A sketch map is a more finished map than the map on page 21. It is done on good paper, using compass directions. The distances are indicated by a scale, and a key or legend explains the signs or symbols, includes the name of maker, and the date.

To make a really accurate map is a science and requires special instruments. However, you can easily make a sketch map.

1. The map you draw as you go is called an "observation" sketch map. You will need a large notebook or a good-sized piece of paper. North will always be at the top of the paper. Select your starting point and if you are going to travel in a northerly direction, put the starting point at the bottom or south end of the paper, and vice versa.

2. Use your ordinary pace as a measure, called "the scale." See page 281 for an explanation of how to find your pace.

3. Sight an object ahead of you and take its direction or "bearing" with your compass. Draw a sketch of the road ahead. Make certain that the North on your paper points to the actual North shown on your compass. Pace the distance to the object sighted and mark the number of paces on your sketch. On the way you will pass objects that are to be shown on your map. Note them on your paper, using the correct map sign or symbol.

4. Take the next bearing from the point at which you stopped pacing. Continue as before, until you have covered the area you wish to map. Then indicate direction, scale, legend, name, and so forth.

5. To make a permanent map, ink in your pencil markings and color some parts of your map. Be sure your map is reasonably accurate before you do this.

The foot traveler will find a detailed map of the surrounding countryside helpful. This can be obtained by writing the

Superintendent of Documents, U.S. Government Printing Office, Washington, D.C. Ask for Catalog No. 53. It lists various types of maps for all parts of the country. The catalog is free and there is only a small charge for the map itself. *Topographical maps*

Have you noticed the signs and symbols on maps? These vary on different maps depending on the purpose of the map. Road maps show the best roads and routes through towns; fire department maps include all the fire hydrants; electric company maps indicate all the power lines.

As you become familiar with maps, each of the symbols and lines will mean something. From them you will be able to determine distances, the kind of country, and other important features.

The first thing we must do with a map is to orient it. This means that the North on the map should be pointed North and should check with the magnetic needle of your compass pointing North.

You can also orient your map by locating the road on which you are standing and then turn your map until the road on it runs in the same direction as the actual road. When a map is oriented, you can follow it cross-country.

A group that has lost the trail should be prepared to find the way by compass, sun, stars, or cross-country guides that lead home. *When lost*

They can follow the river bank, a ridge of hills, an overgrown trail, or cross-country wires, which are usually erected along the shortest distance between two towns. Go down a hill or downstream if uncertain of a direction, since this is most likely to lead you to a settlement or town.

If you should get lost from your troop, do not get panicky or frightened. Stay where you are and don't wear yourself out by aimless wandering. Call or use your whistle at intervals. As soon as the rest of the party misses you, it will begin a

283

search. The members of the searching party will send out agreed-upon whistle signals or calls at stated intervals as they move about. Any call between these intervals they will know belongs to the lost person. When you hear the searchers, repeat your calls frequently in order to help them find you quickly.

Explorer

To explore new places is one of the greatest adventures in the world. To be a good explorer you must learn to follow trails and to use the explorer's tools—compass, maps, and signaling devices. You must know how to take care of yourself and how to meet emergencies. You must be able to keep house in the out-of-doors and know how to feel at home with the animals and plants.

Judging and measuring Girl Scouts have long known the value of being able to judge heights, weights, distances, number, and time with reasonable accuracy. It takes constant practice and real training of eye and hand. Your own measurements are a scale you can often use.

TIME AND DISTANCE. Find out how long it takes you to walk a mile comfortably over fairly level ground. This will give you the rate at which you walk and will help you judge both time and distance.

Personal Measurements
What is your handspread?
What is your armspread?
How long is your foot?
How tall are you?
Which joint is one inch?

HATBRIM MEASURE. Stand facing a lake or river and tip your head until the edge of your hatbrim touches the opposite shore. Turn slowly around, one quarter way, keeping the head in the same position, and note the object in the

distance on your side of the water that your hatbrim touches. Pace to the object. The measurement of paces equals the approximate distance across the lake or river. This can be done with the hand held over the eyes like a visor—instead of with a hatbrim.

PENCIL METHOD. Place a person (or a stick) whose height you know against whatever you wish to measure. Walk off a little distance. Hold a pencil upright before your eye at arm's length. Keep it straight. Measure with your thumb on the pencil the apparent height of the person or stick. Now see how many of these thumb measurements are contained in the object you wish to measure. Multiply this number by the height of the person or stick and you will have a rough estimate of the height of the object.

WEIGHT. Weight cannot be judged by size alone. To learn weight, begin by holding in your hand something that weighs a pound; after holding it a few seconds put it down, then take it up again. Try to sense the weight. Hold it in each hand. Try some objects that weigh an ounce, or several ounces, so that you get the shades of difference. Then take things of which you do not know the weight. Attempt to judge them. Practice until you can at least judge one-half pound; one, five, and ten pounds.

Compass and map

MAGNETIC VARIATION: Now that you are familiar with your compass, you will want to learn other things about its use. Have you heard people use the word "variation"? It means the change in a position of a thing. For example, did you realize that the magnetic needle does not really point to the North Pole? Instead it points to a magnetic deposit known as the Magnetic North Pole. It is about 1500 miles away from the true North Pole.

If you live on a line from the Great Lakes to Georgia, the magnetic needle of your compass in pointing toward the magnetic deposit will also point to the true North Pole. You do not have to worry about variation. However, near Portland, Oregon, the needle will point about 22 degrees East of North, and near Portland, Maine, about 15 degrees West. The rule is: add for westerly and subtract for easterly. Find out what the variation is in your locality from a civil engineer or from the engineering department of your town, city, or county. Record it on the back of your compass on a piece of adhesive tape.

When using your compass and map together you must:
1. Orient map (see page 283).
2. Take the degree reading.
3. Add or subtract as necessary to allow for variation.

DETERMINING MAP DISTANCES. To determine the distance between two points on your map check the map scale. For example, you may find the symbol 1/62,500 which means one inch on the map equals 62,500 inches on the land. Since 62,500 inches are about one mile, one inch on the map would be one mile of hiking. Use a ruler or the plastic scale on your compass to measure the distance. If it reads five inches between two points, you know it will be a five-mile hike.

CONTOUR LINES. The height of certain areas above others is known as the contours of a stretch of country. On a map lines are drawn connecting points of the same height. These lines are called contour lines.

One of the simplest ways to understand contours is to cut an apple or potato in half. Place the flat side down to represent a hill. Then to get the different heights or levels, slice the piece horizontally at regular intervals.

Now take the bottom piece and make an outline of it on a piece of paper, then outline the next piece and so on till all have been outlined. You will find you have a series of rings of the shape of the apple or potato. Notice that the steeper the elevation, the closer the contours come together.

In planning a cross-country hike you must consider both the distance and the contour lines. A two-mile hike up and down hills will be far more time-consuming than a hike of the same distance over fairly level terrain.

How To Pitch a Pup Tent

1. Stretch one side of the tent and peg down at front and back corners.

2. Put in the front pole and peg down the second front corner.

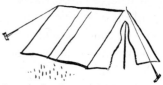

3. Do the same for the back pole and corner.

4. Attach the front and back guy lines. Make a bowline at one end of the rope and place it over the pole. Make a tautline hitch at the other end of the rope. Place this loop around the peg. The tautline hitch is used to tighten or loosen the guy lines.

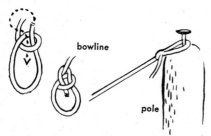

bowline

pole

5. Put in the rest of the pegs. Check to see that the tent is trim. Note that the pegs are driven in so that the top of the pegs lean away from the tent.

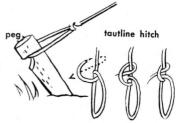

peg

tautline hitch

guy line

peg

tapes

ditch

sod

tent pole

guy line

6. Ditch the tent by making a ditch 6 inches deep so that the rain will roll down the sides of the tent into the ditch and be carried away. Place the sod that has been dug up on the side of the ditch away from the tent.

MOUNTING A MAP. Maps should be mounted so that they will not tear. There are many ways. One is to paste the map on muslin so that it will roll easily; a second is to cut it into sections and mount them on muslin, leaving enough space between sections so the map can be easily folded. Waterproof the map or carry it in a celluloid or plastic case.

Pioneer

One of the greatest dreams of a Girl Scout is to pitch and strike her own camp. The girl who is working for her Pioneer badge is ready for this most advanced form of camping. She will find that the out-of-doors is a "house without windows." Each camping expedition will be full of fun, challenge, friendships, and lasting memories.

Camping is a combination of many things found throughout this book, such as singing, dramatics, sketching, photography, storytelling, hiking, and outdoor cooking. You will find that many other badges besides those in the out-of-doors field will be helpful. These illustrations will show you how to pitch a tent.

A good pioneer camper takes her share in the camp jobs as well as the camp fun; she learns how to take care of herself and her possessions in wind, rain, sun, or snow. She gets acquainted with some of the things of nature, so that she really is at home out-of-doors. A good camper, too, has a feeling of responsibility for the wild things, for the forests, and the places where she pitches camp. Girl Scouts and Guides all over the world say: "You never know a person until you have camped with her." How good a camping companion would you be?

CHAPTER 15

Sports and Games

E VERY nation in the world has its
favorite sports. Baseball is called
the great American game. In England,
cricket rates high. *Jai alai,* of Spanish origin, is popular in Cuba. Archery has been
a sport for centuries. Battledore and shut-
tlecock were as well liked in England in
the sixteenth century as its modern form, badminton, is today. Orienteering has recently become a national sport in
Sweden. It has spread through the Scandinavian countries
and is being taken up by many other countries.

Games, too, are popular with all ages throughout the
world. Did you know that ball-playing was a favorite activity
of the early Egyptians? Playing leap frog and marbles, flying
kites, spinning tops, and jumping ropes are activities enjoyed
by children in nearly every land.

Because you cannot learn to play a sport by reading about
it in a book, you will not find instructions in this chapter.
However, you will find tips and suggestions. Ask someone
who has already become proficient to help you with your
favorite sport. Above all practice it regularly.

Games

There are all kinds of games—circle, relay, singing, dramatic, outdoor, and nature games; games for two teams; contests for three or more groups; pencil and paper games; guessing games, and stunts. There are quiet games and active games. There is a game for every occasion.

How many games do you know? Do you know a good game to make the dishwashing go faster or to play with younger brothers and sisters? Can you teach a game to your family or troop? Have you tried taking a favorite game and changing it for a special occasion or adapting it to Girl Scouting?

Do you know what games are played by Girl Guides in other countries? Often they play the same games but call them by other names. In ancient days, the children of Rome played "Blind Man's Buff" and called it "Murinda." Today, the boys and girls of Germany call it "Blind Cow." The game is known as "Blind Hen" in Spain and "Hoodman Blind" in England.

Take time at troop meetings to learn different kinds of games. You will find suggestions in the Games badge. Read the activities and then borrow a book about games from your leader, school, or public library. Look through the book and select games that you think the troop or your patrol would like to learn.

When you select a game, choose: *Choosing*
1. One that you like yourself and think others would *a game* enjoy.
2. One that will include every member of the group and give each one a chance to do something.
3. One that can be played in the space you have.
4. One that fits the occasion: active, if everyone wants to let off steam, warm up, or get acquainted; quiet, if the day is

hot, players are tired, dressed up, or likely to disturb the neighbors.

Teaching a game   Before you teach a game:

1. Understand all the rules yourself; explain them clearly; make sure the others understand.

2. Have the necessary equipment on hand.

3. Decide on a fair way to divide into teams, if it is a team game.

4. Let the troop play the game for practice before starting to score.

5. Be sure everyone knows how the game is **won**. A referee's business is to see that rules are followed, the game goes smoothly, and is fun for all.

Cyclist

Cycling, like all sports, must be played according to rules. Every cyclist is as responsible for good traffic observances as the driver of a car.

The first safety rule is to see that your bike is in good condition and properly equipped. Check these points and see that:

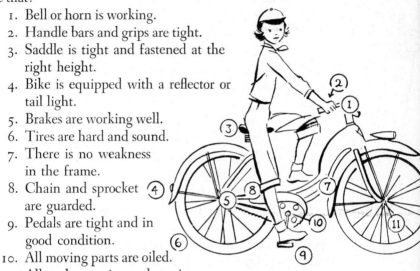

1. Bell or horn is working.
2. Handle bars and grips are tight.
3. Saddle is tight and fastened at the right height.
4. Bike is equipped with a reflector or tail light.
5. Brakes are working well.
6. Tires are hard and sound.
7. There is no weakness in the frame.
8. Chain and sprocket are guarded.
9. Pedals are tight and in good condition.
10. All moving parts are oiled.
11. All spokes are in good repair.

The most common mistake is to have the seat and handle bars incorrectly adjusted. The seat is at the right height when, with your legs straight and the pedal at "six o'clock" your heel is on the lower pedal. Handle bars are right when, with the seat adjusted, and your hands placed on the handle bar grips, you lean slightly forward. Your bicycle repairman, or the salesman from whom you bought the bike, will help check these points.

There are special traffic laws that include bicycles and you should know them. You can find those for your community from your town hall, city hall, or state house.

293

The Bicycle Institute of America has developed a *Safe Riding Code*. Every cyclist should know and follow it. This is it:

1. Obey all traffic signs and rules.
2. Always signal before making turns.
3. Walk across heavy traffic.
4. Ride single file. Don't weave.
5. Ride out of driveways slowly and carefully.
6. Watch carefully at railroad crossings.
7. Keep out of car tracks and ruts.
8. Never stunt or race in traffic.
9. Avoid all hitching.
10. Never carry passengers.
11. Carry parcels in racks or carriers.
12. Use extra caution on sidewalks.
13. Get off the roadway to make repairs.
14. Wear light-colored clothing at night.
15. Want to ride safely.

To cycle correctly, the ball of the foot should be on the pedal. The knees should be kept close to the frame of the bicycle so that your knee joints can bend normally. Practice riding your bike in the driveway or on a street that has little traffic. Be sure to stay away from any people or traffic until you can stop, start, and turn easily.

As you and other members of your troop become skilled cyclists there are many things you can do together—outings, service, trip camping—or you might combine forces with one or more other troops and hold a bicycle rodeo.*

---

* Information on this type of program and bicycle safety tests can be obtained from the Bicycle Institute of America, 122 East 42nd Street, New York 17, N.Y.

Swimmer

Swimming is not only fun and good exercise but makes possible other activities such as boating, canoeing, and sailing. Aim to become a really good swimmer, not just a paddler. You owe it to yourself and other people to know how to take care of yourself in or on the water.

Here are a few common sense rules to follow:

1. Know your swimming ability and remain in the area that is safe for you.

2. Always swim with a buddy (a swimming partner).

3. Wait an hour or an hour and a half after eating before entering the water.

4. Stay out of the water if you are not feeling well.

5. Follow all swimming rules and regulations.

6. Dive only in water when you know how deep it is and you are sure that the area is clear.

7. Leave the water as soon as you feel chilled or tired.

Learn to swim correctly in the very beginning. You can get instruction by taking a course given by a qualified instructor. In this way you will be taught all the skills that will make you feel at home in the water. Have confidence in your instructor and you will go ahead by leaps and bounds.

Try to learn a number of different strokes. Start by becoming proficient in the following strokes and then add others. *Swimming strokes*

SIDE STROKE. This stroke is not speedy but it is relaxing. It is one of the most useful strokes and essential in lifesaving. Your face remains out of the water and each stroke is followed by a long glide. During the glide your arms and legs are motionless.

ELEMENTARY BACK STROKE. This stroke is primarily a rest stroke. It is done while floating on the back. Once again, each stroke is followed by a glide. The leg movement of this stroke is used in one type of swimming rescue.

BREAST STROKE. This stroke is one of the oldest swimming strokes known to man. It is the strongest stroke and the most useful in underwater swimming. The breast stroke is favored in formation and silent swimming since it can be swum with the face above water and requires no breaking of the water with arms or feet. It is invaluable in lifesaving.

CRAWL. This stroke is the fastest of all strokes and the one most commonly used in the United States today. It requires good coordination and rhythmic action. This stroke, when well done, enables a swimmer to cover the greatest distance in the shortest length of time with the minimum of energy.

Swimming and diving go hand in hand. If you can do a good front dive, you know that every entrance into the water will be graceful. It is fun to be able to use a springboard and do a few fancy dives such as the jackknife, backjack and back dive.

Boating

A Girl Scout who can row easily can be of service to others. A well-equipped rowboat has always been one of the important pieces of equipment in lifesaving rescues. Before you start any boating activities, read the safety rules for boating and canoeing on page 300.

When you get into a rowboat, sit so that the boat is "trimmed." That means that your weight is the proper distance from the bow to the stern and the bow is two or three inches higher than the stern. Brace your feet. Frequently you will find adjustable "stretchers" built into the boat for this purpose. Place your oars in the oarlocks so that the grip of the oars comes close together.

There are four parts to the rowing stroke. They are called: the catch, the pull, the feather, and the recovery. As you practice, check these points:

Dip the oars slightly in the water.

Keep your elbows close to your sides at the end of the stroke.

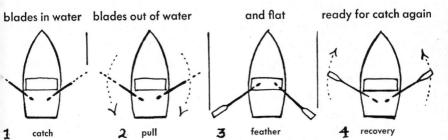

blades in water	blades out of water	and flat	ready for catch again
1 catch	**2** pull	**3** feather	**4** recovery

Lift blade only high enough to clear water during the recovery.

Keep your hands level.

Feather the oars during the recovery.

Rest a few seconds at the completion of each stroke.

No matter what type of boat you row, the four parts of the stroke remain unchanged. There are many different types of rowboats, such as the St. Lawrence skiff, the punt, the dinghy and the fisherman's dory. The type of rowboat that you use will depend on the water in which it is used and the purpose for which it was built. There are different kinds of oars and oarlocks, too. Try to become familiar with a variety so that you will feel at home no matter where you may wish to row.

Skating

Both roller skating and ice skating are good exercise and fun, too. You can enjoy them both indoors and out during many seasons of the year.

Roller skates should fit your shoes securely. Learn to keep them in good condition. Master some basic dance routines

297

and figures. You can start by practicing on a sidewalk. Later you may wish to visit a roller skating rink.

Ice skates with a straight steel blade are the easiest to use. After you have gained some proficiency you may want a pair of rocker skates with a curved blade and toe for figure skating.

Unless you ice skate indoors or on a rink that is open only when the ice is in good condition, you should learn how to judge when the ice is safe. Black ice, from four to six inches thick, is entirely safe. White spots on ice mean air holes. Snow, ice, and slush disguise air holes and therefore are dangerous. Always skate with a "buddy" so that you can keep an eye on each other.

Be courteous when you are ice skating or roller skating. Stick to your own course and stay out of the way of fellow skaters. Keep your skates under control at all times. These simple steps will keep falls and bumps to a minimum.

Ice rescue Every outdoor skater should be prepared for emergencies. Carry a lifeline whenever you go near the ice. Learn what to do if you fall through the ice and how to rescue a fellow skater.

The most important thing in any ice rescue is to keep calm. Think before you act. If possible, throw a rope with something on the end to be grasped by the person in the water. This may be a ring buoy, a knot the size of a person's fist, a piece of wood, or a noose. Hold your end of the rope securely. If you keep the rope taut, the victim cannot go down under the water and usually he can roll out on the ice.

A plank, ladder, or pole may be slid out to the person in the water.

If the victim is helpless, go to him. Tie a rope under your armpits and have someone on shore or on skates hold the other end. When close to the hole, lie down and crawl. Grasp the victim, pull him out, and tell him to lie flat. Remain flat yourself and slide back carefully until you reach firm ice.

After being in icy water, the victim should receive first aid immediately. Send for a doctor if needed. Warmth and dry clothes are important, but if not available, the victim should skate or exercise vigorously if possible, in order to keep warm.

Horsewoman

A horse not only takes you over hill and dale, but he has a real personality of his own. Other forms of transportation can never give you the same feeling of companionship.

There are three types of horses—the small horse, the light horse, and the draft horse. A horse's height is always given in "hands." A hand is four inches. The small horse is under 14 hands and includes Shetland ponies. The light horse is from 14½–16 hands and the one you see most frequently. It is used for riding and pulling sleighs and wagons. The draft horse is over 16 hands and is used for farm work and for drawing heavy wagons.

In addition to the types of horses there are also different breeds. Among the light horses there are the saddle, trotter, and the hackney. The more important breeds of the draft horse are the Morgan, Percheron, Clydsdale, Shire, and Suffolk Punch. It is fun to visit a stable, breeding farm, or horseshow and learn to distinguish the different types and breeds.

The most common colors of horses are bay, brown, and chestnut. You will also find roans, grays, blacks, and piebalds. Have you noticed the different marks on horses? These are known as socks or stockings, stars, blazes, races, and snips, depending upon where they appear.

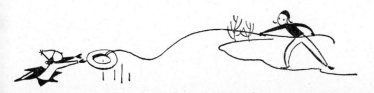

A horse that is in good health and suffering from no injury is called "sound." A good appetite, glossy coat, bright eyes and a soft and pliant skin are indications of a horse's well-being.

As you ride, you will find that horse and rider form a working team. Care and consideration should always be given to the horse. Be firm and kind and your horse will serve you well.

Canoeing

The Indians used birch bark canoes and hollowed-out logs to travel the waterways of America. They always knelt when paddling, as did the explorers and hunters who followed. They knew the truth of the statement, "Load low and trim properly."

Today, you may paddle a canvas or aluminum canoe but you still follow the example of the Indians and kneel. The correct position is to kneel with knees apart and buttocks resting on the thwart. Always use a kneeling pad. It can be made out of rubber or canvas filled with kapok.

To be a proficient paddler, a Girl Scout must be able to paddle in bow or stern position. She must have mastered the different strokes so that she can paddle the canoe in any direction and bring it into any position.

Two people, paddling together, paddle in unison and on opposite sides. The stern paddler is responsible for giving commands. The bow paddler sets the pace and watches for any rocks, logs, or other hazards. It takes time, practice, and perseverance to understand the use of the different combinations of canoeing strokes.

Here are some safety rules for boating and canoeing:

1. Be sure boats and canoes are in good condition and use them only with permission of the leader in charge.

How To Paddle a Canoe

2. Know the number of persons the boat will carry safely and do not overload.

3. Complete the required swimming skills before entering a boat.

4. Never row or paddle without an experienced person in the boat.

5. Use boats only in the designated area.

6. Stick to your boat or canoe if you tip.

7. Stay ashore in bad weather.

8. Obey all boating and canoeing rules and regulations.

Skiing

There is fun, adventure, and plenty of thrill in skiing. In countries such as Norway and Switzerland everyone learns to ski as a matter of course. It is a common method of transportation as well as recreation during the winter months.

The first safety precaution in skiing is the selection of the proper equipment and clothing. You can get help from the National Ski Association of America, the National Ski Patrol System, a ski instructor, or a sporting goods store.

The next important step is to get instruction. Learn to ski correctly in the beginning. If you don't get the right form early, it is hard to change later. If possible, enroll in a ski school and join a ski club.

To enjoy any sport a person must be in good health and skiing is no exception. Start working on the Personal Health badge. Find out from your instructor what exercises you can do to strengthen the muscles you will use in skiing. Do these faithfully for a month or so before you take to the slopes. Take part, if possible, in a "dry school" program during the fall.

Here are a few common sense rules for safe skiing:

1. Learn to ski correctly and be sure your equipment is in good condition.

2. Ski under control at all times.
3. Stick to slopes and trails that are within your ability.
4. Always ski with a buddy.
5. Always wear skis on trails or slopes.
6. Fill in all "sitzmarks" immediately.
7. Take time out when skiing for rests and a good meal at noontime.
8. Always keep poles low and behind while running downhill.
9. Carry your skis over your shoulders with points down.
10. Do preseason exercises to toughen your muscles.
11. Obey the instructions of ski patrolmen at all times.
12. Learn how to recognize safe and dangerous snow conditions.

Sports

How many of the sports listed in the Sports badge have you tried? It is nice to know something about all of them and be skilled in one or two. Choose your sports so that you can play some in teams and others by yourself or with one other person. All sports are good fun and through them you can have happy times and make new friends.

Why not start a tournament ladder for your troop or neighborhood friends in a favorite sport? To do this, you first list names of the entries on heavy paper 2 x 6 inches. Then cut slots in a piece of cardboard and insert the names in any order.

The girl whose name is second on the ladder can challenge the person in No. 1 position. If she wins, she moves up to No. 1, and if she loses she remains in the same position. Each contestant can challenge the girl directly in front of her. A ladder can continue for several months or a year. It's fun to watch the different contestants change places as their skill improves.

Every year, on her birthday, Juliette Low used to send a

303

message to all Girl Scouts. In 1924 she laid down the rules for the Game of Girl Scouting. They apply equally well to all sports and games. She said:

"I hope that we shall all remember the rules of this Girl Scouting game of ours. They are:

To play fair,

To play in your place,

To play for your side and not for yourself.

"And as for the score, the best thing in a game is the fun and not the result, for:

> *When the Great Recorder comes*
> *To write against your name,*
> *He writes not that you won or lost*
> *But how you played the game.*"

Athlete

Do you have any teams at school? If so, try to become a member of one of them. It will be very worth while and will give you an opportunity to learn team play, self-control, and how to use your body skillfully.

A good athlete is good at sports, understands the rules of the game, plays fairly, and never disputes the decision of the referee or coach. Most of all, the popular athlete puts the good of the team ahead of herself. There is no place for the girl who wants to be the "whole show" in sports and games.

Life Saver

The most important things to know in lifesaving are: (1) how to take care of yourself in the water; (2) how to prevent water accidents; and (3) how to help in a water accident. The Life Saver badge will prepare you for all of these.

PART V

You and Your Home

CHAPTER 16   Agriculture

CHAPTER 17   Health and Safety

CHAPTER 18   Homemaking

CHAPTER 16

Agriculture

RAISING and producing food is one of the most important occupations in the world. Without food you would have little use for the other things the world has to offer.

How food—meat, vegetables, dairy products, and so forth —is raised and produced is valuable knowledge for all Girl Scouts. You will find it useful throughout life.

The badges in this field can be done by Girl Scouts living on farms and by those who spend some time each year in the country.

Because the whole field of agriculture is one in which a great deal of work has been done by specialists and scientists, this book does not give detailed information.

What to plant in a garden, how to raise pigs, bees, or blueberries, how to feed a chicken, or how to market milk will be different in various parts of the country. This is true because of the differences in climate, soil, and so on.

If you need particular information, you may write or talk to your county agent at your county seat, or send to the Superintendent of Documents, Washington, D.C., for a list of the government pamphlets on the subject on which you are working.

Farmer

If you are interested in learning more about the farm—the animals, machines, tools, and crops—you will find certain parts of this *Handbook* a help. For instance, the chapters on homemaking, health and safety, and the out-of-doors will be useful. Also look at the arts and crafts and nature chapters.

One of the most important things an agriculturist has to know is how to manage the soil and keep it producing. You can learn a great deal about this by caring for your own garden or doing some simple landscaping or even by raising house plants.

Soil is largely made up of rock and decayed plant and animal life. Types of soil are caused by the kinds of rocks that have broken down in the area during hundreds of years and the kinds of plants and animals that live there.

Topsoil is what we need to grow things. It can only be made by nature. Did you know it takes from three hundred to thousands of years for nature to make an inch of topsoil? The next time you go to the woods dig a hole in the ground. First you will see this year's dead leaves, then last year's dead leaves, and so on. You will have to dig deeply before the leaves cannot be identified as leaves.

Topsoil varies in depth in different parts of the country. In some places it is only a few inches deep and in others several feet. Too much planting takes the life out of shallow topsoil. If too many trees are cut down where the soil is shallow, it becomes exposed to wind and rain, and blows and washes away.

Man can give back to the topsoil what his plants have taken out, and he can plant things which will hasten the formation of topsoil. But we cannot manufacture topsoil as we can vacuum cleaners and automobiles. Today, scientists are working on this. They are experimenting with the making of topsoil from sewage sludge.

Before you plant anything, test your soil. This test will tell you what the soil contains and what you must add to it, if anything, to grow the kind of plants you want to grow.

There are small, inexpensive, soil-testing sets which you can purchase. Or write to your county agent and ask him where you can send a sample of your soil to be tested.

Landscaper

There is no prettier sight than a well-kept yard. You can do something to improve the grounds around your house, school, or troop meeting place. Choose a small section—a place by the steps, a corner of the yard, or a strip along a fence—and see what you can do about it.

Make a plan before you do any planting. Measure the plot and mark it on paper, drawing it to scale. A good scale is to let ¼ inch equal 1 foot. Study seed catalogs and decide what you are going to plant. Allow the proper spaces between rows on the plan. Learn when each thing should be planted and how; when it will flower and what color it will be. Your plan may include trees, shrubs, and flowers or only one or two of these.

Prepare the soil and start your planting. Keep the site weeded and well cultivated. Spray or dust the plants against

destructive insects and plant diseases. Stay with your project during the various seasons. Learn how to mulch your plants. Mulch is any loose material such as straw, grass from your lawn, or dried plants. It is placed around the stalks of plants to protect their roots from injury. Take care of the soil and prepare it for the next planting. You can get help from seed catalogs and garden magazines, and from your county agent.

On page 311 are drawings of some of the tools used in gardening and landscaping. Learn to use the correct names for these tools and use and care for as many as possible.

Home Gardener and Truck Gardener

You will find it a great deal of fun to have a garden—either vegetables or flowers or some of each. You will have things to share with your family and friends. Your garden can be a big one or a small one, or can be several pieces of land in different parts of your front or back yard. A good size is about 10 x 12 feet.

If you cannot garden out-of-doors, garden indoors. There are plans for a window garden on page 240. House plants are not hard to find. They can be raised from seeds, cuttings, or rootings. House plants are inexpensive and respond quickly to good care. Try a window box, too.

You will enjoy many things that are a part of landscaping and gardening, such as learning to arrange flowers and to cook vegetables and fruit in new ways; knowing the birds and small animals that come to your garden. Raise some of your flowers and vegetables from seed. It can be done in pots or boxes on sunny window sills. You might build a cold frame or hotbed. You can get directions from your county agent.

Here are a few tips that will give you an understanding of how things grow.

Take a seed, such as a bean, and plant it in a pot of soil. *Seeds*
Keep it watered and in a sunny place. In a few days the bean
will "sprout" (germinate). After it has its first two foliage
leaves, pull it out carefully. It will look very much like the
picture on this page. The roots and root hairs take in nourishment from the soil and anchor the plant. The stem conducts

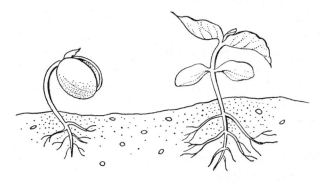

the nourishment to the leaves where, with the help of sun
and light, it is made into the food the plant uses or stores.

Plant other kinds of seeds and see what they look like after
they have their two foliage leaves.

SEED TESTING. When plants are raised for seed, there
is always a chance that seeds from other plants may get mixed
in when the seed is harvested. Separating the kind of seed
you want from other seeds, dirt, small stones, and plant frag-
ments is called "seed testing." First of all you have to know
what the seed you do want looks like.

Use a letter scale and weigh out an ounce of seed from a
bag of grass, wheat, barley, or any other seed that you have
in quantity. Place that ounce on paper. With a magnifying
glass and a pair of tweezers separate the seed you want from
the rest of the matter. Then weigh the seeds again. This will

give you an idea of what is meant by "pure" seed and how important it is to buy pure seed.

GERMINATION TEST. Sometimes you will have seeds left over after planting your garden which you put away for another year. If you want to know what percentage of these leftover seeds will germinate, do the following.

Take twenty seeds of one kind of plant and place them on two or three layers of wet paper toweling. Roll up the toweling carefully and put the roll in a dark, cool, moist place. In a week or ten days open the roll. Some, perhaps all, of the seeds will have sprouted. This will help you estimate the number of seeds from that package that will germinate when planted.

Seed companies often mark seed packages with the percentage of germination that can be expected. All reputable seed companies have tested their seeds for germination.

Fruits and vegetables The seeds of every plant are the fruit of the plant, and it takes a flower to produce a fruit. We eat the fruits of many plants, although we only call a few of them "fruits." What would you call these—apples, tomatoes, cucumbers, cherries, and strawberries? They are all "fruits," but we usually refer to tomatoes and cucumbers as "vegetables," to apples and cherries as "fruits," to strawberries as "berries."

The term "vegetable" is usually used for a plant or any part of a plant that we eat as a main dish or as part of a main dish. Some vegetables we harvest and eat before they bloom, such as carrot, turnip, lettuce, and spinach. Have you ever seen any of these go to flower? Some we eat when they are

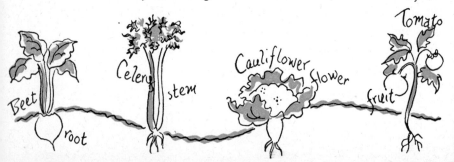

in bud, such as cauliflower and broccoli. We eat some after the flowers have gone and the fruit has ripened, such as cucumbers, strawberries, peppers, and apples. This picture shows some common vegetables and the parts we eat.

On page 237 you will find a drawing of a flower with its parts named and information about the function of the parts.

Did you know that the earthworm is one of the most valuable garden animals? This creature helps to fertilize the soil. He eats soil and decayed life and as they pass through his body certain chemicals are added to them. The earthworm helps to keep good drainage in gardens by making small burrows in the soil. There are farms in this country that specialize in raising earthworms for people to buy and put in their gardens. *Garden animals*

Toads and some snakes are valuable, too. Toads and small snakes, such as the green, garter, and ribbon snake, eat many insects. The larger snakes, such as the black, king, and hog-nosed snake, eat many mice and moles.

Insects that eat other insects are generally considered beneficial to gardens. The best-known are the lady beetles, tiger beetles, and praying mantis. Spiders, though not insects, are considered beneficial in any garden because they, too, feed on insects. Bees are the best pollinators and the honeybee is *the* best. *Garden insects*

Two types of damage can be done in gardens by insects. Some chew off parts of a plant (chewing insects), and some pierce the plant and suck out the juices (sucking insects). To destroy chewing insects, a spray or dust is used that coats the plant and thus is eaten by the insect. To destroy the sucking insect, a dust or spray is used that kills when it comes in contact with the insect's body.

Plant There are many plant diseases. They are caused by one of
diseases the following: (1) unsuitable environment, for example, to-
mato blossom rot; (2) viruses, for example, potato-leaf roll;
(3) bacteria, for example, fire blight; (4) fungi, for example, wheat rust.

Whenever you find a plant that does not seem to be doing well, try to find the reason. Find out what to do for it and
then do it, before the disease or the insect spreads to other
plants.

Notice that disease in human beings is caused by the same
things mentioned above, namely, unsuitable environment,
viruses, bacteria, and fungi.

Fruit Raiser

Instead of having a garden in which you raise many different things, you may wish to specialize. Perhaps you are going
to raise only small fruits, such as currants, blueberries, or
strawberries. Or it may be that you will want to raise only
fruit trees, such as apple, pear, cherry, or peach.

We would not have space in the *Handbook* to give you
help with all sorts of crops. You can get this help by writing
to your county agent, talking to people who know, or sending to the Superintendent of Documents, Washington, D.C.,
for a pamphlet on the subject you are interested in.

Beekeeper

A plant bears the best fruit only when it has been fertilized
(pollinated). We depend upon insects to do a great deal of
this pollination and bees are the best-known pollinators. The
honeybee is the best. Bees feed only on nectar and pollen,
both as larvae and as adults. Most other pollinators feed on
plants when they are in the larval stage—caterpillars, grubs,
maggots.

The honeybee is not native to the United States. It was brought to the eastern part of our country with the early English and Spanish settlers. Honeybees have now become at home in any part of our country.

A unit of bees is called a swarm or colony and its home is a hive. A producing colony has in it a single queen (developed female), thousands of worker bees (undeveloped females), and a few hundred drones (males). A place where bees are raised is called an apiary.

Animal Raiser

There are many different kinds of animals raised on farms and ranches in this country. There are chickens, ducks, turkeys, geese, guinea hens, cattle, swine, goats, sheep, and horses.

There are also many kinds of animals raised in homes and

317

apartments. These are hamsters, white mice, goldfish, turtles, domesticated birds, and tropical fish.

This badge can be done with any kind of animal except the cat and dog, the cow, or poultry. There are special badges which will help you with these animals.

Poultry Raiser

Poultry includes chickens, turkeys, ducks, geese, guinea fowls, pigeons, and pheasants. The turkey is a native American bird. The ancestors of the other kinds of poultry had their origin in Europe and Asia, though some breeds have been developed in America.

Some of the popular breeds of chickens are Barred Plymouth Rocks, White Plymouth Rocks, Rhode Island Reds, Jersey Black Giants, New Hampshires, Leghorns, Minorcas, and Anconas. The last three lay white eggs. The others lay brown eggs. There is no difference in food value between white and brown eggs. The common breeds of ducks are Pekin and Muscovy; of geese, Toulouse and Emden.

The products from poultry have many uses besides food. Egg whites are used in making paints, varnishes, paper sizing, medicines, adhesives, and in tanning leather. Egg yolks are used in soaps, paints, shampoos. The shells are used in fertilizers. The feathers are used in pillows and millinery. And there are other uses for them all.

Dairying

The breeds of dairy cattle commonly used in this country as milk cows are the Ayrshire, Brown Swiss, Guernsey, Holstein, and Jersey. They are quite different in color and markings. You can learn their distinguishing marks and recognize them along the road. Some breeds produce larger quantities of milk than others. Some produce milk in smaller quantities, but richer in cream content.

318

Guernsey

Brown Swiss

Jersey

Ayrshire

Holstein

A cow has teeth only on the lower jaw and must be pastured where the grass or clover is long enough for her to grasp it with her tongue and cut it against her lower teeth. A cow's horns are hollow, fitted over a core of living bone, and are never shed.

The cow's stomach is so constructed that when the animal is feeding the food goes first to the "storage bag" section, where it is formed into cuds. When leisure after feeding comes, these cuds are regurgitated into the mouth, chewed carefully, and swallowed again—going into another part of the stomach.

319

CHAPTER 17

Health and Safety

HAVE you ever stopped to think how important health and safety are in your everyday life? They are a part of everything you do. Can you think how they affect your personal appearance, the sports you play, the camping trips you take and the things you do for other people, such as taking care of children or lending a hand in an emergency?

A healthy person is one who feels fit and looks forward to the day's play and work. The World Health Organization, a special agency of the United Nations, defines health as "physical, mental, and social well-being." This definition is used throughout the world. A safe person is one who uses common sense at all times, does not take unnecessary chances, and knows what to do in the presence of danger.

Health Aid

To take good care of your own health is common sense; to safeguard the health of others is good citizenship. To know what to do in case of an accident is valuable knowledge, but it is even more valuable to know how to prevent accidents.

Safety survey Did you know that the majority of accidents happen in the home? Most of them are caused by little things. They can be prevented. Survey your home from top to bottom and get

How many hazards can you find?

YOU AND YOUR HOME

rid of as many hazards as possible. Check everything, including the closets, the hallways and stairs, window screens, electrical appliances, and so forth.

Then take a look around the porch, yard, barn, or garage. Think of the number of accidents that can be avoided if tools, toys, and bikes are put away, stairs and ladders are in good repair, and ice and snow are promptly removed.

"A safe place for everything and everything in its place and in good repair" is a worth-while slogan. Remember it as you make your safety survey. Your local safety council may have forms on which you can record the results of your survey. They will also give you help on what steps to take next to make your home a safe place for all.

First aid kit   The size of a first aid kit depends on how many people will use it and where. It may be a small package that fits into your pocket on a hike. It may be slightly larger for your own use on a camping trip. It may be a big tin box for the automobile, your home, or camp unit.

Your own pocket-sized kit should have a tiny bottle of antiseptic, a needle, a few individual packages of 1-inch compresses on adhesive, a small tube of sterile petrolatum ointment.

Your patrol or troop kit on a hike should have:

> 2 1-inch compresses on adhesive, in individual packages
> 3 assorted sterile bandage compresses, in individual packages
> 2 triangular bandages
> Small tube of sterile petrolatum ointment
> Small bottle of antiseptic
> Small bottle of aromatic spirits of ammonia
> Small roll of sterile cotton
> 2 needles
> 1 small package of safety matches
> 1 small package of short, sterile, cotton-tipped applicators

322

Your first aid kit in the home, in a camp unit, or in the troop meeting place should include most of the following:

1-inch compresses on adhesive, in individual packages
Sterile gauze squares—about 3 × 3 inches—in individual packages
2 triangular bandages
Sterile gauze—about 1 square yard—in sealed packages
1 tube of sterile petrolatum ointment
1 bottle of antiseptic
1 tube of calamine ointment
1 bottle of aromatic spirits of ammonia
1 box of bicarbonate of soda
1 box of salt
Scissors
1 box of sterile cotton
3-inch splinter forceps (or small tweezers)
Paper cups
1-inch and 2-inch roller bandages
1 box of applicators
1 box of tongue depressors
2 thin board splints
Hot-water bag
Ice bag
2 teaspoons

Most first aid supplies have to be purchased, but you can make the container yourself. Tin boxes and cigar boxes can be painted and fixed up to hold the supplies. An envelope made of waterproof material is good for a pocket-sized kit.

Every day in the field of science new discoveries are being made. In medicine alone, each year sees many advances in the use of new drugs and new treatments. In assembling your first aid kit it is wise to check the contents with your local medical advisers.

323

Good Health Habits

Personal Health

It is not altogether true that "beauty is skin deep." At times you see beauty and at other times you feel it. You may not be born with good looks, but every girl who has good health, who takes care of herself, who is interested in other people and less conscious of herself can become an "attractive personality."

You cannot be perfectly healthy without giving some thought to the way you live. Have you ever stopped to think about your health habits? Have you ever thought of reasons —other than personal ones—why you want to be healthy? Your answer may be a combination of many things.

You may take your strong body for granted, but countless men and women have contributed to your health. They are the people working in medicine, surgery, anatomy, physiology, chemistry, physics, bacteriology, nursing, and engineering. They devote their lives to helping you keep well and happy. Think of how many lives have been saved through the pasteurization of milk, inoculations, vaccinations, "wonder drugs," the iron lung, and new methods in the prevention, control, and treatment of disease.

To know just how healthy you are, you must have an examination. You can go to your family physician, your school health service, or a free neighborhood clinic. It is sensible to have a health examination each year. You must have a yearly examination to take part in swimming, camping, and other strenuous activities in Girl Scouting. Your leader can get a card for you from your local Girl Scout office. *Health examination*

This health examination card has a section for your health history. You and your mother, father, or guardian fill this out. It gives the doctor the story of your health up to the present time. It will help him with your examination.

The other section of the card is filled out when the doctor examines you. A doctor's training makes it possible for him to understand your body and how it works. He is your friend and wants to help you become fit or stay fit. He may recommend rest, diet, more or less exercise, inoculations, or vaccinations. Whatever your doctor advises, it will be your duty to carry it out.

A dentist knows how to help you keep your teeth and gums sound and clean. You should visit your dentist every six months. The kinds of food you eat and your daily health habits also help to keep your teeth and mouth in good condition.

Using your body well When you use your body in the right way at all times, you have a good posture. Watch the people on the streets, buses, and in stores. You can tell a great deal about the way they feel through their posture. You, too, are showing the world every moment of every day much about your own attitude, health, and state of mind through your posture. It affects your appearance, your dress, your voice, and your self-confidence.

Check your own posture by standing with your back to the wall. Stand with feet parallel, heels about three or four inches away from the wall, and the back of your head, shoulders, and buttocks touching the wall. In this position your spine should be sufficiently flexible so that you can bring your back close enough to the wall so that there is just enough room to slip in your extended fingers.

When a person starts to grow quickly she is apt to slouch. Watch out for this. Try always to hold yourself erect. If you find that you are all hunched over, straighten up quickly.

Your feet are the basis of your posture. Look at yours. Do you have straight inner margins from your heel to the big toe? Your footprints should show each print pointing straight ahead and not to the side or the middle.

326

Keep your feet free from corns, calluses, bunions, and in-growing toenails by exercise, good health habits, proper fitting hose and shoes. Your hose should be long enough and broad enough to fit your foot comfortably. They should permit freedom of movement and be free from wrinkles.

Different shoes are worn for different occasions, but they should always be comfortable and fit well, no matter what style you select. A shoe with a straight inner border, flexible shank, adequate toe space and a low, broad heel is the best for people who like to be active. There is an official Girl Scout shoe which meets these standards.

To protect your body and improve your posture, move and lift things properly. Use your judgment about the size and weight of things you move. Do not try to move or lift a heavy object alone. Always stand as close as possible to the object to be lifted, bend at the knees, keep the back straight, grasp the article firmly with both hands, letting leg and thigh muscles do the work. Watch men moving furniture to see how to lift and move objects.

Insurance companies, commercial firms, and other organizations have pamphlets, posters, and movies that will help you understand about your health. Ask your leader to write for these materials.

Home Health and Safety

Home health means a healthy home—a home that is comfortable and in which it is a pleasure to live. A home may have expensive furniture, sterling silver, and oriental rugs but these alone cannot make a comfortable and pleasant home. It is made by the cleanliness, consideration, and working together of a family or any group of people living together. No one member of the family can do this alone. But there are many things that each person can do. Here are a few things that you can do. Chapter 18 has other suggestions.

327

Ventilating and heating   Have a thermometer in your room and try to keep the heat and ventilation regulated. The room should not be warmer than 68 to 70 degrees Fahrenheit. An overheated room lowers body resistance and uses up your vitality.

A room should have moisture in the air. You can help keep a room moist by keeping a pan or bowl filled with water on the radiator. House plants that are well cared for also help to keep moisture in a room.

Lighting   Your eyes are important. Guard them carefully. When you have to use your eyes for close work, do as much as you can during the day. Natural light is better than any kind of artificial light. Too much light may be as bad as too little, so never read, sew, or do handicrafts with the sun glaring on your work.

The best way to place a lamp is just behind your shoulder-line. Turn your chair so that the light falls on the page. When writing, if you are right-handed, place the lamp behind your left shoulder; if you are left-handed, place it behind the right shoulder.

A courteous and thoughtful thing to do is to place your lamp where you and another member of your family can use it together.

328

A home that is pleasant to live in should be both orderly *Cleanliness* and neat. You can help to keep it so by making your own *and order* bed, hanging up your clothes, wiping your shoes before you go into the house, having a place for all your belongings, and putting them away when you have finished with them.

Your medicine chest should be tidy and safe. All medicines *The* should be clearly marked. Put special labels on any poisons. *medicine* Discard all outdated prescription bottles. A diagram of the *chest* contents is helpful. This can be pasted behind one of the shelves or on the door. If there are small children the door should be kept locked at all times. Make it a habit always to read a label three times—before opening, before measuring, and before taking any medicine.

Child Care

It is the right of every baby to be well born and well cared *The baby* for. Doctors, nurses, and those trained in health education work together with parents to make this possible. The baby's birth should be recorded at once by the registrar of birth in the place where the parents live. This certificate is very valuable. It is a proof of citizenship and age. It is needed many times in adult life.

CARE. Every baby should be under a doctor's regular care. The doctor knows what food and rest the baby needs in order to keep strong and to grow strong. In many cities there are free clinics for babies. There are also many free government bulletins on infant and child care.

Taking care of a young baby is great fun if you know how. If you are not nervous or hurried and the baby is kept comfortable and well, both you and the baby will have a good

329

time. He will take his food happily, sleep well, enjoy his play, and grow.

Be quiet and gentle with the baby. If you always play with him, he will soon think of you as an entertainer and will cry for attention every time he sees you. Be satisfied just to fill his needs, except at play time. Then he will be contented when you are in charge. It is natural for a baby to cry at times even when he is given good care. Crying is a form of exercise for a baby just as a game of tag is exercise for you. Before handling a baby, wash your hands carefully and be sure that there are no pins in your clothing that may hurt him.

A little baby cannot support himself. He must be picked up and carried carefully. His mother or nurse can show you the proper way to do this. She can also teach you how to place the baby in a partially sitting position. He should not sit up until his own muscles support him. This is usually at about six or eight months.

To keep a baby comfortable, soiled diapers should be changed as soon as possible. Before putting on a fresh diaper, be sure the skin is clean and dry, especially between the legs. Neglect of this may cause chafing. Baby oil rubbed on will help prevent this.

All the baby's toilet articles should be kept together and used only for the baby. Your hands should be thoroughly washed before you arrange the articles for the bath.

CLOTHES. A baby's clothes should be simple and made to hang from the shoulders. There should be no tight bands or harsh neck or wrist finishings. The season and climate determine to a large extent the weight and amount of clothing a baby needs.

Diapers should be soft and absorbent and not pinned too
tightly.

All the baby's clothes must be carefully laundered and well rinsed to prevent irritating his sensitive skin. Dressing the baby should be done with as little handling, turning, and pulling as possible.

FEEDING. The doctor prescribes the kind of diet and times for feeding. Food in bottles should be warmed in water until it is lukewarm. To test milk, shake a few drops on the inside of your wrist. It should feel neither hot nor cold. When you are giving a baby a bottle, be sure that the neck of the bottle is filled with milk so that he does not suck air. If he drops off to sleep, and when he has finished eating, hold him on your shoulder and pat his back. This is to help him get rid of gas bubbles.

331

A child one year old has usually been taught to drink from a cup. As soon as he can hold a spoon and move it from dish to mouth, let him feed himself.

PLAY AND EXERCISE. The baby needs plenty of fresh air and sunshine. His eyes should be protected from the direct rays of the sun, and he should never be left in a draft. Sunshine on arms and legs helps him grow and helps prevent rickets. Avoid overexposure because of the sensitiveness of his skin.

He needs exercise for his growth and development. He gets most of his exercise by kicking, stretching, and squirming.

A baby likes to put toys in his mouth. Toys should not have sharp edges. They should be painted with harmless coloring and easily washable. Never give a baby any toys or objects small enough to be swallowed.

SLEEP. If possible, a separate room should be set aside for the baby. He should sleep in a crib, bassinet, or basket protected from lights, drafts, and all possible accidents. The baby should not sleep in a bed with his mother or any other person. At night he should sleep the clock around. Rest and sleep are just as important as food or play. Bed clothing should be carefully tucked in and pinned with very large safety pins to the mattress so that the baby will not get wound up in the bedding.

The child If the clothes are simple, a child of three or four usually enjoys dressing himself. Dresses and suits that fasten in the front with a few large buttons or with elastic are best.

Small children like to move and lift objects, to climb and jump. They like to "work," if given a chance. They lift and carry and move things back and forth.

Anything a child may use over and over again, in different ways, makes a good plaything. Here are some things a small child likes: large empty spools, large empty pasteboard boxes, wooden boxes (if not splintery); a sandbox, doll and carriage or bed; a wooden train of cars (without tracks), truck, wagon, digging tools.

From four years on a child likes to make things and do things around the house.

A child likes books and should be taught how to handle them carefully. A child likes the things he sees out-of-doors, the birds and insects, animals and flowers. Help him to know more about them and to go right on liking them.

When you are going to act as a baby sitter, you should have the following information:

Tips for a baby sitter

1. Telephone numbers at which the parents, a relative, or a nearby neighbor can be reached in an emergency. Also the phone numbers of the family doctor, police station, fire station, electric, gas, and water companies.

2. Knowledge of the house, such as the location of light switches, the correct operation of any equipment you may use, for example, the stove.

3. Schedule for the child or children, such as hour for meals and going to bed. Also information on the food to be served, clothing to be worn, temperature and ventilation of rooms.

4. An understanding of exactly what your responsibilities are. Will you only take care of the child or are you expected to do some housework, feed or exercise any pets, and so forth?

5. What is expected of you as far as your personal conduct is concerned? Can you use the radio or television, help yourself to snacks, have personal callers, and make telephone calls?

333

6. Knowledge of what you will be paid (if not done as a service), and how you will return home.

No Girl Scout should sit alone with a sick child. You should never give a child medicine. If you have a cold yourself, or are not feeling well, you should *not* act as a baby sitter that day.

Community Safety

Many persons in your community and in the whole country are helping every day to protect you, your family, and others.

Local In communities throughout the country there are local safety
services councils interested in the welfare of everyone. Find out what your safety council does and help it, if you can.

The police department is there for your safety and needs your cooperation. If you live in a place that is not big enough for a police department or a safety council, there is a board of selectmen, a sheriff, or another group of citizens trying to protect you.

The fire department of a town and the fire wardens of the forestry service protect the lives and property of persons everywhere, from big cities to isolated farms.

In most communities there are building codes for safety. They regulate the materials used, nearness of one building to another, placing of fire escapes, number of entrances and exits, distance from street to front line of building, nearness to water mains, fire-fighting equipment, police protection, and many other health and safety measures.

Many mills and factories have a safety engineer who sometimes has one or more assistants known as safety inspectors. They do such things as give instruction to the workers, develop safety rules, post safety displays, conduct regular inspections, and investigate the causes of accidents.

334

Your state labor department may also inspect mills and factories to be sure they are healthful and safe places for people to work.

Look around your community and see how many other things you can find that are done to protect your health and keep you safe. Is the milk and water supply inspected? Is there a garbage and sewage disposal system? Are the public eating places inspected? If there is a public swimming place, is there a lifeguard?

You can help with the safety in your community by obeying traffic laws and by observing safety and courtesy rules on public beaches, playgrounds, and other places of recreation; by obeying safety rules in buses, trains, streetcars, planes, and buildings, including your own school; by practicing safety rules in all your sports and games; by helping to remove as many hazards as possible from your school, troop meeting place, and home. *What you can do*

It is not just your own safety you risk when you break safety rules. If you walk against a red light, you may get across the street all right, but someone who tries to avoid hitting you may be injured or killed. Your community has highway signs, danger signals, and traffic officers. They are there to protect you and the rest of the community. Know these signs.

If you are in a fire, *keep your head.* Find an exit and go out quietly. More lives are lost from panic than from the actual fire. Keep windows and doors closed to prevent drafts which will fan the blaze. If the room or building fills with smoke, stay close to the floor, and wrap a wet towel around your head and face.

If your clothes catch on fire, roll yourself in a woolen blanket or rug. Do not run—that only fans the blaze. Try to go where a fireman can see you and obey his orders.

335

"Keep
your
head!"

Every Girl Scout should know how to report an accident, how to report a fire, how to give a police alarm. She should know the location of the nearest drugstore, hospital, and doctor; what to do with lost children; and how to direct strangers and children.

Safety depends to a large extent on three *"e's"*: *education, engineering,* and *enforcement of laws.* To help people to learn safety, to appreciate what engineering has done for safety, and to obey the laws of safety is the job of every good citizen. Girl Scouts might well add a fourth: *example.*

Outdoor Safety

Every Girl Scout should be safety-wise in everything she does. Throughout this book you will find material to help you. If you are doing this badge, read Chapters 15 and 16 very carefully.

A safety-wise Girl Scout makes sure that her sports equipment is in good condition; that she swims, skis, and skates in a safe place; that she is in good physical condition and does not become overtired. A person in good health and using safe equipment can still cause an accident when she becomes overtired and her muscles do not respond as they should.

When it is necessary to hike along a road, always walk on the left side facing the oncoming traffic. In this way you can see the cars as they approach and the drivers can also see you more easily. If you are going to be out after dark, wear something white.

Water may appear to be clear, sparkling, and clean but you cannot be sure that it is safe unless it is tested. See page 67 for methods of purifying water on a hike.

Consult your local fire authorities before building an outdoor fire. If necessary, get a fire permit. Always follow the safety regulations for fire building given on page 68.

337

Farm Safety

Even on a safe farm accidents may happen. They are caused by falls, farm machines, animals, motor vehicles, lifting heavy articles, handling tools, stepping on or hitting objects, falling and flying articles, and burns or shock. The first step in farm safety is to list the places where accidents might happen, and the second step is to remove the causes.

Make a list of the danger spots on your farm and present it to all the people who work and live on it. With their help, develop a plan to prevent accidents, correct bad conditions, and improve working habits. Form a Family Safety Council to put your plan into action.

Fires are a major hazard on every farm. Every person on the farm should know what to do if a fire starts in the house, barn, fields, or woods. Hold a fire drill several times a year. Here are some safeguards against fires:

1. Store gasoline, kerosene, or other flammable liquids in red, labeled containers.

2. Have lightning rods put on farm buildings.

3. Be sure not to overload electrical wires. Check to be sure all electrical equipment is in good condition at regular intervals.

4. Never smoke or light a match in the barn.

5. Inspect all heating equipment regularly. See that chimneys are in good condition.

6. Keep the attic and basement free of rubbish.

7. Place ashes in metal containers.

As you work on this badge you will want to add to this list. It is only a beginning to show you how to make up your own list.

First Aid to Animals

The same principles apply in first aid to animals that apply to humans. It is emergency treatment which is given while you wait for the veterinary to arrive. It never takes the place

338

of professional care. The first aid you give should make the animal more comfortable and should prevent the injury from becoming worse.

In first aid treatment it is important to be prepared to do the right thing at the right time. An untrained person may do more harm than good. This badge must be done under the guidance of a veterinary.

First Aid

Girl Scouts believe in being prepared to meet emergencies. Minor accidents sometimes happen at home, in school, or at camp. A person may cut a finger, get a splinter in her hand, or sprain her ankle. Everyone should be able to give first aid, at least until a doctor arrives. The first aider's service stops where the doctor's begins, unless the doctor requests help with a patient.

You should know how to:

Rules for a first aider

1. Prevent accidents.
2. Judge the nature or extent of an injury or illness, in order to apply the proper first aid.
3. Do the proper thing at the proper time.
4. Transport a patient so as to cause no further injury.

Whether you earn the First Aid badge or not, these are the things that every Girl Scout should be able to do in case of an accident or sudden illness.

1. Keep the patient lying down with head level. This prevents fainting and further injury from falling. Turn the head to the side if there is vomiting. This prevents the patient from choking.
2. Keep the patient warm. This prevents serious shock. It is just as important to protect the patient on the underside as it is to cover him over, because he loses his body heat very rapidly when suffering from shock.

339

3. Send someone, or go yourself, to call a doctor or an ambulance. The person calling should tell: what has happened, where the patient is, what first aid is being given, and then listen for the doctor's further directions.

4. Keep your head and do not hurry to move the patient. Proper first aid should be given before a patient is moved.

5. Keep the crowd away from the patient.

6. Never give a patient who is unconscious water or anything to swallow.

7. Make the patient comfortable and keep him from being frightened. A cheerful attitude helps the patient to follow instructions.

8. Avoid letting the patient look at his own injury. This may cause fainting or hysteria.

9. Notify the patient's family or friends.

Bandages The three types of bandages commonly used are the triangular, the four-tailed, and the roller bandage. The triangular bandage can be folded to form a cravat bandage. There are many uses for each type of bandage. Practice is necessary to learn to use them well.

A compress is the sterile gauze or muslin used directly over a wound. Be careful not to touch the surface of sterile gauze when placing it on a wound. The bandage is used to hold the compress in place, to control bleeding by pressure, and to prevent movement when it would cause further injury. It is also used to keep splints in place.

You will find additional information on the use of the triangular bandage and the care of cuts, burns, and splinters on page 75.

You can often be helpful in giving first aid for the common emergencies.

340

NOSE BLEED. Have patient sit in a chair with head rest- *Common*
ing against the back. Apply cold, wet compresses over nose *emergencies*
or on back of neck. Avoid blowing nose for a few hours. If
bleeding does not stop in a few minutes, call a doctor.

BLISTERS (not caused by burns). Apply an antiseptic to
edge of blister, puncture with a sterilized needle (made sterile
by passing through a flame, an antiseptic, or alcohol), gently
push out water or blood, and apply a sterile dressing. If signs
of inflammation or infection occur, call a doctor.

FOREIGN BODIES IN THE EYE. Do not rub the eye.
Close the eye gently, grasp the lashes of the upper lid, pull
out and down over lower lid. Tears may wash out the speck
or move it to the inside corner of the eye, where it may be
removed gently with a piece of sterile gauze or a sterile cotton-
tipped applicator. If this fails after the first attempt, do not
continue. Have the person see a doctor.

If any chemical, such as a strong acid, alkali, or lime, gets
into the eye, immediately wash profusely and for several
minutes with clean water. Call a doctor *at once*. If there will
be considerable delay in securing medical aid, sterile petrolatum ointment may be placed in the eye to relieve discomfort.

FROSTBITE. Warm the injured part by bringing it into
contact with some other parts of the body. For example, place
the open hands over frostbitten face or ears, or put freezing
hands inside clothing, close up under the armpits. Or, place
frostbitten hands and feet in cold water indoors, or apply
cloths wrung out in cold water. If cold water is used, the
temperature of the water should be raised gradually as the
frost disappears, until it is lukewarm. Do not rub frostbitten
parts with snow.

341

INSECT BITES. Remove the "stinger" if present. Apply a compress moistened with ammonia, or baking soda and water. Spider bites may be treated as insect bites with cold application added. See page 345, "Cold Compresses and Ice Bags." Sulphur dusted into shoes and clothes helps to prevent chigger bites. Collodion applied to the bites relieves irritation.

PAIN IN THE ABDOMEN. Call a doctor immediately. Do not give a laxative or any food.

POISON IVY, OAK, SUMAC, AND WOOD. Learn to recognize poison ivy, poison oak, poison sumac, and poison wood. (See picture on page 242). The latter is found in Florida only. Avoid these plants whenever you can. Wash your hands, arms, and legs with yellow soap before you go on a hike in places *where these plants grow*. If a rash appears or you think you have come into contact with them, wash the skin thoroughly with soap and warm water and apply rubbing alcohol, followed by an application of calamine ointment.

SNAKE BITES. If bite is made by a nonpoisonous snake, treat like any wound. See page 75. If the bite is made by a poisonous snake, keep the patient quiet, do not give him any stimulant, and call a doctor immediately.

SPLINTERS. Sterilize a needle and with the needle lift the skin over the splinter. Remove the splinter and apply an antiseptic. Cover the wound with sterile gauze and bandage.

SPRAINS. Sprains are injuries to joints. The picture on page 76 shows how to apply a bandage to a sprained ankle until the patient reaches the doctor. Make patient comfortable, elevate the part injured, apply cold applications, call a doctor. Never attempt to tape a sprain.

SUNBURN. Severe sunburn is dangerous and should be avoided. If you wish to be tanned by the sun, do it gradually. If a severe burn does occur, treat it as any other burn by the use of sterile petrolatum or any good burn ointment. If a large area is burned or fever or chills develop, call a doctor.

Home Nurse

There are many minor illnesses, injuries, and stages of convalescence in the home when you can be of help both to the patient and the doctor. The doctor's job is to diagnose and prescribe, and yours is to help by carrying out his orders. Be sure you understand clearly what it is the doctor would like you to do.

The sick room should be as near the bathroom as possible to save unnecessary steps. It should also be away from the kitchen, because cooking odors are sometimes disturbing to someone who is not feeling well. Your patient needs warmth without weight in covers and circulation of air without danger of drafts. Keep the room clean and "picked up" and the lights well adjusted. Complete rest and plenty of sleep are necessary for a quick recovery. *Patient's comfort*

Flowers, fruit, notes, cards, or other small gifts are better for the patient than visitors. If you want to be a good nurse, be cheerful, walk lightly, be quiet, talk softly, and do not argue with the patient or discuss unpleasant happenings. Serve the meals attractively and on time.

While you are attending a patient, wear a washable dress with sleeves that can be rolled up, a washable apron, and shoes with rubber heels or soles. Your clothes and person

343

should be absolutely clean. Short, smooth fingernails and hands without jewelry are best for the sick room.

A restless patient may be made more comfortable by rearranging the bed clothes, by fanning, by changing the position, by rubbing the back, by putting hot-water bags at the feet, back, and neck. Propping with pillows or using a backrest, rubber rings, and air cushions relieves pressure and gives support to the body.

THE BED. A comfortable bed for a patient should be made with square corners, a drawsheet, and a rubber sheet if necessary. The rubber sheet goes on top of the bottom sheet. The draw sheet goes on next. A drawsheet can be made of an ordinary sheet folded in half, drawn tightly across the bed, and tucked in firmly.

The drawsheet is used to keep the bed smooth and to protect the patient from the rubber sheet. The rubber sheet is used only if there is danger of soiling the mattress.

BATHING AND TOILET CARE. Bathing is just as necessary in sickness as in health. Every patient, unless the doctor orders otherwise, should have one complete sponge bath each day. It stimulates circulation, soothes a feverish condition, keeps the skin in good condition, and gives the patient a little exercise. After the sponge bath, an alcohol rub and powdering will rest the patient.

The patient's hair should be cared for at least once a day. Place a towel under the head to protect the pillow. If the hair is long, it is more comfortable for the patient to have it braided.

Compresses and ice bags

Cold is applied by ice bags and cold compresses. Crush ice into small pieces, place them in a sieve, and run water over them to remove sharp edges by melting. Fill the bag about half-full, expel air, cover with a towel, and place where needed. Ice bags should be aired inside and out, carefully dried, and stuffed with cotton or tissue paper when not in use. Cold compresses are squares of cotton or clean, white cloth pads, soaked in water, wrung out, and placed where needed.

Hot-water bags

The water should never be hot enough to scald the patient if the bag should leak. Fill the bag one-third to one-half full, expel the air by pressing against the bag until the water rises in the neck, screw the top in firmly, and place where needed. Always be sure to test the bag on your own arm or cheek to be sure that it will not burn the patient. The bag should be covered with a towel. When there is no hot-water bag or electric pad, a hot stone or a bag of heated salt or sand may be

345

used. When not in use, a hot-water bag should be dried and hung up by the bottom without a stopper.

Diversions for the sick There are many things you can do to help the time pass quickly for a sick person. Small children can be amused by making figures out of fruits, candy, string, paper. Simple games are fun for any age. Some people will like you to read aloud to them.

Some people enjoy knitting or crocheting or other arts and crafts. Rest for the mind and body are important for a sick person. Be sure your patient does not work too hard or keep at an activity for too long a time.

Communicable diseases A communicable (catching) disease is one in which disease germs may be carried from one person to another. The common cold, scarlet fever, measles, and diphtheria are examples of communicable diseases. A stomach-ache from overeating, heart trouble, and appendicitis, for example, are not communicable.

There are two aims in caring for a person with a communicable disease: one, to cure the patient; the other, to keep other persons from becoming infected. Healthy persons as well as those with communicable disease may spread germs.

Germs from the body are carried in discharges from the nose, throat, bladder, bowels, skin eruptions, and blood. These germ-laden discharges may be transferred to others through water, milk, or other foods, certain insects, unclean hands, common drinking cups, towels, or handkerchiefs. They are also transferred directly from nose or throat spray by coughing, sneezing, and breathing.

Isolation is a method used to prevent a disease from spreading. With common communicable diseases, the patient himself is isolated. Sometimes people who have been exposed are isolated long enough to make sure they have not caught the disease. Sometimes whole households are isolated. The isolation period ends after a stated length of time decided by the state board of health or when the doctor decides that the patient is no longer spreading the germs of the disease.

You have the responsibility of protecting others at all times from communicable diseases. Be considerate of others by covering every cough and sneeze with a clean handkerchief. Avoid spraying others while talking. Never breathe into another person's face.

Public Health

Health is not confined to one person, or a community, or a state, or a nation. It is the concern of the whole world.

Your local health department may have either a county or *Local health* city organization with the work arranged in divisions. You *departments* will find that your department gives the citizens many services. If there are public health nurses, they serve you by bringing nursing aid to the sick in their homes. The patient pays a small fee when possible. The public health nurses also offer courses in the care of the sick.

Every citizen should know and obey the rules that protect community health. However, good health is only half protected if there is constant danger of accidents. Every citizen also has the responsibility to know and obey all the safety laws.

A state health department sets up rules based on the health *State health* laws passed by the state legislature. The department is made *departments* up of: a board of health, sometimes called a public health council; a state health officer, often called a commissioner; a number of divisions or bureaus. Your state health depart-

347

ment offers help in such things as care of infants and children, school hygiene, care and control of communicable and other diseases, sanitation, public health education, the supply of pure water, milk, and food. This department is concerned with the whole state and carries on its work mainly through local departments.

Federal In the Constitution of the United States provision is made *health* for the federal government to help carry out measures that *service* protect public health. The main health agency of the federal government is the United States Public Health Service. Some of the duties of this agency are: to prevent the bringing of disease from other countries; to prevent the spread of disease between states in this country; to study the cause and prevention of diseases dangerous to public health; to supervise the purity of products in interstate commerce; to assist state and local health departments.

The United States Public Health Service has research laboratories and quarantine stations at all airports and seaports handling foreign travel and commerce.

World The World Health Organization is a specialized agency of *health* the United Nations. Its objective as stated in its constitution is "the attainment by all peoples of the highest possible level of health."

CHAPTER 18

Homemaking

YOUR home may be one room, a small apartment, a large or small house, or a trailer. Whatever the size, a happy home is one in which there is warmth and kindness. The members of the family are interested in each others' experiences. They enjoy sharing their skills and abilities. Each person takes part in the household duties.

Your home and family need you to give them just those qualities you are learning through your Girl Scout Promise and Laws. Small things such as being courteous to others, kind and gay with younger children, doing small jobs without being told, doing regular tasks cheerfully, learning how to use your money wisely are all part of homemaking.

Homemaking is an art, a profession, and a business for every girl and woman. Hostesses in restaurants, on airplanes, and in children's homes need to know homemaking skills. Dietitians in hospitals, schools, and camps enjoy working with foods. Fashion designers and store buyers must be well groomed and know about clothing. Manufacturers of home furnishings hire home economists to test and demonstrate their wares.

Whatever you do and wherever you go, you will always be making a home for yourself, your family, and friends. Art and science have given us certain tools, skills, and devices which will prepare you to run your home happily and well.

349

Homemaker

Have you ever stopped to think of all the things the home-maker in your family does? There is the marketing and the meals to prepare, repairs to make, cleaning to do, washing and ironing, the care of small children, and many other things. Who takes care of the plants, makes the beds, sets the table, and washes the dishes? How are birthdays and holidays celebrated? Does the homemaker do any special things to prepare for these days?

A gay touch Window boxes or plants on the window sills make a room cheerful. Select the kinds of plants that like the exposure of your windows. Some prefer north light, like the African violet (Saintpaulia); others need plenty of sun, like the geranium; some must be kept warm, like the cacti; other hardy plants, such as the snake plant (Sanseveria) are not so fussy. On page 240 you will find suggestions for arranging and caring for your houseplants.

Centerpieces A centerpiece gives a festive air to any meal. It may be a colored cloth or mirror glass with pottery or glass animals arranged on it. Or you may like a potted plant. Fall leaves, interesting pieces of wood, and small evergreen branches are effective. A basket or dish with fruit and vegetables makes a pleasant change. Cut flowers are good. Various kinds of ever-lasting flowers, as well as artificial ones, can be used.

Dishwashing Dishwashing takes place in every home. It can be fun if you organize it well. Use plenty of hot water with a detergent. The picture on the following page gives you some pointers.

scraping   rinsing   washing

scalding   draining   cleaning sink

Cook

Cooking is both a science and an art. It can also be a creative experience. Everyone likes to eat, whether indoors or out, so a good cook is always popular.

Recipes and cookbooks

Recipe is the term used in homemaking to describe the directions you follow in preparing foods. Your mother knows many recipes. She can share with you her own and those passed on to her by her own mother and grandmother. You can also find recipes in magazines, such as *The American Girl*. It is fun to exchange them with your pen friends in this and other countries.

Cookbooks are collections of recipes. Keep your favorite, self-tested recipes in a file or cookbook. You will find directions for making a notebook on page 120. Be sure you include some outdoor dishes too. You will find some recipes for these in Chapter 14. Many of them can be cooked indoors as well.

Measures Every cookbook contains a list of standard measures. They
and are very useful in cooking. There are times, for example,
equivalents when you will need to know how many tablespoons there
are in a cup in order to increase a recipe to serve your troop.

3 teaspoons (t) in a tablespoon (T)

16 T in a cup (C)

2 C in a pint (pt.)

4 C in a quart (qt.)

16 C in a gallon (gal.)

You will also want to know some of the equivalents:

3 T cocoa plus ½ T fat equals 1 ounce (sq.) chocolate

1 C uncooked rice equals 3 cups cooked rice

2 T butter or margarine equals 1 ounce

2 C butter equals 1 pound

2 C sugar equals 1 pound

4 C all purpose (wheat) flour equals 1 pound

On page 280 you will find some emergency measurements
to use when cooking out-of-doors.

Cooking tips   1. A piece of waxed paper may be used to line a baking
pan instead of greasing the pan. Waxed paper baking cups
are handy for muffins and cup cakes.

2. Pour cereals slowly into salted, boiling water. Keep the
water boiling to prevent lumps.

3. When you dice apples for a salad, leave on the peel-
ings. They add color.

4. To cut butter into smooth squares, dip your knife into
hot water before cutting each square or put wax paper over
knife.

5. Pour boiling water over tomatoes to make the skin
slip off easily.

6. Use a paper bag to flour or meal chicken or fish. Mix
the flour or meal with salt and pepper in a bag and then add

352

the cut-up chicken or fish. Close the top of the bag and shake gently.

7. Use flour, cornstarch, eggs, rice water, or potato water to thicken sauces or gravies.

8. Rinse egg or milk dishes in cold water before washing. Rinse sugar dishes in hot water.

9. Cut onions under cold running water to prevent tears from coming to your eyes.

10. Cook strong-flavored vegetables, such as cabbage, onions, and turnips, without a cover on the pot. This allows the odor to escape slowly. Or, place a piece of white bread on top of the water to absorb the odor.

11. Use a bread board and spatula for slicing, chopping, or kneading.

12. Use a warm spatula to frost a cake. Dip the spatula into warm water while spreading the frosting.

13. Wash your utensils as you go along so that no large pile is waiting for you at the end. Use as few utensils as possible.

14. Use a kaper chart so that all may share in the work and fun.

A good cook is familiar with the different ways of cooking food. Can you cook something by each of these methods? *Ways of cooking*

 *Boiling* means cooking in water that has reached the boiling point.

Steaming means using a small amount of water in a tightly covered boiler or placing food in the top of a double boiler while water boils in the lower pot.

Baking or roasting means cooking in an oven.

Frying means cooking in fat. There are two kinds of frying —one known as sautéing, or pan-broiling, in a small amount

of fat; and the other deep-fat frying, or French-frying, which requires enough fat to cover all the food.

Broiling means cooking by direct heat—as over the live coals of an outdoor fire or under the heating unit of a stove.

You will discover that some foreign words are used in everyday cooking. Do you know the meaning and origin of words such as sauté, barbecue, casserole, menu, meringue, and soufflé?

Planning pointers   Plan your meals for eye appeal as well as taste appeal. Use a variety of food colors instead of all green, for instance, such as peas and spinach or all white like potatoes and onions. Avoid clashing colors, such as beets and carrots on a purple plate. Different textures in food also lend variety. Many magazines carry pictures of meals that are well balanced and attractively served.

Lunches that travel   There are many times when you must carry your meal with you—a nosebag for a hike, a box supper for a social, or a lunch for school. Choose foods that will make your whole day's meals well balanced. (See the seven basic foods on page 375.)

Your lunch should be appetizing and nourishing. A well-balanced school or picnic lunch includes at least one thing chosen from each of the following:

Bread: brown, date, graham, nut, oatmeal, raisin, rye, enriched white, or whole wheat.

Butter or butter substitute: at least one serving in each sandwich.

Sandwich fillings: chopped eggs; peanut butter or other nuts ground to paste; meat, sliced or chopped; jelly or marmalade; dried fruit paste made of chopped dates, figs, or raisins; fish. Each sandwich should be wrapped separately in waxed paper or aluminum foil.

Fruit: apples, grapes, oranges, peaches, pears, plums, bananas, tomatoes. Stewed fruit in small jars with tight-fitting covers may be carried safely.

Sweets: cookies, gingerbread, cake, candy, dried fruit.

Beverage: milk, a hot drink, or fruit juice. These may be carried in a thermos bottle or tightly covered container.

Pack a lunch neatly with the heaviest articles at the bottom. Include two napkins—one to be used as a tablecloth.

Hospitality

Hospitality is the art of being both a good hostess and a good guest. You can use it every day and every place you go in many different situations. The more you practice it the easier it will become. You play as many roles as an actress on the stage or screen. You must know your lines and cues. There are some basic principles and customs to help you.

Good manners are ways of thinking and acting which show *Manners* that you are interested in the happiness and well-being of *every day* others. They are your ticket to popularity.

What is your score on these everyday manners?

355

Do you listen carefully to what other people are saying? Do you avoid interrupting a conversation?

Are you prompt when you have a date? Do you answer all mail quickly, too?

Are your phone calls short so that others may have their turn?

Do you share the radio and television time at home?

Do you refrain from pushing and shoving even when in a hurry?

Do you show respect for older persons by small courtesies, such as rising when they enter a room, seating them comfortably, opening doors for them to go through first?

Do you behave as nicely to your family as you do to your best friends?

Do you contradict people and pretend to know all the answers?

Do you expect people to wait on you? Do you expect your family to change their plans to fit your own?

How does the bathroom look after you use it?

Do you giggle and whisper at the movies?

Table manners Table manners differ around the world. Here in the United States we have chosen certain rules to guide us. Generally, good table manners are those that draw the least attention to you when you are eating. They include chewing the food with the mouth closed, taking only small portions of food on your fork or from the side of your spoon, chewing and swallowing quietly. They also include sitting straight at the table and carrying on, or helping to carry on, cheerful, pleasant conversation.

In addition, there are specific things which are often done. Water is sipped from a glass, care being taken not to drink too rapidly. Bread is broken and buttered in small pieces. A spoon is never left in the cup but is placed on the saucer. Do not talk with your knife, fork, or spoon waving in the air. The proper place for your knife and fork when not in use is on your plate.

At the close of the meal, the napkin may be partly folded, if not to be used again, or neatly folded and placed at the side of the dessert plate. It should never be left in a heap.

It is good manners to appreciate the food and, if you wish to do so, to accept a second helping and to speak about some particularly good dish.

Unless urged to do otherwise by your hostess, always wait to start eating until she has begun.

Serving a meal

Serve from the side which is most convenient for those being served. Any dish from which a person serves herself should be passed to the left.

Remove dishes from the side which is most convenient. Remove them in this order: (1) serving dishes; (2) soiled china, silver, glassware; (3) clean china, silver, glassware; (4) salt and pepper shakers; (5) crumbs, if necessary, before dessert is served.

There are no hard and fast rules for table setting and serving. Local customs, the number of dishes you have, and common sense must help you decide what to do. The more simply and easily you can entertain, the more fun for the guest, your family, and yourself.

Introduction

1. Introduce the younger person to the older or more distinguished person. For example: "Mr. Brown, this is Esther Smith, a Girl Scout in my troop," or "Mother, this is John Doe. He is in my class and a member of the debating team."

2. Introduce the man to the woman, except when age and distinction indicate that it would show deference to the eld-

357

erly man to introduce a young person to him. For example: "Mrs. Brown, may I present (or introduce) Mr. Adams?" or "Mr. Brown, I would like you to know Esther Smith."

Young people are more informal with one another. However, it is wise to always use first and last names. Add a bit of information about your friends when you introduce them. It will make it easier for them to start a conversation. For instance: "Esther Smith, this is Frank Jones who has just moved to our part of town. Frank, Esther likes camping as much as you do."

Say the name clearly, and when you are being introduced, listen carefully. Make it a point to look directly at the person to whom you are being introduced. Learn to connect the name with the face so that you will remember both when you meet the person again.

It is usual to say "How do you do" when you are introduced. Many people shake hands, others bow slightly, or smile. All are signs of friendliness. The person to whom the introduction is being made decides whether to shake hands or not, and the one being introduced follows the example.

If you are visiting friends and by some oversight have not been introduced to all present, you may speak to them and introduce yourself.

Invitations Invitations are usually answered by using the same form in which the invitation is given. If it is formal, send a formal reply. If it is informal, answer informally. Always answer promptly. It is only courtesy to your hostess to let her know as soon as you can whether to expect you or not.

When you telephone an invitation, give your name and make the date and time very clear. It is far more upsetting to the guest if she makes a mistake in time or place than it is to the hostess.

358

It is as important for you to be a thoughtful guest as it is to be a thoughtful hostess. Remember these things: *Thoughtful guests*

1. Answer invitations promptly.
2. Arrive on time.
3. Enter cheerfully into the plans your hostess has made.
4. Be considerate to all members of the household.
5. Thank your hostess or write a thank-you note afterward.
6. Sometimes you will want to take a small gift to your hostess or send it to her afterward.
7. When your troop or patrol accepts an invitation every member should be a really considerate guest. One girl who forgets spoils everyone's fun.

A wise person builds up friendliness by following the customs of the town in which she lives or is visiting. *Other social customs*

Among the customs that are common in many communities are: gestures of friendliness toward a new neighbor—a short call, an offer of a hot dish for the first meal in the new home, an offer to take care of the children while the unpacking is going on. Or an invitation to attend religious service if she is a stranger in the community.

When neighbors or friends are ill, send them flowers, a book, a delicate dessert, or fruit. When it is not possible to do any of these things, a call, a note, or a card is just as happily received. It is the thought that is important. Think how you would feel as a newcomer or patient. Then do what you would wish someone to do for you.

Seamstress

The girl who can sew can make many lovely and practical things for herself and others. You will need needles in a book, thimble, thread, pins, scissors, darning cotton, tape

359

measure, and so forth. All your sewing articles can be arranged in a box you have decorated or a basket you have woven. You will find help on different kinds of prints on page 130 and weaving on page 131.

Basic
stitches
Every seamstress uses the following basic sewing stitches:

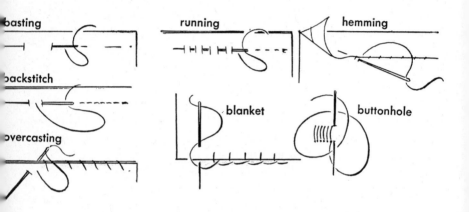

Seams There are a variety of seams used in sewing. The three most commonly used are the plain, the French, and the flat fell.

Darning and Can you weave? Darning and weaving are very much alike.
patching It is handy to be able to put on a good patch. It is smart to be thrifty and it helps the family budget.

Housekeeper

Remember when you were Brownie age and used to say, "Let's play house!" It was lots of fun, wasn't it? Now that you are older you can really become a housekeeper.

Every Girl Scout has some housekeeping duties and should budget her time so that she can do these quickly and well. *Housekeeping duties*

With your mother make a list of all your duties around the house. Then schedule your time so that you set aside certain hours in the day for these duties. Try the schedule given as a sample.

KIND OF WORK	TIME FOR	
	Daily Tasks	*Weekly Tasks*
Meals (buying, cooking, serving, washing dishes)		
Laundry (washing, ironing, sorting clothes)		
Care of Clothing (mending, pressing, remodeling)		
Home Care (dusting, sweeping, making beds)		
Children (helping in any way with younger members of the family)		

Watch the number of steps you take when washing dishes, making beds, cleaning, or any other duty. See if you can rearrange your equipment or make better plans so that you can *Comfort and efficiency*

House-Cleaning Equipment

1. dustpan and brush
2. toilet brush
3. radiator brush
4. whisk broom
5. dusting cloth
6. broom
7. vacuum cleaner
8. dry mop
9. scrub brush
10. pail

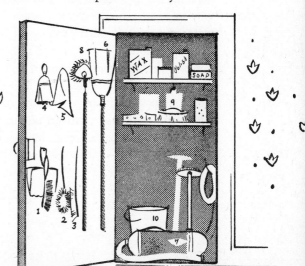

take fewer steps. Try to improve your skill at doing things so that you can reduce the amount of time you spend on them.

If you keep your equipment clean, know how to use it efficiently, store it conveniently, and use your head, you will have a labor-saving idea in operation. If you do not have

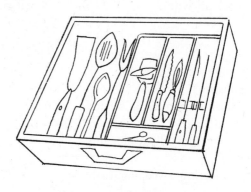

enough storage space make a cupboard from an orange crate. Cover it with gay chintz. Take a look at your closet or the kitchen drawers. Well-arranged ones help you do things more easily.

Keeping the house clean Cleanliness in your home is of great importance. The best way to keep a house clean is with soap or other detergent, water, sunshine, fresh air, plenty of "elbow grease," and family cooperation.

Keep the refrigerator neat. Try to have certain types of food always in the same place. Put things away in as small dishes as possible. Cover as many of the dishes as you can. Clean the refrigerator at least once a week with warm water to which a little baking soda has been added. Defrost when necessary.

The prompt removal of stains or spots not only makes your *Stain* clothes look better but saves expense for dry cleaning. *removal*

Most stains are removed by running cold water through them and then washing in warm or hot soapy water. There are exceptions to this rule. To remove a fruit stain, pour boiling water from a height through the fabric. Rub paint spot with turpentine. Iron rust is removed with lemon juice and boiling water. Always remove spots before pressing a garment.

Carbon tetrachloride is a nonflammable cleaning fluid. Use it in a well-ventilated room. Care must be taken to keep the chemical off your skin. Never use gasoline or benzine for cleaning. They are flammable and explosive.

Dry cleaning at home, except for occasional spots, is not advisable. It is expensive to send your clothes to the cleaners often so try to select clothing that you can launder yourself.

Foods

Food is an interesting subject and vital to our existence. How many foods of other countries have you eaten? Many favorite American dishes have been brought to us from far-away lands. The same is true of the vegetables and fruits we eat.

Milk is the most nearly perfect food. One quart should be *Milk* included in your diet every day. You do not have to drink it all. You may get a part of it in creamed soups, breads, cream-filled pastries, puddings, and ice cream.

In order to safeguard the milk supply, your state has set up certain standards of cleanliness under which dairies operate. The cows, barns, equipment, and attendants must all pass rigid sanitary and health inspection. No milk is absolutely safe until it has been treated to destroy any harmful bacteria. 363

Dried, concentrated, evaporated, or condensed milk may be used. It is economical and convenient to use when you camp.

HOME PASTEURIZATION. If there is any doubt about the milk, follow these steps.

1. Place the bottle of milk with a punctured cap in a boiler or pail on a false bottom. Insert a dairy thermometer through the hole in the cap.

2. Place water in the boiler until it is as high on the outside of the bottle as the milk is on the inside.

3. Boil the water until the thermometer reads 165 degrees Fahrenheit.

4. Cool quickly and store the milk at 50 degrees Fahrenheit until ready to use.

Buying food The choice of the store or stores where you trade is important. Look for honesty, courteous service, nearness, cleanliness, economy, and a good variety of products for sale.

When buying food you must consider grades, sizes, brands, and varieties. United States food and drug laws set standards regarding labeling, quality, and purity of foods.

CANNED AND PACKAGED GOODS. Sometimes the difference in price between two things that look about the same may have to do with size of container and quality of goods.

It is necessary to know how many servings you can get from different size cans when you plan your family or camp shopping list: No. 1 serves 2 or 3; No. 2 serves 4; No. 2½ serves 6; No. 3 serves 8; No. 10 serves 30.

Read the labels on food containers carefully. They describe the contents in detail. They may also indicate the grade and quality.

MIXES. A good cook knows what to mix together to get good results. She uses mixes when they will save time, expense, or work. You can buy many ready-made mixes or make your own for cocoa, biscuits, and so forth. Read the package label to be sure a purchased mix doesn't require almost as many added ingredients as the whole recipe. Mixes are useful on cook-outs, too.

At certain times of the year we often would like foods that *Conservation* are out of season. We can have them whenever we wish if we preserve them when the crop is plentiful. Canning and freezing foods in season are a saving on the food budget if you grow the food or have it easily and cheaply available. The ways to can and freeze foods are always being improved. Write your state college of agriculture and home economics to find out what is recommended in your part of the country.

You can make jams and jellies too. You'll find recipes for these in cookbooks and government bulletins. Some foods are conserved by drying or pickling, and others, such as beans, potatoes, and apples, by putting in cold storage.

Handywoman

A handy person is one who can do many useful jobs. She needs to have on hand the proper tools, know how to use them, and how to take care of them. Your father can help you with this badge.

Keep your tools in a special place such as a closet, basket, *Tools for* or boxes. *home use*

An unused doorway, a corner cupboard, or a closet may be converted into attractive bookcases. Extra space may be obtained by removing doors or adding shelves. A packing box can be converted into a needed closet, and orange crates and large cheese boxes made into cupboards. A little paint can do wonders.

365

Make a list of the things that you can do in your own bed-room to make it more attractive, to give you more space, and to keep it neat. Does the furniture need repairing or refinishing? Would an extra shelf or a picture brighten the room? Are your screens in good condition? Have you any toys that

Tools for Home Use

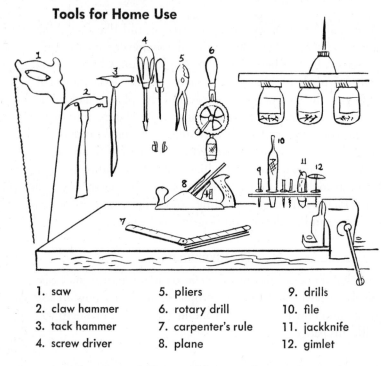

1. saw	5. pliers	9. drills
2. claw hammer	6. rotary drill	10. file
3. tack hammer	7. carpenter's rule	11. jackknife
4. screw driver	8. plane	12. gimlet

you no longer use? You could repair them and give them to a nursery school. This will give you more space and make others happy.

Once you start thinking about fixing up your room many good ideas will come to you. Ask your father or brothers to help. The arts and crafts chapter will give you specific information on interior decoration, textile design, and archi-tecture.

It takes skill to wrap packages neatly and securely. Here *Wrapping* are the steps: *packages*

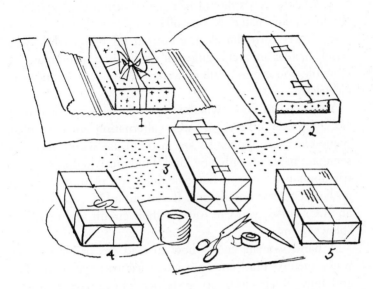

Become familiar with the mailing regulations of your post office. It will save you time, energy, and money.

Can you shut off the water, gas, and electricity in your house? *Water, gas,* Ask your father to show you the correct method. Often *and* serious damage can be avoided by a turn of the wrist, but few *electricity* people know what to do in case of leaking or broken pipes, a flood, or any other emergency. It is important to know the right use of gas and electricity for safety and economy. Learn how to use the gas stoves or heaters in your home.

PLAY SAFE. (See page 327 for other home safety hints.)
1. Always strike the match before turning on the gas.
2. Never look for a leak in the gas supply with a lighted match.

3. Never change a fuse while the electric current is on or use a substitute in place of a real fuse.

4. Electric cords should be repaired or replaced as soon as the insulation materials wear off.

5. Never turn the electric current off or on while your hands or feet are wet, while you are holding metal material, or while you are in a tub of water. Water is a conductor of electricity.

You need to know whether your electric current is on a D.C. (direct current) or A.C. (alternating current) plan. Some electrical appliances are made to use with either, but some are made for only one kind. Find out whether the electric appliances in your home or those you plan to buy work on both currents or only one. If you put a D.C. appliance on an A.C. outlet, you can cause a short circuit and usually it "blows" a fuse.

A handywoman knows how to read gas or electric and water meters. Find out how much gas costs per cubic foot and how much electricity costs per kilowatt hour in your community. Make a ruled card showing the date of each month when the meters are read, write down your own readings, and tack the card up near the meters. You can save the family budget by remembering to turn off lights and faucets when they are not needed and by using gas and water thriftily.

Many of your outdoor skills, such as making Buddy burners, building fires, and purifying water are useful in household emergencies.

Dressmaker

You may like dressmaking because you enjoy sewing or you like the results or you are thrifty, or for all three reasons. You may sew your clothes by hand or machine. Take time and work carefully. Then when you model the finished article you will win smiles of admiration from your friends.

The following are terms used in dressmaking: *Dressmaking terms*

"Selvage" means the closely woven threads at each side of the material.

"Straight of goods" means the threads that run the length of the material and are parallel to the selvage. This can also be called lengthwise grain.

"Crosswise grain" means the threads that run across the width of the material.

When you buy clothes, you consider line, design, and color. *Pattern and material* The same points apply to selecting a pattern. Choose one in which the lines flatter your figure. Check your own measurements against the standard measurements which are given on the pattern envelope and buy the correct pattern size.

Look over the list of fabrics recommended for your pattern on the envelope. Some patterns are best for cotton and others for wool. Check to see whether the material is guaranteed to be preshrunk. Your own color scheme of eyes, hair, and skin make it possible for you to wear certain colors better than others. Buy your material in a color that is most becoming to you.

In addition to your pattern, material, and notions, you will *Equipment* also need to have a full-length mirror, ironing board and iron, pin cushion, straight pins, dressmaker shears, tape measure, yardstick, and your sewing box.

Before you cut your pattern check the following points:

1. Have you studied the pattern work sheet? Do you understand the markings on pattern pieces?

369

2. Have you pinned together the paper pattern and tried it on? Have you made all the necessary adjustments?

3. Have you prepared your material for cutting?

4. Have you placed your fabric on the pattern according to the work sheet?

When all these points have been checked, you are ready to cut out the pattern. If possible, use dressmaker shears. Snip the notches away from the edge of the pattern with small scissors. Make tailor tacks on all marking lines and circles. Fold up the pattern pieces neatly so that you can use the pattern again.

You will find dressmaking tips, patterns, and teen-age styles featured in many magazines such as *The American Girl*.

Good Grooming

Good grooming is not something which is achieved by wishing. It is not just one thing either. It is a combination of many things, chief among them being your own personal health habits. How much exercise do you take daily? Do you eat the proper foods? How many hours of sleep do you get? And how about your personal cleanliness and the care of such articles as your comb, brush, towels, washcloth, closets, and bureau drawers?

Your posture is one expression of yourself. Alert, upright *Posture* posture expresses health and joy. Have you noticed how differently the same dress can look on two different girls? The difference may be a reflection of their posture.

In standing and walking, try to feel a sense of balance and poise. Distribute your weight evenly on your feet, stand tall and hold your head erect. It is a common tendency to walk with one's head slouched forward. If you do this it throws your carriage off balance. In sitting, your balance comes from your hips when you are leaning forward very slightly. This keeps your back straight and prevents slumping.

Is your hair clean and shiny? Do you like your hair style *Appearance* or would you like to try a different one? Do you know how to give yourself a manicure to keep your cuticles soft and your nails trim? Do you use make-up and, if you do, are you sure that you are using it to improve your appearance? There are many tricks to making up. What care do you give your complexion? Do you know what type of skin you have? Ask specialists to visit your troop and help you learn more about these things. Many magazine articles and books tell you how to make the most of your appearance.

371

Clothes　Your clothing can tell friends and strangers a lot about you. They put a label on you marked "careless" when they are mussy, soiled, or badly fitted. You will feel proud and look well when your clothes are right.

When you want to be well groomed, you keep your clothes clean. Wash and iron them as soon as necessary. Sew on loosened buttons and snaps, repair hems and mend rips or tears before wearing the dress again. You sew the badges on your uniform neatly and securely. Your clothes will not become mussy if you arrange your bureau drawer and closet space neatly. Why not try your hand at making some of your own clothes and accessories?

Clothing

Who is the best-dressed girl in town? She is the girl whose clothes suit her style, coloring, and pocketbook, and who looks well in them because she is physically fit, poised, and sure of herself. This confidence comes from the knowledge that she has chosen her clothes well and gives them good care.

Selecting　Combinations such as skirts and blouses, sweaters and jackets
clothes　lend variety to any wardrobe. In buying clothes make a habit of looking at the labels. Is the material preshrunk? Are the colors fast? Do the dresses and skirts have ample hems and seams that will allow you to grow a bit? Choose fabrics that are appropriate for the season and for the purpose for which you plan to use them. Whenever possible select clothes which you can launder easily.

Caring for　SHOES AND STOCKINGS. Shoe trees or crumpled paper
clothes　should be put in shoes as soon as they are removed. This is doubly important when they are wet. Shoes should be polished often to keep the leather in good condition. Stockings
372　or socks should be rinsed out after each wearing. Changing

hose from one foot to the other prevents wear in one place. It is a thrifty idea to buy two or three pairs exactly alike. If one in each pair wears out, you still have a good pair left.

UNDERWEAR. These should be washed out after each wearing because perspiration and soil destroy the material.

DRESSES. After taking off a dress, hang it on a coat hanger, air thoroughly, and press if necessary. When it is put on the hanger, straighten the collar and sleeves, and hang it straight so that it keeps its shape. Examine the dress for rips and loose buttons and repair them before you wear the dress again.

Knitted wool suits, dresses, and sweaters should not be hung on a hanger but carefully aired, patted back into shape, and laid in a drawer or on a shelf.

COATS. A coat should be brushed and hung up when removed. It is our most expensive item of clothing and the one most often left in a heap by the girl who is careless.

HATS. These should be placed on stands to protect the brim and trimmings. Round pasteboard boxes, such as oatmeal boxes, covered with hand-decorated paper, make excellent stands.

GLOVES. Pull your gloves back into shape when you take them off. Washable gloves should be washed on the hands and dried on a glove form or pulled into shape while still damp.

RUBBERS AND RAINCOATS. These protect your clothes as well as yourself.

Washing clothes

It is easier to wash a lot of clothes that are lightly soiled than a few that are badly soiled. If garments are washed or cleaned often, the wear on the fabric is less and the garments last longer. Use warm water and a mild soap or other detergent to remove ordinary dirt. Wash carefully, rinse thoroughly, and shake into proper shape before hanging to dry. When you dampen them fold the clothes carefully to keep them as smooth as possible. They will be easier to iron. Woolens or articles that stretch out of shape easily should be squeezed gently to remove water, pulled into shape, and wrapped in bath towels to absorb moisture. Using a flat surface, place the article on a dry towel, pinning it in shape. Let it dry in this position. Spots and stains should be removed before washing.

Nutrition

It is not enough to be able to prepare and serve a meal well. You must also know something about the nutritional needs of your family and yourself. Do you know the meaning of proteins, carbohydrates, fats, and vitamins?

The seven basic foods Over the years, scientists have made studies to determine what foods are necessary to insure a person's well-being. Today we have the benefit of their knowledge in planning our menus. Use the seven basic food groups in this chart in choosing each day's food.

Menus A menu is all the courses of food used to make up a meal. It is different from a recipe which simply means the different foods that are used to make up one particular dish such as custard or pancakes. Courses are commonly grouped together in the following fashion: appetizer, main course, salad, dessert, beverage. They are not always eaten or served in this order.

374   When you make your own menu be sure to balance the

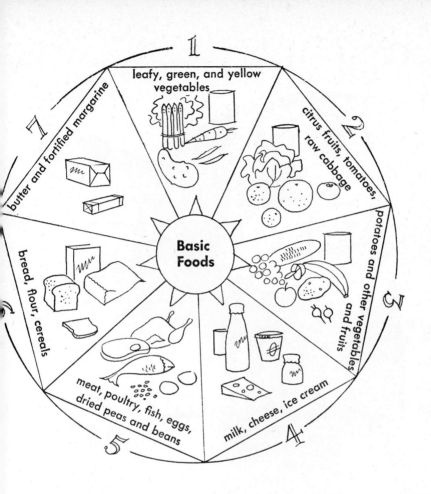

1
leafy, green, and yellow vegetables

2
citrus fruits, tomatoes, raw cabbage

3
potatoes and other vegetables, and fruits

4
milk, cheese, ice cream

5
meat, poultry, fish, eggs, dried peas and beans

bread, flour, cereals

7
butter and fortified margarine

Basic Foods

amounts with the variety of food served. Choose some foods each day from each of the seven basic food groups. Do not repeat flavors or color in the same meal, for instance, pineapple juice, pineapple salad, and pineapple ice cream. Try to have different textures. Combine soft foods, such as mashed potatoes or scrambled eggs, with something crisp and chewy, such as red cabbage, slaw, radishes, or fried foods.

375

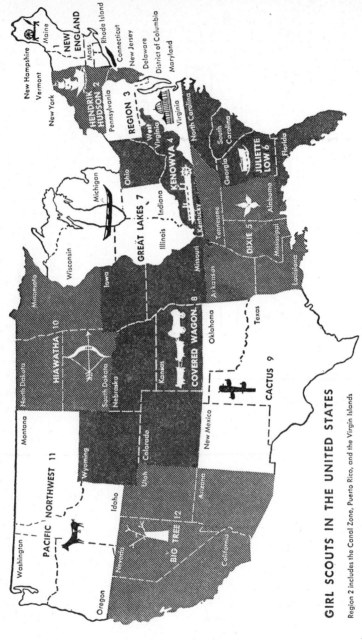

GIRL SCOUTS IN THE UNITED STATES

Region 2 includes the Canal Zone, Puerto Rico, and the Virgin Islands

Region 11 includes Alaska

Region 12 includes Hawaii and Guam

PART VI

Proficiency Badge
Activities

CHAPTER 19   *Adventuring in the Arts*

CHAPTER 20   *Citizens Here and Abroad*

CHAPTER 21   *Fun and Exploration in the Out-of-Doors*

CHAPTER 22   *You and Your Home*

CHAPTER **19**

Adventuring in the Arts

Arts and Crafts

Architecture
Basketry
Bookbinding
Dabbler
Drawing and Paint-
ing

Glass
Interior Decoration
Leather
Metal
Needlecraft
Photography

Pottery
Prints
Textile Design
Weaving
Wood

Literature and Dramatics

Bibliophile
Dramatic Apprecia-
tion
Journalist

Magic Carpet
Play Producer
Player
Puppeteer

Reader
Storyteller
Troop Dramatics
Writer

Music and Dancing

Dancer
Folk Dancer

Group Musician
Minstrel

Music Appreciation
Musician

ARTS AND CRAFTS

As you do a badge in arts and crafts, read Chapter 8.

The following badge from literature and dramatics may be applied toward an arts and crafts major in the First Class rank:
Puppeteer.

Dabbler To earn this badge, do eight of these activities.

1. Take colored chalk and see how many different ways you can use it.

2. Make a drawing or painting of something such as a story you like, a song you like, a place you have been.

3. Make a pinch pot out of clay.

4. Make a hike stick, simple toy, whistle, cook spoon, or darning egg out of wood.

5. Make a candle holder, corn popper, cookie cutter, or imaginative animal out of tin.

6. Take bunches of grass, pine needles, or like material and make a sit-upon by coiling and sewing with raffia or long grass.

7. Learn something about how the American Indian and other folk arts have influenced arts and crafts of today.

8. Cut a leaf pattern or other design into a piece of potato, linoleum, wooden block, or stencil. Print your design on a smock or apron.

9. Make hand puppets of characters from favorite stories and have each puppet act.

10. Make an imaginative fish or animal form from wire.

11. Make a peepshow or a diorama.

Drawing and Painting To earn this badge, do nine of these activities including the three that have a star.

1. Explore the quality of color by doing the following:

    a. Mix any two poster or tempera colors and see what you get. Add a third color and see what you get.

    b. Take a single color and see how much you can change it by adding black, white, or another color.

*2. There are many different ways of applying color. Try all of these:

    a. Dip your drawing paper into water. Dab brushfuls of poster paint on the wet sheet. Tilt the paper and let colors blend. Name three new colors you were able to make this way.

    b. Apply thick colors to your paper. With a hairpin, pencil, or other instrument, scratch a design into it.

380

     c. Put a thin wash of color on paper. When dry, take a brush and dot over it.

  3. Make a finger painting.

 *4. Color expresses moods and feelings. Take any of the following topics and express your feelings about them through the colors you choose: rain, summertime, bridges, a storm, a circus, wind, the hospital, your town.

 *5. Paint two pictures of activities or things you see around you: flowers in the rain, your pets playing, places you have been, your friends.

  6. Know how to do four of the following: care for and store your brushes and paintings; mix powdered poster paint in the amounts you need; make paste; "fix" a charcoal or pencil drawing; make your own fingerpaint mix.

  7. Visit a museum, art gallery, studio, or home, to see drawings and paintings. Choose one of the artists whose work you like and tell about his or her ideas on art, why he paints the way he does. If you are not near museums or studios, look for reproductions of paintings in magazines.

  8. Look through magazines and newspapers for different kinds of lettering. Clip them and use various letters to make new arrangements. Choose the one you like best and make a poster.

  9. Arrange on paper some natural materials. Paste them in a combination that is most interesting to you.

  10. Make a mask of papier-mâché. Color, shellac, and put a headdress on it. Use in your dramatic activities.

  11. Make an original soft pencil, crayon, charcoal, or colored chalk drawing.

To earn this badge, do ten of these activities including the three that have a star.

Bookbinding

 *1. Make one section of a book—fold the paper, cut and sew it into a paper cover.

 *2. Make some hand-decorated end papers, using any method desired: blockprinting, marbling, finger painting, stenciling.

 *3. Know the meaning of the following and help make an exhibit: first edition, volume, manuscript, autographed copy, bookplate, end paper, signature, parchment, vellum, sewing in, deckle edge, and headbands.

4. Know in what countries bookbinding began and name two kinds of material used before paper.

5. Make a simple design you would use to tool a leather book cover.

6. Design and make a bookplate.

7. Make a hand-carved book cover of wood using your own design.

8. Bind a series of magazines or a collection of sheet music.

9. Make a simple portfolio or bind envelopes between strong covers to make a file.

10. Visit a bindery, and see how books are bound by machinery.

11. Visit the workshop of a professional bookbinder.

12. Visit public libraries, museums, private homes, to see examples of well-bound books. Be able to distinguish hand-bound from machine-bound books.

13. Know the names of two American book publishers and the kind of books they publish.

14. Know the difference between a case-bound and a regular bound book.

15. Visit the mending department of your public library to see how books are preserved and repaired. Help do this for your school, church, or synagogue.

Wood To earn this badge, do seven of these activities including the three that have a star.

1. Design and make of wood something that will be useful to you.

*2. Make some article of wood for the comfort of your animal friends.

3. Gather pieces of driftwood, old roots, burls. Carve and complete the form they suggest to you. Make a table centerpiece or lamp base using some of these pieces.

4. Make a child's toy. Sandpaper and paint it.

*5. Demonstrate the correct and safe use of four of the following: chip carving knife, whittling knife, saw, ax, vise, chisel, oilstone, miter box, hammer, plane, sandpaper, screwdriver, T square.

*6. Carve and whittle a set of wooden buttons, belt buckle, pin, earrings, or letter opener.

7. Chip carve your own design on an article made of wood.

8. Carve in relief your own design on an article made of wood.

9. Apply your own design in gesso on some article made of wood.

10. Know the meaning of the terms veneer, stain, marquetry, grain, plywood.

11. Be able to identify five or more woods and know their uses. Know where they grow, what makes the grain, which are soft and which hard.

12. Visit a wood carver, a cooper, a cabinetmaker, a furniture factory, a box factory, lumberyard, or carpenter shop. Discuss what you see there.

13. Use a miter box to make a picture frame. Finish the wood by polishing or staining it.

To earn this badge, do ten of these activities including the two that have a star. *Glass*

1. Know how the work of Casper Wistar, William Henry Stiegel, John Frederick Amelung, and Deming Jarves affected the history of glass-making in this country.

2. Tell the meaning of at least five of the following; pontil mark, annealing, cutting, etching, engraving, stem, foot, bowl, South Jersey-type, portrait flasks, prunts.

*3. Describe three of the following and tell their uses: cut glass, blown glass, pressed glass, stained glass, pattern glass, milk glass, crystal, plate glass, safety glass.

*4. Etch an original design or monogram on glass.

5. Make a small medallion of stained glass.

6. Measure and carefully cut a piece of glass for use in framing one of your paintings, for a window pane, or a terrarium.

7. Make a figurine by fusing glass tubing.

8. Design a table centerpiece in which you use glass, such as a bowl, mirror, or plaque.

9. Design and make a belt, earrings, or bracelet using glass beads. Tell how the Indians use glass beads.

10. Read a book on how to polish, clean, and care for glassware in your home.

11. Know how stained glass is made and find good examples of it in your community.

12. Select a tableware glass pattern you would like for your home and explain why.

13. Start a collection of pictures or examples of American glass.

14. Visit a glass factory or glass blower in your community. Learn how glass is made and colors produced.

Pottery To earn this badge, do eight of these activities including the three that have a star.

*1. Make a study of Indian, early American, and Pennsylvania-German pottery. Learn about Chinese porcelain and some of the well-known French and English wares.

*2. Model a figure or form in clay. If possible, glaze the piece and have it fired.

*3. Make a pinch pot and apply a design of your own to it, using one of the following: slip decoration, carving, incising, sgraffito, or an Indian design in tempera.

4. Know the meaning of the following terms and demonstrate the method used in one: glaze, potter's wheel, slip, embossing, pressed mold, sgraffito, underglaze, bisque firing, wedging.

5. Make a tile. Apply an abstract design using slip tracing. If possible, glaze it and have it fired.

6. Make a piece of pottery using coil method and finish it with an opaque glaze.

7. Make a wedging board, plaster bats, and some simple pottery tools. Explain their uses.

8. Build a simple outdoor kiln for troop, school, camp, or community use.

9. Know the process by which clay is fired and made permanent.

10. Know these different glazes: majolica, matt, luster. Learn one formula for a simple low fire glaze.

11. If there is a clay bed in your community, obtain some of the clay and prepare it for use. Know how to recondition clay.

12. Show with a lump of clay the difference between modeling and carving.

13. Learn about the different types of pottery such as china, porcelain, earthenware, stoneware. Know an appropriate use for each.

14. Visit a commercial pottery or potter's studio and observe methods used.

To earn this badge, do eight of these activities including the three that have a star.

Leather

1. Tell something about the history of leather carving in this country.

2. Visit a museum or private collection to see how leather was used in other times for household articles, musical instruments, weapons.

*3. Make a simple leather article such as an eyeglass case or small purse, and use your own pattern.

4. Make a simple leather article and tool it, using your own design. Finish the edges carefully.

5. Carve a piece of leather for a wallet, belt, portfolio, purse, book cover, or wastebasket.

*6. Demonstrate the uses of five of the following: tracer or scriber, skiving knife, leather modeler, spring and revolving punch, snap setter, leather needle, awl, drive punch, slit punch, leather stamps.

7. Clean, preserve, and polish several articles of leather for your family.

8. Tell the difference between tooling and nontooling leathers and name two animals from which each type is taken.

9. Make two different useful articles by braiding leather.

385

*10. Make a leather article using three of the following: thonging, tooling, stitching, lacing, carving or stamping, lining, snap or eyelet setting.

Needlecraft To earn this badge, do six of these activities including the three that have a star.

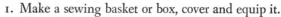

1. Make a sewing basket or box, cover and equip it.
*2. Darn a sock, and mend a hole in a sweater.
*3. Embroider two articles you can use in your home.
*4. Make a sampler that shows you know how to do the following stitches: outline, chain, satin, cross, buttonhole, and French knot.
5. Appliqué a simple design on an article for the home.
6. Work out an all-over design that can be used in needlepoint, crochet, or other type of handwork that uses small squares in building up the design.
7. Make a needlepoint chair seat, cushion, or sampler. Or, make a petit point picture and know in what country this originated.
8. Study pictures of early American appliqué quilt patterns. Pick ones you like and either copy them or make up patterns of your own. With your troop, make a quilt as a service project.
9. Create a design in two or three colors and make a border for a household article using the cross, hardanger, needle-weaving, darning, crewel, or Florentine stitch.
10. Look up and know the meaning of the following kinds of needlecraft: Florentine, Assisi, Jacobean, hedebo. Demonstrate how to do one of these and tell in what country it originated.
11. Choose a suitable pattern and make a knitted or crocheted article.
12. Learn something about the history of hooked rugs. Study pictures of originals, noting the patterns used. Design and make a hooked rug.
13. In cross-stitch, or other suitable stitch, make a picture map of some place familiar to you.

To earn this badge, do eight of these activities including the four that have a star. *Textile Design*

1. Look for good examples of textile design in home furnishings and clothing. Tell some of the standards by which you can judge good and bad design.

2. Tell something of the origin, history, and method of one of the following processes: batik, stick-tied, tied-and-dyed work. Make an article using one of these processes.

*3. Create a design for silk screen, stencil, or block prints. Print material using your design and one of these methods.

*4. Show how an abstract design may be repeated, and print an original over-all pattern on paper or cloth using potatoes, sea shells, or sticks.

5. Name at least two modern textile designers. Bring an example or pictures of their work to show your patrol or troop.

*6. Learn the methods of preparing and using natural and commercial dyes. Use one of these methods to dye or tint a piece of cloth.

7. Add five new words used in textile design to your vocabulary and know their meaning.

8. Visit the studio of a textile designer and watch him work.

9. Visit a textile mill or wholesale fabric house to find out how fabrics are processed, printed, and distributed to retailers.

*10. Make an article of clothing or household linen using your knowledge of textile design.

To earn this badge, do eight of these activities including the four that have a star. *Weaving*

*1. Make your plan for an article and weave it on a standard loom.

2. Demonstrate how interesting textures may be obtained by using various sizes or kinds of threads in warp or woof.

*3. Make and thread a simple loom and weave something on it.

4. Explain the use of these knots: snitch, loop, bow. Tie a fringe on a piece of weaving you did.

*5. Know the meaning of: loom, heddle, beater, treadle, harness, reed, beam, warp, woof, web, pattern weaving, finger weaving, rug weaving, tapestry weaving.

6. Beam the warp for your woven article and know how to tie a broken warp thread.

7. Make some natural dyes and use them to dye materials for your weaving.

8. Use at least three colors to make an article of tube weaving.

9. Make a wooden shuttle.

*10. Weave a piece of material in a pattern of simple stripes.

11. Find out what materials for weaving grow in this country, and what new materials have been used by modern weavers.

12. Learn about some of the weaving industries in the United States and in one other country.

13. Find examples of weaving in shops, private homes, and textile mills. Arrange an exhibit of woven articles. Compare machine-woven and hand-woven ones.

14. Make a collection of pictures of patterns and types of weaving for your use.

Basketry

To earn this badge, do five of these activities including the two that have a star.

1. Find out what natural materials are plentiful in your community for basketmaking. Gather, prepare, and weave some of this material into a basket using your own design.

2. Design and make a basket, coaster, or tray from prepared materials, such as reed and raffia.

3. Tell about two of the ways in which basketry plays an important part in Indian life. Learn how these baskets compare with those commercially manufactured as to materials, decorations, and patterns.

4. Describe how basket materials are used in the making of furniture. If possible, watch someone cane a chair or weave a basket.

5. Make a design for an article made of splints, such as a tray or basket. Make one using your design. Explain what types of wood are best for making splints and how they are made.

*6. Create a design in two or more colors for some article. Make it using your design.

7. Make a woven reed tray with a wooden base.

8. Know how to take care of materials you use in basketry.

9. Borrow baskets made all over the world from friends. Exhibit them and be able to tell something about each.

*10. Show by articles you have made or by demonstration a method used in basketry—weaving, coiling, plaiting, braiding.

To earn this badge, do eight of these activities including the three that have a star. *Metal*

*1. Make a small bowl or tray of pewter, copper, lead, or aluminum.

2. Make an item of jewelry using .040 (or 18 B and F gauge) sterling silver wire.

3. Experiment with at least three or four designs for metal. Etch the best design on a pewter or copper article.

4. Design and make an article of pewter, silver, aluminum, tin, or copper, using a sawed-out pattern.

5. Design and make a simple article which requires soldering such as a pin, buttons, a lantern, or a candle holder.

*6. Know how to use and care for metal work tools, including a drill, soldering iron, simple blow torch. Demonstrate setting of saw blade and the correct filing strokes of round, half round, triangle, and flat files.

*7. Know what metals are used in a household for kitchen equipment and utensils, tableware, water pipes, electric wiring, and screens. Give reasons for the use of each kind of metal.

8. Show how to clean and polish different kinds of metals.

9. Choose a table silver pattern you like and tell why. Find out something about the origin of the pattern and the name of the designer.

10. Locate in your community examples of the following: wrought-iron gates, grilles, balconies, lampposts, fences, signs; bronze statues, doors, memorial plates, fountains.

11. In your museum or library, find examples of old and new hand-wrought objects.

389

12. Make a simple sculpture out of metal wire, screening, copper foil, or other metals.

13. Help assemble an exhibit of good examples of metalcraft. Prepare a short talk to explain the exhibit.

14. Know one metal in ore form. Find out how it is mined, smelted, and prepared for use.

15. Find out what metals have been used structurally or ornamentally by architects.

Prints

To earn this badge, do eight of these activities including the three that have a star.

1. Know what equipment is needed and how it is used in making a linoleum print.

*2. Create, cut, and print with a linoleum block a simple design for two of the following: bookplates, gift wrapping, end papers for books, or wallpaper pattern.

3. Make a linoleum print using two or more colors.

*4. Using leaves or other forms, make as many different kinds of prints as possible: spatter prints, smokeprints, sunprints, blueprints, shell prints, stick prints, apple, turnip, and potato prints.

5. Know how to make your own stencil paper, take care of cut stencils and protect edges from softening, handle and take care of your tools.

6. Cut a design. Stencil a border in two or more colors on a useful article.

7. Know how stenciling was used by early settlers in this country, for example, Hitchcock chairs, Early American wall decorations, textiles, tole ware.

8. Know the woods and tools used for wood blocks. Make a wood-block print.

*9. Tell the method of making the following and if possible watch the process: lithograph, etching, mezzotint, dry point, aquatint. Collect pictures of these.

10. Make a drawing for a dry point and know how to care for and clean plate and prints.

11. Know the meaning of: ground, burr, burnisher, scraper, acid bath, proof, needle, and bite in etching and dry point.

12. Find out all you can about a well-known print maker.

13. Know what your community offers in print collections and classes in print making. Join a class if possible. Attend exhibits.

14. Make a print collection of your own. Choose suitable mats and frames for them.

To earn this badge, do ten of these activities including the three that have a star.

Interior Decoration

*1. Cut out pictures of home furnishings from magazines. Combine lamps, tables, draperies, and other furnishings to decorate a new room. Show principles of arrangement.

*2. Tell how different periods of history affected the styles of furniture. Identify the characteristics of: Louis XIV, Georgian, Colonial, Victorian, Contemporary. Note any similarities in the furnishings in your home or school.

*3. Make a scale model of a room. Exchange models with a member of your troop and discuss with each other colors for draperies, walls, and grouping of furniture.

4. Obtain a book of wallpaper samples and select a pattern that will look well in the room you have planned. Design a wallpaper pattern of your own.

5. Tell what colors brighten a dark room, give warmth to a cold room, and tone down a room with too much light.

6. Make something for your home or a friend's home, such as a rug, draperies, a painting, woven place mats, a block-printed tablecloth, coasters.

7. Refinish a piece of furniture or a wooden bowl.

8. Learn and tell how wallpaper is printed today. Tell how wallpaper was made in early Pennsylvania-German towns.

9. Tell how Venetian blinds originated and why they are so called.

10. Cut out pictures of several types of floor coverings and show which you would use in different rooms of a house.

11. Explain how to use wood filler, stain, enamel, shellac, varnish, and lacquer. Tell how to remove paint from various surfaces.

391

12. Know how rugs, furniture, draperies, and Venetian blinds are cleaned.

13. Visit a department store, and look at and feel some textiles for draperies and upholstery. Collect swatches.

14. Make an attractive arrangement of flowers for a living room.

15. Help decorate your troop meeting room or a room in a children's hospital, or a room in a service club.

Photography To earn this badge, do eight of these activities including the two that have a star.

*1. Know the parts of a camera. Tell what happens to the shutter in a time exposure and a snapshot. Understand time-setting, distance-measuring, and light-controlling devices.

*2. Take at least two pictures in each of the following groups: pictures of one or more objects; pictures of things happening in your community; pictures of group activities, such as camping, sports, games.

3. Take a photograph that would serve as a design motif for a linoleum print, wood block, or painting.

4. Develop or print some of your own pictures.

5. Enlarge some of your own pictures.

6. Know the different types or speeds of film you can use in your camera. Explain the purpose of each speed and the cautions for handling fast film.

7. Show how to clean the lens of a camera.

8. Know the causes of underexposed, out-of-focus, light-struck, and fogged prints. Explain how to avoid these faults.

9. Take at least six properly exposed color pictures.

10. Be an active member of the school camera club for at least one term or help organize one.

11. Make a collection of at least twenty good photographs or reproductions. Examine them for effective composition and other good points.

12. Take six pictures of some of your Scout activities. Help start a home-made album using your pictures and those of other troop members, or write a letter illustrated with your pictures.

13. Set up a file of your negatives. Show how to properly mount finished photographs in an album.

To earn this badge, do eight of these activities including the three that have a star.

Architecture

*1. Make a scrapbook of pictures showing buildings typical of at least five different sections of the country. Learn how location and weather influenced their design.

2. Collect pictures of public buildings and memorials. Know how their purpose and use influenced their design.

3. Locate pictures of the work of some present-day architects. Tell about these architects. Find out and explain the differences in style and design for which each is well-known.

*4. Make a house plan for your family or some family you know. Consider the family's needs in the location and size of the living room, sleeping quarters, kitchen, bath, laundry, storage, heating, and delivery service. Make your plans in relation to sun, garden, outlook, privacy, and size of lot.

*5. Make a model of the kitchen or workshop in your house designed for greatest efficiency. Indicate the height of work surfaces.

6. Make up a simple house plan to scale and tell how scale is used so that the different parts of a room or building will be the proper size; that is, what determines the size of a door, a room, a window, a fireplace.

7. Learn how a blueprint is made from the tracing of your plan. Read a blueprint.

8. Know the use of various building materials.

9. Tell how modern inventions change the design of buildings and how the airplane may affect your city's planning in the future.

10. Visit, with your troop or patrol, buildings that are examples of types of architecture in your community.

11. With your troop or patrol study a new building under construction. Discuss the kinds of materials used and the design of the building.

393

12. Tell about the contractor's and architect's part in building a house from ground-breaking until actual completion.

13. Find out what building codes are and why they are made.

LITERATURE AND DRAMATICS

As you work on a badge in literature and dramatics, read Chapter 9.

The following badges from other fields may be applied toward a literature and dramatics major in the First Class rank: Minstrel, Drawing and Painting, Radio and Television, Speaker.

Magic Carpet To earn this badge, do ten of these activities including the four that have a star.

*1. Bring a few of your favorite books to a troop meeting and tell the troop why you like them. Listen to the other girls tell about the books they like. Read some of those books that sound interesting to you.

2. Help plan and carry out a book party.

3. Learn about the authors of your favorite books. Write the story of the life of one. Tell what books he or she has written and why you like the ones you have read.

4. Make an anthology of poetry or quotations that you like. Share your anthology with the troop or help make one with your troop.

5. Know what is meant by folklore and read some of the folk tales of different countries. Find a folk tale that belongs to more than one country.

*6. Tell a story to younger children or to other members of the troop.

7. Learn and tell something about storytellers and minstrels of early days and the place of honor they held before books were printed.

*8. Help dramatize a folk tale or ballad, making your own costumes. Present it to an audience.

9. Select the illustrations you like best in books you have read, and tell why you like them. Find other books illustrated by the same artist and arrange an exhibit.

10. Draw your own illustrations for a favorite story.

11. Learn how to take care of books. Make paper covers for your own or borrowed books.

*12. Have a membership card in your public library and know how to make the best use of it and your school library. If there is no library in your community, find out where you can get books.

13. Help plan and start a troop library.

To earn this badge, do ten of these activities including the three *Reader* that have a star.

1. List some of the books you have read. Give the author, illustrator, and publisher of each. For five of your books, write briefly what the book is about and why you like it.

2. Classify the books on your list under the subject about which they are written. Find other books on the same subjects. Learn about the authors whose books you enjoy most.

3. Select a Girl Scout activity and find some books on the subject. Make an annotated booklist for your troop of the ones you like best.

4. Select a place in your home where you can read in comfort with proper light. Arrange your bookshelves and care for your books.

5. Add to your poetry reading. Look through poetry anthologies and find new poems you like. Share them with your troop.

*6. Learn about and use your public library. Know how to find a book through the card catalog; use reference books to find specific items; find magazine articles on special subjects; use the dictionary and encyclopedia; find the publisher and price of a book.

7. Know what services are offered by the Library of Congress in Washington, D.C., the United States Superintendent of Documents, and your state library. Learn how to use them. Visit bookstores in your community that have children's departments.

*8. With the help of someone who knows books, make a reading plan. Add to your reading list as you work on this badge. Use your public or state libraries and other sources.

9. Select poems or stories for reading aloud. Interest the troop in reading together at troop meetings or at camp.

10. With your troop, select books from the library to put on a Girl Scout shelf or a troop reading list. Or help set up a troop library.

11. Take part in the observance of Book Week.

12. Invite an author or illustrator to talk with your troop about how he works and how books are produced.

13. Read book reviews in magazines and newspapers. Tell what you think makes a book "good" and well written.

14. Compare the different magazines you read in both content and style. Write a review of some story, feature, or article in *The American Girl*.

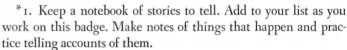

*15. With your troop find ways you can help your library or people who like to read.

Storyteller To earn this badge, do ten of these activities including the three that have a star.

*1. Keep a notebook of stories to tell. Add to your list as you work on this badge. Make notes of things that happen and practice telling accounts of them.

2. Listen to good storytellers and watch the listeners. Observe ways in which the storyteller adds to the interest of the story.

*3. Find new and different kinds of stories. List them in your notebook. Read one of each kind. Tell some of them and find out which you can make most interesting.

4. Learn something about the storytellers and minstrels of the early days, the importance in which they were held, the kinds of stories they told.

5. Read a story anthology from three of the following: folk tales, legends or mythology, animal stories, stories of adventure, modern stories of everyday life, stories of great men and women. Select one story from each of the three and tell it.

*6. Learn new and interesting words from the stories you read. Pronounce and use them correctly. Learn how to use your voice and speak clearly.

7. Select a story told in poetry or a ballad that would make a good choral reading for a troop meeting or around the campfire and use it.

8. Tell stories you think the troop would enjoy at troop meetings and campfire.

9. Learn how to select good stories for younger children. Tell them to children in your family, in your neighborhood, at a nursery school, children's home, or a library.

10. Study one book on how to tell stories.

11. Keep notes on your own storytelling and add to your list of stories to tell.

12. Decide what you think makes a good story to tell. Make up original stories and tell them.

To earn this badge, do ten of these activities including the three that have a star.

Writer

1. Keep a notebook in which you record daily descriptions, verse, or ideas you would like to write about.

2. Serve as troop scribe or secretary of a group. Learn how to write good minutes and accounts of what happens.

3. Practice good letter-writting by corresponding with a pen pal in some other part of the country or in another country.

4. Select a subject you are interested in and write a story, a poem, and a short play or skit about it. Compare what you have written and see which form you like best.

*5. Write a poem, story, or article telling your thoughts and feelings about something which impressed you deeply.

6. Select a favorite story and rewrite it as a poem or play.

7. Write a story of a trip you have taken with your family or troop.

8. Write a description or true story about someone you know or a great person whose life you have read or studied.

9. Study words—their meaning and where they come from. Find ten that have the same "root" and are similar in at least three different languages.

*10. Read at least one book on the art of writing or the use

397

of language. Know how to use the dictionary and other reference books.

11. Visit a library, bookstore, or publishing house and find out what happens between the time the author completes the manuscript and the book is published.

*12. Select one story, poem, description, or play that you have written. Prepare it in correct manuscript form. Learn how to count number of words in your manuscript.

13. Write a letter or submit a story or article you have written to a suitable magazine.

Junior High

Bibliophile Before starting this badge, it is suggested that you complete the Magic Carpet and Reader badges.

To earn this badge, do ten of these activities including the four that have a star.

*1. Know the origin and meaning of the word bibliophile; the difference between a bibliography and an annotated booklist; the value of the title page of a book, of the index and how to use one; what a copyright is and what is meant by books in the public domain; the meaning of manuscript, format, printer's mark, signature; what is meant by classics.

*2. Select one kind of book you enjoy reading or one subject you are interested in and make an annotated booklist for your own use. Check the ones you would like to own.

3. Find out what interesting or unusual collections of books or manuscripts there are in your community, in the public library, the museum, or private collections. Visit as many of them as possible and learn all you can about them.

*4. Learn about some of the famous books and manuscript collections in libraries and museums in different parts of the United States.

5. Learn about at least one well-known book collector and his collection. Read at least one book about the art of book collecting.

6. Learn about the history of book-making—early materials

used to write on, discovery of paper-making, invention of printing. Learn about the early great printers.

7. Make a collection of alphabets or pictures that illustrate the history of writing and arrange an exhibit.

8. Find out how libraries mend and rebind books. Mend one of your own books or one belonging to the troop or school library.

9. Observe the way libraries and bookstores arrange books on their shelves. Arrange and care for your own books.

10. Learn about the work of several famous illustrators. Select one of your favorites and show examples of his work, telling about him and why you like his work.

11. Be able to identify the following leathers used on books: Morocco, calfskin, pigskin, seal, Russia, and ooze.

12. Learn about special awards for distinguished books. Arrange an exhibit of books that have received an award or tell the troop about several awards.

13. Design and make a bookplate for yourself, a friend, or your troop.

*14. Start your own book collection.

Junior High

To earn this badge, do ten of these activities including the three that have a star.

Journalist

1. Visit a newspaper and observe the various departments. Learn how news is gathered, including international news, and how newspapers are made.

*2. Help produce a school, camp, or troop newspaper.

*3. Know the basic rules for writing a news story. Write one based on local events or troop activities.

4. Know proofreader's marks. Read and correct your own copy or proof.

5. Interview some person and write up the interview in newspaper style.

6. Write a feature story or article on some subject appropriate to your papers.

7. Write an editorial of approximately three hundred and fifty words.

8. Write a review of a movie or play you have seen or a book you have read.

9. Know what a copyright means, how it is obtained, and for how many years it is given. Learn what is meant by libel and plagiarism.

10. Tell your troop about vocational opportunities in the field of journalism. Know the qualifications for at least one newspaper job.

11. Read about how newspapers are made, the history of early newspapers, or the life of a famous journalist, and tell your troop about it.

12. Compare different newspapers. Keep a scrapbook of good examples of news stories, cartoons, editorials, headlines, and layouts.

13. Make a quiz game of newspaper words. Explain the meaning of the terms and play the game with your troop.

*14. Make a legible copy of one of your articles. Proofread and correct it.

15. Prepare and submit an article, feature story, review, or news story to some newspaper other than your school or troop paper.

Troop Dramatics   To earn this badge, do ten of these activities including the three that have a star.

1. With your friends see a play, opera, ballet, or movie. Discuss the performance.

2. Take part in three short pantomimes or tableaux based on scenes from well-known stories or real life.

3. Help plan and act a scene with impromptu dialogue.

*4. Help dramatize a fairy tale, legend, historical event, or scene from a favorite book. Make your own costumes and stage setting.

5. Help dramatize a folk song or ballad. Make your own costumes and stage setting.

*6. Explain what the following acting terms mean: stage right, stage left, apron, up-stage, down-stage, entrance, exit, cue, script.

7. For your troop library compile a list of poems and prose selections for choral speaking.

8. Arrange two selections for choral speaking. Either direct or take part in presenting these.

9. Help plan and carry out an international program.

10. Help plan and carry out a program built around American folklore.

11. Help plan and carry out a ceremony for some special occasion in the troop or at camp.

*12. Help find short plays or scenes from great plays suitable for your troop to act. Help produce and take part in one.

13. Help write and present a play for an audience.

To earn this badge, do ten of the activities; choose six in Section A and two each in Sections B and C. Do the activities in Section A first. The activities that have a star are required.

Player

SECTION A

*1. Learn to walk, sit, rise, run, relax, and dance with ease and grace. Practice making a good entrance and exit and moving about the stage.

2. Walk across the room in such a way that your friends can guess the type of character you represent. Pantomime at least six different persons who are engaged in some activity such as a small boy learning to ride a bicycle.

3. Pantomime situations to show different sensations so that your friends can guess what it is that you see, hear, touch, taste, and smell.

4. Make up simple sentences and demonstrate different moods or feeling by speaking the same lines differently.

*5. Read aloud poems, newspaper articles, and lines from plays. Discuss with listeners the rhythm, tempo, and tone of your speech, and what practice you need in using your voice effectively.

6. Read several plays and select the roles you would like to

play. Practice reading aloud some of the lines of parts you selected.

7. Take part in a choral reading.

8. Act out a short scene portraying in words and action one or two characteristics of a famous person or someone the troop knows so that the audience can recognize the person.

9. Help plan and take part in a short scene using speech and action, with each member portraying a different kind of person

SECTION B

In a program that your troop presents:

10. Act in the dramatization of a ballad.

11. Act in the dramatization of a story.

12. Act in a pageant.

*13. Act in a play.

SECTION C

14. Find out about an organized theatre group in your community; a national theatre group; or a theatre group of another country. See a performance given by a dramatic group.

15. Find out all you can about a well-known actor and actress and their successful plays. Share your information with the troop through pictures, stories, and reviews.

16. Learn about theatrical make-up and how to use it.

Puppeteer

To earn this badge, do eight of these activities including the two that have a star. The badge will be more interesting if you do the activities in the order listed.

1. Know the four main types of puppets—hand, shadow, rod, and marionette—and how they work.

2. Tell what kind of plays and characters can be presented easily and effectively and explain why.

3. Read about the history of puppets in different parts of the world. Tell the troop about "Mr. Punch."

4. See a puppet show. Talk to the puppeteer about how the puppet is made and operated, and the show produced.

5. Do Activity 6 in Troop Dramatics and Activity 1 in Play Producer. Know how these apply to puppet shows.

*6. Make and operate a hand puppet and a shadow puppet.

7. Help select and arrange the story, poem, or play, and make the stage for a hand puppet or shadowgraph show. Help produce it.

8. Learn to operate the puppet in time with the action of the story being told. Learn to speak the part of your puppet in a play in time with his action.

*9. Make, dress, and learn to operate a simple marionette.

10. Take part in the production of a marionette show using the marionette you have made and dressed. Help select and arrange the story or play and make the stage.

Junior High

To earn this badge do any ten of the activities.

Dramatic Appreciation

1. Discuss moving pictures you have seen. Select three favorites and compare them with those of your friends.

2. Read reviews of moving pictures in your local newspaper and recommended lists in *The American Girl* and other magazines. Discuss with the troop the standards of good plays and how they should apply to movies.

3. Attend a Little Theatre, school, or other play, and write a review of it. Read reviews of plays in newspapers and magazines.

4. Learn something about the history of the theatre. Find out about: the early strolling players, the miracle plays, the theatrical guilds, the Greek dramas, the plays of Shakespeare's time. Select a scene and with other members of the troop present it as it was originally acted.

5. Learn something about each of the following: great actors and actresses, theatres of different ages or nations, costumes of different periods, great playwrights. Make a collection of pictures, sketches, or articles about one of these.

6. Find different kinds of plays that are important in the theatre and as literature. Read some of them and learn why they are considered great. Select a few passages or scenes from one of them and interest the troop in reading them aloud. Discuss the

403

action, setting, characterization, and language of those you read together.

7. Help select and write for acting in pantomime a folk tale, a Bible story, or legend. Choose appropriate background music. Present it and discuss the results with the troop.

8. Write a short play in correct form.

9. Make a list of several one-act plays you feel your troop would like. Include different kinds to provide a varied program.

10. Find out some of the plays that are successes today, who wrote them, and what actors and actresses have roles in them. Read some of the reviews.

11. Listen to opera music. Select one opera you like and learn all you can about it, the composer, and singers.

12. Listen to a play on the radio. Talk about the differences in presenting a play on the stage, the screen, the radio, and television.

13. Compare the way in which plays are written and staged today, and in earlier days of the theatre. List some of the great dramas that are still being played and learn something about the dramatists.

Junior High

Producer   To earn this badge, do ten activities: choose three from Section A, four from Section B, and two from Section C. The three that have a star are required.

*1. Know how a stage is built and learn the names for its parts. If possible, visit a theatre backstage and see how to operate curtains, scenery, and lights.

SECTION A

For any play or program presented by your troop:

2. Draw sketches of suitable stage-sets.

3. Help construct stage-sets.

*4. Learn about the jobs of the "backstage crew" and be responsible for one during a performance.

5. Help design and make or collect the costumes.

6. Learn to create make-up for various types of characters,

using both dry and grease paint. Help to make up the players.

7. Help with the lighting for your play using regular equipment or constructing your own.

SECTION B

8. Practice using your voice to read poems, prose selections, or short scenes from plays.

9. Act in a troop dramatic program.

10. Learn how a play is produced and for what things the director is responsible. If possible, attend a rehearsal of a theatrical group.

*11. For a troop dramatic program, help choose the cast, direct, conduct the rehearsals, or supervise the committees in charge of staging and costuming.

12. Choose a play for your troop. Plan the casting, directing, settings, and lighting.

13. Attend a radio broadcast of a play. Take part in producing a one-act radio play. Use either a real or property microphone.

14. Help your troop decide on the plots for one or more impromptu scenes and produce them.

15. Know how plays were produced in the great periods of theatrical history.

SECTION C

For any one of the plays or programs presented by your troop:

16. Help with: the selection of a theatre or auditorium, ticket distribution or plan of admission, training ushers in seating procedure, acting as head usher.

17. Help with publicizing the play.

18. Help draw up a budget for the entire cost of production.

19. Make up a sample play program, giving credits, cast of characters, and other information.

MUSIC AND DANCING

As you do a badge in music and dancing, read Chapter 10.

The following badges from other fields may be applied toward a major in the First Class rank: Storyteller, Player.

Minstrel To earn this badge, do eight of these activities including the three that have a star.

*1. Learn to sing and know the source of: two American folk songs; two folk songs from other countries (one in another language); two art songs; and two rounds or descants.

2. Tell and dramatize interesting facts about one of your songs.

3. Learn to play the accompaniments for one song and one dance for your troop.

4. With others, learn and take part in an American singing game and two from other countries.

*5. Teach a folk song, a singing game, or tell a folk legend about one of your songs to your troop or to a group of younger children.

6. Select songs you think can be used for opening or closing of the troop meeting, ceremonies, a hike.

7. Help plan and give an entertainment around the life and work of a great composer for some troop occasion.

8. Help dramatize a folk ballad. Assist in making suitable costumes and stage settings for it.

9. Help make and show a shadowgraph based on a song.

10. Tell a folk tale or local legend about which folk songs are sometimes built.

*11. Learn about the customs, manners, and culture of one country. Plan a troop event which includes some of the music and dances of your selected country. Show some of the things it has contributed to the world.

12. Make a design symbolizing the art of a country whose music you like. Put the design on an invitation or program for a troop event.

13. Join a trio, quartet, or chorus that sings for various occasions.

14. Write a story about the meistersingers in Germany, troubadours in France and Spain, or minstrels of England. Learn several of their songs.

To earn this badge, do eight of these activities including the *Group*
two that have a star. *Musician*

*1. Sing well in a group the following songs and give their
sources: an art song; a folk song; two-, three-, or four-part rounds;
and a song with a descant.

2. Help present a dramatic performance in which there is
music.

3. Using a handmade or manufactured instrument, help to
accompany several musical selections.

4. Make an album about one or two great composers. Include
such things as pictures, a list of best-known works, samples of
songs or other music, stories about his life.

5. Sing or play by yourself or with a group two of the works
of the composer chosen for the album in Activity 4 above.

*6. Select suitable music, and direct the chorus or orchestra
for a performance which your troop or another group is giving.

7. Visit a factory, music store, private home, or museum and
find out all you can about four or more musical instruments you
like.

8. Select one musical instrument you like and learn all about
its origin, development, and uses.

9. Discuss good manners for a concert in a public hall or
during a radio or phonograph program in a home.

10. Join, or help to organize, a Girl Scout glee club. Sing at
community affairs.

11. Help arrange a dancing party that includes dances from
pioneer times up to the present. Be able to explain the dances.

12. Help give a musical program made up of music of the
United States: Indian, Negro, music of the early settlers, and
modern music.

To earn this badge, do eight of these activities including the *Musician*
two that have a star.

*1. Do the following:

    a. Play or sing a major scale and be able to give its rel-
    ative and parallel minor. 407

b. Listen to a few bars and tell whether they are in a major or minor key.

c. Learn to recognize the third, fifth, and seventh intervals in the octave above middle C when played singly or in combination.

d. Draw symbols for ordinary notes and rests. Explain their value.

e. Explain five time signatures. Write a measure for each one, using both notes and rests.

*2. Play or sing simple music at sight. Beat its rhythm and explain all signs and terms in it.

3. Examine several musical compositions and list all the terms like staccato, crescendo, or legato that you find. Know why Italian terms are used.

4. Read about a great composer whose work you like. Learn to play or sing one of his works.

5. Beat the time and tempo to a tune after hearing it played. Make up a simple dance step to suit the time.

6. Make a musical instrument such as a drum or a pipe. Learn to play on it. Accompany your troop in songs or dances.

7. Learn to play or sing in a simple chorale or similar group.

8. Look up four types of dances for which classical composers have written music.

9. Write on music staff notepaper the songs of birds; the tunes played by church bells; or the notes sounded by boat and factory whistles; and so forth.

10. Select a song or instrumental piece and teach it to others so that they can sing or play it with you.

11. Write down a musical accompaniment for words written by yourself or another person.

12. Listen to a piece of music while looking at the score. Pick out the themes and notice the number of times and ways in which they are introduced and varied.

13. Help to organize a string trio, band, or orchestra. Practice conducting it. Play for dancing or singing entertainments.

14. Act as accompanist for your troop singing or dancing, or for some other part of its program.

To earn this badge, do ten of these activities including the two that have a star. *Music Appreciation*

*1. Listen to symphonic, sacred, solo, and chamber music over a period of several months. Keep a log of what you hear.

2. Start a record collection, or make a list of records you would like to own, from among the music you have heard.

3. Collect pictures of symphony orchestra instruments. Know which instruments are a part of each section. Recognize the lead instrument in each as you listen.

*4. With others plan and present a musical program for invited guests. Use in your program recorded music, choral or instrumental music by troop members.

5. Write a short story or play based on the life of a great composer.

6. Choose any four works of a great composer and listen to them until you can recognize them.

7. Find out how folk songs originate and tell some of their general charactistics. Learn some of the folk music of the United States.

8. Collect words and music of at least ten folk songs and art songs. Make them available to your troop or other troops. Add them to your log.

9. Learn the story of one opera. Listen to the opera on radio or phonograph until you can recognize the main theme, the arias, and the characters who sing them. Read about the composer.

10. Arrange a phonograph concert for a group of friends. Play music in which one or two instruments take the lead. Decide on the things you like most about the music they make.

11. Explain the following: madrigal, chorale, oratorio, opera, concerto, symphony, and ballet. Learn the titles and composers of one composition of each type.

12. Dramatize good manners for a concert in a public hall or during a radio or phonograph program in a home.

13. Show how to care for musical instruments, phonographs, and records.

Folk Dancer To earn this badge, do eight activities including the two that have a star.

*1. Learn eight dances: four United States country dances and four folk dances from other countries. Teach two to your troop.

2. Learn to call a simple square dance.

3. Demonstrate three of the following: the polka, schottische, jig, step-hop, and the peasant waltz.

4. Learn to sing at least three folk songs that could serve as accompaniment to folk dancing.

5. Play for your troop to dance at least four tunes on the piano, violin, accordian, shepherd's pipe, or other instrument.

6. Make an appropriate costume for folk dancing.

*7. With your troop give a folk dance party. Invite guests and teach at least one dance at the party.

8. Find pictures of several musical instruments that are used for folk and square dancing.

9. Find several well-known compositions based on folk tunes. Play some of these for your troop or play records of them.

10. Dance correctly one court dance, such as the minuet, the Viennese waltz, the Polish mazurka, or the polonaise.

11. Take part in a community or intercommunity square dance or folk dance festival.

12. Help plan and give a program of your dances for another group in your community.

13. Learn at least three singing games and teach them to a group of Brownie Scouts or young children.

14. Learn about the ways collectors of folk music discover and record tunes. Learn how the copyright law protects them and how it applies to you.

Junior High

Dancer To earn this badge do seven activities including the three that have a star.

*1. Practice to music: walking, running, skipping, jumping, hopping, sliding, and leaping. Using your favorite music, put foot and arm movements into a dance which expresses the mood and rhythm which you feel.

*2. Learn to dance the waltz, fox trot, rumba, and one other popular dance step.

3. Plan a program for an evening of dancing with appropriate music.

4. Help to give a brief skit showing good manners at a dance.

5. Show two things you do to get people to mix and feel at home at a dance.

*6. Learn and teach an "ice breaker" that may be used at a party.

7. Help give a square dance or other kind of dance for boys and girls. Know appropriate dress for different kinds of dances.

8. Compose a tune which can be used for dancing.

9. With your leader and troop arrange for lessons in ball-room dancing.

10. Ask your dancing teacher to discuss with you the vocational possibilities in dancing.

11. Help dramatize, in a pageant or shadow play, some part of the history of the dance.

12. Collect for yourself or troop library one of the following:

a. Names of well-known dance orchestras, symphonies, and choral groups. Include names and pictures of music composers and some of their outstanding works.

b. Pictures and information of famous dancers and something about their work.

13. See a movie, ballet, or musical play in which there is dancing.

CHAPTER 20

Citizens Here and Abroad

Community Life

Active Citizen	My Community	My Troop
Aviation	My Country	Radio and Television
Clerk	My Government	Speaker
		Traveler

International Friendship

Conversationalist	Pen Pal	World Neighbor
Language	Western Hemisphere	World Trefoil
My World	World Gifts	

COMMUNITY LIFE

As you do a badge in community life, read Chapter 11.

The following badges from other fields may be applied toward a community life major in the First Class rank: Community Safety, Public Health, Weather, My World.

Active Citizen To earn this badge, do ten of these activities including the two that have a star.

1. Dramatize some right and wrong ways to make a newcomer in your town feel at home.

2. Ask people who have come from other towns and other countries to help you plan ways to help newcomers feel at home. Do something about it.

3. Ask your parents or teachers how people get together to improve their town. Make a directory of such groups in your town or areas.

4. Learn how a person not born in the United States becomes an American citizen.

*5. Talk over with your family and then with your troop how the Bill of Rights affects your daily life.

6. List names of some of the people in your town who are considered "good citizens." Tell why you feel this way about them. Name some of the "good citizens" in your community's history and tell what they did.

7. Explain how people are elected to office. Use as examples your troop, adult clubs, and public officials.

8. Plan ways your troop can help adults get out the vote, and put your plans into action at the next election.

*9. Make a simple map of your town which would be useful to a newcomer.

10. Look into the history of town meetings, the secret ballot, elected leaders.

11. Through a game or story show how gossip changes facts. Discuss with your troop some good rules to follow when making up your mind about something.

12. Study advertisements and commercials on radio and TV to see how companies influence you to want to buy their products. Group your examples according to those which tell about the quality of the products and those which play on the emotions only.

13. Care for your school's flag; plan a ceremony and serve in the color guard for your school or for some special occasion; or show your knowledge of the care and use of the flag to another group.

To earn this badge, do ten of these activities including the two that have a star.

My Troop

*1. Know something about the lives of the founders of Girl Scouting and Girl Guiding in Great Britain and the United States. Find out about the Juliette Low World Friendship Fund, the World Flag, Our Chalet, Girl Scout Week, the Girl Scout Birthday, the history of your Girl Scout council.

413

2. List the persons who have helped your troop within the year. Plan an appropriate way to thank them.

3. Do something to improve your meeting place, your troop camp cabin, or Girl Scout headquarters.

4. Give or lend a book or magazine to your troop library, or serve as troop librarian, or arrange for a Girl Scout shelf in your public library.

5. Help a group make plans for welcoming a new troop member.

*6. Take an active part in your Court of Honor, patrol, or troop discussions or business meeting. Help to put on a skit showing successful ways of taking part in a discussion.

7. Find ways to improve the rules or traditions of your troop.

8. Work on a community service project, or have a hike or party with another group.

9. On a map, show all the places in your community where your troop may go to have fun. Indicate resources for different types of troop activities.

10. Make an exhibit which shows something about your troop activities.

11. Help work out a system of record-keeping or a budget for your troop. Or, for a period of a month or two, keep some of the troop records.

12. Show that you know how to wear the Girl Scout uniform and where to place insignia. Dramatize several situations to show how Girl Scouts can create good or bad public opinion.

My Community

To earn this badge, do ten of these activities including the three that have a star.

*1. Before working on this badge, list the things you think make a good community. Discuss your list after completing the badge to see if there are any changes.

*2. Start a file of places where you can get help for troop program.

3. Present some of the history of your community through shadowgraphs, puppets, tableaux, murals, or dramatics.

4. Find out how your public school system works and how

much it costs to run it. Invite someone in your school system to visit the troop or go and talk to him about how the school is used outside of class time.

5. Check your town for examples of how public property has been damaged or misused. Discuss with your troop what can be done to prevent this misuse.

6. Know how the work of the social agencies in your community is financed and how the agencies work together.

7. Learn about government officials who direct the special services needed for your family's comfort and protection and what they do.

8. Know what religious groups there are in your town. Find out the ways your own church or synagogue works for a better community.

9. Find out what your community does for the physically handicapped, mentally ill, orphans, old people, poor, unemployed.

*10. Select one thing which would make your community a nicer place in which to live. Discover why it has not been done, how it could be done, and try to do something about it.

11. From a list of the main occupations of people in your community, choose several which interest you. Talk with people in those jobs, or give service that will help you find out what future opportunities there are for you.

12. Dramatize how you would get help for several types of possible emergencies in your home or community.

13. Prepare yourselves to help with the community events in which your Girl Scout council usually cooperates. Know places in your community which would be of interest to visitors.

14. Pick one community problem that adults are studying. Gather all the information you can. Have a troop forum when you feel you know the facts. See if the community decision agrees with yours.

To earn this badge, do ten of these activities including the four that have a star.

My Country

415

1. Find out what historical and current information you should know about your country if you should be hostess to an international guest or represent Girl Scouts at an international event.

2. Make several maps of the United States. Record on them places and facts about your country such as national parks and forests, typical crafts, industries, agriculture, geography, nationality background, music, or typical foods.

*3. Name the freedoms people in this country enjoy. Know what documents give us these freedoms and tell what they mean in your daily life.

*4. Find pictures of at least six symbols of your country and learn about their origin and meaning.

5. Make or study a collection of commemorative stamps and learn how the subjects for stamps are selected.

6. Choose one subject to study in the romance of our heritage, such as: (a) the riverboats on the Mississippi; (b) cattle brands of the West; (c) the "forty-niners"; or (d) the story of one of our legendary heroes.

*7. Find out your state's nickname, motto, flower, bird, song, and flag. Learn the same things about several other states where you have friends.

8. Read some of the folklore and history of at least two of our Indian tribes, learn about how and where Indians live today, visit a reservation if there is one near you.

9. Ask a naturalized citizen to tell you about the questions he had to answer to become a citizen, and see if you would be able to pass his test.

*10. Write down your attitude and opinions about a part of your country you have never visited. Check the accuracy of your views with books and with people who have been there. Plan and carry out a troop discussion about "generalizations" and about "fact-finding."

11. Find out what taxes *you* pay. Know at least one service *you* use which is paid by federal, state, and local taxes.

12. Learn about some large government project which helps people such as reforestation, conservation, agricultural experiments.

13. Do at least one service suggested by the activities in this badge; or help with a current service project for a group within this country; or assist in some way with the citizenship education classes for people born in another country.

To earn this badge, do ten of these activities including the four *Traveler* that have a star.

*1. Plan an overnight trip by train, bus, boat, or airplane. Show how to: read timetables, buy tickets, handle baggage, tip porters, order food, select clothes to travel in and to include in your overnight bag.

*2. Plan a trip by car. Show how to read a road map and road signs; arrange for overnight stops; pack and stow baggage; observe safety rules in the car; be courteous to the other passengers; entertain younger children; care for animals on the trip.

3. Dramatize the courteous and correct use of the telephone and show how to use a telephone directory.

4. Show how to send a telegram, and money order, and how to use traveler's checks.

5. Know what to do when stranded in a strange place.

6. Find out where emergency and first aid equipment is located on trains, buses, boats, or planes and learn how to use them.

*7. In a skit, show courteous conduct to other travelers and employees on a public conveyance. Show that you know how to use and care for waiting rooms and washrooms and how to ask for special services.

8. Find out the duties of some of the people who work for transportation companies.

*9. Pack a suitcase neatly and efficiently. Determine how heavy a bag you can handle with ease.

10. Show how to pack, tag, and fasten baggage for shipment by express, freight, or on a ticket. Know how to insure baggage and what to do if it is lost.

11. Know the rules about taking small animals on trains, buses, and planes. Learn how they are shipped in a baggage car, and how you plan for their care.

12. Explain how the fare on buses, trains, and planes varies according to age of traveler and type of accommodations.

Speaker To earn this badge, do eight of these activities including the three that have a star.

*1. Listen to people talk. Notice how student leaders, salespeople, public speakers, teachers, members of your family and your troop speak. Decide what things you like or dislike about their speech.

2. Record your voice on a tape recorder or practice speaking over a public address system. Decide what you need to improve.

3. Experiment with seating arrangements and decide which ones help people discuss most freely. Dramatize ways in which you would bring out the opinions of the ones who hesitate to talk and discourage the ones who do all the talking.

4. With others make a list of subjects to discuss in your patrol, committee, or troop. With your leader select one that requires troop action and conduct a discussion. Use parliamentary procedure to get a fair expression of opinion.

5. Attend some meeting or listen to a discussion group over the radio. Discuss methods used by the leader, the way the group took part, and when possible, the physical setup of the room.

*6. Preside over a meeting and introduce a speaker.

*7. Choose a subject that will interest a group of people. Prepare and give a five-minute talk.

8. Represent your group at a conference or Court of Honor showing that you know how to speak for others.

9. Play a game with the group in which members make one-minute unprepared speeches on subjects chosen for them.

10. Use what you have learned in this badge for community service.

Junior High

Clerk To earn this badge, do ten of these activities including the three that have a star.

*1. Dramatize the courteous way to approach salespeople, to wait on people, and to receive visitors in an office.

*2. Learn how to use and care for the following: typewriter, hand-stapling machine, fountain pen, and automatic pencil. Be able to read a postal scale.

3. Demonstrate use of a home and pay station telephone. Show that you can take a message, ask and answer questions, and give courteous, clear directions.

4. Know how a cashbook, journal, and ledger are used.

5. Show that you can handle the following bank procedures: make out a check and record stub, and a withdrawal and deposit slip. Explain a bank statement.

6. Learn how to make out a receipt.

7. Learn to write simple business letters, requesting information, placing orders, and expressing thanks.

8. Learn to cut a stencil, plan an attractive page arrangement, including copy and illustrations.

9. Demonstrate the use and care of a mimeograph or other duplicating machine using the stencil made in Activity 8.

10. Show how to file things neatly. Know several common systems for organizing files.

11. Do some kind of service in your community where you can use one or all of the above skills.

*12. In a skit show how to apply for a job.

Junior High

To earn this badge, do seven of these activities including the three that have a star.

My Government

It is hoped that every girl who holds or is working on this badge will serve as an aide to voters every year during registration, primary, and election time.

*1. Know the following facts about voting: dates for registration, primaries, and election; polling places for your neighborhood; who is eligible to vote; and how to obtain and use an absentee ballot.

*2. Before an election find out: the major duties of the jobs being filled; what parties have candidates in the election; what issues are being voted upon.

419

3. Learn about the Girl Scout aides to voters. Register for service. Know about the other nonpartisan groups in your community.

*4. With others, select and do at least two of the following:

a. Compare the ways candidates are nominated for office in your state, your Girl Scout council, and your troop.

b. Know one duty that is the same in the job of a troop treasurer, town treasurer, state treasurer, and Treasurer of the United States. Describe two jobs in government that resemble that of a patrol leader.

c. Know which of the following services are paid for by federal, state, local funds: fire and police protection, post office, immigration service, schools, public parks, highways, public higher education.

d. Make a list of at least twelve duties of citizens of the United States. Star the ones that affect you.

e. Read aloud the Declaration of Independence, and the Preamble to the United States Constitution and its Bill of Rights. Explain what these documents mean to you and why they are so important to your country.

5. Do at least one of the following:

a. Gather all the information you can on one issue in the coming election. After the election, see how the voters voted and whether you would have voted that way.

b. Listen to several news commentators reporting on the same news item. Notice if they use the same words, if they give you the same idea about the event, if they seem impartial.

6. Find out how your representative in your city, state, or federal government learns the opinions of the public. Learn how people express their opinions to their representatives.

7. Know your local laws regarding speed limits, special zones, bicycles, learners' and drivers' licenses, dog taxes, and restrictions on pets.

8. Select a recent law that affects you directly, find out who sponsored it, when it was passed, and who is responsible for en-

forcing it. Find one law in your city or town that is out of date. Learn how such laws can be removed from the statute books.

9. Find out about some nonpartisan group in your community. Ask this group or some other civic group to help you with this badge.

Junior High

To earn this badge, do ten of these activities including the three that have a star.

Aviation

*1. Visit the nearby airports or landing strips. If none exist, make a model airport including runways, hangars, windsock, and control tower.

2. Identify a glider, helicopter, jet-propelled plane, transport type plane, and private personal planes from at least five different manufacturers.

3. For a specific model of one type of aircraft selected in Activity 2 find out:

    a. Name of manufacturer and popular name of plane
    b. Passenger or cargo capacity
    c. Number and horsepower of engines
    d. Material used in construction of wings and fuselage
    e. Top, cruising, and landing speeds
    f. Cruising range

*4. Know the uses of ailerons, elevators, and rudder of an aircraft; flaps of an airplane; and spoilers of a glider.

*5. Explain the four major factors governing flight—lift, thrust, drag, gravity.

6. Know how many people are concerned with the flight of one transport plane and what each individual or group does. Invite one of these people to tell of his training and experience.

7. Hold a quiz program on aviation terms.

8. Find out how aircraft is used in flood, fires, and other emergencies; agriculture, air mail, air freight.

9. Practice at least ten safety rules to be observed at an airport and around a plane.

421

10. Make a flight or solid model airplane.

11. Learn when a parachute is worn, how to open one, the difference between a pack and seat chute.

12. Record weather conditions for flying for at least three weeks through radio and newspaper reports, weather maps, and your own weather devices; or earn the Weather badge.

13. Tell how the airplane has brought the peoples of the world together. Compare travel times and routes between a city in the United States and three cities on other continents.

14. Get information from airlines, travel bureaus, and experienced travelers and chart a plane trip from your nearest commercial airport to a city in another country.

Junior High

Radio and Television

To earn this badge, do ten of these activities including the two that have a star.

1. Keep a record of radio or television programs heard in your home for a week. Classify them as: entertainment; educational; a good blend of both.

2. Report to your troop on your favorite program. Write to a broadcasting station and give your reactions to a program.

3. Plan a listening party with your troop. Tune in at least three different types of programs. After listening discuss what you have heard. Decide how radio and television affect your daily living.

*4. Visit a radio or television studio. Find out how a program is produced and how many people are involved.

5. Find out how at least five sound effects are produced.

6. Demonstrate the difference in acting on the stage, in the movies, on the radio, on television.

7. Talk with people who work in radio and television or ask them to talk with your troop. Find out what they do, how they became interested in and trained for their jobs.

8. Discuss the techniques used by announcers on different programs. If possible, obtain from your local station the script of a typical announcer's audition.

9. Write a short announcement for one of the following: a commercial advertisement, a commentary for a serious music program or a popular music concert, a spot announcement on Girl Scouting.

10. Take part in a radio or television broadcast *or* do Activity 13 in the Play Producer badge.

*11. Write a fifteen-minute quiz program on Girl Scout history and activities. Give the program on the air if you can or give it as a mock broadcast.

12. Know the meaning of at least five of the following: ad lib, audition, PA, continuity, on the nose, commercial, web, platter, voice level, ham operator. Know some of the signs used for communication during a broadcast or telecast.

13. Organize a mock quiz broadcast based on information about radio or television terms, such as microphone, transmitter, relay station, kilocycle, broadcasting band, very high frequency, ultra high frequency, FCC, network, transcription, kinescope, television, coaxial cable, frequency modulation.

14. Know the use of radio in police work, by ships at sea, in news transmission, operation of airplanes, aerial photography, radio telephone, and radiogram.

15. Find out how radio and television are used throughout the world. Explain how this communication plays a vital role today in international affairs.

INTERNATIONAL FRIENDSHIP

As you do a badge in international friendship, read Chapter 12 and check yourself on "A Friend to All" checklist, page 221.

The following badges from other fields may be applied toward an international friendship major in the First Class rank: Traveler, Aviation, Folk Dancer, Pioneer.

To earn this badge, do ten of these activities including the three that have a star.

World Gifts

*1. Find out the countries from which the ancestors of troop members came. Make a troop family tree to illustrate this.

423

2. Share with your troop an expression, custom, recipe, or object in your family which came from one of your ancestor's countries.

*3. Learn where the people in your community come from and why. Demonstrate some crafts, songs, dances, customs, and holiday celebrations they brought to your community.

4. Invite an old inhabitant of your neighborhood to talk to your troop about the early days. Dramatize a story or legend about this.

5. Learn folk dances and songs from the girls in your troop who were born in other countries or whose parents were.

6. Plan a World Gifts party for your parents or another troop, using the songs and dances, stories and games from other countries.

*7. Tell why the United States is called the "melting pot." Show on a map or chart the sections of the United States where various nationality and racial groups settled.

8. Tell the troop at least one thing that each of the groups you marked on the map in Activity 7 has contributed to the United States.

9. Know at least fifteen trees, plants, and flowers that were brought to the United States from other countries.

10. Prepare an exhibit to show basic foods needed by all peoples. Learn what countries grow them and how they are exchanged through foreign trade.

11. Learn to cook a main dish from another country that has become popular in the United States.

12. Set an international table for a troop party using articles made in other countries.

13. Plan a joint meeting, hike, or party with girls from another troop, whose nationality, racial, or religious backgrounds are different from yours.

14. Decide on things you and your troop will do to help newcomers feel at home in your community.

15. Plan or take part in an international or intercultural festival. Demonstrate some of the things you have learned from this badge.

To earn this badge, do ten of these activities including the five that have a star.

World Trefoil

*1. Find out how Girl Scouting began in this country. Tell how Juliette Low showed her interest in international affairs.

2. Contribute to the Juliette Low World Friendship Fund. Tell three things for which it has been used. Explain what Juliette Low representatives do.

*3. Dramatize incidents showing how Lord Baden-Powell introduced Scouting to the world.

*4. Locate on a map all the countries that have Girl Guides and Girl Scouts. Describe some typical activities in three of these countries. Explain why some countries have two different associations.

*5. Give a three-minute talk on the World Association.

6. Dress dolls in the uniforms of countries in the World Association. Exhibit or lend them to interested groups.

7. Learn the "World Song" and several other favorite songs of Guides and Scouts.

8. Ask a member of an International Friendship Troop to tell you about its program.

*9. Write a ceremony explaining the things we hold in common with Guides and Scouts all over the world. Use it for a special occasion.

10. Explain what is meant by Thinking Day and International Month. Describe the way Thinking Day is celebrated in at least three other countries.

11. Locate Our Chalet on a map. Describe or sketch it. Know its purpose and history. Sing "Our Chalet" with the whole troop.

12. Compare camping customs of Latin-American and European Guides with ours. See how many reasons for the differences you can find.

13. List three kinds of international gatherings Guides and Scouts may attend. Know the basic requirements for United States representatives.

14. Make a scrapbook on international Scouting. Use clippings from magazines such as *The American Girl* and *The Council Fire,* letters from pen pals, Thinking Day cards.

Junior High

Pen Pal To earn this badge, do ten of these activities including the two that have a star.

*1. Correspond with a pen pal from another country.

2. Keep a file of all letters in the order in which you receive them.

3. Find out about the government, the capital, the occupations of the people, the landscape, and the famous people of your pen pal's country.

4. Learn the Girl Scout Promise, motto, and slogan in your pen pal's language.

5. Find out your pen pal's hobbies and main interests and help by sending her information about them.

6. Exchange pictures of your country, yourself, Girl Scout activities, your town, family, and friends with your pen pal.

7. Send an American gift on birthdays or Christmas or make a gift for your pen pal.

8. Ask your pen pal what Girl Guides do in her country, how they dress, how they camp, what songs they sing. Tell about the Girl Scouts of the U.S.A.

9. Share letters from your pen pal, and any articles you might receive, with friends.

10. Inform other interested troop members of the International Post Box and how they can get a pen pal.

*11. Keep up to date on happenings in your pen pal's country.

12. Obtain a map of your pen pal's country and locate approximately where she lives.

Western Hemisphere To earn this badge, do ten of these activities including the four that have a star.

*1. Show on a map the countries in the Western Hemisphere belonging to the World Association. Know the flags of these countries. Locate the Western Hemisphere Center.

*2. Learn the Girl Scout Promise and motto of one country in the Western Hemisphere whose language is not English. Find out what official languages are spoken in the Western Hemisphere.

3. Make an article, typical of a Latin-American craft. Give this to someone as a present.

4. Invite a person who has traveled or lived in Canada to talk to your troop. Find out in what ways our country is like Canada and how it is different. Discuss across-the-border camping.

5. Demonstrate two popular dances that have come to us from Latin America.

6. Trace the journey of an imaginary air mail letter from your home town to a girl living in a South American city. Tell how much postage you need and how long it would take to get there.

7. Bring to a troop meeting three books that show how our country was influenced by other Western Hemisphere countries in its early development. List as many ways as possible in which we are linked.

*8. Select a country in which you are interested and read articles about it. Report to your troop.

9. Listen to records or the radio and make a list of musicians from other Western Hemisphere countries. Collect pictures of them.

10. Dramatize how you would entertain in your home girls from two different countries in the Western Hemisphere.

11. Play a game using the names of cities, towns, and streets in the United States taken from Latin-American countries.

12. Plan to celebrate one or several religious or patriotic holidays as they would be celebrated in their native country. Invite another troop to share in this celebration.

*13. Explain the work of the Pan American Union. Learn when and how Pan American Day is celebrated.

14. Prepare an exhibit of crafts, food, songs, flags, and stamps that come from Western Hemisphere countries.

15. Learn to sing in the national language a simple song from a Latin-American country.

427

World To earn this badge, do ten of these activities including the
Neighbor three that have a star.

1. Read the preamble to the charter of the United Nations, and discuss with your troop its statement on neighborliness.

2. Present a patrol skit showing what it means to be good neighbors in your community, in your country, and in the world.

*3. Plan an imaginary trip to a country you would like to visit and prepare for it by finding out:

    a. The way you would go; passports and visas necessary; and cost of travel.

    b. Points of interest you would want to see.

    c. Ways children and adults dress.

    d. How families live; schooling for children; favorite recreation.

    e. Something about the men and women whose work is of importance to the world.

    f. How its past and present history is related to our country's.

    g. Something about the climate and how you would dress while there.

    h. Something about the government, current events, and important officials including the ambassador to the United States.

4. Present the plan for your trip to an interested group.

5. Learn the names and locations of the Girl Guide and Scout hostels.

6. Collect stamps and coins of your chosen country. Display them for the troop and explain the value of the coins in relation to ours.

7. Ask a person who has lived in the country or a girl who has a pen pal there to tell the troop about it.

8. Teach your troop a few courtesy phrases in the language of that country.

*9. Take part in at least one international project to demonstrate your troop's neighborliness to another country.

10. Know the correct form for writing a letter to a United

States ambassador. Know what a consulate is and tell where there is one.

11. Demonstrate how you would greet and make friends with a Girl Guide of another country, without knowing her language.

*12. Show your troop the things a traveler should do in order to be a good representative of her own country.

To earn this badge, do ten of these activities including the three that have a star. *Language*

*1. Learn to pronounce correctly the names by which Girl Scouts are known in at least ten countries.

*2. Repeat the Girl Scout motto in five other languages.

3. Play a game using the language of another country.

4. Listen to a radio program, phonograph records, or attend a movie in which another language is spoken.

5. Secure a menu written in another language. Teach your troop to order a meal from it.

6. Make a collection of words, phrases, and expressions originating in another language but now commonly used in English.

7. Learn to sing three different folk songs, each in a language other than English. Teach one of the simple ones to a Brownie troop.

*8. Find out what languages are required for United States girls attending the Juliette Low Session at Our Chalet. Compare the need to speak foreign languages between United States girls and girls from other countries.

9. Interview someone who speaks a foreign language fluently to find out in what ways his ability has been useful.

10. Find out the *official* and *working* languages of the United Nations. Ask someone to explain the system of simultaneous translations they use.

11. List at least five different types of jobs open to people who know several languages. Talk with someone who holds such a job.

12. Make a list of everyday courtesy expressions in other languages.

13. Plan and carry out a party based on customs of one country. Use the language of that country as much as possible.

14. Learn to count to ten in two other languages.

15. Explain to your troop the meaning of linguistics and *esperanto*.

Conversationalist

To earn this badge, do ten of these activities including the two that have a star.

*1. Show ability to read, write, and converse in a language other than English.

2. Compile a book of pictures and information about the country where your chosen language is spoken. Write your explanations in that language.

*3. Report to your troop on some article which you translate from another language.

4. Get copies of Girl Scout books and pamphlets in your chosen language. Display them, and explain the material in English.

5. Write a diary account of a day and night you might spend sight-seeing in the country where your chosen language is spoken. Include common expressions you would need in that language.

6. Serve as hostess or interpreter to a foreign visitor whose language you speak.

7. Lead a discussion about the country whose language you speak.

8. Talk with a person who was born, or who has lived, in a country whose language you speak. Ask her to tell you in that language about things she did as a girl.

9. Help a friend translate correspondence from a pen pal or someone in the country whose language you know.

10. Get acquainted with several of the new methods of teaching languages.

11. Investigate the vocations open to women who read, write, or speak a foreign language. Write a sample letter of application in your foreign language for one of these positions.

12. Help someone else with the requirements for the Language badge.

Junior High

To earn this badge, do ten of these activities.

My World

1. Discover how many hours it would take you by air to reach Guides living on any continent. Trace on a map your journey to one of these continents. List the things you should know before starting.

2. Take the same imaginary trip by ship. Compare routes, length of time, cost.

3. Lay or follow an international trail where interesting things from other countries can be seen.

4. Help prepare a reading list of books for Intermediate Girl Scouts or Brownie Scouts on children in other lands. Or arrange a display of books suitable for an international bookshelf for a troop or Girl Scout office library.

5. Make a survey to learn the number of people in your neighborhood who have traveled or lived in another country. Invite one of them to talk to your troop.

6. Find out about one of the specialized agencies of the United Nations, and how it works.

7. Decide on a specific service project for children made possible through the United Nations. Carry it out in your patrol or troop.

8. List the organizations that are working together for the benefit of people in all countries. Tell about the work of one in detail.

9. Exhibit stamps of foreign countries. Include an explanation of the stamps and of the work of the Universal Postal Union.

10. Teach your troop a game that is popular in other countries.

11. Trace on a pictorial map the world's food supply. Discuss the distribution of food.

12. Make friends with an individual or group different from yourself.

13. Attend several movies or read books about other countries. Discuss things which made the people seem familiar to you, and things which made them seem different.

431

14. Make up a quiz game on the World Association of Girl Guides and Girl Scouts.

CHAPTER 21

Fun and Exploration in the Out-of-doors

Nature

Bird	Mammal	Salt Water Life
Cat and Dog	Rambler	Star
Conservation	Reptile and Am-	Tree
Garden Flower	phibian	Weather
Insect	Rock and Mineral	Wild Plant

Out-of-Doors

Adventurer	Campcraft	Outdoor Cook
Back-Yard	Explorer	Pioneer
Camper	Foot Traveler	

Sports and Games

Athlete	Games	Skiing
Boating	Horsewoman	Sports
Canoeing	Skating	Swimmer
Cyclist	Life Saver	

NATURE

As you do a badge in nature, read Chapter 13.

The following badge from agriculture may be applied toward a nature major in the First Class rank: Animal Raiser.

Rambler   To earn this badge, do nine of these activities including the two that have a star.

*1. Go on several hikes or trips with your troop to learn about or collect the things you need to carry out this badge. If they grow in your part of the country, know the poison ivy, poison sumac, and poison wood (Florida).

2. Make a terrarium and put in it small common wild plants. Keep the terrarium in good condition.

3. Make a chart to be used by your troop or patrol and write on it the names of flowers you have seen.

4. Have some troop members join you and have each person plant a seed of any kind in a flower pot. Compare your plants at the end of a month.

5. Find or make a game that uses pictures of birds to help your troop to learn six common birds.

6. Make some tree leafprints that can be used for stationery, decorations, invitations, or games.

7. Make an insect cage to house comfortably a cricket, a caterpillar, or a web-building spider. Feed it, watch it, and tell your troop about it.

8. Make a star theatre and show at least six different constellations.

*9. Make one of the following collections to give to a hospital, institution, or special school group: nature games, songs, poems, mounted leaves or leafprints, rocks and minerals, wood samples, cloud charts, flower pictures, bird pictures, shells.

10. Explore a stream, pond, lake, or seashore, and make a list of the different kinds of things you find. Make up a game that will help you remember what you saw, or that will help other members to know what you found.

11. Dramatize an animal story that will help other people to know more about animals or a particular animal.

12. Plan and carry out a nature trail for your troop that will have at least ten things labeled with their names and some interesting fact about each.

13. Have a fruit show in the troop or some public place. Include seeds, nuts, berries, and the larger fruits.

14. Plan and carry out a nature quest for your troop for at least four weeks.

15. Help to plan a nature treasure hunt for your troop. Do not put anything on the list for the treasure hunt that is uncommon or that might be hurt.

16. Decorate a living Christmas tree or your old Christmas tree for the birds.

To earn this badge, do ten of these activities including the one that has a star.

Tree

*1. Identify, out-of-doors, fifteen trees.

2. Visit a park, botanical garden, forest, tree nursery, or estate to see trees that are not native in your section of the country.

3. Know how to plant and care for a young tree. Know the proper way to cut a branch from a tree and how to care for the wound.

4. Know some of the local, county, state, and federal organizations or departments that are interested in forestry.

5. Learn the common causes of forest fires, what can be done to prevent them, and how such fires are handled when they occur.

6. Raise a tree from seed and care for it until it can take care of itself.

7. Learn how to clear an area or cut a trail properly. If possible, do one of these after obtaining permission from the owner.

8. Show that you know how, where, and when to cut sticks for outdoor cooking, shelter, and crafts.

9. Know some of the insects and plant diseases harmful to some or all of the trees you choose in Activity 1. Know some of the helpful insects.

10. Locate in your community the kinds of trees and shrubs that attract birds, both as food and nesting sites. Plant some, if possible.

11. Help to arrange an exhibit about trees in some public place, such as a library or school; include leaves, books, pictures, photographs, and things you or your troop have made of wood.

12. Collect some good poems about trees.

435

13. Know the value of trees in flood prevention and erosion control.

14. Record the shape of the leaves of your fifteen trees by making prints, plaster casts, collections, or drawings.

15. Make something out of wood that shows its grain and texture. Know the kind of wood you use and where it grows.

16. Photograph, sketch, or paint three of your trees, showing their characteristic shapes.

Garden Flower   To earn this badge, do ten of these activities including the one that has a star.

*1. Identify twenty-five flowers grown in gardens, greenhouses, or houses.

2. Know three garden flowers that are or have been used medicinally.

3. Make a "slip" or cutting from a plant; root it, and grow it for at least two months.

4. Show the correct way to cut flowers, and how to combine colors and arrange flowers for home decoration.

5. Know the part of the world in which five of your twenty-five plants are native.

6. Know and identify six herbs commonly used for garnishing or seasoning.

7. Be able to identify five plants by their scent.

8. Plant a flower seed and learn how to care for a seedling. Know when and how plants are repotted.

9. Know one annual plant, one perennial plant, and one biennial plant.

10. Do something with plants and flowers to make your home, neighborhood, or school more attractive.

11. Know three insects that trouble cultivated plants and three that are beneficial to them.

12. Sketch, paint, or photograph some of the flowers.

13. Make and carry out a plan for a window of potted plants.

14. Be able to recognize five of the common weeds to be found in lawns, gardens, or both.

To earn this badge, do ten of these activities including the two *Wild Plant* that have a star.

*1. Identify, out-of-doors, twenty wild plants. Do not pick or dig them.

2. Find several different kinds of seeds and notice how some are prepared to travel. Plant some of these seeds and watch them grow.

3. Learn what organizations in your community, such as the local garden club, are working for the protection of wild plants. Do something to help.

4. Photograph or sketch some wild plants. Or, make some craft object using some part of a plant in the design.

*5. Be able to recognize the following plants if they grow in your part of the country: poison ivy, poison oak, poison sumac, and poison wood (Florida). Know how to protect yourself against them and what to do for such poisoning.

6. Know what edible wild plants and fruits grow in your section and how to prepare one of them to eat.

7. Know the uses of three plants for dyes or medicines.

8. Make a troop chart for wild plants found.

9. Know the proper way to cut common flowers and care for them.

10. Fill a terrarium and show that you understand how to keep the plants in good, healthy condition. Use only common plants.

11. Take a trip to the grounds of someone who has a wild plant garden.

12. Visit a botanical garden to see the wild plants uncommon or unknown in your section.

13. Make a list of the plant life in an area a yard square.

14. Find at least three relatives of wild plants in your local flower shops, greenhouses, or gardens.

To earn this badge, do ten of these activities including the *Cat and Dog* five that have a star.

*1. Be responsible for the care of a dog or cat for at least three months. Keep a chart with the following headings: feeding hours;

kinds of food; exercise; coat care; illnesses or accidents; good manners learned; approximate cost of caring for your dog or cat for a week.

2. Be able to identify five different breeds of dogs or three different breeds of cats.

3. Know the humane and sensible ways to housebreak a dog or cat.

4. Read at least two books or see two movies in which the dog or cat is a major character.

*5. Know how to put a safety muzzle on a dog.

*6. Know what first aid to use in at least three of these accidents until a veterinary can get there: broken leg; chill; burns or scalds; thorn or glass imbedded in foot pad; severe bleeding; cuts and bruises.

*7. Know how to give liquid medicine or a tablet.

8. Know how to bathe a dog, and how often.

9. Explain how you would teach a dog the following: walk to heel; stop; lie down; sit; stay. Or, explain how you would teach a cat to keep off the furniture and not to claw things.

*10. Find out your state and county laws and municipal ordinances governing the ownership of dogs or cats in at least three of the following: licensing, humane treatment, leashing, curbing, loss or theft, desertion, poisoning, strays.

11. Know the work that your local humane society or SPCA is doing in protecting the dog and cat and in assisting owners in the better care of animals. If there is no humane society in your locality, find out what your municipal government does in animal welfare.

12. Know how the female dogs and cats should be cared for before and after they produce their young. Know the food care of puppies and kittens.

13. Know what should be done to keep the house cat from being a danger to birds.

14. Make a collection of dog or cat pictures and show them to your troop.

To earn this badge, do ten of these activities including the two *Bird* that have a star.

*1. Identify, out-of-doors, at least fifteen birds.

2. Visit a bird sanctuary.

*3. Learn what is being done to protect birds in your state. Do something to help.

4. Make a birdhouse, feeding tray, or birdbath.

5. Know at least five kinds of trees and shrubs that attract birds.

6. Know the nests of at least five birds.

7. Gather printed material on birds. Read it.

8. Know in what way the English sparrow and starling are beneficial.

9. Know why hawks and owls are of value to men.

10. Visit a zoo or pet shop and learn about the birds you see.

11. Learn about domesticated birds raised on farms.

12. Read stories and articles about people interested in birds.

13. Arrange an exhibit of bird books, pictures, and photographs in some public place.

14. Know the songs or calls of at least five birds.

To earn this badge, do eight of these activities including the *Mammal* one that has a star.

*1. Be able to identify ten wild mammals native to your state. Know the life history of one and the food of all ten.

2. Know the type of home used by five of the mammals.

3. Be able to identify the tracks of two of these mammals.

4. Know the ways in which bats, skunks, and foxes are beneficial to man.

5. Know the trapping and hunting laws in your state.

6. Know what mammals, if any, in your state are in danger of extinction.

7. Know the proper care and feeding of one wild mammal and one domesticated mammal.

8. Visit a circus or zoo. Learn how the mammals are fed, cared for, and housed.

9. Visit a farm to learn the care of some domesticated mammals.

10. Be able to describe two breeds of horses, cattle, dogs, cats, pigs, sheep, or rabbits. Know the country from which they originated.

11. Make a collection of some of the postage stamps of the world that have mammals pictured on them.

12. Do something in your community to help in the protection of wild mammals.

13. Make an exhibit of pictures, books, pamphlets, clippings, and so forth that will help other people to know more about mammals.

14. Select a story about a mammal and be able to tell or dramatize it.

Insect To earn this badge, do ten of these activities including the one that has a star.

*1. Identify, out-of-doors, twenty insects.

2. Identify at least three different kinds of galls.

3. Know three different insects that are found in houses or on domestic animals, and know their life histories.

4. Make two different types of insect cages. Know how to care for any insects you put in them.

5. Raise at least one insect from the egg or young (larva) to the adult insect.

6. Know the difference between a spider and an insect.

7. Know at least three near relatives of insects other than spiders.

8. Know one mammal and three birds in your vicinity that are insect eaters.

9. Know six kinds of insects that are harmful to the trees and gardens in your community and three that are beneficial or not harmful.

10. Go out at night to learn about some night-flying insects.

11. Tell something about the life of the ant or the bee.

12. Distinguish between the following better-known orders of insects: flies, beetles, and moths and butterflies.

13. Find the homes of at least six kinds of insects.

14. Know four kinds of water insects.

To earn this badge, do eight of these activities including the two that have a star.

Reptile and Amphibian

*1. Be able to identify six reptiles and six amphibians and explain some differences between them. Know why they are called cold-blooded. Know the life history of two different kinds and the food of all of them.

2. Raise to adult stage the tadpole of a toad or frog.

3. Know how and why a snake sheds its skin.

4. Know the laws in your state, if any, that protect any reptiles or amphibians.

5. Be able to identify the poisonous snakes in your state, and explain the use the poisonous snake makes of its fangs.

*6. Know the benefit to mankind of reptiles and amphibians, especially those you have chosen.

7. Make a terrarium or fix an aquarium and show that you know how to care for an adult amphibian or reptile.

8. Know ten of the false beliefs about reptiles and amphibians.

9. Do something in your community to help protect the non-poisonous reptiles and amphibians.

10. Be able to explain the difference between alligators and crocodiles, toads and frogs, salamanders and lizards.

11. Know the precautions to take where there are poisonous snakes, and what to do if you are bitten.

12. Know some of the mammals and birds that feed on the reptiles and amphibians you have chosen.

13. Make an exhibit of pictures, maps, clippings, and books that will help others to learn about reptiles and amphibians. Display it where others can see it.

14. Be able to identify three toads or frogs from their voices.

15. Know some of the ways the nonpoisonous snakes protect themselves.

16. Know the shape and texture of turtle eggs; where and how they are laid. Do not disturb them.

17. Know two prehistoric animals that were reptiles.

441

Star   To earn this badge, do ten of these activities including the one that has a star.

   *1. Be able to identify, out-of-doors, ten constellations.

   2. Make a star theatre or other device to help other people learn about stars.

   3. Learn some constellations which make up the zodiac and know their signs.

   4. Visit an observatory to learn what you can about the way the instruments work.

   5. Learn the planets contained in our solar system, and be able to locate at least two of them in the skies.

   6. Find interesting legends about some of the constellations and tell or dramatize the story of one.

   7. Know how stars are used in navigation.

   8. Know what causes the phases of the moon.

   9. Know what causes an eclipse of the moon and the sun.

   10. Show that you know what is meant by magnitude and degrees. Find things in the sky to illustrate them.

   11. Take a group of people out-of-doors to show them the six constellations you like best and teach them how to find them.

   12. Plan or help to plan a party using games and other entertainment based on the subject of stars.

   13. Know what meteors are and when the largest "star showers" appear.

Rock and   To earn this badge, do eight of these activities including the
Mineral   one that has a star.

   *1. Identify five rocks and ten minerals in their natural state. Make a collection of ten and label them properly.

   2. Know the common rocks and common minerals in your section.

   3. Visit at least two places of geological interest in your community.

   4. Find three different kinds of building stones used in your community and, if possible, learn where they were quarried.

   5. Find a fossil plant or animal in your community and know what kind of rock contained it.

442

6. Visit a jewelry store to learn about some precious and semi-precious stones, or visit a lapidary (gem cutter).

7. Know what is meant by igneous, sedimentary, and metamorphic rocks.

8. Know some ways that weather affects rocks.

9. Know ten rocks and minerals we use and see every day.

10. Find out what makes soil.

11. Visit a museum or private collection to see rocks and minerals not common in your vicinity.

12. Make an exhibit based on things you have learned in this badge and display it in some public place.

To earn this badge, do ten of these activities including the two that have a star.

Weather

*1. Keep a daily record of directions of the wind, temperature, cloud formations, and the weather that accompanied them. Do this for a month. For another month, try your hand at predicting the weather and keep a record. (West of the Rockies and in parts of the Southwest, this activity should be done in the winter months.)

2. Know five trustworthy "weather wisdoms."

3. Make rain or snow measure cans and list measurements and dates for two months.

4. Know first aid for sunstroke, heat exhaustion, shock, and frostbite.

*5. Know the rules of safe conduct during a thunderstorm—out-of-doors and indoors.

6. Select and share with your troop some poems or stories about weather, wind, rain, snow, clouds, sky.

7. Make a collection of pictures of rain, snow, clouds, and frost and the effects of these. Exhibit the pictures at troop meetings.

8. Collect (or draw) pictures of instruments for weather forecasting, and know how they work.

9. Make a simple wind vane and a simple barometer and use them for a month.

10. Know the definition of air masses.

443

11. Be able to interpret Beaufort's scale and estimate wind velocity from things you see, such as grass blowing, flags, smoke, sails.

12. Be able to read a weather map and explain it to someone else. Define a "high" and a "low" and know the wind direction of each in the Northern Hemisphere.

13. Post a series of weather maps and note the movement of storms from west to east for a week.

14. Know the five weather flags, and be able to read them in six combinations.

Salt Water Life   To earn this badge, do eight of these activities including the one that has a star.

*1. Identify at least ten shells.

2. Identify at least three seaweeds.

3. Identify three water birds.

4. Know the uses man has made of some of the plant and animal life in or near salt water.

5. Know the laws that protect the salt water animals.

6. Find the homes of at least three different kinds of shore and water animals.

7. Draw a cross-section map of a stretch of beach or rocky shore and show the location of some of the plant and animal life.

8. Learn what causes the tides and know the times of them in your locality.

9. Visit a fish or lobster hatchery and learn how the animals are cared for and distributed.

10. Visit a fish market several times and be able to recognize some of the fish commonly for sale. Learn ways to prepare and cook them.

11. Sketch, paint, or model some of the animals and plants that live near salt water.

12. Identify at least three rocks found on the beach.

To earn this badge, do eight of these activities including the *Conservation* one that has a star.

1. In your locality find four illustrations of erosion and explain the cause, effect, and cure of each.

2. Know which plants in your state may never be cut or picked; which may be cut or picked sparingly; and which may be cut or picked at any time.

3. Find out which birds and fur-bearing animals are protected by the nation and by your state.

4. Explain how hawks, owls, and snakes are helpful to man.

5. Know the part trees and forests, grass and grasslands play in conservation of wildlife, soil, and water supply.

6. Explain how plants and animals are dependent on each other.

7. Learn all you can about the national park or national forest nearest you.

8. Visit a forest station; find out what the forest ranger does and how you can help him. Learn especially about forest fire prevention.

9. Visit a fish hatchery and learn what your state and federal government do to protect and increase fish in your state. Learn what water pollution means.

10. Visit a dam, and find out why it was placed there.

11. Form a Junior Audubon Club in your troop or school and be active in it.

12. Learn the values of having community forests.

13. Take an active part in any conservation project that is going on in your Girl Scout established camp, day camp, or troop camp.

14. Help plant and care for at least twenty young trees or seedlings for a season.

*15. Do one of the following:

    a. Maintain a bird or mammal feeding station for at least four months. Keep a record of the wildlife that come to the station.

    b. Assist in maintaining a wildlife sanctuary for at least two months. Keep records of wildlife seen in the sanctuary.

445

c. Help with a soil erosion problem in a garden, orchard, river bank, or worn-out lawn. If possible, submit "before and after" pictures or drawings showing what you have done.

d. With the consent and support of your local highway commissioner, plant a cover crop on the sides of a new highway cut.

16. Learn the Conservation Pledge.

17. Make an exhibit to show what you have learned about conservation. Display it where others can see it.

OUT-OF-DOORS

As you do a badge in out-of-doors, read Chapter 14.

The following badges from other fields may be applied toward an out-of-doors major in the First Class rank: any badge from the nature field, except Dog and Cat, and Garden Flower badges; First Aid; Outdoor Safety; Personal Health.

Adventurer To earn this badge, do eight of these activities including the two that have a star.

*1. On a hike show that you know good manners in the out-of-doors and observe the rules of the road.

2. Assemble a first aid kit and explain the care of a simple cut, burn, and splinter.

3. Hold a fashion show and model the correct clothes for different kinds of outdoor activities in various types of weather.

4. Use your compass to take and follow degree readings. Show how to find the four cardinal points using sun or stars as guides.

5. Whip the ends of a rope. Demonstrate the use of a square knot and clove hitch.

6. Demonstrate how to open, close, pass, oil, and sharpen a jackknife. Make something with your knife that you can wear or use.

7. Send and receive the alphabet in International Morse code.

*8. Lay and light a foundation fire. Demonstrate five points of fire safety.

9. Prepare, cook, and serve a simple one-pot meal.

10. Know the Conservation Pledge and show that you understand it.

11. Learn three games that can be played while you are hiking or at a cook-out.

To earn this badge, do ten of these activities including the two that have a star.

Back-Yard Camper

*1. Select a back yard or a vacant lot for your camp. Plan and set up an outdoor fireplace. Demonstrate your knowledge of fire regulations, permits, and community rules.

2. Camp overnight, planning and cooking two meals out-of-doors.

3. Help to waterproof material for a shelter half, or groundcloth.

4. Make and use a set of tin-can cooking utensils, a tin-can stove or charcoal stove.

5. Learn how charcoal is made and use it for a cook-out.

6. Waterproof matches and prepare emergency fuel.

7. Make simple furniture from scrap lumber for your back-yard camp.

8. Make a sketch map showing how to reach your back-yard camp.

9. Plan with your patrol or troop at least six outdoor programs. Hold one each month.

*10. Help plan and carry out a cook-out for at least ten people.

11. Make an artistic map of your back-yard camp, pacing off and marking on it the location of all trees, plants, flowers, and shrubs.

12. Plan entertainment suitable for your back yard such as games, songs, folk-dancing, or a campfire program. Lead at least one of these.

13. Hold a cook-out for your family using the back-yard fireplace.

14. Set an attractive table or make and use an efficient outdoor dishwashing system.

447

Campcraft   To earn this badge, do ten of these activities including the four that have a star.

   *1. Plan and carry out an overnight or week-end troop camp at a cabin or lodge.

   2. Demonstrate ways of heating, cooking, and lighting when gas and electricity are not available.

   3. Build a fire in a stove or indoor fireplace and help cook a meal over it.

   4. Show how to care for and use safely an oil lamp, lantern, or stove.

   *5. Plan and pack your own equipment for the troop camp. At camp make a comfortable bed and arrange your personal belongings neatly.

   6. Pack food for transportation. Build a cache at the troop camp.

   7. Demonstrate at least one method of purifying water. Show how to prime a pump or thaw out a frozen water pipe.

   8. Show your skill in using a knife, hammer, saw, and hatchet or lightweight ax by building something for your camp site or cabin.

   9. Split or saw enough wood to keep a fire going for an hour. Make a neat woodpile.

   10. Make and use four of the following, choosing one from each section:

        a. For cooking: broiler, pothook, plank, crane, fuzz stick.

        b. For lighting: candleholder, lantern, waterproof matches, emergency fuel.

        c. For carrying equipment: packbasket, knapsack, waterproof cover for any equipment.

        d. For housekeeping: collapsible wash basin, grease pit, dishwater drain, incinerator, food cache.

   11. Show how to dispose of garbage and waste and how to keep a latrine clean.

   *12. Help lash an article for use during the troop camp. Whip the ends of a rope and show the use of two of the following: sheetbend, sheepshank, bowline, double half hitch.

13. Help build and care for three of the following: a quick hot fire, a reflector fire, a fire for broiling or roasting, a beanhole fire, a barbecue fire, a council fire. Demonstrate fire prevention and safety rules.

14. Help assemble a troop first aid kit, or make your own individual kit. Demonstrate the use of the triangular bandage. Know how to call the nearest doctor.

*15. Help plan a campfire program and conduct part of it.

To earn this badge, do ten of these activities including the four that have a star.

Outdoor Cook

*1. Build a fire by yourself for a troop or patrol cook-out. Demonstrate safety precautions and explain conservation laws.

2. Identify and collect samples of tinder, kindling, and fuel. Make a chart or exhibit that will help others learn about soft and hard woods and how they are used.

3. Make cooking utensils and gadgets from natural materials. Use at least two for a cook-out.

*4. On a cook-out take care of the cleanup. Demonstrate the way to put out a fire, dispose of garbage, and wash utensils.

5. Teach a less experienced person how to select fuel, build, light, and put out a fire.

6. Build and light a fire without paper when (a) tinder is scarce, (b) it is windy, and (c) wood is damp or it is rainy.

7. Demonstrate first aid treatment for burns, cuts, bruises, and bites. Know how to protect these injuries after they have been treated.

8. Make a list of troop outdoor cooking equipment. Decide what items can be made and determine the cost of articles that must be bought. Present the plan to your troop.

9. Help plan and cook meals for hot weather and cold weather, and a quick meal and a leisurely meal. Explain the differences. Include in your plan costs, amounts of food, packing and carrying, and kapers on the cook-out.

10. Know edible wild plants and fruits in your area and serve a meal that includes at least two. Know what poisonous plants to avoid.

449

*11. Cook a one-pot meal. Show how to protect and clean your kettle.

12. Toast bread and broil meat or fish over hot coals.

13. Show your ability to roast or bake over an open fire.

14. Start a collection of outdoor recipes. Try at least three of these.

*15. Learn some recipes for traditional dishes of the United States and other countries. Plan, prepare, or clean up after an outdoor meal using one or more of these recipes.

Foot Traveler To earn this badge, take a series of walks that will make a total of one hundred miles. Do ten of these activities including the three that have a star.

A hike should cover at least one mile, or one-half hour of walking, and be increased gradually. Keep a record of each trip. The following rules should be observed:

Find out from your leader whether adults should go with you or whether several girls may go together, and how far you should try to hike.

Get permission from your parents. Return at the time agreed upon.

Get permission to cross or use private property and know the rules governing use of public property. Leave the places in as good a condition as your found them, or better.

The walks should be selected from at least three of the following areas: town or city streets; city parks; country roads; trails in state or county parks and reservations; cross-country trails.

*1. Show how to stand, walk, breathe, dress, and rest on the trail.

2. Know the length of your regular pace. Compare the time it takes you to go a half mile using your regular pace and a half mile using Scout's pace.

3. Help make a list of hiking routes within a two-mile distance. Follow the routes and make a simple sketch map of one.

4. Make a list of places for cook-outs, outdoor games, or nature study that are less than a mile from streetcar or bus line.

Give directions for reaching them, time it would take, and tell about the things that can be done or seen.

5. Show on hikes the way to observe rules of the road, traffic regulations, safety rules for drinking water, and conservation laws.

6. Make a knapsack or a hike stick.

7. Discuss with your patrol health and safety practices for hiking. Draw up a list of the most important ones and present to the troop through a skit, exhibit, poster, or discussion.

*8. Keep a record of at least one hike by means of a sketch map, nature notes, sketches, story, poems, or photographs.

9. Estimate the distance and time it would take to walk to five places of interest.

10. Using compass and map, lay out and lead a cross-country hike of at least two miles.

11. Prepare and pack a nutritious trail lunch. Know the foods that cause thirst and those that quench thirst.

12. Know common weather signs and predict weather conditions twenty-four hours in advance every day for a week.

13. Find out about the organized groups interested in walking in your community. Follow one of their trails, if possible.

*14. Plan and go on an all-day hike. Make sure that everyone is adequately equipped and that all equipment is packed correctly.

15. Teach one or more hiking songs or games.

Junior High

Earn the Foot Traveler badge before working on this one. Do six activities including the two that have a star. *Explorer*

*1. Go on five all-day exploration trips.

2. Demonstrate your ability to read a road, city, or topographical survey map. Use one of these to plan and go on a trip with your family or troop.

3. Show by playing outdoor games that you can move quietly in the woods and observe accurately.

4. With a member of your troop send and receive messages using International Morse code.

451

5. Make a map, drawn to scale, of a favorite hiking trail or camp site. The trail should be at least two miles long or the area a quarter mile square.

6. Learn and demonstrate your ability to judge satisfactorily any three of the following: time, distance, weight, height, number.

7. Help keep a log of at least one of your trips.

8. Help plan and present a campfire or other program based on the lives of famous explorers or pioneers.

*9. Organize your patrol as an exploration party with a leader, outfitter, navigator, cartographer, botanist, geologist, log keeper, photographer or artist and explore an unfamiliar place.

10. Plan with your group an imaginary trip camp. Include necessary preparations, routes, transportation, and possible adventures or emergencies you might meet along the way.

Junior High

Pioneer

Note: Because this is the most advanced form of camping you should earn the Campcraft badge before starting these activities. To earn this badge, do ten of these activities including the five that have a star.

*1. Explain and demonstrate the things to consider in selecting a camp site.

*2. Plan and carry out a primitive troop camp of at least two nights.

*3. Help plan well-balanced menus, and buy and pack the food for the trip. Construct caches at the camp site.

*4. Pack all personal equipment for transportation. At camp, prepare a comfortable sleeping place and arrange your personal equipment. Lash any necessary gadgets.

5. List the tools and equipment needed. Help assemble, pack, and check the articles before and after the camp. Demonstrate your ability to use the tools and equipment.

6. Demonstrate your understanding of nature conservation by:

a. Explaining the part trees and forests play in conservation of wildlife, soil, and water supply.

     b. Picking only common wild plants and fruits for foods or decorations.

     c. Giving respectful attention to the homes and families of birds, insects, snakes, and other animals.

   7. Help make a pup tent, hike tent, or other small tent.

*8. Pitch a small tent, help with the construction and care of one of the following: temporary shelter, latrine, incinerator or grease pit, primitive shower, work table.

   9. Demonstrate in rain or snow your ability to prepare a meal on a fire built with materials found in nearby woods or fields.

   10. Cook and serve at least one meal for your group using one of the following fires: quick hot fire, reflector fire, coals for broiling, ashes for roasting, beanhole fire, barbecue fire.

   11. Help present a program based on a theme connected with your camp site or present a dramatization showing the importance of fire to man.

   12. Start a collection of poems, songs, and stories for use in outdoor programs.

   13. Make a list of personal equipment needed for troop camping. Decide what can be made from inexpensive materials and make at least two articles.

   14. Make a list of troop equipment needed for troop camping. Decide what articles can be made and determine the cost of articles that must be bought. Present your plans to the troop and, if the troop approves, help make or buy this equipment.

SPORTS AND GAMES

As you do a badge in sports and games, read Chapter 15.

The following badges from other fields may be applied toward a sports and games major in the First Class rank: First Aid, Personal Health, Foot Traveler, Folk Dancer.

Any girl wishing to take part in the activities of the Swimming and Life Saving badges must give evidence of good health by presenting a record of a health examination by a licensed physician within the last year, and a statement of present health signed by her parents or guardian.

453

If you have had a serious illness or operation since you last took part in a sports program, you should bring a note from your doctor giving permission to take part in active sports.

Games To earn this badge, do eight of these activities including the three that have a star.

*1. Play at least one game from each of the following groups: (a) games for two teams, (b) interpatrol contests, (c) circle games, (d) singing or dramatic games, (e) nature games, (f) games for young children.

2. Select three games from the above groups and adapt them to include Girl Scout program activities.

*3. Teach at least four games at different troop meetings.

*4. Make a notebook of games that would be fun on hikes, at camp, at troop meetings, on rainy days, at home, at parties and family gatherings. Include the number of persons, equipment needed, and the rules.

5. Help to make some permanent game equipment.

6. Make a game that you and your friends would enjoy, using inexpensive materials.

7. Participate in an outdoor playday.

8. Explain three games to play with a handicapped or convalescent friend.

9. Play at least one game from four of the following groups: treasure hunts, tracking and stalking games, guessing games, icebreaker games, and games from other countries.

10. Make up with your patrol safety rules for playing games. Present these to the troop.

11. Know first aid treatment for floor burns, turned ankles, scraped knees, and splinters.

12. Be a member of a committee to plan and lead the games at a troop party.

454

To earn this badge, do eight of these activities including the *Cyclist*
three that have a star.

*1. Know the parts of a bicycle and how to keep them in good
condition. Be able to make minor repairs and know where you
can have major repairs done.

*2. Show your ability to ride a bicycle by demonstrating bal-
ance at slow speed, steering, circle riding, braking, and maneuver-
ing.

*3. Know and observe the rules for safe bicycling. Find out
what your local and state traffic regulations are.

4. Decide on and carry out a troop, school, or community
bicycle safety project.

5. Plan and take part in three bicycle trips. Use a map to
determine your route.

6. Learn about the safety equipment used on bicycles or
worn by riders, and make sure you are properly equipped.

7. Help to erect a shelter using ponchos and bicycles.

8. Teach another person how to ride a bicycle.

9. Learn about the work of the Bicycle Institute of America,
the National Safety Council, and the American Youth Hostel.
Find out how bicycles are used in other countries.

10. Invite a member of the traffic department or the local
safety council to talk with your troop.

11. Plan three nutritious lunches suitable for an all-day bicycle
trip and prepare one.

12. Learn about the history of bicycles. Explain the advantages of the different models in current use.

To earn this badge, do eight of these activities including the *Swimmer*
four that have a star.

*1. Show your ability to:

    a. Swim for 40 yards each the side stroke, the elemen-
tary back stroke, and the breast stroke.

    b. Swim 100 yards using one or more of these strokes.

    c. Float for two minutes with minimum amount of
movement.

455

d. Submerge feet first in water, 6 to 8 feet, and swim 20 feet underwater.

*2. Recover yourself after falling into the water with your clothes on from a boat, canoe, dock, or side of the pool. Stay with your craft or stay afloat for five minutes.

3. Do a standing front dive in good form.

*4. Tread water for one minute, using hands if necessary.

5. Play three water games, or teach three stunts in the water.

6. Demonstrate the back-pressure arm-lift method of artificial respiration.

*7. Discuss with your troop or unit various types of safety practices and swimming regulations and the reasons for them.

8. Take part in a water pageant, water sports, or playday, or practice swimming in formation or to music.

9. Swim the crawl in good form for at least 40 yards.

10. Demonstrate two types of shore assists used in lifesaving.

11. Plan and carry out a project to improve your waterfront.

12. Help prepare and present a dramatic skit on water.

Boating To earn this badge, do eight of these activities including the four that have a star.

Before starting these activities a girl must demonstrate her ability to jump into water over her head, recover, tread water, and swim with ease.

*1. Demonstrating good form

a. Cast off and board a boat.

b. Row a triangular course of 440 yards using the regular stroke, the fisherman's "alternate" stroke, sculling, and the back water stroke.

c. Make pivot turns to port and starboard.

d. Land, debark, and moor the boat.

*2. Row over the triangular course with a partner using paired oars.

3. Show how to handpaddle a rowboat and to scull and to paddle a boat with a single oar.

*4. Take part in a deliberate upset of a rowboat. With the

aid of others right the boat and propel it to shore in swamped condition.

*5. Be able to back the transom of the boat to within reach of a tired swimmer and to tow the swimmer ashore while rowing.

6. Explain: proper bracing and use of stretchers, selection of oars of correct length and balance, feathering oars.

7. Learn and use correctly the names for the parts of a boat and oars. Know the different types of rowboats and oarlocks. Explain their advantages and disadvantages.

8. Learn the proper care of a rowboat. Help keep or put a boat in good condition.

9. Make and use four knots, hitches, or splices that are helpful in boating.

10. Help plan and participate in a short rowboat trip.

11. Take part in a project to improve boating facilities.

To earn this badge, do eight of these activities including the *Skating* three that have a star.

*1. In good form skate forward, turning corners clockwise and counter-clockwise. Stop and start quickly and skate backward.

*2. Know how to select and care for your skates. Explain the safety rules for roller or ice skating.

*3. With a friend skate forward, backward, and in dance position.

4. Participate in a skating show, carnival, or competition.

5. Learn to play three games on skates.

6. Demonstrate the cross tango, society blues, or glide waltz.

7. Demonstrate one or more of the following figures: Mohawk turn, three turn, one-foot spin, waltz jump, bunny hop, leap jump.

8. Know the terms used in figure skating and the method of scoring used in competitions.

9. Execute a figure eight on the right foot and the left foot, and practice skating to music.

10. Plan and take part in a wintertime cook-out and skating party. Or plan with others an afternoon of outdoor fun.

11. Make and wear some article of clothing for skating.

457

12. Demonstrate ice rescue methods and tell what treatment should be given the victim.

Horsewoman To earn this badge, do eight of these activities including the three that have a star.

*1. In good form mount and dismount; ride at a walk, trot, and canter; illustrate the use of the "aids" with stops and turns at three gaits.

*2. Show the correct way to saddle and bridle a horse, to halter, lead, hitch, feed, water, and to return a horse to a stable.

*3. Explain safety regulations for riding. Demonstrate your understanding of equestrian etiquette and the Fifth Girl Scout Law.

4. Know the parts of the saddle and bridle, their correct use and care. Name the principal parts of a horse.

5. Groom a horse and know the names of the implements you use.

6. Explain how to detect, and remove, a stone from a horse's foot; how a horse should be shod and why. Describe the different types of shoes.

7. Talk with a veterinary and learn the symptoms of common ailments and diseases of horses.

8. Know how to select and care for your riding equipment.

9. Learn about the history and the development of the horse. Collect or take pictures of four leading breeds and tell about their distinctive features and uses.

10. Draw with dimensions the plans for a stall and its fittings or a tackle room.

11. Take part in one of the following: a trail ride, all-day-cross-country ride, breakfast or supper ride, riding drill or demonstration, horse show, gymkhana.

12. Know the daily care of a horse and explain how it varies. Find out approximate cost of the monthly care of a horse.

13. Halter a horse, using a suitable knot and the correct length of rope. Explain how to tie a group of horses and how to lead one horse while riding another.

To earn this badge, do eight of these activities including the *Canoeing* four that have a star.

Before starting these activities a girl must demonstrate ability to jump into water over her head, recover, tread water, and swim with ease. In addition she must take part in a canoe tip-over in company with an experienced canoeist and assist in propelling the canoe along the shore line while using it for support.

*1. In good form:

    a. Launch or board a canoe.

    b. Demonstrate in bow position the pushover, draw, sweep, bow, and back-water strokes.

    c. Paddle in stern position a triangular course of 440 yards.

    d. Beach or dock the canoe.

*2. In water over your head, jump out of a canoe without losing contact with it and climb in without shipping water.

*3. With a friend show the procedures to use in the rescue of two canoeists who are clinging to a capsized canoe.

*4. Explain the importance in canoeing of the kneeling position, the painter, remaining with an overturned canoe in case of accident.

5. With a friend tip over a canoe, right it, get in and hand paddle 100 yards along the shore line. Show "safety" use of a swamped canoe.

6. Explain the care of canoes and paddles. Know how to make temporary repairs to a punctured canoe and a broken paddle shaft. Assist, if possible, in refinishing paddles or a canoe.

7. Know and use correctly the names for different parts of a canoe and paddle. Learn about the different types of canoes and paddles. Explain their advantages and disadvantages.

8. Help plan and participate in a short canoe trip.

9. Know common weather signs and predict weather conditions twenty-four hours in advance every day for a week. Learn about tides and currents.

10. Learn several songs, the rhythm of which is suited to paddling.

459

11. Make something useful for boating such as kneeling pads, a checkboard, course markers.

12. In stern position, paddling on port and then starboard, make good head-on and broadside landings.

Skiing To earn this badge, do eight of these activities including the four that have a star.

*1. Show your ability to ski on the level, to use poles properly, and execute kick turns to the right and left.

*2. Demonstrate the side-step and herringbone.

*3. Make a controlled downhill run. Do three connected snow-plow turns and demonstrate two traverses.

4. Know how to select and care for your equipment. Know the correct care of wet clothing. If possible, take part in a fashion show to illustrate the proper clothing and equipment for different types of winter sports.

5. Learn about the National Ski Association of America and the National Ski Patrol System. If possible join one of these organizations.

6. Explain and use the following terms correctly: stem turn, side-slipping, Christiania, jump turn, Telemark, slalom course.

7. Know first aid treatment for snowblindness, sunburn, frost-bite, chilblains, bruises, and sprains. Explain how these injuries might be avoided.

8. Plan and carry out a cook-out in the snow.

*9. Explain the safety precautions for skiing, skiing etiquette, and how to select a place to practice.

10. Lay a cross-country trail through the snow, using a compass, tracks, or trail signs, or follow one made by an animal or human being.

11. Plan and take part in an evening of songs, games, dancing, and storytelling after a day of skiing.

Sports To earn this badge, do eight of these activities including the four that have a star.

*1. Show your ability to play well a sport such as tennis, badminton, ping pong, golf, archery, bowling, shuffleboard, paddle tennis, waterskiing.

*2. Know the rules of your sport. Explain the types of competitions or tournaments that are held.

3. Participate in a tournament between your troop and another group. After the event decide how you can improve your play.

*4. Know the health and safety rules and the proper clothes to wear for your sport.

5. Practice one sport daily for at least two weeks or more.

6. Know the history and development of three organized sports and the countries in which they are most popular.

7. Help plan and run off a tournament in one of these sports or organize a ladder for your neighborhood.

*8. Officiate as a referee, umpire, timekeeper, or scorekeeper during a sports event.

9. Explain the points to be considered in selecting, caring for, using, and storing the equipment needed for your sport.

10. Read a book featuring some aspect of sports you are interested in and give a report to your troop.

11. Find out what sports' facilities are available in your community. Locate them on a map of your town so your findings can be used by other troops and groups interested in sports.

12. Make a piece of sporting equipment.

To earn this badge, do eight of these activities including the *Athlete* five that have a star.

*1. Be a member of a school, club, or troop team in a sport such as volley ball, softball, basketball, or field hockey.

*2. Demonstrate your skill in the sport and your understanding of team play.

*3. Know the rules governing the sport.

4. Take part in an intermural, interclub, or intertroop game. After the event analyze with your team the good and bad points of your play.

5. Know the health and safety rules and the proper clothes to wear for this sport. Know first aid treatment for floor burns, turned ankles, scraped knees, and splinters.

6. Officiate as a referee, umpire, timekeeper, or scorekeeper during a sports event.

461

7. Make a scrapbook or be responsible for a bulletin board with information about your favorite sport which will interest others.

*8. Discuss with your troop the value of regular exercise and develop a six months' plan for yourself, or earn the Personal Health badge.

*9. Read about the method of play, rules, and formations used in boys' games such as baseball, basketball, football, ice hockey. Discuss with your troop the differences and the reasons for the differences between girls' and boys' rules for sports.

10. Learn about the different type of school sports in other countries such as lacrosse, cricket, calisthenics.

11. Be a member of a school athletic or games committee or take part in a project to improve or increase interest in your school athletic program.

Junior High

Life Saver To earn this badge, do two of these activities including the one that has a star.

*1. Successfully complete a Junior Life Saving Course given by the American Red Cross, Boy Scouts of America, or Y.M.C.A.

2. Assist a lifeguard or waterfront counselor for at least three swimming periods. Discuss with your troop the principles of water safety that were demonstrated.

3. Assist either your troop, unit, or the American Red Cross in making waterfront safety equipment, such as checkboards, torpedo buoys, and kickboards.

CHAPTER 22

You and Your Home

Agriculture

Animal Raiser	Farmer	Landscaper
Beekeeper	Fruit Raiser	Poultry Raiser
Dairying	Home Gardener	Truck Gardener

Health and Safety

Child Care	First Aid to Animals	Home Nurse
Community Safety	Health Aid	Outdoor Safety
Farm Safety	Home Health and	Personal Health
First Aid	Safety	Public Health

Homemaking

Homemaker	Foods	Housekeeper
Clothing	Good Grooming	Nutrition
Cook	Handy Woman	Seamstress
Dressmaker	Hospitality	

AGRICULTURE

As you do a badge in agriculture, read Chapter 16.

The following badges from other fields may be applied toward an agriculture major in the First Class rank: Conservation, Farm Safety, First Aid to Animals, Foods, Weather.

Farmer To earn this badge, do ten of these activities including the two that have a star.

1. Learn how to bridle, lead, and tie a horse.
2. Learn how to drive cows or sheep.
3. Learn how to draw and cut up a chicken.
4. Learn how to gather, candle, and grade eggs.
5. Learn how to hoe and how to run a hand cultivator.

*6. Get acquainted with the members of a farm family (other than your own) and find out how they prepare the soil, plant, and tend crops or stock.

7. Learn how to cook six substantial meals for farm workers. Prepare one.
8. Drive a nail and saw a board.
9. Sharpen household knives, a hatchet, and an ax.
10. Know the various uses of a tractor on a farm.
11. Become familiar with the farm journals and magazines published or widely read in your locality.
12. Know the location of your state or county fair and attend, if possible.

*13. Do some kind of service to help improve farming for your own family, a neighbor, or your community.

14. Be able to recognize the various machines used in planting, cultivating, and harvesting crops.
15. Know how to act when working around farm animals.

Landscaper To earn this badge, do ten of these activities including the two that have a star.

*1. Landscape a piece of land. If you have no land around your house, perhaps someone will lend you a piece nearby. You may be able to get your troop to help landscape some piece of public land.

2. Learn the names of the things that already grow there.
3. Note the amount of sunshine the piece of land gets and have the soil tested.
4. Look at seed catalogs and make a list of some of the things you could use in your landscaping. Figure the cost.

5. Plan, on paper and to scale, what you would like to do to

your piece of land. Use as much as possible of what already exists there.

6. Through the year, remove plants, prepare soil, plant, and replant, working toward your landscape goal.

7. Know three kinds of trees that are good for home planting. Know three kinds of plants that make good hedges.

8. Help prune a bush, a vine, and small limbs from trees, and cut a hedge.

9. Be able to identify and to tell the use of and care of these tools: pruning knife, pruning shears, lopping shears, hedge shears, pole shears, pruning saw, spade, shovel, prong shovel, hoe, iron rake, wooden rake, lawn rake, cultivator, sickle, scythe, lawn mower, and hose.

10. Plant a tree or a bush and care for it until it is well established.

11. Use leaves and grass for mulch or compost. Know the fire laws of your community in regard to the burning of grass and leaves, and know the safety methods for both.

12. Name six annuals that bloom in the spring, six in the summer, and six in the fall. Do the same for six perennials and three biennials.

13. Know the country, or the part of this country, to which three of your plants are native.

*14. Use the knowledge you have gained from landscaping to help a friend, a neighbor, or the community to beautify another spot.

15. Keep a list of the birds that visit your piece of land.

16. Visit and, if possible, take part in your state or county fair.

To earn this badge, do ten of these activities including the one that has a star.

Home Gardener

*1. Make a garden at least 10 x 12 feet in a place where the soil is good for raising vegetables and flowers. Make it one plot or the equal number of feet in various parts of a piece of ground. Make a plan showing what vegetables and flowers are to be grown and where. Take care of your garden.

2. Raise at least one kind of plant from seed for your garden.

3. Know three different types of soil and the plants that prefer these. Learn the proper use of three different types of fertilizers.

4. Learn six weeds that grow in your garden.

5. Visit some gardens in your neighborhood and make a list of the plants growing in them.

6. Watch how the insects gather nectar and pollen. Explain cross-pollination and self-pollination.

7. Visit your garden after dark and note what insects are abroad and which flowers are closed or open.

8. Find out which vegetables can be stored for winter use and how. Can or freeze at least one of them.

9. Know the insects and plant diseases from which you must protect your vegetables or flowers.

10. Find out the native country of at least two vegetables and two flowers (or four of either one) in your garden. Know something of the history, lore, legend, or use of these plants.

11. Pot something from your garden at the end of the summer and grow it indoors.

12. Understand some of the occupants of your garden other than insects, such as earthworms, snails, toads, and snakes. Learn what they do.

13. Know the tools necessary for a small garden and show how to use and care for them in summer and winter.

14. Learn how to gather and care for seeds and bulbs over the winter.

15. Know what garden or farm clubs there are in your community and do something to help one of them; or help your troop to plan and hold a flower or crop show.

16. Learn how to cut and arrange flowers.

Truck Gardener

To earn this badge, do ten of these activities including the two that have a star.

*1. Find a truck garden in your community to work in for at least fifty hours; or observe one over a period of three of the growing months. Do the rest of the activities in relation to six vegetables grown there.

2. Learn how to plant seeds and transplant seedlings.

3. Recognize and describe some of the machines used on truck farms.

4. Learn the insect pests and plant diseases that trouble your six vegetables and know the controls for them.

5. Find the approximate retail market "in-season" and "out-of-season" price of your six vegetables.

6. Know the type of soil, amount of water, and cultivation methods, including mulch and fertilizers, for your six vegetables.

7. Harvest your vegetables and prepare them for market.

8. Know the work of the honeybee in a truck garden.

9. Know the uses and differences between a cold frame and a hotbed.

10. Learn the value of earthworms, beneficial insects, toads, and some of the snakes in a truck garden.

11. Describe one method of irrigation or watering.

12. Know the best method of home preservation for your vegetables and preserve one.

13. Prepare some of your vegetables for the table.

14. Know the countries from which your vegetables originated.

15. Find out what migratory labor is and how it is housed in your community. If possible, invite some of the girls from a migrant camp to join in your troop activities.

*16. Use some of the information you have learned, or the produce you have raised, for a troop, school, church or synagogue, or other community service.

17. Visit and, if possible, take part in your state or county fair.

To earn this badge, do ten of these activities including the two that have a star.

*1. Take part care of a fruit orchard, a vineyard, or a small fruit farm for two months, or full care of a fruit tree and a grapevine and three berry bushes for a year.

2. Learn the soil, exposure, and moisture necessary for the fruit you are working with, including mulching, trenching, irrigating, fertilizing.

3. Learn the insect pests, plant diseases, and animals that attack the fruit you are working with and the sprays, powders, and other means used to combat them, and when these are used.

Fruit Raiser

467

4. Learn the use of smudge fires and other devices to protect fruit from frost.

5. Learn how to trim or prune the trees, bushes, or vines you are working with, and know how grafts and cuttings are made.

6. Know the names and the care of the tools you use with your fruits.

7. Know how the fruit you are working with is harvested and prepared for market.

8. Learn to recognize some of the fruits that are not grown in your part of the country.

9. Learn the approximate "in-season" and "out-of-season" retail market price in your community for the type of fruit you are working with, and learn to recognize the various sizes of boxes and baskets used for large and small fruits.

10. Learn ways that will protect your fruit from birds but will not harm them.

11. Know what insects are valuable to you in pollinating the flowers of your fruit, and the effects, if any, of sprays.

12. Learn the home preservation methods for the fruit you have chosen, and preserve some of it.

13. Know ways to prepare each of your chosen fruits for the table.

14. Learn the native homes of your fruits and what their names mean.

*15. Use some of the information you have learned, or the produce you have raised, for a troop, school, church or synagogue, or other community service.

16. Visit, and if possible, take part in your state or county fair.

Beekeeper To earn this badge, do ten of these activities including the two that have a star.

*1. Tell what constitutes a colony of bees and how it lives.

2. Know how nectar is gathered, stored, and how the honeycomb is built.

3. Explain what part the queen, drones, and workers play in the life of the colony.

4. Be able to recognize and describe each of the following:

468

queen, drone, worker, egg, larva, pupa, honey, wax, pollen, brood-nest, comb, queen cells, bee glue.

5. Assist in having a swarm, examining a colony, removing the comb, finding the queens, putting foundations in sections, filling and removing supers, and preparing honey in comb and straining for market. Be able to identify different parts of a hive.

6. Help fix the hives for the winter months.

7. Tell which flowers afford the best food for bees, and how honey varies in color and flavor according to the flowers. Know effect, if any, of insect sprays on bees.

8. Know how to keep from being stung by a bee and what to do for a bee sting.

9. Learn at least three recipes in which honey may be used in place of sugar.

10. Read Maurice Maeterlinck's *Children's Life of the Bee* or some book or pamphlet on the bee, and tell your troop about it.

11. Find out about the habits of wild bees and how you go about finding a colony of them.

12. Know the value of having bees wherever plants are grown for food or for pleasure.

13. Know how to introduce a new queen into a hive.

14. Know what gear is necessary in beekeeping.

15. Learn the diseases of bees and some of the things that destroy colonies of bees.

*16. Use some of the information you have gathered, or produce you have raised, for a troop, school, church or synagogue, or other community service.

17. Visit and, if possible, take part in your state or county fair.

To earn this badge, do eight of these activities including the one that has a star.

Animal Raiser

This badge can be earned using any animal, except a cat or dog (see Cat and Dog badge), cow (see Dairying badge), or poultry (see Poultry Raiser badge).

*1. Take full charge of an animal (or several animals) for at least six months. At all times treat it with kindness and understanding.

2. Know the foods needed to keep it healthy.

3. Give it the proper amount of sun, air, sleep, and water.

4. Keep it in a temperature in which it is safe and comfortable.

5. Make or find it the proper kind of shelter. Make it a real home. Keep it clean.

6. Know the breeding season of your animal.

7. Know some of the sicknesses and diseases from which you have to protect it.

8. Know the treatment needed if it is ill. Before administering treatment, talk with a veterinary or with someone who knows more than you do about the animal.

9. Know the proper way to transport your animal from one place to another.

10. Learn what is being done by your local humane society or the Society for Prevention of Cruelty to Animals for the protection of animals.

11. Draw, paint, model, or photograph your animal.

Poultry Raiser To earn this badge, do ten of these activities including the two that have a star.

*1. Raise a flock of chickens (at least six) and keep records on the cost of chicks, feed, fuel, litter, labor, and so forth. Record the average weights of the chickens at five weeks, ten weeks, twenty weeks.

2. Know the value in egg production, fattening, and resistance to disease of different types of feed.

3. Study the types of poultry houses in your community and in the U.S. Department of Agriculture publications. Learn the best features of each.

4. Know the symptoms of three chicken diseases and what to do if they appear in your flock.

5. Recognize and point out the difference between at least six kinds of poultry.

6. Keep an egg record, recording the number of hens, the eggs gathered each day, the average production record. Learn to cull out nonlayers and broody hens.

7. Learn about blood-testing and leg-banding of hens.

8. Learn what is meant by U.S. Approved, U.S. Certified, R. O. P. Learn the egg-grading laws of your state, if any.

9. Learn to dress and draw a chicken; how to prepare a chicken for frying; and how to prepare a chicken for roasting.

10. Learn about moulting—why a chicken moults, what will shorten or lengthen a moult, feeding requirements during moulting.

11. Learn the names of the organs of a hen and how an egg is formed.

12. Learn the names of the parts of an egg.

*13. Use some of the information you have learned, or the produce you have raised, for troop, school, church or synagogue, or other community service.

14. Visit and, if possible, take part in your state or county fair.

15. Know what animals attack poultry and how to protect poultry from them.

To earn this badge, do ten of these activities including the two that have a star.

Dairying

*1. Take part care of a milking (fresh) cow for a period of one month.

2. Know the difference, in females, between a calf, a heifer, and a cow, and the quantity and type of feed for each.

3. Explain how butter and cottage cheese are made and approximately how much milk it takes to make a pound of each. Make some of each, if you can.

4. Be able to recognize and describe three different breeds of dairy cattle.

5. Tell what is meant by butterfat content and how it is measured.

6. Describe three diseases of cows, the prevention, and the cure, if any.

7. Milk a cow by hand or strip one after machine milking. Know the care of the udders before milking.

8. Know the sanitary care of milking machines, pails, and other equipment used in milking.

9. Explain how and why milk is pasteurized and how it can be done in the home.

10. Know the difference between the two market kinds of milk, and the usual three grades of each.

11. Visit a dairy and learn how milk is handled before and after pasteurizing and how it is prepared for delivery.

12. Be able to describe the food values of milk and milk products. Know three recipes using milk.

13. Learn what you can about your state and local laws that govern the sanitation of a dairy barn and the marketing of milk.

14. Know the wholesale and retail costs of various grades of milk, and, if possible, how the prices are set.

*15. Use some of the information you have learned, or produce you have raised, for troop, school, church or synagogue, or other community service.

16. Visit, and if possible, take part in your state or county fair.

HEALTH AND SAFETY

As you earn a badge in health and safety, read Chapter 17.

The following badges from other fields may be applied toward a health and safety major in the First Class rank: Life Saver, Handywoman.

Health Aid To earn this badge, do ten of these activities including the two that have a star.

1. Make a safety survey of your home and yard. With your family correct as many hazardous conditions as possible.

2. Make a home telephone card for emergency calls. Know how to make the proper calls and to give the necessary information.

3. Find out and practice five different things you can do in order to help when there is sickness in the family.

4. With your patrol assemble a first aid kit to carry on hikes and for your troop meeting place. Know how to use it.

*5. Demonstrate how to give first aid for fainting, small cuts, blisters, bruises, scratches, and splinters. Know three ways in which a triangular bandage is used.

6. Prepare and demonstrate the use and care of a hot-water bag and an ice bag.

7. For one week keep a record of your observance of simple health rules. Tell what you can do to improve your record.

8. Pantomime fifteen things you would do for a safe and comfortable all-day outing.

9. Learn the health and safety precautions for a children's playroom. Practice several games, stories, and songs you can use with small children.

10. Learn the rules for the safe use of your play equipment.

11. Prepare a scrapbook or posters illustrating the seven basic food groups. Know why each of these foods are important for health.

12. Visit a grocery store and learn the names of fruits and vegetables, either canned or fresh, that are new to you. Learn how and where they are grown and one way to prepare at least five.

13. Become acquainted with a farm family. Learn what foods are produced on their farm and how they are cared for until they are used by the family or sold.

*14. Plant and grow a few seeds or a bulb. Discuss three things important both to its growth and to your growth.

To earn this badge, do ten of these activities including the three that have a star.

Personal Health

1. Take part in a seasonal sports program. Discuss with your troop how this activity contributes to your physical and mental well-being.

2. Pantomime good posture in several daily activities.

*3. Have a health examination. Make a record of the things the doctor advises and carry out his suggestions.

4. Help plan a cold prevention campaign. Describe the best things to do to avoid common colds and three things to do to care for yourself when you have a cold. Tell why a cold should not be neglected.

*5. Discuss what is necessary in a well-balanced diet for a girl of your age.

6. Make an exhibit of good and poor types of shoes and hose.

7. Show the proper care of the teeth, hair, skin, hands, and nails.

8. In a style show, demonstrate how posture, health, and grooming help make you appear more attractive.

*9. Help plan and carry out a program to demonstrate the rules of good health, using posters, games, skits, songs, exhibits, dramatizations.

10. Know the occupational opportunities for women in health work. Know the qualifications for one.

11. Find out what part nutrition plays in building sound teeth and healthy gums. Discuss with your dentist or dental hygienist what to do to keep your teeth in good condition.

12. Learn what health services your community offers. Visit a health agency.

13. Demonstrate good lighting for reading and sewing.

14. Know five diseases from which you can be protected by inoculations. Keep a record of the inoculations you have had. Learn how serums are made.

15. With others, write a play showing how your responsibility for your health increases as you grow older. Show what you can do as a good citizen for the health of your family, your community, nation, and the world.

Home Health and Safety

To earn this badge, do ten of these activities including the three that have a star.

*1. Make a survey of your home and yard to discover fire and accident hazards. Organize a Family Safety Council.

2. With others, plan a series of window displays on home safety.

3. Demonstrate the safe care and use of heating and cooking stoves in your home.

4. Make or draw a model of a bathroom or kitchen showing safety features.

5. With your mother, label and arrange neatly the contents of your medicine chest.

6. Help plan and carry out a continuous safety campaign for your troop meeting place.

7. Demonstrate the safety measures to take in five of the following: baking; canning; washing dishes; waxing floors; laundering with electricity; turning on electric lights in the bathroom; using long-handled saucepans; hanging a picture; filling a hot-water bottle; disposing of broken glass, nails, tacks, tin cans, pins, needles, razor blades; burning of paper out-of-doors.

*8. Demonstrate the safe use and care of knives, can opener, scissors, ice pick. Make a protective covering, container, or rack for them.

9. Discuss with your patrol common hazards connected with two of our holidays. List things you do to keep yourself and your family safe at holiday time.

10. Make and put in a safe place noninflammable containers for used and unused matches.

11. Draw a floor plan for a home, showing furnishings and equipment. Consider health and safety aspects of heating, lighting, ventilation, sunlight.

12. Visit a model home. Tell what you think of its location, design, equipment, and furnishings from a health and safety standpoint.

*13. Make and carry out a schedule for the care of the following: refrigerator and food containers; dishes, silver, dish cloths; waste and garbage containers; brooms and brushes; dusters, waxing and polishing cloths; vacuum cleaner and carpet sweeper.

To earn this badge, do ten of these activities including the three that have a star.

Child Care

1. Help collect or make several safe toys for infants and young children.

2. Know how birth certificates are made out, why they are important, and where yours is kept.

*3. Watch or help give a baby its bath. Using a doll, show how you would bathe, dress, and feed a baby.

4. Assemble a baby's bath tray.

5. Help to make and equip a bed for a baby.

6. Know what signs to look for in babies or small children for health and for illness.

*7. Find out what foods an infant and a small child need and how often they eat. Prepare one food for an infant and one for a small child.

8. Display infants' and children's clothing borrowed from home or store. Point out the good features of each piece. Make an infant's or child's garment to give away.

9. Find three approved books that answer the usual questions about an infant's and child's everyday life and use them for these activities.

10. Discuss safety measures in the home where there are small children.

11. Visit a Brownie troop or a group of small children to see what games and songs they like best. Teach a song or game to the group.

*12. Dramatize an interview with a mother who has asked you for the first time to care for her child for four hours. Include the things you need to know about the child, the house, and equipment.

13. Visit a day nursery or kindergarten or arrange to have a movie shown on child care. Observe the care and attention given to the small child.

14. Learn how a mother animal takes care of her young. Know what she does to protect their health and safety.

15. Help plan and carry out a party for a small group of preschool children. Serve simple refreshments. Play active and quiet games.

16. Help an adult care for a child for a whole day.

Community Safety

To earn this badge, do ten of these activities including the three that have a star.

1. With some of your troop, plan and carry out a neighborhood clean-up campaign.

*2. Visit a fire department. Learn about its services and how it protects you.

3. Dramatize or make posters illustrating safety rules for hikers and cyclists.

4. Discuss the public services you would use if you found a lost child at a large gathering; had been exposed to a communicable disease; had been bitten by a dog; injured your ankle while on a public playground.

*5. Visit four public buildings. Tell how they provide for public safety.

6. Inspect the places in your neighborhood where small children play. List the safety hazards and make plans to help to correct them.

7. Show how to use garden tools safely.

*8. With others inspect your meeting place or camp site for any safety or health hazards. Serve on a committee to make necessary improvements.

9. Collect stories of accidents on the street, in homes, schools, or play areas. Discuss how they might have been prevented.

10. Make a list of safety rules for your playground, school gym, community center, or swimming pool. Observe these rules.

11. Ask the police department or other community group to help you plan and give bicycle tests to children in your neighborhood.

12. Make an exhibit to show safe practices in the following: crossing the street; obeying traffic lights; playing in a safe place; closing doors, gates, and drawers; picking up toys.

13. Make a map, diagram, or illustration of the busiest corner in your community. Indicate all safety devices.

14. Visit your local health department and learn about the accident rates from various causes. Compare the rates for your town with several other localities. What could you do to help improve these records?

Outdoor Safety

To earn this badge, do ten of these activities including the three that have a star.

*1. At an outdoor meeting or on a camping trip, help plan, organize, and carry out a fire drill.

2. Identify and know the precautions for poisonous plants, insects, and snakes found in your area.

*3. On a cook-out, wash dishes in a sanitary way.

4. On a hike or camping trip, show the correct way to dispose of garbage, waste liquids, paper, and tin cans.

5. Help put on a troop fashion show. Model clothing for the out-of-doors for various kinds of weather.

6. Store food properly in the out-of-doors. Name three types of outdoor caches.

7. Make a skit or game that teaches what to do: (a) to avoid getting lost when hiking; (b) if you are lost in the woods; (c) when a member of your group is lost.

*8. Find the hazards at your favorite outdoor meeting place or your camp site. Help eliminate them or put up warning signs.

9. Know the safety rules to observe in using a bicycle, canoe, rowboat, horse, skates, skis.

10. Make a sheath for an ax, hatchet, or hunting knife. Show that you know how to hold, carry, use, and sharpen your tool.

11. Make a collection of games that teach or review outdoor first aid facts and skills. Teach one.

12. Learn how and where water is tested. Demonstrate two ways to purify water.

13. Know the safety precautions to use in a thunderstorm and in high winds.

14. Know the work done by several of the following: Coast Guard, American Red Cross, lifesaving station, lighthouse, park authority, forest ranger, fire warden, safety council, state police.

15. Prepare a chart or exhibit to teach safety rules for the building and control of outdoor fires.

16. Make a first aid kit for outdoor activities. Demonstrate how to behave in an emergency, and how to get help in case of accident.

Farm Safety

To earn this badge, do ten of these activities including the three that have a star.

*1. List the places where accidents occur on your farm. With your family organize a Family Safety Council.

2. Observe safe behavior around farm machinery.

3. Know safe use and care of three kinds of ladders.

4. Drive a nail and saw a board.

478

5. Show the safe use and care of common hand tools.

6. Know the safe use and care of oil heating and lighting equipment.

7. Dramatize how to approach farm animals with safety for yourself and without frightening them.

8. Demonstrate the knots to use in tying livestock especially in case of fire.

9. Sharpen a knife.

10. Explain the precautions to take for yourself, your home, buildings, and farm animals before and during any kind of storms common in your locality.

11. Identify poisonous plants that grow on or near your farm.

*12. Know the first aid treatment for blisters, burns (including sunburn), chill from exposure, cuts or scratches, animal bites, poisoning from plants, nosebleed, punctured wound.

13. With others prepare and display an exhibit on prevention of home accidents.

*14. Learn the common causes of farm fires; how to extinguish small fires; and how to make a safe exit in a serious fire.

To earn this badge, do ten of these activities including the two that have a star.

First Aid to Animals

This badge must be done under the guidance of a veterinary. It may be done with any kind of domestic animal.

*1. Know the types of injuries and diseases to which your animal is susceptible, and the means of prevention.

2. Demonstrate how to approach the animal if it is injured.

3. Show how to catch, carry, muzzle, tie, hold, or confine your animal when giving treatment.

*4. Explain the first aid treatment for hysteria, bruises, suffocation, burns and scalds, shock, wounds, gases, drowning, hemorrhage, fractures, electric shock, internal injuries. Know the care of newborn animals.

5. Demonstrate how to take its pulse and temperature.

6. Know how to administer medicine in liquid or tablet form.

7. Make and know how to use a dog lasso.

8. Be able to name the parts of your animal.

479

9. Find out what is being done in your community for the control of the communicable diseases of animals.

10. Know the work and some publications of the American Humane Association, and find out the location of the nearest unit of the Society for the Prevention of Cruelty to Animals.

11. Know the local and state laws governing the treatment, use, and ownership of your animal.

12. List the address and telephone number of a veterinary and and of the nearest SPCA or Humane Society Shelter.

13. Give a talk to some group on the value of learning first aid to animals.

14. Know the accepted, humane method of disposing of animals when this becomes necessary.

Junior High

First Aid

To earn this badge, do ten of these activities including the six that have a star.

Instruction for this badge should be given by one of the following: licensed doctor of medicine, nurse with first aid experience, or a person who has received a Standard or Advanced First Aid Certificate within the past three years.

1. Dramatize or tell a story showing: the four main purposes of first aid; why emphasis is on prevention of accidents; why everyone should know first aid; how to behave in an emergency; the quickest way to get professional help in case of a serious injury.

*2. Demonstrate the uses of: roller bandage, sterile gauze dressing, triangular bandage, cravat bandage.

3. For at least four weeks, serve on a troop safety committee for prevention of accidents in all troop activities.

4. Learn about the history, work, and financing of the American Red Cross and the activities in the junior branch.

*5. Make a telephone card for emergency calls for the following: family physician, local public health representative, fire department, police department, ambulance service, nearby hospital. Know how to make the proper calls to each giving the necessary information.

6. Demonstrate the first aid to give a person who has: fallen down a flight of stairs; has been hit on the head by a heavy object; has been overexposed to cold or heat.

*7. Demonstrate: the proper cleansing of the hands for giving first aid treatment; how a wound should be treated; how to apply splints for a fracture of the forearm, for a fracture at the wrist; treatment for nosebleed, fainting, bee sting; treatment for a cinder in the eye, a minor burn, poison ivy rash, or minor cuts and scratches.

*8. Demonstrate how to apply pressure to the two main digital points. Tell when you would use each.

9. Make and equip a first aid kit.

10. Show how you would improvise and use a stretcher, a chair as a carrier. Demonstrate a two-man carry, an eight-man carry.

11. Make up a first aid quiz game.

*12. Demonstrate how to recognize and care for a patient suffering from shock.

13. Show how to give proper first aid for a simple fracture of the leg. Or demonstrate what should be done when a person has come into contact with an electric current.

*14. Demonstrate back pressure—arm lift method of artificial respiration.

Junior High

To earn this badge, do ten of these activities including the four that have a star. *Home Nurse*

1. Select a room in your home in which you would care for a sick person. On a floor plan, show present arrangement and how you would need to adapt it. Demonstrate care of the room.

*2. Show how to make a comfortable bed for a patient. Make or improvise a back rest, body supports, device for supporting bed clothes, night light, bedside light, bed jacket, bed table, door silencer, ventilating screen.

3. Demonstrate arrangement and use of a bedside table and of trays for medicines, toilet articles, and meals.

*4. Tell how to care for a mild infection, such as a cold (a) when you are sick yourself (b) when caring for another person.

481

Know precautions to be observed. List equipment and supplies to collect or make.

5. Demonstrate the care and use of a mouth thermometer.

6. Explain six early symptoms of illness and what precautions are needed if an illness is diagnosed by the doctor as contagious.

7. Explain what is meant by liquid, soft, and light diets. Prepare and serve a typical meal from each.

*8. List safe and interesting things with which to entertain convalescents. Make or collect one for a child and one for an adult and give them to people who need them.

9. Show how to help patients to turn over, sit up, get out of bed, wash their faces and hands, brush their teeth.

10. Study types of uniforms used by nurses. Make a simple type of apron for your own home nurse outfit. Model it for your patrol.

11. Discuss and dramatize scenes from the life of one of the following: Clara Barton, Robert Koch, Sir Joseph Lister, Florence Nightingale, Louis Pasteur, or Walter Reed.

12. Visit your public health nursing center and find out about its services.

*13. Demonstrate the use and care of a regular and an improvised hot-water bottle, ice bag, inhalator.

14. With others, present a home nursing exhibit or tableau showing what a home nurse does. Invite a speaker to your troop meeting to talk about nursing.

Junior High

Public
Health

To earn this badge, do ten of these activities including the two that have a star.

*1. Draw a map of your neighborhood—within five blocks. Show its health, safety, and recreational facilities. If these facilities seem inadequate, discuss what your troop or community might do about it.

2. Know the health and recreational services in your community for the physically handicapped, aged, and others needing special facilities. Help with a service project for one of these organizations or for a shut-in.

3. Visit a camp site and inspect the health and safety facilities. Find out which regulations are necessary because of the recommendations of the state and local public health departments.

4. Visit a county health department or health center. Talk with at least two members of its staff to find out what they do.

5. Know how your own state helps to keep people well.

6. Find out the communicable diseases and learn what your community does to prevent them.

7. Know what your health department does to prevent contamination of foods and who inspects foods. Visit a public market or eating place to see how these rules are enforced.

8. Help organize a troop health council to improve the health and safety practices in your troop.

9. Learn what the World Health Organization is and its purpose. Choose one of the countries where it is operating and learn all you can about what is being done there. Discuss with others how this affects you.

10. Choose one department or agency of the federal government and learn what it does for national health.

11. Find out about the Pure Food and Drug Act. Study labels on packaged foods and drugs, and tell how labels help you buy wisely.

*12. Get to know several voluntary groups that are working for health in your community. Set up an exhibit to explain the work of one of these organizations.

13. Visit the local water works or incineration and sewage plant.

14. Cooperate with your health department in a mosquito, fly, or rat control campaign in your neighborhood.

HOMEMAKING

As you do a badge in homemaking, read Chapter 18.

The following badges from other fields may be applied toward a homemaking major in the First Class rank: Home Health and Safety, Home Nurse, Home Gardener, Interior Decoration, Child Care.

PROFICIENCY BADGES

Homemaker To earn this badge, do ten of these activities including the three that have a star.

*1. Discuss in your patrol, family customs or holidays that you enjoy such as Christmas, birthdays, or the Fourth of July.

2. Visit a dairy. See how milk is kept safe for us. Know why milk is a good food.

3. Hammer a nail, put in a screw, and sharpen a knife.

4. Plant and care for bulbs or plants indoors or outdoors. Use them in your home or troop meeting place.

*5. Make a personal budget including an item for troop dues.

6. Make a bed for regular use and show how to adapt it for a sick person. Make your own bed each day.

7. Cook one of your favorite foods to serve at a troop party.

8. Dramatize using the telephone for special calls such as taking a message for someone in your family, reporting a fire, calling a doctor. Dramatize introducing a friend.

*9. Set a table for a troop event or a family supper. Wash the dishes at home for at least one meal each day for a week.

10. Wearing a thimble, put a hem in an article such as a skirt, dish towel, a baby diaper.

11. Make a safe toy for a child and teach a game or tell a story to a young child you know.

12. Arrange a dresser drawer or kitchen drawer so it will be convenient and help keep it that way.

Cook To earn this badge, do ten of these activities including the two that have a star.

*1. Prepare a breakfast, lunch, or supper for your family or patrol.

2. Know basic cooking equipment and its uses, including the stove you use.

3. Make up a cooking quiz or game with words and abbreviations found in recipes.

*4. Learn and discuss the importance of the seven basic food groups in your diet.

5. Cook eggs in three different ways.

6. Cook and eat a cereal as part of a good breakfast.

484

7. Make cocoa with three kinds of milk and decide which kind you prefer.

8. Prepare a cook-out dish that combines foods from at least three of the seven basic foods.

9. Prepare for lunch or supper a main dish containing meat, cheese, or eggs.

10. Prepare a dish that is typical of your part of the United States or of your ancestors' country.

11. Cook a main dish of fish, meat, cheese, or eggs that can also be cooked in the outdoors.

12. Learn several ways to use leftover meat or chicken and use two of them.

13. Help make a patrol or troop cookbook. Try out and contribute at least five recipes of which one should be from another country or from another part of the United States.

14. Help plan, cook, and serve a meal, indoors or outdoors, for your troop committee or parents. Keep an account of costs and time needed for preparation and cleanup.

15. Bake something for a troop service project.

16. Choose good lunches at the school cafeteria or prepare your own for at least a week. See how many of the seven basic foods you include.

To earn this badge, do ten of these activities including the two that have a star.

Hospitality

*1. In your troop discuss everyday good manners and getting along with people as a hostess and as a guest.

2. Act out introducing your troop leader and your mother, your friends to your mother, boys to girls, and starting a conversation after an introduction.

3. Discuss and practice good conversational topics to use with teachers, family at dinner, or troop visitors.

*4. Have troop members ask questions that puzzle them on social behavior. Have a committee decide which to present to the troop for discussion.

5. Discuss and dramatize shaking hands with a new acquaintance, joining or leaving a group, sitting or rising gracefully.

6. Discuss "What is a friend?" and how to make friends with new troop members; in a new troop; at a party where you know only the hostess.

7. Give a party with a theme such as games or songs around the world, books, special events for your parents or friends, or for those who have helped your troop.

8. Plan a birthday party for yourself and for another member of your family. List what you would do before, during, and after the party.

9. Visit a jewelry store or a home to see table silver and china. Set a table for all three meals a day and for special ones like buffets or teas. Use a suitable centerpiece.

10. Demonstrate and discuss table courtesies to use when you are a guest or a hostess.

11. Plan and prepare the menu and entertainment for half the troop as guests. Be their guests in return.

12. List things that would be fun for an out-of-town friend visiting you for a week.

13. Know how to act as an overnight guest in a home. Write a letter to your hostess after your visit.

14. Make a list of foods to have on hand for unexpected guests. Prepare two recipes using these foods.

15. Plan a gathering with a group of boys who enjoy some of the same activities as your troop.

Seamstress To earn this badge, do ten of these activities including the three that have a star.

*1. Collect sewing equipment for your sewing box or basket.

2. Learn the sizes of needles and numbers of thread. Use the right size for the activities you do.

*3. Know seven stitches and use five of them in these activities.

*4. Have a sewing bee at troop meeting to repair your clothes.

5. Shorten a dress by putting in a deeper hem.

6. Lengthen a dress by letting down a hem.

7. Wear to a troop meeting either socks or stockings that you have darned.

8. Know when to use three different kinds of seams. Use one on something you make.

9. Put on a *needed* patch or mend a torn place in a garment.

10. Make a pouch bag, mittens, or calotte.

11. Sew, knit, or crochet something for your home.

12. Sew, knit, or crochet a scarf for yourself or to give away.

13. Dress a doll for a child or dress a doll in the uniform of another country.

To earn this badge, do ten of these activities including the two that have a star.

Housekeeper

*1. Discuss in troop meeting what a good housekeeper does. Choose which of the jobs you can do daily, weekly, or occasionally to help at home. Report to your troop.

2. Know the equipment needed for various household tasks. Describe commercial labor-saving devices, preparations, and supplies, and your own labor-saving methods.

3. Demonstrate cleaning of enamelware and aluminum; mirrors or windows.

4. Help organize a system for dishwashing at home.

5. Reorganize a clothes closet, kitchen closet, or closet in a troop room so that everything is arranged for greatest convenience.

6. Clean bedsprings, turn a mattress, and make the bed. Mend a torn sheet or bind a blanket.

7. Clean your refrigerator or ice box, store contents conveniently; learn how to defrost and regulate a mechanical refrigerator.

*8. Help give a thorough cleaning to a room at home or your troop meeting place.

9. Help protect family clothing and household goods from moths and other pests.

10. By patrol or troop, collect examples of cleaning supplies and compare them by cost, use, and convenience.

11. Know the care that should be given to floors, woodwork, walls, furniture, rugs, and curtains. Demonstrate in carrying out Activity 8.

487

12. Find out how to remove spots and stains from fabrics. Practice removing five of them several times.

13. Visit a supermarket and a small store. Compare the prices of familiar brand articles. Discuss the reasons for price differences.

14. Help your mother plan meals for three days. Check food supplies on hand and do the necessary marketing.

15. Discuss with your family how you will receive or earn your spending money. Make your personal spending plan and try it out for two months.

16. Assist in regular laundering.

Foods To earn this badge, do ten of these activities including the two that have a star.

*1. Show on a world map where major food crops grow. Find out the native name for these foods. Point out which countries export or import food.

*2. Find out what the United Nations is doing about food.

3. Discuss the effect of railroad, steamship, refrigeration, trucking, airplane, canning and freezing industries on the foods we eat.

4. Know where food packaging materials come from: tin, paper for labels, printing dye, plastics for containers.

5. Ask your family to try one or more vegetables fresh, canned, dried, and frozen. Compare cost per serving, taste, labor, time in preparation, and family preference.

6. Bring five examples of labels from food products for a display. Know what information helps you make a wise selection.

7. With the help of a meat dealer or other qualified person, learn how to select the best buys of meat for various methods of cooking. Recognize one cut for each method.

8. Visit a place where fish is sold and list the kinds of fish, their sources, and cost.

9. Go through a dairy or milk processing plant. Find out about the grades of milk and what makes price differences.

10. At an egg market watch grading and storing. Learn why egg prices vary, and why eggs are refrigerated.

11. Select ten favorite fruits or vegetables and make a calendar

showing the months of the year in which each is a good buy for eating and for canning.

12. Know six ways of preserving food and the advantages and disadvantages of each. Preserve foods using at least two methods such as canning, freezing, drying, salting, storing.

13. Find out why meats, poultry, fish, and vegetables need very high heat when being canned. Help can one of these foods using a pressure cooker.

14. Visit a community or commercial canning, freezing, or drying center.

15. Learn how to store at least two foods in storage pits, basements, cellars, garages, or back yards. Know what foods grow the year around in your locality.

16. Find out which fruits are natural jelly makers. Explain how pectin can be added when necessary. Make jelly.

To earn this badge, do eight of these activities including the three that have a star.

Handy-woman

1. Demonstrate the best way to use and care for electrical and mechanical appliances in your home.

2. Ask a licensed electrician to explain precautions in handling electrical appliances and fixtures and how to check for trouble.

3. Ask an experienced person to demonstrate the correct method of painting furniture. Paint some yourself.

4. Learn how to refinish a small piece of furniture.

5. Know how to read a gas, electric, or water meter, and learn how to compute the costs. Discuss with your family ways to reduce the bills.

6. Locate a place where a shelf or a handy article would be useful and assist in making it.

7. Inspect your home for minor repairs you could make. With the aid of a friend make the repairs. In turn assist her.

8. Learn how to rewind and reset the spring of a window shade; how to put a new shade on a roller or turn an old one.

*9. Describe a situation in which the gas, electricity, or water in a house should be turned off. Find out how to do this and

489

whom to notify in case of trouble with any of these services. Show two ways to provide each of the following: emergency light, heat, and safe drinking water.

10. Visit a home workshop to see how others care for and use their tools. Check your own equipment. Suggest to your parents any inexpensive, handy article that might be added.

11. Put up any three of the following in wood or plaster: drapery fixtures, cup hooks, picture hooks, clothes hooks, towel rods, shelves.

12. Know how to oil any two of the following: an electric fan, sewing machine, door hinges, lawn mower, mechanical toy or implement.

13. Find out how window screens, awnings, storm doors, or storm windows are stored.

*14. Help arrange the storage space at home or in a troop meeting place. Put up new shelves, divider, or hooks for added convenience. Help keep the space neat.

*15. Give a demonstration of two ways to put a good cutting edge on knives.

Junior High

Dressmaker

To earn this badge, do ten of these activities, including the two that have a star, and either Activity 7 or Activity 8.

*1. Have the Seamstress badge, or equip a conveniently arranged sewing box. Know seven stitches. Know how to make three different kinds of seams.

*2. Thread and run a sewing machine, stitch evenly in line and turn corners.

3. Find the lines and types of clothing that are most becoming to you. Find your pattern size. Show how to make necessary alterations. Invite an experienced dressmaker to the troop to tell how to have "the custom-made" look.

4. From the various fabrics on sale in a store, choose one you might use for a school dress.

5. Demonstrate how to read a pattern direction sheet, how to lay out and cut a pattern, how to mark your cloth.

6. Find out how to press and iron different materials. Explain why it is best to press-as-you-go in dressmaking.

7. Make a skirt and blouse from simple patterns. Keep track of your time and the cost.

8. Make a basic dress from a simple pattern. Keep track of your time and the cost.

9. Knit, sew, or crochet accessories for the garment you made.

10. Sew, knit, or crochet something for your room.

11. Compare ready-made clothes with those you make yourself.

12. Make an article for a layette, or for a child, or for a service project.

Junior High

To earn this badge, do ten of these activities including the two starred.

*1. Discuss the importance of good health and good grooming in your everyday life.

*2. Make a "Good Grooming Chart" on which you arrange the points your troop has decided every girl should check daily, weekly, once a month.

3. Test yourself with some of the score sheets found or advertised in magazines. Make up your own.

4. Have someone discuss shampooing, care of the hair, and hair styles. Try out different ways of doing your own hair. Have a hair style show in your troop.

5. Ask anyone experienced in food to tell you how to improve your looks and health by eating the right kind of food. Plan a day's menu for yourself.

6. Have an expert or someone especially interested discuss types of faces and skin; demonstrate proper skin cleansing and protection; discuss the effect of diet on complexions.

7. Put on a troop demonstration to show how care of wraps, outer clothing, underclothing, shoes, hats, and accessories adds to the well-groomed look.

8. Discuss with your dentist, or an oral hygienist, what you can do to make your teeth more attractive.

Good Grooming

491

9. Learn how to keep your nails and hands clean, well groomed, and in suitable condition for the things you do.

10. Discuss how sleep contributes to the way you feel and look, factors that affect sleep, and the amount of sleep needed by girls of your age.

11. Learn about the care of the feet; proper fit of shoes and types for various activities.

12. In pantomime, interpret the slogan, "Better light, better sight" for sewing, reading, and studying.

13. Demonstrate how to wear the Girl Scout uniform with a well-groomed appearance.

14. Act out "Stand tall, sit tall" to show good and bad posture.

15. Hold a quiz on good grooming, good health, poise, good manners.

16. Have an "ensemble" fashion show, demonstrating the things you have learned in this badge.

Junior High

Clothing

To earn this badge, do ten of these activities including the two that have a star.

1. Put on a skit showing the right and wrong way to dress for various occasions.

2. Find pictures or examples of clothes worn by girls your age: when Scouting first started in 1912; 100 years ago; and 500 years ago. Explain to the troop the advantages of your present-day clothes, including your Girl Scout uniform.

3. Collect outgrown and used clothing. Put them in good wearable condition for a service project.

4. Demonstrate to the troop: ironing, cleaning, darning, mending, polishing shoes, good posture, and personal cleanliness.

5. Dramatize being a good customer and good salesgirl.

6. Do your weekly clothes repair jobs together in a troop or patrol sewing bee.

7. Ask an experienced person to demonstrate effective color combinations for different members of your troop. Choose colors best for you.

8. Pack a suitcase for an overnight visit and for a week's visit.

*9. Discuss basic wardrobe needs with girls in your troop. Plan your year's basic wardrobe. Illustrate with pictures or draw your own designs.

*10. Make an inventory of your own wardrobe and list what you already have for the wardrobe in No. 9.

11. Plan a school outfit for yourself. Show the advantages of interchangeable sets of accessories.

12. Have a clothes clinic at troop meeting. Discuss how to fix garments which can be worn another year.

13. Sew, knit, or crochet an accessory for your wardrobe.

14. Ask a clothing expert or a well-dressed Senior Scout to tell the troop how to buy clothes wisely, and discuss good taste in clothes versus fads.

15. Of the many jobs in the "fashion world" find out about five.

16. Design and construct a costume for a play your troop is giving.

17. Have a fashion show to display either your remodeled clothing or an ensemble you have assembled from your present wardrobe.

Junior High

To earn this badge, do ten of these activities including the three that have a star.

Nutrition

*1. Invite a nutritionist or home economist to talk with your troop about body building foods, energy foods, and protective foods. Find out why milk is a "good buy" nutritionally, and how to include it in the diet in five different ways.

*2. Help make or collect posters on the seven basic food groups. Arrange an exhibit of your posters for troop and explain what is included in a well-balanced meal.

*3. Cook the food you plan in at least three of the nutrition badge activities you do.

4. Keep a record, for two weeks, of everything you eat and drink. Using the posters collected in Activity No. 2, check your

record to see whether you are getting what you need and what changes you should make.

5. Help plan several one-dish meals for cook-outs or troop events that combine three or four of the basic foods.

6. Plan menus for a supper and breakfast for an overnight trip.

7. Plan three lunches that travel using foods from five of the seven basic food groups.

8. Plan meals for your family for one week.

9. Know what agencies in your community help people learn about foods. Interview a representative of one agency.

10. Act out a cheerful breakfast time in a healthy, happy home.

11. Know what foods are nutritional and satisfying for snacks.

12. Get menus from various eating places. Choose a well-balanced meal for the money you plan to spend.

13. Make up a game that will help you to know the meaning of such terms as fortified, enriched, hidden hunger, protective foods, homogenized, the sunshine vitamin, malnutrition, irradiated, the basic seven, and Food and Agriculture Organization of the United Nations.

14. Find out about jobs in the "food world." Invite a specialist to talk to your troop about her job and her training.

15. Visit a place where food is commercially prepared. Find out the state or local food laws that protect you.

INDEX

This index to the *Girl Scout Handbook* does not include all the subjects in the proficiency badges. The Handbook index will be most helpful if you look under several related titles to get all the information you need on a subject. For example, in looking up "Camping" you will find some information under the word "Camping," more under "Campcraft" and under "Fires," and still more under "Out-of-Doors." When using your index, look under related headings for homemaking, health and safety, citizenship, or any other subject for which you need information.

Accident prevention, 320–321
Active Citizen, 190–191
  badge, 412–413
Adventurer, 263–268
  badge, 446–447
Agriculture, 309–319
  Animal Raiser, 317–318
  Animal Raiser badge, 469–470
  Beekeeper, 316–317
  Beekeeper badge, 468–469
  Dairying, 318–319
  Dairying badge, 471–472
  Farmer, 310–311
  Farmer badge, 464
  Fruit Raiser, 316
  Fruit Raiser badge, 467–468
  Home and truck gardening, 312–316
  Home Gardener, 312–316
  Home Gardener badge, 465–466
  Landscaper, 311–312
  Landscaper badge, 464–465
  Poultry Raiser, 318
  Poultry Raiser badge, 470–471
  proficiency badges in, 463–472
  Second Class Rank requirement in, 74–75
  Truck Gardener, 312–316
  Truck Gardener badge, 466–467

Alcott, Louisa, vi
America. *See* United States of America.
"America the Beautiful," 176, 196, 197
American Girl, The, 31
Amphibians, 253–255
Animal Raiser, 317–318
  badge, 469–470
Animals
  cats and dogs, 243–245
  garden, 315
  mammals, 249–251
Annual national membership dues, 24
Apiary, 317
Architecture, 142–144
  badge, 393–394
Ark, Our, 212
Arts and crafts, 115–144
  Architecture, 142–144
  Architecture badge, 393–394
  Basketry, 135–136
  Basketry badge, 381–382
  Bookbinding, 120
  Bookbinding badge, 381–382
  chalk and crayon, 116
  clay modeling, 125–126
  Dabbler, 116–117
  Dabbler badge, 380
  design, 50–51, 129–131

Arts and crafts (*Continued*)
Drawing and Painting, 118–120
Drawing and Painting badge, 380–381
Glass, 123–124
Glass badge, 383–384
Interior Decoration, 140–141
Interior Decoration badge, 391–392
Leather, 126–127
Leather badge, 385–386
Metal, 138
Metal badge, 389–390
Needlecraft, 128–129
Needlecraft badge, 386
Photography, 141–142
Photography badge, 392–393
Pottery, 116, 124–126
Pottery badge, 384–385
Prints, 138–139
Prints badge, 390–391
proficiency badges in, 379–394
Second Class Rank requirements in, 50–52
Textile Design, 129–131
Textile Design badge, 387
Weaving, 131–135
Weaving badge, 387–388
Wood, 121–123
Wood badge, 382–383
Assistant patrol leader, 35
Athlete, 305
badge, 461–462
Audubon, John James, 248
Audubon Society, National, 248
Aviation, 204–205
badge, 421–422
Ax, use and care of, 273

Babies, care of, 329–332
Babysitters, tips for, 333–334

Back-Yard Camper, 268–272
badge, 447
Bacon twisters (recipe), 280
Baden-Powell, Agnes, 10
Baden-Powell, Lady Olave, 46
Baden-Powell, Lord Robert, 10, 46
Badge
First Class, 28
sash, 31
Second Class, 28
Badges, proficiency
Agriculture, 463–472
Arts and crafts, 379–394
Community life, 412–423
for older Intermediate Scouts, 102–103
Health and safety, 472–483
Homemaking, 483–494
how to earn, 81–86
International friendship, 423–432
Literature and dramatics, 394–405
Music and dancing, 405–411
Nature, 434–445
Out-of-doors, 446–453
placement of, 28, 31
Sports and games, 453–462
Ballads, dramatizing, 54
Bandages, types of, 76, 340
Bandanna, uses for, 264
Basketry, 135–136
badge, 388–389
Batik work, 130
Bed-making, 18, 344
Bedroll, how to make, 268–270
Beekeeper, 316–317
badge, 468–469
Bibliophile, 155–158
badge, 398–399
Bicycling. *See also* Cylist.
safety rules for, 294
Big Dipper, 256

Bill of Rights, 191, 192, 413, 420
Bird, 245–248
  badge, 439
  nest of, 247 (*ill.*)
Birthday, Girl Scout, 45
Birthday, troop, 43
Blisters, first aid for, 341
Blockprints, 130–131
Blushing bunny (recipe), 268
Boating, 296–297
  badge, 456–457
Bookbinding, 51–52, 120
  badge, 381–382
Books
  binding of, 51–52, 120
  care of, 52–53
  early printing, 155–156
  exhibits and collections, 156
  kinds of, 148–150
Bowline (knot), 73
Brazil, Guide uniform and pin
  in, 216
Bread twisters (recipe), 280
Broadcasting signals, 206
Brownie Scouts
  age of, 2
  fly-up for, 44
  progression to Intermediate
    troops for, 2
  uniform for, 2
  Wings, 31
Budget, troop, 39–41
Buitenzorg, 212
Burns, first aid for, 76
Butterflies, 252
Buzz (game), 72

Caldecott Award, 157
Campcraft, 273–277
  badge, 448–449
Camping. *See also* Out-of-Doors.
  back-yard, 268–272
  pioneer, 287–289

Canada, Guide uniforms and pins
  in, 216
Canning, 365
Canoeing, 300–302
  badge, 458–459
Cassiopeia, 256
Cat and Dog badge, 437–438
Caterpillars, 252
Cats, care of, 243–245
Cattle, 318
Centerpiece, table, 350
Cepheus, 256
Ceramics. *See* Pottery.
Ceremonies
  flag, 12, 25–26, 42, 44, 48, 54,
    59–60, 176
  investiture, 25–26
  Scouts' Own, 45
  troop, 43–46, 163
Chalet, Our, 212
Charcoal stoves, 271–272 (*ill.*)
Cheese toast (recipe), 279
Cheese twisters (recipe), 280
Chickens, common breeds of, 318
Child Care, 329–334
  badge, 475–476
Choral speech, 165
Citizenship
  contributions to, vii
  Day, 45
  in community life, 61, 104,
    189–198, 202–204, 222–
    223, 334–337, 412–415
  in first *Girl Scout Handbook*,
    11
  in Girl Scout program, 50
  in government, 202–204, 223,
    415–417, 419–421
  in Girl Scout Laws, 6–9, 78–
    80, 92–98
  in Girl Scout motto, 9, 94
  in Girl Scout Promise, 6, 85–
    86, 92–93

Citizenship (*Continued*)
  in rank requirements, 48, 50, 87, 90, 102, 107
  in Girl Scout slogan, 9, 93
Clerk, 201
  badge, 418–419
Clothing, 372–374
  badge, 492–493
  care of, 372
  for hiking, 264
  removing stains from, 363
  selection of, 372
  washing, 373–374
Cloud formations, 65–66
Clove hitch, 74
Club form of government, 38
Code, international Morse, 266
Coed activities, 104
Color guard, 60
Communicable diseases, 346–347
Community. *See also* Community life.
  health, 347–349
  know your own, 194–196
  service to, 85–86, 104, 110–111
  what it is, 189–190
Community life, 48, 59–61, 189–206
  Active Citizen, 190–191
  Active Citizen badge, 412–413
  Aviation, 204–205
  Aviation badge, 421–422
  Clerk, 201
  Clerk badge, 418–419
  My Community, 194–196
  My Community badge, 414–415
  My Country, 196–198
  My Country badge, 416–417
  My Government, 202–204
  My Government badge, 419–421

Community life (*Continued*)
  My Troop, 193–194
  My Troop badge, 413–414
  proficiency badges in, 412–423
  Radio and Television, 205–206
  Radio and Television badge, 422–423
  Second Class Rank requirements in, 59–61
  Speaker, 200–201
  Speaker badge, 418
  Traveler, 198–199
  Traveler badge, 417–418
Community Safety, 334–337
  badge, 476–477
Compass, 19–21, 286
Compresses
  cold, 345
  for wounds, 340
Conservation, 261–262
  badge, 445–446
  of food, 365
Constellations, Polar, 256
Constitution, United States of America, 191, 192, 348, 420
Contour lines, 287
Conversationalist, 225–226
  badge, 430
Cook, 351–355
  badge, 484–485
Cooking, 351–355. *See also* Food *and* Meals.
  meal planning, 354
  measurements, 352
  out-of-doors, 267–268, 277–281
  tips, 352–353
  ways of, 353–354
Copyright laws, 180–181
Correspondence with Girl Scouts
  in other communities, 198
  in other countries, 218
Council Fire, The, 218

Council, Girl Scout, 41–42
Court of Awards, 43–44
Court of Honor, 33–37
Cows, 318–319
Crabs, 260
Cravat bandage, 76
Criss-cross fire, 70
Curie, Marie, v
Curved Bar Rank, 106–108
  pin, 28
  requirements, 106–107
Cuts, first aid for, 75. See also
  Wounds.
Cyclist, 293–294
  badge, 454–455

Dabbler, 116–117
  badge, 380
Dairying, 318–319
  badge, 471–472
Dancer, 184–185
  badge, 410–411
Dancing, 58, 182–185
Declaration of Independence,
  202, 420
Democracy, 37, 93, 193
  in troop government, 32–38
Design, 50–51, 129–131
Directions, finding, 19–22, 264
  when lost, 283
  with map, 283–284
Diseases
  communicable, 346–347
  plants, 316
Dishwashing, 350–351
Dogs, 243–245. See also Cat and
  Dog badge.
Doughboys (recipe), 280
Dragon, 256
Dramatic Appreciation, 170
  badge, 403–404

Dramatics, 53, 159–172. See also
  Literature and dramatics.
  ceremonies, 163
  choral speech, 165
  impromptu, 164–165
  nosebag, 160
  pantomime, 163–164
  producing plays, 170–172
  puppets, 165–169
  shadowgraph, 167–168
  troop entertainments, 160
Drawing and Painting, 118–120
  badge, 380–381
Dressmaker, 368–370
  badge, 490–491
Dues
  annual national membership,
    24
  troop, 39
Dyes, making natural, 134–135

Eagle, American, 196 (ill.)
E Pluribus Unum, 190
Earhart, Amelia, vi–vii
Earthworms, 315
Egg on a rock (recipe), 279
Egypt, Guide uniform and pin in,
  217
Electricity, safe use of, 367–368
Embroidery stitches, 128–129
Entertaining. See Hospitality.
Equipment
  for bicycles, 293
  for housecleaning, 361–362
  for sewing, 369–370
Equipment Service, National, 28
Etiquette. See Manners.
Examination, health, 325–326
Explorer, 284–287
  badge, 451–452

Fainting, first aid for, 75
Farm Safety, 338
  badge, 478–479
Farmer, 310–311
  badge, 464
Farming. See Agriculture.
Feet, care of, 326–327
Field of interest
  Girl Scout, 50
  choosing major for First Class, 88–89
Finance, troop, 39–41
Fingerpainting, 119
Fire
  prevention, 338
  safety, 68–70
  what to do in case of, 335
Fires
  basic A, 69–70
  building of, 68–70, 270–272, 277–278
  criss-cross, 70
  hunter's, 278
  reflector, 278
  tepee, 70
  trench, 278
First aid, 75–76, 339–343
  badge, 480–481
  basic rules for, 339–340
  for blisters, 341
  for burns, 76
  for cuts, 75. See also Wounds.
  for fainting, 75
  for foreign bodies in the eye, 341
  for frostbite, 341
  for insect bites, 342
  for nose bleed, 341
  for pain in abdomen, 342
  for poison ivy, oak, sumac, wood, 342
  for snakebites, 342
  for splinters, 76, 342

First aid (Continued)
  for sprains, 76, 342
  for sunburns, 343
  for wounds, 75, 340
  kits, 321–322
  use of bandages in, 76, 340
First Aid to Animals, 338–339
  badge, 479–480
First Class Rank, 87–98
  badge, 28
  pin, 28
  requirements, 87
Flag, United States of America
  ceremony, 12, 25–26, 42, 44, 48, 54, 59–60, 176
  how to display, 13–14, 60
  how to fold, 14
  meaning of, 13
  "O Beautiful Banner," 55, 176
  Pledge of Allegiance to, 14–15, 59–60
  respect due to, 13–14
  school's, 413
  "Star-Spangled Banner, The," xvi, 176, 197
Flag, World Association, 15, 211
Flowers
  cultivated, 237
  from other lands, 238 (ill.)
  parts of, 236, 241
  wild, 240–242
Fly-Up, Brownie Scout, 44
Folk Dancer, 182–184
  badge, 410
Folk songs, 176
Folk tales, 147–148
Foods, 363–365. See also Cooking and Meals.
  badge, 488–489
  buying of, 364–365
  canned, 364
  raising and producing. See Agriculture.

Foods (*Continued*)
  selection for menus, 374–375
  seven basic groups, 374
Foot Traveler, 281–284
  badge, 450–451
Forestry, 261–262
Frogs, 254–255
Frostbite, first aid for, 341
Fruit Raiser, 316
  badge, 467–468
Fruits and vegetables, 314–315

Games, 71–72
  badge, 454
  singing, 183
Garden Flower, 237–239
  badge, 436
Gardening, 312–316. *See also* Flowers.
Gas, safe use of, 367–368
Gesso craft, 122–123
Germination, 313–314
Girl Scout
  Birthday, 45
  Laws, 6–9, 79–80, 93–98
  Promise, 5–6
  stories, 149
Girl Scout Organization, National
  history of, 10–12
  twelve regions of, 376 (*ill.*)
Girl Scout Week, 45
Girl Scouting
  history of, 10–12
  in other countries, 63–64. *See also* International friendship.
  what it is, 2
Girl Scouts. *See also* Intermediate Girl Scouts.
  age range of, 2
  how to join, 2–3
Glass, 123–124
  badge, 383–384

Good Grooming, 371–372
  badge, 491–492
Government. *See also* My Government.
  troop, 33–38
  United States, 37, 93, 198, 202–204, 413, 419–421
Great Britain, Guide uniform and pin in, 216 (*ill.*)
Groundcloth, how to make, 268, 270
Group discussion, 193
Group Musician, 177–179
  badge, 407
Guide Cottage, 212
"Gypsy Song," 57

Half hitches, two, 74
Handshake, Girl Scout, 13
Handywoman, 365–368
  badge, 489–490
Hatbrim measuring, 285
Hatchets, use and care of, 273
Health. *See also* Health and Safety.
  community, 334–337, 347–348
  examination, 325–326
  home, 327–329
  personal, 76–77, 324 (*ill.*), 325–327
  public, 347–348
Health Aid, 320–322
  badge, 472–473
Health and safety, 320–348
  Child Care, 329–334
  Child Care badge, 475–476
  Community Safety, 334–337
  Community Safety badge, 476–477
  Farm Safety, 338
  Farm Safety badge, 478–479

Health and safety (*Continued*)
   First Aid, 339–343
   First Aid badge, 480–481
   First Aid to Animals, 338–339
   First Aid to Animals badge, 479–480
   Health Aid, 320–322
   Health Aid badge, 472–473
   Home Health and Safety, 327–329
   Home Health and Safety badge, 474–475
   Home Nurse, 343–347
   Home Nurse badge, 481–482
   Outdoor Safety, 337
   Outdoor Safety badge, 477–478
   Personal Health, 324 (*ill.*), 325–327
   Personal Health badge, 473–474
   proficiency badges in, 472–483
   Public Health, 347–348
   Public Health badge, 482–483
   Second Class Rank requirements in, 75–77
Heating, home, 328
Hiking
   application of Laws when, 66–67
   clothing for, 264
   first aid kit for, 321–322
   lunches for, 354–355
   permissions needed, 67
   purifying water when, 67
   rest during, 67
   rules of the road, 66–67
Home. *See also* Homemaking *and* House.
   first aid kit for, 322
   hazards, 323 (*ill.*)
   health, 327–329
   housekeeping duties in, 361

Home (*Continued*)
   keeping clean, 362
   safety, 320, 322, 367–368
Home Gardener, 312–316
   badge, 464–466
Home Health and Safety, 327–328
   badge, 474–475
Home Nurse, 343–347
   badge, 481–482
Homemaker, 350
   badge, 484
Homemaking, 349–375
   Clothing, 372–374
   Clothing badge, 492–493
   Cook, 351–355
   Cook badge, 484–485
   Dressmaker, 368–370
   Dressmaker badge, 490–491
   Foods, 363–365
   Foods badge, 488–489
   Good Grooming, 371–372
   Good Grooming badge, 491–492
   Handywoman, 365–368
   Handywoman badge, 489–490
   Homemaker, 350
   Homemaker badge, 484
   Hospitality, 355–359
   Hospitality badge, 485–486
   Housekeeper, 360–363
   Housekeeper badge, 487–488
   Nutrition, 374–375
   Nutrition badge, 493–494
   proficiency badges in, 483–494
   Seamstress, 359–360
   Seamstress badge, 486–487
   Second Class Rank requirement in, 77–78
Horsewoman, 299–300
   badge, 457–458
Hospitality, 355–359
   badge, 485–486
Hostels, 212

Hot-water bags, 345–346
House
  gas and electricity systems in, 367–368
  plants, 74, 238–241, 350
  structure of a, 143 (*ill.*)
  ventilation of, 328
  water system in, 367–368
Housekeeper, 360–363
  badge, 487–488
Hunter's fire, 278

Ice
  bags, 345
  rescue, 298–299
  skating, 297–299
Identification emblem, troop, 30
Illustrators, xiii, 156
India, Girl Guide uniform and pin in, 217
Insect bites, first aid for, 342
Insect badge, 440–441
Insects, 252–253
  garden, 315
Insignia, Girl Scout, 28–31, 29 (*ill.*)
Interior decoration, 140–141
  badge, 291–292
Intermediate Girl Scouts
  age of, 2
  insignia for, 28–31
  program for older, 99–111
  troop for. *See* Troop.
  uniform for, 28–31
International friendship, 207–228
  Conversationalist, 225–226
  Conversationalist badge, 430
  Language, 224
  Language badge, 429–430
  My World, 226–228
  My World badge, 431–432

International friendship (*Cont.*)
  Pen Pal, 218–219
  Pen Pal badge, 426
  proficiency badges in, 423–432
  Second Class Rank requirement in, 62–64
  Western Hemisphere, 219–220
  Western Hemisphere badge, 427–428
  what Girl Scouts can do for, 62–63
  World Gifts, 207–211
  World Gifts badge, 424–425
  World Neighbor, 220–224
  World Neighbor badge, 428–429
  World Trefoil, 211–218
  World Trefoil badge, 425–426
International Friendship Troops, 214
International gatherings, 215
International Guiding and Scouting, 63–64, 211–218
International Month, 45
International Morse Code, 266
International Post Box, 218
Introductions, how to make, 357–358
Invalid, care of, 343–347
Investiture, 25–26
Invitations, giving and answering, 358

Jackknives
  how to use and care for, 22, 23 (*ill.*)
  whittling, 121, 265
Journalist, 158–159
  badge, 399–400
Juliette Low. *See* Low, Juliette.

Juliette Low World Friendship Fund, 212–213 (*ill.*), 214–215

Kabobs (recipe), 279
Kapers, 277
Kindling, 69
Knives, how to use, 22, 23 (*ill.*)
Knots, 72–74

La Nef, 212
Landscaper, 311–312
  badge, 464–465
Language, 324–325
  badge, 429–430
Lashing, 274–277
Laws, Girl Scout, 6–9, 79–80, 93–98
  citizenship in, 6–9, 78–80, 92–98
  fourth Law and international friendship, 221
Leader, patrol. *See* Patrol leader.
Leader, troop, 41
Leaf Hunt (game), 71
Leather, 126–127
  badge, 385–386
Leaves
  deciduous and evergreen, 236
  simple and compound, 236
Letterwriting, 219
Liberty Bell, 196
Libraries, 146–147
Life Saver, 305
  badge, 462
Lighting, 328. *See also* Electricity.
Linoleum blocks, 131
Literary awards, 157

Literature and Dramatics, 145–172. *See also* Dramatics.
  Bibliophile, 155–158
  Bibliophile badge, 398–399
  Dramatic Appreciation, 170
  Dramatic Appreciation badge, 403–404
  Girl Scout stories, 149
  Journalist, 158–159
  Journalist badge, 399–400
  literary awards, 157–158
  Magic Carpet, 146–148
  Magic Carpet badge, 394–395
  Player, 163–165
  Player badge, 401–402
  Producer, 170–172
  Producer badge, 404–405
  proficiency badges in, 394–405
  Puppeteer, 165–169
  Puppeteer badge, 402–403
  Reader, 148–150
  Reader badge, 395–396
  Second Class Rank requirement in, 52–54
  Storyteller, 151–152
  Storyteller badge, 396–397
  Troop Dramatics, 160–163
  Troop Dramatics badge, 400–401
  Writer, 152–154
  Writer badge, 397–398
Little Dipper, 256
Loom, 132–134
Lou Henry Hoover Memorial Forests and Sanctuaries, 262
Low, Juliette, 11–12, 11 (*ill.*)
Lunches, suggestions for, 354–355

Magic Carpet, 146–148
  badge, 394–395

Major field, choosing, 88–89
Make-up for plays, 172
Mammal, 249–251
  badge, 439–440
Manners, good, 355–359
  for guests, 359
  in invitations, 358
  in making introductions, 357–358
  in the community, 195–196
  table, 356–357
  when hiking, 66–67
Marionettes, 168–169
Mapping, 21, 282–283, 286–289
Meals. *See also* Cooking *and* Food.
  one-pot, 267–268
  planning, 354
  serving, 357
  without dishes, 279–281
Measurements
  cooking, 352
  emergency cooking, 280
  hatbrim or hand, 285
  of time and distance, 284
  pencil method, 285
  personal, 284
  weight, 286
Meeting places, troop, 32
Meetings, troop, 24, 32, 42–43
  attending as Tenderfoot requirement, 24
Membership card, 24, 28, 43
Membership dues, annual national, 24
Membership star, 30
Menus, how to plan, 374–375
Metal, 138
  badge, 389–390
Mexico, Guide uniform and pin in, 216
Milk, 363–364
  home pasteurization of, 364
Minerals, 257–258

Minstrel, 174–176
  badge, 406
Mock angel food cake (recipe), 281
Mollusks, 259
Moon, 257
Morse code, international, 266
Moths, 252
Motto, Girl Scout, 9–10
  citizenship in, 9, 94
Music and Dancing, 173–185
  Dancer, 182–185
  Dancer badge, 410–411
  Folk Dancer, 182–184
  Folk Dancer badge, 410
  Group Musician, 177–179
  Group Musician badge, 407
  Minstrel, 174–176
  Minstrel badge, 406
  Music Appreciation, 181–182
  Music Appreciation badge, 409
  Musician, 179–181
  Musician badge, 407–408
  proficiency badges in, 405–411
  Second Class Rank requirements in, 54–59
  songs, 174–179
Music Appreciation, 181–182
  badge, 409
Musical instruments, 58
Musician, 179–181
  badge, 407–408
My Community, 194–196
  badge, 414–415
My Country, 196–198
  badge, 415–417
My Government, 202–204
  badge, 419–421
My Troop, 193–194
  badge, 413–414
My World, 226–228
  badge, 431–432

505

National Equipment Service, 28

National Girl Scout Organization. *See* Girl Scout National Organization.

Nature, 233–263
  Bird badge, 439
  birds, 245–248
  Cat and Dog badge, 437–438
  cats and dogs, 243–245
  collections, 234
  Conservation, 261–262
  Conservation badge, 445–446
  Garden Flower, 237–239
  Garden Flower badge, 436–437
  Insect badge, 440–441
  insects, 252–253
  Mammal badge, 439–440
  mammals, 249–251
  observing, 65
  names in, 234
  proficiency badges in, 434–445
  Rambler, 233–235
  Rambler badge, 434–435
  Reptile and Amphibian badge, 441
  reptiles and amphibians, 253–255
  Rock and Mineral badge, 442–443
  rocks and minerals, 257–258
  Salt Water badge, 444
  salt water life, 259–260
  Second Class Rank requirement in, 65–66
  Star badge, 442
  stars, 256–257
  three kingdoms in, 234–235
  Tree badge, 435–436
  trees, 236–237
  weather, 258–259
  Weather badge, 443–444
  Wild Plant badge, 437
  wild plants, 240–242

Needle, how to sterilize, 76
Needlecraft, 128–129
  badge, 386
Newberry Award, 157
Newspapers, 158
Nightingale, Florence, v
Nobel Prize, 158
North Star, 256
Nose bleed, first aid for, 341
Numeral, troop, 30
Nursing, home, 343–347
Nutrition, 374–375
  badge, 493–494

O Beautiful Banner," 55, 176
Officers, troop, 38–39
One-pot meals, 267–268
Orienteering, 19–20
Orienting map, 283
Our Ark, 212
Our Chalet, 212
"Our Chalet Song," 56–57
Outdoor Cook, 277–281
  badge, 449–450
Outdoor cooking, 267–268, 277–281
Outdoor Safety, 337
  badge, 477–478
Out-of-Doors, 263–289
  activities for older Intermediates, 103
  Adventurer, 263–268
  Adventurer badge, 446–447
  Back-Yard Camper, 268–272
  Back-Yard Camper badge, 447
  Campcraft, 273–277
  Campcraft badge, 448–449
  Explorer, 284–287
  Explorer badge, 451–452
  Fire building in the, 68–70, 270–271, 277–278
  Foot Traveler, 281–284

Out-of-Doors (*Continued*)
Foot Traveler badge, 450–451
Outdoor Cook, 277–281
Outdoor Cook badge, 449–450
Pioneer, 287–289
Pioneer badge, 452–453
proficiency badges in, 446–453
Second Class Rank requirement in, 66–70

Pace, 281
Packages, how to wrap, 367
Pain in abdomen, first aid for, 342
Pantomime, 163–164
Pasteurization, 364
Patrol
assistant leader, 35
first aid kit for, 321
leader, 35
meetings, 33–34
system, 33–37
"Peace of the River," 56
Peepshow, building a, 117
Pen Pal, 218–219
badge, 426
Pencil method measuring, 285
Personal health, 76–77, 324–327
badge, 473–474
Personal measurements, 284
Pets, care of, 19, 243–245
Photography, 141–142
badge, 392–393
Pigespejderhuset, 212
Pins
Curved Bar, 28
First Class, 28
Girl Scout, 25, 28
of Girl Guides and Girl Scouts
of other countries, 216–217

Pins (*Continued*)
World Association, 15, 26, 28, 211
Pioneer, 287–289
badge, 452–453
Planets, 256–257
Plants
diseases of, 316
in window boxes, 240–241 (*ill.*), 350
parts of, 236–237, 240–241
poisonous, 242
potted, 74, 239–240, 350
rooting a cutting from, 75
seeds of, 241, 313–315
wild, 240–242
Player, 163–165
badge, 401–402
Plays. *See also* Dramatics.
costumes for, 172
production of, 170–172
Pledge of Allegiance, 14–15, 59–60
Pocket stew (recipe), 268
Poetry, 149
Poison ivy, oak, sumac, wood, 242
first aid for, 342
Polar constellations, 256
Post Box, International, 218
Posture, 326–327, 371
Pottery, 116, 124–126
badge, 384–385
Poultry Raiser, 318
badge, 470–471
Printing, 155–156, 158–159
Prints, 138–139
badge, 390–391
textile, 129–131
Producer, 170–172
badge, 404–405
Proficiency badges. *See* Badges, proficiency.

Program, Girl Scout
  choosing major field in, 88–89
  citizenship in, 50
  consultants, 41
  eleven fields of interest. *See* Fields of interest.
  ranks in. *See* Ranks.
Promise, Girl Scout, 5–6, 78, 92–93
  citizenship in, 6, 85–86, 92–93
  made in investiture ceremony, 25
Proofreader's marks, 159
Public health, 347–348
  badge, 482–483
Public Health Service, United States, 348
Pulitzer Prize, 158
Puppeteer, 165–169
  badge, 402–403
Pup tent, how to pitch, 288

Quiz, "How Do You Rate As a Friend to All," 221–224

Radio, 205–206
Radio and Television badge, 422–423
Rambler, 233–235
  badge, 434–435
Ranks
  Curved Bar, 106–108
  First Class, 87–98
  Second Class, 47–80
  Tenderfoot, 4–26
Reader, 148–150
  badge, 395–396
Reading. *See* Literature and Dramatics.
Recipes, 268, 279–281

Reflector fire, 278
Refrigerator, care and defrosting of, 362
Regions, Girl Scout, 376
Reptile and Amphibian badge, 441
Reptiles, 253–255
Rock and Mineral badge, 442–443
Rocks and minerals, 257–258
Roller bandage, 340
Roller skating, 297–298
Rowing, 296–297
Rules of the road, 66–67

Sacajawea, vi
Safety. *See also* Health and Safety.
  community, 334–337
  farm, 338
  home, 320–321, 327–329, 367–368
  in bicycling, 293–294
  in boating and canoeing, 300, 302
  in fire building, 68–70
  in skating, 297–298
  in skiing, 302–303
  in swimming, 295
  in using a knife, 22, 23 (*ill.*)
  in using an ax or hatchet, 273
  in using gas and electricity, 367–368
Salt Water Life badge, 444
Salt water life, 259–260
Salute, Girl Scout, 12
Sandwich fillings, 355
Scouts' Own, 45
Scout's pace, 281
Scribe, troop, 38
Seamstress, 359–360
  badge, 486–487

Seaweed, 260
Second Class Rank, 47–80
  badge, 28
  requirements, 47–49
Seeds, 74, 313–315
Senior Girl Scouts, 108–111
  graduation to, 44
  uniform, 2
Service, 45, 61, 85–86, 104–105
Sewing, 78, 128–129, 359–360
Shadowgraphs, 167–168
Shaw, Anna, v
Sheepshank (knot), 73
Sheet-bend (knot), 73
Shells, 259–260
Shoes, 327
Shrubs, 237
Sick, care of the, 343–347
Sign, Girl Scout, 12
Signaling, 266–267
  in broadcasting, 206
  when lost, 283–284
Silk screening, 130
Sit-upon, how to make a, 67
Skating, 297–299
  badge, 457
Sketching, 119
Skiing, 302–303
  badge, 459–460
Slogan, Girl Scout, 9
  citizenship in, 9, 93
Snakes, 253–254, 315
  first aid for bites of, 342
Social customs. See Manners.
Social dancing, 185
Soil, care of, 310–311
Some-mores (recipes), 280–281
Songs
  beating time for, 178
  choosing and teaching, 177–178
  every troop should know, 54–57
  types of, 176

Speaker, 200–201
  badge, 418
Speech, how to make a, 200–201
Spiders, 252
Splinters, first aid for, 76, 342
Sports and Games, 290–305. See also Games.
  Athlete, 305
  Athlete badge, 461–462
  Boating, 296–297
  Boating badge, 456–457
  Canoeing, 300, 301 (ill.), 302
  Canoeing badge, 458–459
  Cyclist, 293–294
  Cyclist badge, 454–455
  Games, 291–292
  Games badge, 454
  Horsewoman, 299–300
  Horsewoman badge, 457–458
  Life Saver, 305
  Life Saver badge, 462
  proficiency badges in, 453–462
  Second Class Rank requirement in, 71–74
  Skating, 297–299
  Skating badge, 457
  Skiing, 302–303
  Skiing badge, 459–460
  Sports, 303–304
  Sports badge, 460–461
  Swimmer, 295–296
  Swimmer badge, 455–456
Sports badge, 460–461
Sportsmanship, good, 303–304
Sprains, first aid for, 342–343
Square knot, 72
Squaw corn (recipe), 268
Stains, removal of, 363
Star badge, 442
"Star-Spangled Banner, The," xvi, 176, 197
Stars, 256–257
  finding direction by, 264

509

Statue of Liberty, 196 (*ill.*)
Stenciling, 130
Storrow, Mrs. James J., 212
Storyteller, 151–152
    badge, 396–397
Stoves, 272
Suitcase, how to pack, 199
Sunburn, first aid for, 343
Swimmer, 295–296
    badge, 455–456

Table
    centerpieces, 350
    manners, 356–357
    setting, 17
    silver, 17
Tadpoles, 254–255
Taxes, 202–203
Television, 205–206
Tenderfoot Rank, 4–31
    meaning of, 5
    requirements, 4–5
Tepee fire, 70
Terraria, making, 255
Textile Design, 129–131
    badge, 387
Thinking Day, 46, 212, 214
Tin-can stoves, 271–272 (*ill.*)
Toads, 254–255, 315
Tools
    for home use, 365–366
    garden, 311–312
Topographical maps, 282–283
Tournament ladder, how to
    make, 303–304
Trails and trail signs, 21–22
Traveler, 198–199
    badge, 417–418
Treasurer, troop, 39
Treasury, troop, 39–40
Tree badge, 435–436
Trees, 236–237

Trefoil, xiv (*ill.*), 25
Trench candles, how to make,
    270–271
Trench fire, 278
Triangular bandage, 76
Troop Dramatics, 160–163
    badge, 400–401
Troop, Girl Scout (Intermedi-
    ate), 32–46
    adult leader for, 41
    birthday, 43
    budget, 39–41
    ceremonies, 25–26, 43–46
    committee, 41
    Court of Awards in, 43–44
    Court of Honor in, 36–37
    crest, 30
    dues, 39
    first aid kit for, 321–322
    government of, 33–38
    how to join, 2–3
    investiture of, 25–26
    library, 146–147
    meeting places, 32
    meetings of, 24, 32, 42–43
    numeral, 30
    planning in, 33–38
    scribe, 38–39
    size of, 32
    treasurer and treasury, 39–40
Truck Gardener, 312–316
    badge, 466–467
Twisters (recipe), 280
Turtles, 254

Uncle Sam," 197
Uniforms
    Brownie Scout, 2
    disposing of outgrown, 28
    how to get, 28
    how to wear, 27
    Intermediate, 2, 27

Uniforms (*Continued*)
  of Girl Guides and Girl Scouts in other countries, 64, 216–217 (*ill.*)
  Senior Girl Scout, 2
  when to wear, 28
United Nations, 227 (*ill.*), 228
United States of America
  citizenship in, 190–191, 196–198, 202–204, 223, 412–413, 415–417, 419–421
  Constitution, 191–192, 348, 420
  flag of, 13–15. *See also* Flag, United States of America.
  government of, 37, 93, 198, 202–204, 413, 419–421
  heritage of, 196–198, 207–208
  map of, 376
  Public Health Service of, 348
  some famous men of, 46, 197–198
  songs of, 197
  symbols of, 196–197

Vegetables, 314–315
Ventilation, 328
Voting, 32, 202–204

Waterproof matches, how to make, 270
Water system, house, 367–368
"Wayfarer's Grace, The," 55
Weather badge, 443–444
Weather forecasting, 65–66, 258–259

Weaving, 131–135
  badge, 387–388
Western Hemisphere, 219–220
  badge, 427–428
  Regional Committee, 15, 220
Wheatley, Phyllis, v
"When E'er You Make a Promise," 54
Whifflepoof (game), 71–72
Whipping a rope, 265–266
Wild Plant, 240–242
  badge, 437
Window boxes, 240–241
Wire forms, 116–117
Wood, 121–123
  badge, 382–383
Woodpiles, 69
World Association Gallery (game), 71
World Association of Girl Guides and Girl Scouts, 15–16, 211. *See also* International Guiding and Scouting.
  Bureau, 15
  Committee, 15
  Conference, 15, 218
  flag, 15, 211
  pin, 15, 26, 211
  Regional Committee, 15
World Gifts, 207–211, 209 (*ill.*)
  badge, 424–425
World Health Organization, 348
World Neighbor, 220–224
  badge, 428–429
World Trefoil, 211–218
  badge, 425–426
Wounds, care of, 75, 340
Wrapping packages, 367
Writer badge, 397–398
Writing, 152–154